A

TREATISE

ON THE

RIGHT OF PERSONAL LIBERTY,

AND ON THE

WRIT OF HABEAS CORPUS

AND THE

PRACTICE CONNECTED WITH IT:

WITH A VIEW OF THE

LAW OF EXTRADITION OF FUGITIVES.

BY

ROLLIN C. HURD.

THE LAWBOOK EXCHANGE, LTD.
Clark, New Jersey

ISBN 9781584773221 (hardcover)
ISBN 9781616190910 (paperback)

Lawbook Exchange edition 2010

The quality of this reprint is equivalent to the quality of the original work.

THE LAWBOOK EXCHANGE, LTD.
33 Terminal Avenue
Clark, New Jersey 07066-1321

Please see our website for a selection of our other publications and fine facsimile reprints of classic works of legal history:
www.lawbookexchange.com

Library of Congress Cataloging-in-Publication Data

Hurd, Rollin C. (Rollin Carlos), b. 1815.
A treatise on the right of personal liberty and the writ of habeas corpus and the practice connected with it : with a view of the law of extradition of fugitives / by Rollin C. Hurd.
p. cm.
Originally published: Albany : W.C. Little & Co., 1858.
Includes bibliographical references and index.
ISBN 1-58477-322-7 (cloth: alk paper)
1. Habeas corpus—United States. 2.Extradition—United States.
3. Liberty. I. Title: Writ
of habeas corpus. II. Title.

KF9011 .H8 2003
347.73'5—dc21 2002044397

Printed in the United States of America on acid-free paper

A

TREATISE

ON THE

RIGHT OF PERSONAL LIBERTY,

AND ON THE

WRIT OF HABEAS CORPUS

AND THE

PRACTICE CONNECTED WITH IT:

WITH A VIEW OF THE

LAW OF EXTRADITION OF FUGITIVES.

BY

ROLLIN C. HURD.

ALBANY:
W. C. LITTLE & CO., LAW BOOKSELLERS.
1858.

WEED, PARSONS & Co., Printers,
Albany, N. Y.

HENRY STANBERRY, Esq.,

DISTINGUISHED AMONG THE FEW WHO, AMIDST THE TEMPTATIONS TO PROFESSIONAL INCONSTANCY PECULIAR TO OUR TIMES AND COUNTRY, CONTINUE, WITH UNWAVERING DEVOTION, TO DIGNIFY AND ADORN THE

PRACTICE OF THE LAW,

BY THE DISPLAY OF PROFOUND AND VARIED LEARNING AND THE GRACES OF POLISHED ELOCUTION, THIS WORK IS RESPECTFULLY

INSCRIBED

BY

THE AUTHOR.

PREFACE.

The jurisdiction exercised under the writ of habeas corpus embraces many interesting and important subjects. It is invoked to remove alleged illegal restraint of personal liberty; but as all restraint is not illegal, it becomes important to a ready and just administration of the law, that there should be a clear apprehension of the nature and extent of the right of personal liberty and the limitations to which it may, legally, be subjected.

Restraint may be imposed under legal process emanating from a federal court, or under color of federal authority without process. In such cases it is important to understand the nature and extent of the jurisdiction of the state courts under the writ of habeas corpus.

The restraint may be imposed under legal process emanating from a federal or state court when the legality of the imprisonment may depend on the extent or rightful exercise of the jurisdiction of the court granting the process, or on the sufficiency of the process itself. Process may be irregular and yet the prisoner may not be entitled to be discharged, for the writ of habeas corpus is not a remedy in all cases of false imprisonment. It may be regular and yet the prisoner may be entitled to be discharged, for the imprisonment under it may, notwithstanding its regularity, be illegal.

The restraint may be imposed under a claim of private authority, and that authority may be denied, or there may be conflicting claims for the custody of the person restrained; and the restraint may be imposed in the exercise of the duty of extradition of fugitives from justice or from service, and in such cases not only the validity of the process employed may be brought in question, but also the constitutional powers of congress and of the states.

Thus, under the writ of habeas corpus, it may become necessary to decide as to the extent and legal exercise of the jurisdiction of a federal court or officer, or of a state court; the validity of legal process in respect to any or all the many grounds on which it is liable to be impeached; the constitutionality of state and federal laws; the right of prisoners to be admitted to bail, and the right and sometimes the expediency of continuing private custody.

This jurisdiction, so extensive and important and, when in competent hands, so beneficent, has in some states been committed to inferior officers not learned in the law; and there have not been wanting magistrates of this class, ambitious of the distinction of *Habeas Corpus Judges*, who have cherished the pleasing illusion that, though destitute of every other qualification for the judicial office, they were quite sufficient for a proceeding in which the law appeared to them to be concerned only for the release of prisoners. And there have not been wanting magistrates of higher rank, who, though acknowledging their subjection to the law in all other proceedings, have, when acting under the writ of habeas corpus, deluded themselves with the idea that they were, judicially, omnipotent. In such hands there is reason to fear that the law has suffered violation in the discharge of prisoners as often as in the commitments which they have reviewed.

The practitioner who has undertaken to investigate, and the judge who has been required to administer the law under this writ have doubtless, at times, felt a regret that some one had not lessened their labors by a careful collection and methodical arrangement of the principles of law commonly involved in the proceeding, the rules of practice by which it is governed and the decisions wherein they have been applied and illustrated. The profession has, hitherto, been without such aid. The only service of practical value which has been rendered is the learned note in 3 *Hill's Reports*, 647, by NICHOLAS HILL, Jr., Esq., to which as well as to the encouraging counsel of its generous and accomplished author, I have been greatly indebted. I desire also to express my obligations to FRANCIS WHARTON, Esq., the learned author of the valuable work entitled, "American Criminal Law," for his interesting article on the extradition of fugitives from justice, found in 6 *Penna. Law Journal*, 412, which he kindly placed at my service.

The object of the following pages has been to supply a work of the description above indicated, which no one else has found inclination or leisure to execute. With no predecessor in this field to encourage by his success or warn by his failure, I have been compelled in the choice and discussion of the topics considered, to assume the responsibility and incur the risk, and may therefore, perhaps not in vain, ask for the performance the indulgence usually extended to the labors of a pioneer.

ROLLIN C. HURD.

MOUNT VERNON, OHIO,
September, 1858.

CONTENTS.

BOOK I.

THE RIGHT OF PERSONAL LIBERTY.

CHAPTER I.

GENERAL NATURE AND LIMITATIONS OF THE RIGHT.

SECTION I.

SECTION II.

CHAPTER II.

LIMITATIONS OF A PUBLIC NATURE.

SECTION I.

SECTION II.

SECTION III.

B

CHAPTER III.

LIMITATIONS OF A PRIVATE NATURE.

SECTION I.

SECTION II.

SECTION III.

SECTION IV.

SECTION V.

SECTION VI.

SECTION VII.

BOOK II.

THE WRIT OF HABEAS CORPUS.

CHAPTER I.

NATURE OF THE WRIT OF HABEAS CORPUS, AND SOURCES AND EXTENT OF JURISDICTION OVER IT.

CHAPTER II.

PRACTICE IN PROCURING AND SERVING THE WRIT.

SECTION II.

SECTION III.

SECTION IV.

CHAPTER VI.

JURISDICTION IN RESPECT TO THE VALIDITY OF LEGAL PROCESS WHEN ASSERTED AS CAUSE OF DETENTION.

SECTION I.

SECTION II.

SECTION III.

SECTION IV.

SECTION V.

CHAPTER VII.

VALIDITY OF LEGAL PROCESS.

SECTION X.

SECTION XI.

SECTION XII.

CHAPTER VIII.

RIGHT TO BAIL.

SECTION I.

SECTION II.

SECTION III.

SECTION IV.

CHAPTER IX.

CLAIMS FOR PRIVATE CUSTODY FOUNDED ON THE DOMESTIC RELATIONS.

SECTION I.

SECTION II.

SECTION III.

CHAPTER XI.

SECTION I.

BOOK III.

THE LAW OF EXTRADITION OF FUGITIVES.

CHAPTER I.

EXTRADITION OF FUGITIVES FROM JUSTICE FROM FOREIGN STATES.

SECTION I.

SECTION II.

SECTION III.

CHAPTER II.

EXTRADITION OF FUGITIVES FROM JUSTICE FROM THE SEVERAL STATES OF THE UNION.

SECTION I.

SECTION II.

SECTION III.

INDEX TO CASES CITED.

D.

E.

F.

G.

S.

Y.

BOOK I.

THE RIGHT OF PERSONAL LIBERTY.

THE RIGHT OF PERSONAL LIBERTY.

CHAPTER I.

GENERAL NATURE AND LIMITATIONS OF THE RIGHT.

Section I. General nature of the right.
II. Nature of the limitations.

SECTION I.

GENERAL NATURE OF THE RIGHT.

Personal Liberty is the power of unrestrained locomotion. The right to exercise it springs from the fundamental laws of our being. The ever-recurring wants of the body, requiring continual labor for their provision, and the necessity of exercise to the healthy action of all its vital processes, render locomotion indispensable to animal existence. Man shares these wants with inferior animals, and, were he their equal only, should share their freedom also. But he has other wants no less imperious than those of the body: knowledge, the aliment of the soul; and happiness, the object of its unceasing aspiration. To supply these varied wants, he is constrained to employ his powers with unremitting care. Acting upon that enlightened sense of independence, which a knowledge of his nature and destiny alone can inspire, he pursues happiness in whatever paths it invites him; gives his days to labor, to study or to pleasure; remains in one place or visits all; in a word, in the exercise of liberty attains the full enjoyment of life.

A survey of the nations of the earth, to discover where the right of personal liberty has been, and now is, most generally understood, most highly prized and most effectually secured to every walk in life, and to observe the liberalizing and elevating influence which a just sense of it exerts upon the government which fosters and secures it, the vital energy which it imparts to the administration of public affairs, and the unfailing stimulus which it supplies to private enterprise, would prove alike grateful to the spirit of philosophic inquiry and flattering to the pride of an American citizen. But it is the object, rather, of the following pages to ascertain what are the limits of this right; how it is secured, and how, when illegally assailed, it may most speedily be vindicated.

The right of personal liberty, thus inhering in man as an independent sentient being, though absolute and of inestimable value, is not without material qualifications. "Man," says Montesquieu, "is born in society and there he remains." Government is essential to the preservation of society, and, in some form, everywhere prevails. Thus, born in society and under government, enjoying the privileges of one and the protection of the other, he cannot rightfully exercise any power incompatible with the well-being of either. Hence, each member of society, in the exercise of his right of liberty, as well as of his other absolute rights, is subject to such limitations and penalties, as the common welfare and the just ends of government may require.

SECTION II.

NATURE OF THE LIMITATIONS.

The limitations of the right of personal liberty are either of a public or private nature.

I. Limitations of a public nature are those which are,

1. Punitive of crime;
2. Coercive of duties to the state; or
3. Executive of duties to the citizen.

II. Limitations of a private nature are those which are,

1. Coercive of private obligation; or
2. Incident to certain civil relations, viz.:
    1. Husband and wife;
    2. Parent and child;
    3. Guardian and ward;
    4. Master and apprentice;
    5. Master and servant;
    6. Master and scholar;
    7. Principal and special bail.

CHAPTER II.

LIMITATIONS OF A PUBLIC NATURE.

SECTION I.

LIMITATIONS PUNITIVE OF CRIME.

In 1765 it was written of the English law: It is a melancholy truth that, among the variety of actions which men are daily liable to commit, no less than a hundred and sixty have been declared by act of Parliament to be felonies without benefit of clergy; or, in other words, to be worthy of instant death. 4 *Bl. Com.*, 18. And in 1810 it was declared by Lord Holland, in debate in the House of Lords, that the list had been increased to nearly double that number. 4 *Am. Jurist*, 7.

In 1844 this "dreadful list" had been reduced to twelve. 4 *Bl. Com., Wend. ed., App. A.*

The same severity did not prevail in the American Colonies as in England; yet in them many crimes were punished capitally which are now punished with imprisonment. In the United States more than half the States, and these among the foremost in point of the general completeness and the considerate humanity of their criminal codes, have in effect abolished the punishment of death for all other crimes than the single offence of murder. *Law Rep.*, 490.

Although doubts have been suggested as to the right of the State to inflict capital punishment in any case, and elaborate arguments urged against the policy of it, the right to imprison for crime in all cases is unquestioned. It is not that crime has become less odious in the sight of legislators, but the rights of life and liberty more precious, that the severity of the penalties of the criminal codes of England and America has been so greatly mitigated. It may be said now, that in the United States the personal liberty of offenders supplies the principal revenue of Penal Justice. She inflicts, indeed, pecuniary fines for slight offences, and exacts the forfeit of life for the most atrocious; but the great multitude of felons are required to expiate their crimes in prison.

Of Contempts. The right of liberty is also subject to restriction as a punishment for contempts of court, which may, without impropriety, be classed with crimes.

A court of justice represents the judicial majesty of the people. Through the forms of law it utters their mighty voice in judgment. Property, character, liberty and life itself, are involved in the issues before it; and it needs all the aid which composure can lend to reason to enable it to discharge wisely and impartially its manifold and momentous duties. Contempts, therefore, tending to interrupt or disturb the court in the administration of justice, have always been held to deserve instant and severe punishment. 4 *Bl. Com.*, 284.

SECTION II.

LIMITATIONS COERCIVE OF DUTIES TO THE STATE.

1. *The duty of supporting and defending the state.*
2. *The duty of testifying for the state in criminal cases.*
3. *The duty of obedience to judicial mandates.*

1. *The duty of supporting and defending the State.* It is no less the duty of the citizen to support the State than it is of the State to protect the citizen. And although our army and navy are now supplied by volunteers, it is the undoubted right of the State, whenever in her judgment the public emergency requires it, to compel the citizen to enter her service. And when engaged in that service, whether by compulsion or voluntary enlistment, he becomes subject to her control under officers acting within their appointed spheres.

Whatever charms the life of the soldier or marine may possess, it is not one of perfect liberty. The restraints to which they are subjected, though necessary to that rigor of discipline which the art of war demands, are oftentimes felt to be serious and sometimes annoying if not oppressive restrictions.

2. *The duty of testifying for the State in Criminal Cases.* Besides the obedience which a witness owes to a subpœna, for neglect of which he is exposed to punishment, he may also, in criminal cases, be compelled to enter into a recognizance to appear at a future day to give evidence in behalf of the State; and in case of his refusal, he may be committed to prison. Such appears to have been the common law,

1 *Chitt. Cr. Law*, 76, and such is the statute law of several states.

It may seem harsh thus to imprison a man not only innocent of crime but not even charged with it. But it is of the highest interest to the community that offenders should be brought to justice; and he who refuses to be laid under bonds to give evidence against them is delinquent in public duty. The witness was not, however, at common law required to procure any surety. His own recognizance was all that was exacted. To require him, as has sometimes been done, to procure sureties in addition, is certainly an extraordinary exercise of legislative power. 4 *Bl. Com., Wend. ed.*, 296.

3. *The duty of obedience to judicial mandates.* The judiciary would hold but a barren scepter if their powers ceased with declaring the law. They are vested with a power to enforce as well as pronounce their judgments. In many cases of contumacious conduct they secure obedience to their orders by attachment and commitment of the delinquent party. Imprisonment in such cases is not regarded merely as a punishment for a contempt, but as a necessary means of enforcing compliance with the decision of the court.

SECTION III.

EXECUTIVE OF DUTIES TO THE CITIZEN.

It would be a very narrow view of the obligations of the state to suppose that her protection should be limited to such as may be able in return to render aid to her. The lunatic, the idiot and the helpless pauper, no less than the industrious citizen and the valiant soldier claim her fostering care.

The irresponsible lunatic must not be allowed a liberty fraught with danger to himself and others—nor must he or the idiot be left exposed to the cupidity and rapacity of designing and heartless relatives. Neither must the invalid pauper be suffered to starve in a land overflowing with plenty.

This obligation of Government has long been recognized, but not so long efficiently discharged. There is, however, no more gratifying evidence of the progress of society than is afforded by the asylums which a just sense of public duty has, in many of the states, provided for these unfortunate classes.

Irrespective of any statutory provision, the custody of such persons would, especially in case of infants, devolve upon the nearest in blood; but in view of laws enacted to provide for their support and custody, the right of private restraint must yield to the call and benevolent design of the state. Hence it has been held that a lunatic could not be kept in close confinement by his relatives or friends, except on the ground of temporary necessity, and that only so long as may be reasonably required to obtain the benefits provided by law. *Colby v. Jackson*, 1 *N. Hamp.*, 181; *Hinchman v. Richie*, *Brightly Rep.*, 143; *see In re Shuttleworth*, 9 *Ad. & El.*, 651, *N. S.*

In the exercise of this power the legislature may prescribe and cause to be enforced such regulations as in its judgment the public good may require.

The lunatic may be made a close prisoner, or suffered to go at large under the custody of a committee; and the pauper may be required to perform moderate labor and abide in the public infirmary, or become the servant of the "lowest bidder."

The restrictions in these cases being designed for the benefit of the unfortunate subjects and for the safety of the community, should cease when the cause which required them is removed; as, when the lunatic recovers his reason, or the pauper acquires property adequate for his maintenence by gift or otherwise, or gains sufficient health and strength to earn his support.

CHAPTER III.

LIMITATIONS OF A PRIVATE NATURE.

SECTION I.

LIMITATIONS COERCIVE OF PRIVATE OBLIGATIONS.

The duty of the state to provide some means of redress for private wrongs, has long been recognized by all civilized nations. Pecuniary demands, whether springing from contracts, express or implied, or from injuries to the person, property or reputation, have been made the subjects of various civil remedies, in some of which a heavy hand has, not unfrequently, been laid upon the right of personal liberty.

1. *Demands arising out of contracts, express or implied.* The relation of debtor and creditor has long been a matter of legislative concern; and the principles of freedom and avarice have, in their persons, for ages struggled with each other for the mastery. Legislative favor seemed at last to declare against freedom; and in England, and even under American skies, the victims of a cruel and oppressive

policy could be reckoned by thousands locked in prisons built and guarded by the state.

The distinctions of age and sex were disregarded, and not even the decrepid patriot soldier could excite the pity or escape the rapacity of the merciless creditor. It almost surpasses belief that ever on American soil and under the sanction of American law, a helpless woman, innocent of fraud, with her infant child at the breast, could, for a pitiful debt of six dollars, be cast into prison and kept in close confinement.

And yet, not only was that done in 1824, in Massachusetts, but in 1818 a captain in the revolutionary army, then more than seventy years old, was kept in close confinement in a jail in New Hampshire for a debt of eight dollars, *and had been for more than four years.* 14 *Niles Reg.*, 423; 26 *ib.*, 400.

In the year 1828 there were confined in the prison of the city of New York, 1,085 persons for debt; and between the 6th of June, 1829, and the 24th of February, 1830, there were imprisoned for debt in the city of Philadelphia 817 persons, of whom 80 were committed for debts less than one dollar each. 38 *Niles Reg.*, 174.

The right of personal liberty was held no more sacred in Great Britain. On the 29th of April, 1826, there were confined for debt in England, Scotland, Wales and Ireland 3,820 persons, of whom 228 had been confined more than two years and 104 more than four years. 32 *Niles Reg.*, 230.

But the day of deliverance for honest debtors in America was drawing nigh. From the boundless west a champion had come.

Born in 1781, in the then almost unbroken wilderness of Kentucky, inured to the hardships and privations of a pioneer life, possessing the lively sense of the right of personal liberty which that life of peculiar self-dependence always inspires, having the warmest sympathies for the laboring classes, to which he was attached both by inclination and habit, and wearing, not without pride, the laurels he had gained on the field of battle in defence of the liberties of his country, Col. RICHARD M. JOHNSON appeared in 1822, on the most conspicuous theater of the nation, the acknowledged and resolute champion of the long oppressed right of personal liberty—a right dear to all, but doubly dear to the poor.

Important reforms in the law of imprisonment for debt had been proposed in some of the states, and partially adopted in others; the subject, also, on account of the great severity of the times, had recently been brought forward in Congress; but there was wanting a public leader to enlighten, concentrate, extend and make effectual the favorable opinions in regard to it which had begun to be entertained in different sections of the country. Such a leader was found in Col. JOHNSON. On the 14th day of December, 1822, then a Senator from Kentucky, he introduced in the Senate of the United States a bill for the abolition of imprisonment for debt. The measure was delayed by various fortune for several years, but was finally successful. During its pendency before Congress it was defended with great zeal and ability by the distinguished mover, who plead earnestly for the natural rights of man, and pointed with just pride to the example of his own noble state.

Although it was beyond the power of Congress to affect the condition of a debtor imprisoned under the authority of the several states, yet the agitation of the subject, the discussion which it elicited, and the action of Congress could not but exert a favorable influence upon the popular mind, and lead to an amelioration of the laws of the states; and so thought the imprisoned debtors of the city of New York, when on the 8th day of January, 1830, their prison resounded with the Kentuckian name, for his philanthropic labors in the cause of liberty.

Our prisons now, in most of the states, have no terrors for the poor and honest debtor; and it is just to record that to Col. JOHNSON, more than to any other statesman, are we indebted for the restoration of so much valuable ground to freedom.

In one of his reports to Congress, there is a sketch of the condition of the debtor in the republics of Greece and Rome, and of the origin and gradual extension of imprisonment for debt in England, drawn by a master hand, and which deserves to be preserved not only as evidence of the spirit and thoroughness with which the subject was discussed, but also as depicting in striking, and, with one or two immaterial exceptions, truthful colors the character of the thraldom from which thousands of our citizens have been delivered.

"In ancient Greece," says the report, "the power of creditors over their debtors was absolute; and, as in all cases where despotic control is tolerated, their rapacity was boundless. They compelled their insolvent debtors to cultivate their lands like cattle, to perform the service of beasts of burden, and to transfer to them their sons and daughters, whom they exported as slaves to foreign countries.

"These acts of cruelty were tolerated in Athens, during her more barbarous state, and in perfect consonance with the character of a people who could elevate a Draco, and bow to his mandates, registered in blood. But the wisdom of Solon corrected the evil. Athens felt the benefit of the reform; and the pen of the historian has recorded the name of her lawgiver as the benefactor of man.

"In ancient Rome, the condition of the unfortunate poor was still more abject. The cruelty of the Twelve Tables against insolvent debtors should be held as a beacon of warning to all modern nations. After judgment was obtained, thirty days of grace were allowed before a Roman was delivered into the power of his creditor. After this period he was retained in a private prison, with twelve ounces of rice for his daily sustenance. He might be bound with a chain of fifteen pounds weight; and his misery was three times exposed in the market-place, to excite the compassion of his friends. At the expiration of sixty days, the debt was discharged by the loss of liberty or life. The insolvent debtor was either put to death or sold in foreign slavery beyond the Tiber. But, if several creditors were alike obstinate and unrelenting, they might legally dismember his body, and satiate their revenge by this horrid partition. Though the refinements of modern criticisms have endeavored to divest this ancient cruelty of its horror, the faithful Gibbon, who is not remarkable for his partiality to the poorer class, preferring the liberal sense of antiquity, draws this dark picture of the effect of giving the creditor power over the person of the debtor: No sooner was the Roman empire subverted than the delusion of Roman perfection began to vanish, and then the absurdity and cruelty of this system began to be exploded—a system which convulsed Greece and Rome, and filled the world with misery, and, without one redeeming benefit, could no longer be endured—and, to the honor of humanity, for about one thousand years, during the middle ages, imprisonment for debt was generally abolished. They seemed to have understood what, in more modern times, we are less ready to comprehend, that power in any degree, over the person of the debtor, is the same in principle, varying only in degree, whether it be to imprison, to enslave, to brand, to dismember, or to divide his body. But as the lapse of time removed to a greater distance the cruelty which had been suffered, the cupidity of the affluent found means again to introduce the system; but by such slow gradations, that the unsuspecting poor were scarcely conscious of the change.

"The history of English jurisprudence furnishes the remarkable fact, that, for many centuries, personal liberty could not be violated for debt. Property alone could be taken to satisfy a pecuniary demand. It was not until the reign of Henry III., in the thirteenth century, that the principle of imprisonment for debt was recognized in the land of our ancestors, and that was in favor of the barons alone; the nobility against their bailiffs, who had received their rents and had appropriated them to their own use. Here was the shadow of a pretext. The great objection to the punishment was, that it was inflicted at the pleasure of the baron, without a trial; an evil, incident to aristocracies, but obnoxious to republics. The courts, under the pretext of imputed crime, or constructive violence, on the part of the debtor, soon began to extend the principle, but without legislative sanction. In the eleventh year of the reign of Edward I., the immediate successor of Henry, the right of imprisoning debtors was extended to merchants—Jewish merchants excepted, on account of their heterodoxy in religion—and was exercised with great severity. This extension was an act of policy on the part of the monarch. The ascendancy obtained by the barons menaced the power of the throne; and, to counteract their influence, the merchants, a numerous and wealthy class, were selected by the monarch, and invested with the same authority over their debtors.

"But England was not yet prepared for the yoke. She could endure an hereditary nobility; she could tolerate a monarchy; but she could not resign her unfortunate sons, indiscriminately to prison. The barons and the merchants had gained the power over their victims; yet more than sixty years elapsed before Parliament dared to venture another act of recognizing the principle. During this period, imprisonment for debt had, in some degree, lost its novelty.

"The incarceration of the debtor began to make the impression that fraud, and not misfortune, had brought on this catastrophe, and that he was, therefore, unworthy of the protection of the law, and too degraded for the society of the world. Parliament then ventured, in the reign of Edward III., in the fourteenth century, to extend the principle to two other cases, debt and detinue. The measure opened the door for the impositions which were gradually introduced by judicial usurpation, and have resulted in most cruel oppression. Parliament, for one hundred and fifty years afterwards, did not venture to outrage the sentiments of an injured and indignant people, by extending the power to ordinary creditors. But they had laid the foundation, and an irresponsible judiciary reared the superstructure. From the twenty-fourth year of the reign of Edward III., to the nineteenth of Henry VIII., the subject slumbered in Parliament. In the mean time all the ingenuity of the courts was employed by the introduction of artificial forms and legal fictions to extend the power of imprisonment for debt in cases not provided for by statute. The jurisdiction of the court called the King's Bench extended to all crimes or disturbances against the peace. Under this court of criminal jurisdiction, the debtor was arrested by what was called the writ of Middlesex, upon a supposed trespass or outrage against the peace and dignity of the crown. Thus, by a fictitious construction, the person who owed his neighbor was supposed to be, what every one knew him not to be, a violator of the peace, and an offender against the dignity of the crown; and while his body was held in custody for this crime, he was proceeded against in a civil action, for which he was not liable to arrest under statute. The jurisdiction of the Court of Common Pleas extended to civil actions arising between individuals upon private transactions. To sustain its importance upon a scale equal with that of its rival, this court also adopted its fictions, and extended its power upon artificial construction, quite as far beyond its statutory prerogative; and upon the fictitious plea of trespass, constituting a legal supposition of outrage against the peace of the kingdom, authorized the writ of capias, and subsequent imprisonment, in cases where a summons only was warranted by law.

"The Court of Exchequer was designed to protect the king's revenue, and had no legal jurisdiction, except in cases of debtors to the public. The ingenuity of this court found means to extend its jurisdiction to all cases of debt between individuals, upon the fictitious plea that the plaintiff, who instituted the suit, was a debtor to the king, and rendered the less able to discharge the debt by the default of the defendant. Upon this artificial pretext, that the defendant was debtor to the king's debtor, the Court of Exchequer, to secure the king's revenue usurped the power of arraigning and imprisoning debtors of every description. Thus these rival courts, each ambitious to sustain its relative importance, and extend its jurisdiction, introduced as legal facts, the most palpable fictions; and sustained the most absurd solecisms as legal syllogisms.

"Where the person of the debtor was, by statute, held sacred, the courts devised the means of construing the demand of a debt into the supposition of a crime, for which he was subject to arrest on mesne process; and the evidence of debt into the conviction of a crime against the peace of the kingdom, for which he was deprived of his liberty at the plesure of the offended party. These practices of the courts obtained by regular gradation. Each act of usurpation was a precedent for similar outrages, until the system became general, and at length received the sanction of Parliament. The spirit of avarice finally gained a complete triumph over personal liberty. The sacred claims of misfortune were disregarded, and, to the iron grasp of poverty, were added the degradation of infamy and the misery of the dungeon."

But English cupidity did not exhaust the resources of ingenuity, nor set the only example of laws too barbarous for barbarians. The judges of Scotland were not to be surpassed in matters of fiction. They discovered that the delinquent debtor by being unable to pay his debt, had not committed a trespass, or a breach of the peace merely, as in England, but treason, and was accordingly to be proceeded against as a *rebel.*

Lord Kames, in his *Historical Law Tracts*, p. 336, written in 1761, says of the law of Scotland: "There is not in the law of any country a stronger instance of harshness, I may say of brutality, than occurs in our present form of personal execution for payment of debt; where the debtor, without ceremony, is declared a rebel, merely upon failure of payment. To punish a man as a rebel, who, by misfortune, or be it bad economy, is rendered insolvent, betokens the most savage and barbarous manners. One would imagine love of riches to be the ruling passion in a country where poverty is the object of so great a punishment."

It can hardly be necessary to remind the reader that it is recorded in the *Antiquary*, that Eddie Ochiltree expressed great disgust at the Scottish process of personal execution.

There has been some amelioration of the law of imprisonment for debt in Scotland, at least in the mode of administering it, for it is now said to be "slow, cautious and tolerant in its operation." 2 *Kent*, 511.

In the United States the law of imprisonment for debt has not only been modified by statute, but important securities against a return to its former barbarism, have been gained by provisions in the fundamental law of more than half of the states.

The constitutions of Ohio, Iowa, New Jersey and California forbid imprisonment for debt in all cases except those of fraud. The constitutions of Pennsylvania, Kentucky, Tennessee, Georgia, North Carolina, Alabama, Mississippi, Arkansas, Rhode Island, Vermont and Illinois forbid it, except in cases of strong presumption of fraud, *after* the debtor delivers up his estate for the benefit of his creditors, in the manner prescribed by law. The constitution of Missouri forbids it after such surrender of his estate by the debtor, without regard to the question of fraud. In Texas and Wisconsin, imprisonment for debt is forbidden in all cases by their constitutions.

There is reason also to believe that the poor and honest debtors of England, judging from recent efforts in that country, may before long be allowed that exemption from imprisonment for poverty, which was enjoyed by their ancestors eight hundred years ago.

2. *Demands arising out of injuries to the person, property or reputation.* Although imprisonment partakes of the nature of punishment, it is not inflicted with that view when allowed in aid of civil remedies. The theory is, that the state having, for the sake of the public peace, denied to the citizen the right to redress his own wrongs, should make the remedies which it proffers for private injuries so prompt and effectual as to remove as far as possible all motive to seek satisfaction by unlawful means. Hence it is, that for fraud practiced in making contracts or in attempting to evade their just obligation, imprisonment, as a coercive means to protect or redress the innocent and injured party, continues an approved element of remedial justice. And hence, also, in cases of injuries to the person, property or reputation, where they are instigated by malice or committed willfully, the wrong-doer has no more meritorious plea for exemption from imprisonment than the fraudulent contractor. Accordingly in some of the states this distinction is recognized to some extent, and no good reason is seen why it should not generally prevail. 2 *Kent,* 511, *n ; Holcomb's Law of Debtor and Creditor.*

SECTION II.

LIMITATIONS ARISING FROM THE RELATION OF HUSBAND AND WIFE.

1. *The husband's right of custody.*
2. *His supposed right of chastisement.*
3. *His right of confinement.*
4. *His right of recaption.*

1. *The husband's right of custody.* Of all the domestic relations, that of husband and wife is the first in the order of nature, the most intimate and the most enduring. Marriage, by some described as a "status," is truly a contract, though it differs in some respects from all other agreements. It is the only one that cannot be legally dissolved by the mutual consent of the parties; and the only one by which one human being can lawfully acquire dominion over another for life.

The extent of the power which the husband acquires over the person of his wife is not very distinctly marked. The courts have not been frequently called on to define with strict precision the limits of the power, partly because, in most cases, mutual affection banishes all thought of inequality; and partly because the labors and trials of life, common to both, beget a sense of mutual dependence which does not nourish controversies for personal supremacy.

Endowed with superior physical power, man is properly chargeable with, what he has in all ages and in all countries assumed, the protection of woman. But it is in his character as the responsible head and governor of the family that he acquires his right of private restraint over the wife.

The law favors industry, economy and a well regulated household. It requires the husband to maintain the wife and to repair whatever injuries she may inflict upon others. It holds domestic habits to be befitting the wife and mother, and it abhors a dishonored bed.

For these reasons it arms the husband with power to regulate his household. If his wife inclines to extravagant living he may protect his estate and prevent her from squandering it. If she forsakes her duties to her family and gads about to scandalize her neighbors or reform the race, he may bring her home and keep her there. If she burns with "free love" he may protect his honor and exclude her from all associations by which it is endangered.

By what means the husband is permitted to enforce this right of restraint, and with what effect, will be seen as we proceed.

2. *The husband's supposed right of chastisement.* "By the old law," *says Blackstone*, 1 *Com.*, 444, "the husband might give his wife moderate correction, for, as he is to answer for her misbehaviour, the law thought it reasonable to intrust him with the power of restraining her, by domestic chastisement, in the same moderation that a man is allowed to correct his apprentices or children, for whom the master or parent is also liable in some cases to answer. But this power of correction was confined within reasonable bounds. The civil law gave the husband the same or a larger authority, over his wife.

But with us in the politer reign of Charles the Second, this power of correction began to be doubted; and a wife may now have security of the peace against her husband; or in return a husband against the wife. Yet the lower rank of people, who were always fond of the old common law, still claim and exert their ancient privilege; and the courts of law will still permit a husband to restrain a wife of her liberty in case of any gross misbehavior."

The right to chastise the wife is repudiated in Ireland and Scotland, *Bishop on Marriage and Divorce*, § 485; and has met with but little favor in the United States.

In Kentucky, in 1822, it was thought that "the law countenanced the husband in the exercise of needful chastisement of the wife or restraint of her liberty." *Humphrey Compend.*, 137. In 1824, in the State of Mississippi the Supreme Court expressed themselves faintly in favor of the right, saying that the husband "should perhaps be permitted to exercise that power moderately in cases of great emergency." *Bradley* v. *The State*, *Walker Rep.*, 156.

The Chief Justice of New Jersey discards the rule. In the case of *The State* v. *Barnhard*, 2 *Wes. Law Jour.*, 301, the defendant was tried for an assault and battery upon his wife. It appeared in evidence that she interfered with his correction of his children and got slapped in the face, but not very hard.

Green, Ch. J., said: "There was a time in the history of the common law, in which a man was allowed to beat his wife with a rod no larger than his thumb; and a time still earlier than that when he was allowed to beat his wife at discretion and turn her out of doors; but in this enlightened and christian age and country, no man has a right to strike his wife at all. If she interferes with a proper discipline in his domestic relations he may restrain her; but the law will not justify him in striking a blow."

It was also held by the court in that case that the defendant could not protect himself under the plea that a man might lawfully whip his wife in Germany where they were married. Such a plea would have proved equally unavailing before the Scotch judge who by his question, suggestive of an interesting contrast, in *Duntze* v. *Levett*, 3 *Eng. Eccl. Rep.*, 504, doubtless meant to affirm that the English emigrant could not carry with him the laws of England and exercise on Scottish soil a power so barbarous.

"If a man in this country," asks Lord Robertson "were to confine his wife in an iron cage, or to beat her with a rod the thickness of the judge's finger, would it be a justification, in any court, to allege that these were powers which the law of England conferred on a husband, and that he was entitled to exercise them because his marriage had been celebrated in that country?"

In Delaware, the Supreme Court intimated in the case of *The State* v. *Buckley*, 2 *Harr.*, 552, that the husband was only indictable for "undue or excessive battery of his wife, either in degree or with improper means."

The Supreme Court of Massachusetts, in *Atkins* v. *Atkins*, cited in Bishop on Divorce, § 465, note, quoted with approbation the observation of Chancellor Walworth of New York, that such corporeal correction of the wife was not authorized by the laws of any civilized country.

In the case of *The People* v. *Winters*, 2 *Parker's Cr. R.*, 10, the defendant was indicted for an assault and battery on his wife.

It appeared on the trial that the prisoner attempted to correct one of his children, and that his wife interfered and made such a noise as to alarm the neighborhood. She testified that he struck her on the head with his hand and bruised her severely.

Walworth, Circuit Judge, said: A husband has no right to beat his wife or to inflict punishment upon her. But he may defend himself against her, and may restrain her from acts of violence towards himself or others, for he is accountable for her acts which injure others.

The jury thinking the defendant was only acting on the defensive, acquitted him.

It may be doubted whether a slight "slap in the face" of the wife by the husband is an indictable offence anywhere out of New Jersey; but it may safely be affirmed that the right of chastising the wife has no foothold in American law.

The right of the husband, however, to restrain the wife of her liberty to some extent and for several causes is recognized in all the cases, English and American.

3. *The husband's right of confinement.* Where the wife will make an undue use of her liberty, either by squandering his estate, or going into lewd company, it is lawful for the husband, in order to preserve his

honor and estate, to lay such a wife under restraint. *Rex.* v. *Lister, Str.*, 478; 8 *Mod.*, 22; *The State* v. *Craton*, 6 *Iredell*, 164.

Lord Hale construed the "salva moderatio castigatione" in the Register, not to mean a beating of the wife, but only admonition and confinement to the house, in case of her extravagance. 3 *Salk*, 139; *Vin. Abr., tit. Baron and Feme, U.*

It seems also that he is authorized to impose restraint upon her when she interferes to prevent his discipline of his children. *The State* v. *Barnhard*, 2 *Wes. Law Jour.*, 301; also when she gads about unreasonably, *Barlow* v. *Heine*, 3 *Law Rep.*, 453; also when he has reason to fear that she intends to elope. *In re Cochrane*, 8 *Dowl. P. C.*, 630. The manner in which this right may be exercised is not clearly defined.

The restraint is not viewed in the light of a punishment, but as a preventive remedy merely. The marriage contract does not *extinguish* the natural rights of the wife. It does not abridge her right of life nor deprive her of the right of its reasonable enjoyment. The restraint, then, which the husband may impose, must be limited in degree and duration, not only by the object for which it is permitted, but also by the natural rights of the wife, of which coverture has not deprived her.

When "imprisonment" was "accounted in law a civil death, where a man is deprived of society, of wife, home, country, friends; and liveth with wicked and wretched men," 5 *How. St. Tr.*, 373, it was held that the husband might "confine" his wife but could not imprison her. *Atwood* v. *Atwood, Gilb. Eq. Rep.*, 149; *Vin. Abr., tit. Baron and Feme, U.* He might then confine her to the house. *Freem. Rep.*, 376; *Vin. Abr., Baron and Feme, U.*

The law in England upon the point was very fully considered in a case before Mr. Justice Coleridge, in 1840, *In the matter of Cochrane*, 8 *Dowl., P. C.*, 630. In this case the wife obtained a writ of habeas corpus directed to her husband, who made return to the writ in substance as follows: "That before the coming of the said writ of habeas corpus my said wife was, and she still is, in my custody and under my care and protection, living with me in the same rooms and apartments with myself at No. 11 Great Castle-street, occupying with me the drawing room apartment there and the adjoining rooms on the same floor;"— that they were married in 1833—had two children, and afterwards "on the 29th May, 1836, she left me, without any just cause, and remained absent, nor could I learn where she was until 21st May, 1840, when she was induced, by stratagem I admit, to come to my lodgings where I have lived with her since. During her absence she attended, as I learn, masked balls at Paris, &c., and she says if she could regain her liberty she would run away from me—and to prevent this I have refused to permit her to leave the rooms in which we are now residing." The return also showed that there was no deed of separation. Coleridge, J. "The question raised in this case is, simply, whether by the common law the husband in order to prevent his wife from eloping has a right to confine her in his dwelling-house, and restrain her from her liberty, for an indefinite time, using no cruelty nor imposing any hardship or unnecessary restraint on his part; and on hers, there being no reason from her past conduct to apprehend that she will avail herself of her absence from his control to injure either his honor or his property. * * The language used in the case of *Rex.* v. *Lister*, 8 *Mod.*, 22, must be understood with reference to the case before the court, in which violence and actual imprisonment in the popular sense had been made use of for an unlawful purpose. If it could be fairly extended to such a case as the present, it would deny the *general* right of the husband to the control and custody of his wife, and restrict it to those cases, comparatively few in number, in which her misconduct made it palpably unsafe to allow her to be at large. This would, however, be inconsistent with the doctrine clearly laid down by the older authorities. The general rule would then be, that the wife, as to her residence and manner of spending her time, was independent of her husband. But our law has not so limited his rights, nor rested them on so narrow a foundation; although expressed in terms simple almost to rudeness, the principle on which it proceeds is broad and comprehensive—it has respect to the terms of the marriage contract, and the infirmity of the sex. For the happiness and the honor of *both* parties it places the wife under the guardianship of the husband and entitles him for the sake of both to protect her from the danger of unrestrained intercourse with the world by enforcing cohabitation and a common residence. It is urged that by refusing to discharge her I am sentencing her to perpetual imprisonment. Cases of hardship will arise under any general rule, and so long as there are, unfortunately, ill-assorted unions there will be cases in which wives will find it hard to be compelled to reside with their husbands. But our law for the wisest reasons allows of no divorce on such grounds; and I cannot doubt that a greater amount of human happiness is produced in the married state, from the mutual concession and forbearance which a sense that the union is indissoluble tends to produce, than could be enjoyed in the carelessness and want of self-government which would arise when the tie was held less firm. But if there be anything painful to Mrs. Cochrane in the present state of things she cannot properly complain of it, for it arises from her own breach of duty, and she may end it whenever she will cheerfully and frankly resolve on performing the contract she has entered into. The moment she makes restraint of her person unnecessary for keeping her in the path of duty it will become illegal, and nothing I have said to-day will prevent her from coming to this court for protection. Let her be restored to Mr. Cochrane."

A late writer, remarking upon this case and the restraint which it permits the husband to exercise, observes: "But this, I apprehend, does not mean that he is to lock her up, because *that*, as coming under the head of cruely, would justify her in escaping from him, and leaving him entirely; and would be a ground of divorce. For the same reason he is not to deprive her of the benefits of air and exercise." *McQueen's Husband and Wife*, 339.

In the case of *Atkins* v. *Atkins, cited Bishop on Divorce,* § 465, *note,* Mr. Justice Wilde, of Massachusetts, said he had "decreed a divorce where the husband accused the wife of adultery *and locked her up.*"

Chancellor Kent, 2 *Com.*, 181, says, that the husband may put gentle restraints upon the liberty of his wife if her conduct be such as to require it; but that for any unreasonable and improper confinement by him, she will be entitled to relief upon habeas corpus. In the case of *Barlow* v. *Heine,* 3 *Law Rep.*, 453, it appeared that on the morning of the separation of the parties there was some difficulty, when the husband told his wife not to go out. The court said: "A husbaud has the right to regulate such matters to a reasonable extent. He has no right to imprison his wife or treat her as a slave, but he has a right to regulate her locomotion, and if, for good reasons, he thinks proper to prevent her gadding abroad she ought to obey him."

It would seem, then, that the husband has authority to confine his wife to his dwelling, if necessary to prevent her from squandering his estate, or from going into lewd company, or from eloping, or from defeating him in the reasonable administration of discipline to his children, or from dissipating her time and neglecting her duties to her family by idly "gadding about," or from inflicting personal violence.

But in exercising this right he may not lock her up as a close prisoner; he may not deprive her of the benefit of light and air and exercise; nor of the

5

society of himself or the family, nor may he exclude her entirely from all intercourse with her neighbors, where there is no ground to apprehend any injurious consequences.

But while he may not deprive her of these rights he may prescribe the mode of their enjoyment. His power may be summed up in these words, he may "*make her live with himself at home as his wife.*"

The precise value of a wife requiring such surveillance, the law furnishes no rules for estimating.

4. *The husband's right of recaption.* At common law if the wife eloped or was forcibly carried away the husband might lawfully retake her, provided the act of recaption was not done riotously or in a manner to occasion a breach of the peace.

In 1840, the husband was allowed in England to recapture his wife by stratagem and to maintain the custody so regained. *In the matter of Cochrane*, 8 *Dowl. P. C.*, 630.

The American reports furnish a single case on the point, but it is probable the common law rule as above stated would be applied in all cases *where the husband was in no fault* and *had not consented to a separation.*

1*st. Agreement to separate, bars husband's right of recaption.*

Such an agreement is held to be a renunciation of the husband's marital rights. *Rex* v. *Mead*, 1 *Burr.*, 542; *Sanders* v. *Rodway*, 13 *Eng. Law and Eq.*, 463.

2*d. The husband may forfeit the right by misconduct.*

Cruelty or other conduct on his part, constituting a ground for divorce, gives authority to the wife to leave the husband and he cannot retake her whether she applies for a divorce or not. And it has been held that he cannot retake her if she leaves him to obtain a divorce, honestly believing that his treatment afforded sufficient ground for divorce, although it should appear that the facts did not warrant the belief.

In a late case in Rhode Island, *The State* v. *Tillinghast*, the defendant was found guilty of an assault upon his wife under the following state of facts. She had left the defendant to obtain a divorce, and fled to her mother, with her infant. The defendant, accompanied by four associates, demanded the infant, and being refused and also refused admission to the house, lifted the latch and forced open the door, took his wife by the arm, pulled her out of doors (with her child in her arms) lifted her into his wagon—the child in its night gown, the wife bareheaded—and drove to the house of his brother, about three-fourths of a mile distant. The wife resisted to the extent of her ability, but was not hurt, was treated kindly at the house of the brother and entertained until the next morning, when without opposition from any quarter, she returned with her child to her mother's. Chief Justice Ames is said to have charged the jury: "that when, as in this case, a woman has left the husband for such cause as she thinks entitles her to a divorce under the statute, and with a view to applying for a divorce, the husband has no right to use any force or means to control her or influence her action which he could not rightfully use towards any other lady in the community, and this, no matter how commendable may be the purpose of the husband or kindly his feelings."

Where, also, the husband compels the wife to live separate from him, either by abandoning her or forcing her by any means to leave him, and such separation is not merely temporary and capricious, but permanent and without expectation of living together again, leaving the wife wholly unprovided for, he forfeits his right to control her person, even if she seeks lewd company. *Love et al.* v. *Moynehan*, 16 *Ills.*, 277.

Ordinarily, the right of recaption cannot be exercised where it will occasion a breach of the peace. Nor can the husband justify a trespass to retake his wife where she seeks the protection of her parents or friends against him. And such protection will be lawful where it is afforded at the request of the wife and without any improper solicitation on the part of the parent. The rule of the father's liability for harboring his daughter who leaves her husband is thus laid down by Kent, Ch. J., in the case of *Hutcheson* v. *Peck*, 5 *Johns.*, 196: "It ought to appear that he detains the wife against her will, or that he entices her away from her husband from improper motives. Bad or unworthy motives cannot be presumed. They ought to be positively shown or necessarily deduced from the facts and circumstances detailed. This principle appears to me to preserve, in due dependence upon each other, and to maintain in harmony the equally strong and sacred interests of the parent and husband." And it was said in the case of *Bennett*

v. *Smith*, 21 *Barb. Sup. Ct.*, 439, that even strangers may receive the wife into and allow her the comforts of their house, where the conduct of the husband is such as to endanger her personal safety, or so immoral and indecent as to render him grossly unfit for her society.

But although he may not commit a breach of the peace or a trespass under ordinary circumstances, he may, it seems, when he has reasonable ground of apprehension of his dishonor, employ force to rescue his wife from her paramour.

Thus in the case of *The State* v. *Craton*, 6 *Iredell*, 164, the defendant was indicted and found guilty of the murder of Harrison. The defendant, Harrison, and some of their neighbors had been attending court some distance from their place of residence, and towards evening, when preparing to go home, Harrison desired his wife to ride with him. She objected, saying the horse was too small; and declared she would go with the defendant. Harrison did not consent. But she mounted behind the defendant and started with the others—leaving Harrison. He afterwards overtook them, and found them some distance behind the rest of the company. The defendant and Harrison's wife had been seen lying on a bed together a short time before. When Harrison overtook the defendant he demanded his wife. The defendant not surrendering her, Harrison rode in front and stopped him. This was repeated several times, Harrison all the time demanding his wife. The defendant finally dismounted, got a bludgeon and broke Harrison's skull. Harrison was somewhat in liquor, and had his knife out.

The leading question before the Supreme Court was, whether there was provocation shown in the facts proved to extenuate the killing. The legal power of the husband over his wife necessarily came under review. Ruffin, Ch. J., in delivering the opinion of the court, said: "In general, a man has a right to the exclusive custody of his wife. It may be true that any person has a right to protect her from the violence of her husband, and to take her from cruel usage under his hand. And it may also be true that the husband would not have a right to take her by force from the house of a parent or any proper protection during a difference between them, nor indeed, to confine her where there is not plainly a sufficient reason for imposing the restraint upon her. *Lister's case*, 8 *Mod.*, is a full authority, and founded, as we think, on the best reason, that Harrison might have restrained his wife by force from criminal conversation with the prisoner; and by consequence, that he might compel her to leave the society of the prisoner, if he had any reasonable grounds to suspect that those persons had perpetrated, or that they were forming the guilty purpose of perpetrating a violation of his rights and honor, or were contracting those regards towards each other, which would probably result in that stigma. The circumstances in this case leave no room to doubt that the husband entertained the belief, and that upon strong grounds of presumption, that it was essential to his wife's purity and his honor, that he should separate her from the company of the prisoner. Such a cause would justify the husband in effecting that end by compulsion on his wife; for it was obvious that nothing short of it would be effectual. And it would seem necessarily to follow that he might use actual force towards the paramour also, in order to regain his wife from him. But we need not consider that, as we have already seen there was no actual assault by the deceased. There was merely a stopping of the prisoner by the deceased drawing up his horse in front of the prisoner several times, accompanied by a demand of his wife and a declaration that the prisoner should not go on unless he gave up the wife. Those acts, we think, were not an injurious restraint on the prisoner's liberty, but only a lawful impediment to his carrying away the deceased's wife to her ruin and the husband's dishonor. There was consequently no provoction to extenuate the killing of Harrison."

The softening and elevating influence of christianity is nowhere more perceptible than in the relation of husband and wife. If it has not entirely banished, it has greatly ameliorated the marital tyranny of the common law. This just though long delayed enfranchisement of the wife is thus noticed by the French jurist, M. De La Croix:

"This unfortunate power was undoubtedly derived from the Roman law which permitted chastisement to be inflicted on the wife by the husband, who, according to the author of the Persian Letters, 'began by alarming her modesty and led her back in a manner to a state of childhood flagellis et fustibus acriter verberare uxorem.'

" But the dignity of the marriage has been exalted in the eyes of legislators in proportion as time has discovered to them the respective rights of two beings equally free, who are united for their mutual benefit; who in forming the sweetest and first of all natural societies, could never intend that one should become the slave of the other, but that both should equally depend on each other for a mutual interchange of duties and affections." 2 *La Croix, Rev. Cons. Europe,* 1790, *p.* 305.

SECTION III.

LIMITATIONS ARISING FROM THE RELATION OF PARENT AND CHILD.

1. *The grounds of parental custody.*
2. *The parent's right of chastisement.*
3. *The parent's right of confinement.*
4. *The power of emancipation.*
5. *The mother's right of correction.*

1. *Grounds of parental custody.* A parent is vested with power over the person of his child to enable him to discharge those duties towards the child which are imposed upon him by the law of nature or the state.

The duties of parents to their legitimate children, and of mothers to their illegitimate children, principally consist in three particulars: their maintenance, their protection, and their education. The duty of parents, says Blackstone, to provide for the maintenance of their children is a principle of natural law; an obligation, says Puffendorf, laid on them not only by nature herself, but by their own proper act in bringing them into the world; for they would be in the highest manner injurious to their issue if they only gave their children life that they might afterwards see them perish. By begetting them therefore they have entered into a voluntary obligation to endeavor as far as in them lies that the life which they have bestowed shall be supported and preserved. And thus the children have a perfect right of receiving maintenance from their parents. 4 *Bl. Com.*, 447. The wants and weaknesses of children, says Chancellor Kent, render it necessary that some person maintains them, and the voice of nature has pointed out the parent as the most fit and proper person. The laws and customs of all nations have enforced this plain precept of natural law. The Athenian and Roman laws were so strict in enforcing the performance of this natural obligation of the parent that they would not allow the father to disinherit the child from passion or prejudice, but only for substantial reasons to be approved in a court of justice. The obligation on the part of the parent to maintain the child, continues until the latter is in a condition to provide for its own maintenance, and it extends no further than to a necessary support. The obligation of parental duty is so well secured by the strength of natural affection that it seldom requires to be enforced by human laws. According to the language of Lord Coke, it is "nature's profession to assist, maintain and console the child." A father's house is always open to his children. The best feelings of our nature establish and consecrate this asylum. Under the thousand pains and perils of human life, the home of the parents is to the children a sure refuge from evil and a consolation in distress. In the intenseness, the lively touches and unsubdued nature of parental affection, we discern the wisdom and goodness of the great Author of our being, and the Father of Mercies. 3 *Kent. Com.*, 182.

The duty of *protection* is a natural duty, but rather permitted than enjoined by any municipal laws; nature, in this respect, working so strongly as to need rather a check than a spur. 1 *Black.*, 450. The *education* of children in a manner suitable to their station and calling, is another branch of parental duty, of imperfect obligation generally in the eye of the municipal law, but of very great importance to the welfare of the state. 2 *Kent's Com.*, 189.

These obligations rest upon a step-father when "he takes the wife's child into his own house, for he is then considered as standing *in loco parentis*, and is responsible for the maintenance and education of the child so long as it lives with him, for by that act he holds the child out to the world as part of his family."

Although the common law did not afford any adequate means of *enforcing* these duties, yet it conferred adequate power upon the parent to enable him to discharge them. 4 *Ad. and El.*, 899.

The rights of parents result from their duties. As they are bound to maintain and educate their children the law has given them a right to such authority and, in the support of that authority, a right to the exercise of such discipline as may be requisite for the discharge of their sacred trust. This is the true foundation of parental power." * * "The father (and on his death, the mother) is generally entitled to the custody of the infant children, inasmuch as they are their natural protectors, for maintenance and education." 2 *Kent*, 203.

This power over the person of the child ceases on its arrival at the age of majority, which has been variously established in different countries.

It thus appears that the parent is entitled to the custody of his child for certain important ends chiefly affecting the welfare of the child. When necessary to the discharge of his parental duty he may resort to corporeal discipline. He may and should in proper cases inflict moderate chastisement. He may impose such temporary confinement as may be necessary to secure obedience to his reasonable commands, so that it is not prejudicial to the life, limb or health of the child.

The law prescribes no form of parental discipline. It designates the purposes for which it may be employed, and confers adequate power for its administration; yet while it authorizes confinement or chastisement, it exacts moderation and punishes cruelty as a crime. *Fost*, 262; 1 *East P. C.*, 261; 1 *Hale P. C.*, 454; *Johnson* v. *The State*, 2 *Humph.*, 283.

2. *The parent's right of chastisement.* It is admitted to be a point of some difficulty to determine with precision when a parent has exceeded the bounds of moderation. An eminent author arrives at the following conclusion: "The true ground on which this ought to be placed is, that the parent ought to be considered as acting in a judicial capacity, when he corrects; and of course not liable for errors of opinion; and although the punishment should appear

to the triers unreasonably severe and in no measure proportioned to the offence, yet if it should also appear that the parent acted conscientiously, and from motives of duty, no verdict ought to be found against him. But when the punishment is in their opinion thus unreasonable, and it appears that the parent acted *malo animo*, from wicked motives, under the influence of an unsocial heart, he ought to be liable to damages. For error of opinion he ought to be excused; but for malice of heart, he must not be shielded from the just claims of the child. Whether there was malice, may be collected from the circumstances attending the punishment. The instrument used, the time when, the place where, the temper of heart exhibited at the time, may all unite in demonstrating what the motives were which influenced the parent. These obligations are equally applicable to the case of a schoolmaster, or to any one who acts *in loco parentis*." *Reeves' Dom. Rel.*, 287.

Express malice is justly made the test of parental liability; but is it the true test of the liability of the schoolmaster and others who act *in loco parentis?* Are there not weighty reasons for holding the schoolmaster, especially, to a stricter accountability than the parent?

There is a material difference in their relations. *One* has the custody of the child from a natural and undeclinable duty. He is actuated by a peculiar, ever-wakeful solicitude for his offspring. The idea of paternity, which is allied to that of property, suggests a claim of dominion, which, though reduced by law to a mere right of custody, remains a hidden but active principle in parental government, sometimes prompting to cruel punishment, sometimes to fatal indulgence. *The other* is a volunteer. He has ample leisure to count the cost before he incurs responsibility, and generally has an eye to the profit. His obligation arises from express contract. He may feel an interest in the welfare of the child, but how unlike that which pervades the parent's breast! Moreover he undertakes the care and custody of the child, whether it be for instruction in some art, in letters, in manners or in general industry, as a special business, for which he claims to be qualified in knowledge, in judgment and the needful art of government—a qualification required by law in some of the domestic relations and to be overlooked in none.

In view of these considerations and others that might be named, ought the substitute of the parent, especially the schoolmaster, to be allowed the full benefit of the parent's plea of infirmity of temper and error of judgment for unreasonable chastisement of the child?

Ought not the substitute in all cases to be held responsible when he inflicts punishment without probable cause—that is, a reasonable ground, under the circumstances of the particular case, for its infliction? At the least should he escape responsibility where he inflicts it wantonly, though there may not be express malice?

3. *The parent's right of confinement.* Temporary confinement is allowed as a means of enforcing obedience to reasonable commands. But this power

must also be exercised in moderation. The life of the child must not be endangered, nor its health sacrificed or unreasonably exposed; nor its limbs paralyzed or injured; nor can it be imposed to the prejudice of the child from sheer malice of heart.

The right of custody ceases, as we have seen, on the arrival of the child at majority. The rule admits of no exception but that of idiocy or other grievous disability of the child, where, in the absence of the intervention of the state, the custody should remain with the parent while the disability continues. *Upton* v. *Northbridge*, 15 *Mass.*, 237; *The Town of Oxford* v. *The Town of Rumney*, 3 *N. H.*, 331.

4. *The power of emancipation.* The child may be emancipated by the express consent of the parent, or by his conduct; as, by sending the child away or suffering it to go forth to shift for itself or to contract matrimony. *Chitty Con.*, 154 *note, 9th ed.;* 2 *Kent*, 194, *note ; Dick* v. *Grissom*, 1 *Freem. Ch. R.*, 428.

It may be emancipated also by the gross neglect of the parent; also by cruel treatment. "A father who turns his daughter out of his house upon the world to shift for herself, thereby relinquishes his paternal right in relation to her person and absolves her from filial allegiance." *Stansbury* v. *Berton*, 7 *Watts and Serg.*, 362.

It does not follow, however, that because he may forfeit his right of custody by gross neglect or cruelty he at the same time absolves himself from his obligation of maintenance. Where an infant child escapes from his father for fear of personal violence and abuse and cannot with safety live with him, the father is liable for necessary support and education furnished to such child by a stranger. *Stanton* v. *Willson*, 3 *Day*, 37 ; 2 *Kent*, 193.

Such liability may not arise, perhaps, in such a case, where there are statutory provisions for enforcing the duty of maintenance. *Gordon* v. *Potter*, 17 *Verm.*, 348.

Besides the liability to lose the right of custody of their children in the ways above noticed, parents may also for other reasons be deprived of it by "courts of justice, which may in their sound discretion and when the morals or interests of the children strongly require it, withdraw the infants from the custody of the father or mother, and place the care and custody of them elsewhere." 2 *Kent*, 205.

The jurisdiction of the courts in such cases and the principles upon which it is exercised will be considered hereafter.

5. *The mother's right of correction.* Where the father and mother reside together the general custody of the children is vested in him as the head and governor of the family. The mother, however, has a share in that custody; not independently of the father nor of equal extent, but sufficient to demand of her, the father not forbidding, an active part in the discipline of the children.

It has been said that "a mother, as such, is entitled to no power, but only to reverence and respect." 1 *Black*, 453 ; *Commonwealth* v. *Murray*, 4 *Binn.*, 487.

The Roman law not only enjoined the duty of reverence and respect to the mother but "punished any flagrant instance of the want of it." *Cod.*, viii., *tit.* 47, § 4 ; *Forsyth on Infants*, 5.

Reeves, *Dom. Rel.*, 295, says: "Mothers, during coverture, exercise authority over their children; but in a legal point of view they are considered as agents for their husbands, having no legal authority of their own."

Whatever may be the exact legal character in which she holds the rod, she generally applies it with as much freedom and spirit as if she were acting upon an inherent right of her own. Indeed, it is one way she has of securing that reverence and respect which are admitted to be her due.

On the death of the father, the mother remaining at the head of the family, succeeds to his rights of custody and control over the children. 2 *Kent*, 203; *Dedham* v. *Natick*, 16 *Mass.*, 135; *Nightingale* v. *Whittington*, 15 *Mass.*, 272; *Jones* v. *Tevis*, 4 *Litt.*, 25.

And this principle applies in case of the civil death of the father; as where the father was convicted of felony and in custody under sentence of transportation, a writ of habeas corpus was granted to the mother to take their child from its aunt and deliver it to the mother. *Ex parte Bailey*, 6 *Dowl. Pr. Cas.*, 311.

SECTION IV.

LIMITATIONS ARISING FROM THE RELATION OF GUARDIAN AND WARD.

1. *General nature of the relation of guardian and ward.* The relation of guardian and ward usually applies only to infants. The guardian may be invested with authority over the person and not the property, or over the property and not the person, or over both the person and property of his ward. The relation, however, with similar powers, has been extended in some states to idiots and lunatics of whatever age; and in others, to inveterate drunkards, though as to them power has only been given over their estates.

There were several kinds of guardianship at common law, but the only one subsisting in this country, independent of statutory provision, is that of guardianship by nature. This denotes nothing more than the relation of parent and child, the nature of which and the reciprocal obligation of the parties under it, have already been sufficiently considered.

In all other cases than that of guardianship by nature, the relation is created by judicial or testamentary appointment, under statutes prescribing the mode and conditions of the appointment, and defining, with various degrees of particularity in different states, the powers and duties of the guardian.

2. *Guardianship over idiots and lunatics.* In some of the states these unfortunate persons are committed to the custody of public officers and kept in asylums maintained at the public expense. In such cases there is not, technically speaking, the relation of guardian and ward. There is, however, a power of restraint involved and necessarily conferred.

In other states the custody is committed to private persons of suitable qualifications, who are sometimes denominated "committees."

The relation being of statutory origin in both cases, reference must be had to the statutes to ascertain what measure of power of personal restraint has been conferred.

3. *Guardianship over infants.* This too is a relation created by statute; for, as we have seen, the common law guardianship by nature is embraced in the relation of parent and child. But the statutory relation of guardian and ward in the case of infants, where it is not otherwise provided by statute, has some common law incidents which it is proper to notice.

Where the guardianship includes the custody of the person, and is not otherwise limited by statute, "the power and reciprocal duty," Blackstone says, "of the guardian and ward are the same, *pro tempore*, as that of a parent and child." But there are some important distinctions between these relations which deserve notice.

"A guardian," says Mr. Justice Woodbury, in the case of *Hancock* v. *Hamstead*, 1 *New Hamp.*, 265, "though *in loco parentis* as to a few purposes, has no absolute control over the person or services of the ward." The guardian is under no obligation to maintain the ward with his own funds; nor is he entitled to the services of the ward; nor can he bind him out to service, unless under particular statutory provisions. The ward is not the servant of the guardian in the same sense that a child is of the parent, or that an apprentice is of the master. *Velde* v. *Levering*, 2 *Rawle*, 269; *Leech* v. *Agnew*, 7 *Barr*, 21. Accordingly, Kent, with more caution, says: "The relation of guardian and ward is *nearly allied* to that of parent and child." 2 *Kent*, 236. And Swift, in his Commentaries says: "The power and duty of guardian and ward, *in a great measure*, correspond to that of parent and child."

There is nothing expressly said by Blackstone, Kent or Swift touching the guardian's right to administer moderate corporeal correction to the ward. This right, or rather duty, undoubtedly exists. By the laws of most of the states males of the age of fourteen years and females of the age of twelve, are authorized, their parents being dead, to choose guardians. And at those ages children may be said to have arrived respectively at what is called the "age of discretion." Where the ward is within this "age of discretion" it is plain enough that the guardian possesses the right and that it is clearly his duty, on proper occasions, in a reasonable manner, to correct his ward for misbehavior, with the rod if in his judgment that mode of correction be necessary. And especially is this true where the ward resides in the family of his guardian. In such a case it is important to allow the guardian to employ the usual means of discipline not only for the benefit of the ward but also to enable him to execute his reasonable plan of family government. For no man fit to be entrusted with the training up of a child, would take the infant stranger under his roof to educate with any privilege to misbehave, or escape the punishment usually inflicted on his own children for misconduct.

It would not be safe, perhaps, to deny that in a case of flagrant misbehavior the guardian possesses the right to chastise his ward when of somewhat riper years. But when, by reason of the advanced age of the ward this mode of correction becomes deeply humiliating, as well as painful, it is safe perhaps to say that the right cannot lawfully be exercised unless it appear that there was probable cause for it, and that all other means of correction less severe were inadequate.

4. *The guardian's right to change his ward's domicil.* The power of the guardian in respect to changing the domicil of his ward is more restricted than that belonging to the parent. Whether the guardian can change it at all out of the general territorial jurisdiction of the court from which he receives his appointment has been a controverted point. It has been held in Massachusetts that he could, and in Pennsylvania that he could not; but it seems to be agreed that he cannot do it wantonly, but must act in good faith and reasonably in his character as guardian. 2 *Kent's Com.*, 227, *note.*

Viewing the guardianship simply as a personal relation, it would seem difficult to maintain the right of personal control beyond the jurisdiction where it is created, and where, only, the obligations arising under it can be properly enforced.

SECTION V.

LIMITATIONS ARISING FROM THE RELATION OF MASTER AND APPRENTICE.

This relation is a contract of service for a term of years, to learn some art or trade, which owing to the temptation and abuse to which it is liable has been made the subject of special legislative regulation in the several states.

The operation of the contract is local. The apprentice cannot be taken out of the state unless such removal is provided for in the indenture, or arises from the nature of the contract, as in the case of seafaring men. *Commonwealth* v. *Edwards*, 6 *Binn.*, 202; *Commonwealth* v. *Deacon*, 6 *Serg. & Rawle*, 526.

In both of these cases the apprentices, brought from other states, one from Virginia and one from England, were discharged on habeas corpus.

"The relation of master and apprentice was in its original spirit and policy an intimate and interesting connection, calculated to give the apprentice a thorough trade and education, and to advance the mechanic arts in skill, neatness and fidelity of workmanship, as well as in the facility and utility of their application. The relationship if duly cultivated under a just sense of the responsibility attached to it, and with the moral teachings which belong to it, will produce parental care, vigilance and kindness on the part of the master, and a steady, diligent, faithful and reverential disposition and conduct on the part of the apprentice." 2 *Kent*, 266.

"A master may by law correct his apprentice for negligence or other misbehavior, so it be done with moderation." 1 *Black.*, 428. But he cannot depute another to give such correction. 1 *Wheeler, Crim. Cas.*, 159.

As in the case of parent and child there is also a power to impose temporary confinement, subject to similar limitations.

SECTION VI.

LIMITATIONS ARISING FROM THE RELATION OF MASTER AND SERVANT.

This relation rests altogether upon contract. The one is bound to render the service and the other to pay the stipulated price. Notwithstanding passages which may be found in the books apparently to the contrary, 1 *Hawk. P. C. C.*, 29, § 5; 3 *Salk.*, 47; 4 *Burns' J.*, 119, it is the opinion of a late English writer upon the subject that no master would be justified by the laws of England, even in moderately chastising a hired servant of full age, for dereliction of duty; and that when the books speak of a master being justified in moderately chastising his servant or apprentice, they must be taken to apply only to the case of a servant or apprentice under age.

It is stated in *Viner. Abr*, *tit. Master and Servant*, *K*, that if a servant departs from his master he cannot put his hands upon him nor bring him back by force.

There are numerous provisions in the English statutes for the regulation of laborers, domestic servants, and servants in husbandry, prescribing certain duties, regulating wages and inflicting corporeal and other punishments, which would seem to be unnecessary if the power of corporeal chastisement existed in the master or employer.

Chancellor Kent says: "This power does not grow out of the contract of hiring, and its lawfulness has been questioned on the ground that it is not agreeable to the genius and spirit of the contract. And, without alluding to seamen in the merchant service, it may safely be said to be confined to apprentices and menial servants while under age, for then the master is to be considered as standing *in loco parentis*." 2 *Kent*, 258.

It may be doubted whether this limitation is sufficiently restricted. Should not the power be limited to cases where the master contracts with the parent, or other person legally representing him for that purpose, for the service of the child under circumstances to afford ground to presume a delegation of the parental power of chastisement? At least ought not the power to be denied to the master in cases where servants have reached years of discretion, are emancipated from parental control and assume to and do contract for themselves?

SECTION VII.

LIMITATIONS ARISING FROM THE RELATION OF MASTER AND SCHOLAR.

The schoolmaster, also, is invested with a portion of parental authority. Whether his authority is derived from the parent, or, in case of public schools maintained at the public expense, from the state, is a matter of little consequence, as he stands in all cases for the time being *in loco parentis*; and is authorized to direct the application, regulate the conduct and require the obedience of his pupil to reasonable rules.

This authority does not ordinarily extend beyond the limits of the premises appropriated to the use of the school; nor does it attach to the pupil before the time appointed for opening the school or continue after it is dismissed. It is competent, however, for the parents, and perhaps in public schools for the officers charged by law with their management, to extend the authority of the master over the pupil on his way to and from school, and, out of school hours, over the school premises; but in the absence of special stipulations to this effect the child is in the parent's custody until it arrives at school and as soon as he leaves it.

Obedience to all proper rules and requirements may be enforced by stripes in moderation, as a last resort; or, within school hours, by temporary confinement. And, perhaps, in the absence of special and agreed regulations, a delinquent may be detained after the school is dismissed to complete a reasonable task which might with proper application have been accomplished in the regular hours of school; provided the time of such detention embrace only such period as would be given to play or idleness. In most cases parents require the services of their children morning and evening, and the right to exact them will not be presumed to have been waived or surrendered by the mere sending of the child to an ordinary day school. The power of the master to inflict punishment upon the pupil came under review in the case of *The State* v. *Pendergrass*, 2 *Dev. and Bat.*, 365, and the rules of law governing the relation were fully considered. With the exception of the test of responsibility, an "actual wicked motive" which it approves, the case exhibits satisfactorily the law upon this point.

The defendant was indicted for an assault and battery. She kept a school for small children. On one occasion, after mild treatment towards a little girl of six or seven years of age had failed, the defendant whipped her with a switch so as to cause marks upon her body, which disappeared in a few days. Two marks also were found to have existed, one on the arm and one on the neck, which were apparently made with a larger instrument, but they also disappeared in a few days. The court below had instructed the jury "that as the child was of tender years, if they believed the defendant had whipped her with either a switch or other instrument so as to produce the marks described to them, she was guilty." The Supreme Court held that this instruction was erroneous, and that the correction was not immoderate.

Gaston J., delivered the opinion of the court "It is not easy," says the judge, "to state, with precision, the power which the law grants to schoolmasters and teachers with respect to the correction of their pupils. It is analogous to that which belongs to parents, and the authority of the teacher is regarded as a delegation of parental authority. One of the most sacred duties of parents is to train up and qualify their children for becoming useful and virtuous members of society. This duty cannot be effectually performed without the ability to command obedience, to control stubbornness, to quicken diligence and to reform bad habits; and, to enable him to exercise this salutary sway, he is armed with the power to administer moderate correction when he shall believe it to be just and necessary. The teacher is the substitute of the parent; is charged in part with the performance of his duties, and in the exercise of these delegated duties is invested with his power. The law has not undertaken to prescribe stated punishments for particular offences, but has contented itself with the general grant of the power of moderate correction, and has confided the graduation of punishments, within the limits of this grant, to the discretion of the teacher.

"The line which separates moderate correction from immoderate punishment can only be ascertained by reference to general principles. The welfare of the child is the main purpose for which pain is permitted to be inflicted. Any punishment, therefore, which may seriously endanger life, limbs or health, or shall disfigure the child, or cause any other permanent injury, may be pronounced in itself immoderate, as not only being unnecessary for but inconsistent with the purpose for which correction is authorized. But any correction, however severe, which produces temporary pain only, and no permanent ill, cannot be so pronounced, since it may have been necessary for the reformation of the child and does not injuriously affect its future welfare.

"We hold, therefore, that it may be laid down as a general rule, that teachers exceed the limits of their authority when they cause lasting mischief; but act within the limits of it when they inflict temporary pain only. When the correction administered is not in itself immoderate, and therefore beyond the authority of the teacher, its legality or illegality must depend entirely, we think, on the *quo animo* with which it was administered. Within the sphere of his authority, the master is the judge when correction is required, and of the degree of correction necessary; and like all others entrusted with a discretion, he cannot be made penally responsible for error of judgment, but only for wickedness of purpose. The best and the wisest of mortals are weak and erring creatures, and in the exercise of functions in which their judgment is to be the guide, cannot be rightfully required to engage for more than honesty of purpose and diligence of execution. His judgment must be *presumed* to be correct, *because he is the judge*, and also because of the difficulty of proving the offence or accumulation of offences that called for correction; of showing the peculiar temperament, disposition and habits of the individual corrected; and of exhibiting the various milder means that may have been ineffectually used before correction was resorted to.

"But the master may be punishable when he does not transcend the powers granted, if he grossly abuse them. If he use his authority as a cover for malice, and, under the pretence of administering correction, gratify his own bad passions, the mask of the judge shall be taken off; and he will stand amenable to justice as an individual not invested with judicial power."

SECTION VIII.

LIMITATIONS ARISING FROM THE RELATION OF PRINCIPAL AND SPECIAL BAIL.

The relation of principal and bail is created where a party arrested or in prison on civil or criminal process procures sureties who undertake by bailbond or recognizance for his return or appearance at a place and on a day certain. 4 *Inst.*, 178; 3 *Black.*, 128; 4 *id.*, 297.

A man's bail are looked upon as his gaolers, of his own choosing; and the person bailed is in the eye of the law, for many purposes, esteemed to be as much in the prison of the court by which he is bailed, as if he were in the actual custody of the proper gaoler. 2 *Hawk. P. C., ch.* 15.

The term "bail" as used in this connection does not extend to all cases of suretyship. It imports a delivery of the person arrested or imprisoned out of public into private custody for safe keeping. Nor does it extend to all cases of imprisonment. It does not apply to the case of a "surety for the gaol liberties, which is not matter of record, but exists only *in pais.*" *Ex parte Bagley*, 7 *Cow.*, 472.

It is said it did not include the case of mainpernors at common law. 3 *Black.*, 128. "Every bail," says Coke, 4 *Inst.*, 179, "is mainprize (for those that are bail take the person bailed into their hands and custody), but every mainprize is not bail, because no man is bailed but he that is arrested, or in prison: for he that is not in custody or prison cannot be delivered out, as before it appeareth. But a man may be mainperned which never was in prison, and therefore mainprize is more large than bail."

"These words, 'mainpernors and bail,'" says *Petersdorf*, in his work on Bail, 7, "have been used indiscriminately without attending to the distinction, that *bail* have the power of imprisoning the principal, or surrendering him before the stipulated day of appearance; and that mainpernors can do nothing, but are barely and unconditionally sureties for his due attendance in court on the day mentioned in the writ. Bail are only sureties that the party will be answerable for the special matter for which they stipulated. Mainpernors are bound to produce him to answer all charges whatsoever."

The law relating to this distinction has become a matter rather of speculative curiosity than of practical interest. It is practically unknown with us, and the reasons assigned for it would seem to require the rejection of the distinction if the writ of mainprize was still in use.

This species of bailment is called a "living prison," 4 *Inst.*, 178, and the bail have the power, of their own motion, to detain or surrender the principal. They are his keepers and are said to have him always in a string, which they may pull whenever they please, and render him in their discharge; and this "because the court of justice doth deliver him unto them to be safely kept." 4 *Inst.*, 178.

A doubt seems to be intimated in *Ex parte Bagley*, 7 *Cow.*, 472, whether bail in a criminal case have power to surrender the principal. The case is briefly reported; but if the doubt be meant of the general rule it seems to be without foundation. 2 *Hawk. P. C.*, 140; *Com. Dig.*, *tit. Bail*, *Q.* 2; *Petersdorf on Bail*, 515; *Harp* v. *Osgood*, 2 *Hill*, 216.

The principal may be taken on Sunday. The dwelling-house ceases to be a castle to defend him, and if the door should not be opened the bail may break it down and drag him from his bed at midnight. *Commonwealth* v. *Bricket*, 8 *Pick.*, 138.

This power of the bail is not limited to the territorial jurisdiction of the court before which the relation is contracted; but is at least coextensive with the limits of the state.

If, however, after the letting to bail, other rights attach against the principal, the right of the bail may be suspended until those are determined: As where a debtor is in the jail bounds in one district and an applicant there for the benefit of the insolvent debtor's act, he cannot be taken by his bail out of that district to be surrendered in another; nor will a habeas corpus be granted at the instance of the bail for that purpose. For the court, it was said, never grants a habeas corpus for an illegal purpose. And in such a case it would be an escape, would make sureties on the prison-bounds-bond liable; would prevent the prisoner from obtaining his discharge under the insolvent debtors' act *where* he applied for it and *where* he was entitled to have it. *Breeze* v. *Elmore*, 4 *Rich.*, 436.

The question as to the power of the bail to arrest the principal beyond the state in which the bailment is made, is one of practical importance, though not of very frequent occurrence since the general abolition of imprisonment for debt. It is interesting also as it involves questions of state sovereignty and comity. There is a remarkable concurrence of judicial opinion in favor of its extra-territorial exercise.

In New York the question has twice been before the Supreme Court and the power sustained.

In the case of *Nicolls* v. *Ingersoll*, 7 *Johns.*, 144, it appeared that Pierpont Edwards was special bail for the plaintiff in Connecticut; that by a letter of attorney on the back of a copy of his recognizance he empowered Asa Morgan to call all necessary aid and in his behalf to arrest the plaintiff and surrender him in discharge of his recognizance; that Morgan, with the defendant, at midnight broke into the house of the plaintiff in the State of New York, seized him under the authority of the bail-piece and forcibly carried him off half dressed; that the defendant acted at Morgan's request and as his assistant.

The plaintiff brought this action of trespass, assault and battery and false imprisonment. The court held, First. That the bail may depute another to take the principal; Second. That the bail or his deputy may take the principal in another state and at any time and place.

In speaking to the latter point, the court say: "The power of taking and surrendering is not exercised under any judicial process; but results from the nature of the undertaking by the bail. The bail-piece is not process, nor anything in the nature of it; but is merely a record or memorial of the delivery of the principal to his bail on security given. It cannot be questioned, but that bail in the Common Pleas would have the right to go into any other county in the state to take his principal; this shows that the jurisdiction of the court in no way controls the authority of the bail; and as little can the jurisdiction of the state affect this right, as between the bail and his principal. How far the government would have a right to consider its peace disturbed, or its jurisdiction violated, or whether relief would not be granted on habeas corpus, where a citizen of this state was about to be carried to a foreign country, are questions not now before the court." After quoting 3 *Black.*, 290; 6 *Mod.*, 231; 1 *Atk.*, 237; and *Show.*, 214, the judge concludes: "The cases I have referred to show that the law considers the principal as a prisoner, whose gaol liberties are enlarged or circumscribed at the will of his bail; and according to this view of the subject it would seem necessarily to follow, that as between the bail and his principal, the controlling power of the former over the latter may be exercised at all times and in all places; and this appears to me indispensable for the safety and security of bail."

In a subsequent case, *Harp* v. *Osgood*, 2 *Hill*, 216, both of the above points were substantially reaffirmed. In that case it appeared that the bail in New York sent a deputy to Virginia, to bring back the principal to be surrendered. Being arrested, he obtained, on account of sickness in his family and urgent business engagements, his release from the arrest by paying the deputy $100, being the expenses of the journey and procuring the defendant to execute his note for $200 conditioned for the principal's appearance at court in discharge of the bail. The principal failing to appear, suit was brought on the note, and the action sustained to the extent of $65, being the necessary expenses of the bail in attending court, employing attorneys.

In Connecticut the same doctrine is recognized. *Howard* v. *Lyon*, 1 *Root*, 107; *Pease* v. *Burt*, 3 *Day*, 485; *Parker* v. *Bidwell*, 3 *Conn.*, 84; *Ruggles* v. *Corey*, *id.*, 421.

In Massachusetts the point was determined in the case of *Commonwealth* v. *Bricket*, 8 *Pick.*, 138. This was a case in habeas corpus sued out at the instance of Samuel Thompson for whom the defendant was bail in a civil proceeding before a justice of the peace in Vermont. Thompson fled and Bricket pursued and arrested him in Massachusetts to remove him to Vermont in his discharge as bail.

The court held that the liability of the principal to arrest by his bail arose from the contract and that the bail was entitled to remedy according to their laws. "There is no statute provision here," says the court, "for the granting of a warrant for the bail. He is to act here, if at all, under the provisions of the common law, and we are satisfied that they are sufficient. The obligation which the principal entered into to the bail was not discharged by stepping across the line of his state. The relation between bail and principal exists here as it did in Vermont, in full force." The prisoner was remanded to the custody of the defendant.

In Pennsylvania, the question for the third time came under review of the Supreme Court in 1837, and was fully discussed in the case of *Halsey* v. *Trevillo*, 6 *Watts*, 402. In that case the relator Smith Halsey showed a bail-piece, duly certified, from the inferior court of Common Pleas of Essex county, New Jersey, in a suit of *R. W.* v. *A. R. Woolley*, in which suit the relator and J. Allen were bound as special bail for said Woolley, who was a citizen of Kentucky. The relator had met the said Woolley on his road to New Jersey, and by virtue of his bail-piece had him in custody at Pittsburgh: He was taken from the custody of his bail by E. Trevillo. On the return to the writ of habeas corpus, the sheriff returned that he had arrested Mr. Woolley on a capias ad respondendum, issued by the administrators of O. Ormsby, deceased, in which special bail was required in $300. This writ was issued after the bail arrived in the city with his principal, and on it he was taken from the custody of the bail, who sued out this writ of habeas corpus. The relator had also a regular deputation from J. Allen, the other special bail.

The court said: "It seems that special bail may depute another to act for him in executing a bail-piece, 3 *Conn.*, 84; 7 *Johns.*, 145; but I take it, where there are two persons special bail, one may take out a bail-piece and bring and surrender his principal in discharge of his bail, at all events in discharge of himself. The writ of habeas corpus may issue at the instance of the party restrained of his liberty or at the instance of any other person who has the right to the custody of such person; and the English books abound with cases of habeas corpus at the instance of special bail; and this in civil cases is matter of course. When confined on a criminal charge, it must be on motion; but in either case it is not matter of favor, but *ex debito justitiæ*. 7 *Durn. & E.*, 222.

The power of the special bail over the principal is very great. They may arrest in the night; on Sunday; force doors; and in case of resistance, use any force necessary to overcome the resistance.

In England the government is one. In the United States, the citizens of every state are constantly passing to other states; and many have contracts and liabilities in several states. Hence a man may be sued and give special bail in one state and before that suit is ended become indebted in another state, and arrested and confined or give special bail there, and this presents a case different perhaps from what is found in the English books. Taking into view our general and state governments, the jurisdiction of the several courts is such that we need not expect to find, out of our Union, decisions in point in all cases. If we look to the constitution of the United States we find that full faith and credit shall be given in each state to the public acts, records and judicial proceedings of every other state."

Without pretending to state the effect of this provision in all cases, it may have some bearing on a case like the present; and the harmony of the Union might be endangered if any one state should become a city of refuge to the debtors of all other states, and if crossing the line of any state should secure any principal debtor from his special bail. It has been said that "the bail has the principal on a string and may pull it when he pleases." I do not believe that legal rights are made clear by metaphors, or comparison with material things. It seems settled that either by the nature of the agreement or by the operation of law on the agreement, the bail has rights over the personal liberty of the principal of the most positive kind, and that a sheriff is bound to assist in enforcing them; and we have authority for saying this right of the bail extends beyond the state in which bail was entered. 7 *Johns.*, 145; 8 *Pick.* 138.

This matter is not new in this state. As early as 1798, 2 *Yeates R.*, 263, a habeas corpus issued to the keeper of the prison in Philadelphia, who returned that he held the prisoner on two several writs of capias as mesne process, one of which had been executed before the bail came from Virginia with his bail-piece. The case is not very accurately reported; but the court say: "In the relation in which the several states composing the Union stand to each other, the bail in a suit entered in another state have the right to seize and take the principal in a sister state, provided it does not interfere with the interests of other persons who have arrested such person. But where actions have been brought against the party, previous to such seizure, the same right does not exist." I then understand the case that the debtor had been arrested and was in custody of the sheriff *before* the seizure on the bail-piece, and for that reason was not delivered to his bail. See also 3 *Yeates*, 37, where the right of bail in another state to take the principal here is again recognized, but the right to remove him was suspended until the sentence of a court-martial, passed against him, was executed."

Woolley was restored to the custody of his bail that he might proceed with him.

In the case from 2 *Yeates*, 263, the court intimate that the bail could not be deprived of his rights by collusion between his principal and other parties, saying, in addition to what is above quoted from the decision: "Nevertheless if the actions originated by collusion with the defendant and merely to protect him from being surrendered to his bail, the court, on good grounds, would interfere and prevent such improper practice." 1 *Str.*, 416.

In Louisiana the same general doctrine has been twice sustained. In *Lafonta's case*, 2 *Rob.*, 495, it was also further held that the bail was entitled to the aid of the sheriff and might apply to the court for an order to arrest the principal. In that case, which was one of habeas corpus, the judge in stating the case and delivering the opinion of the court says: "Bruce and Hays are appellants from a judgment which discharges Lafonta on a writ of habeas corpus from their custody as his bail in a suit brought against him in the State of Massachusetts, where he was arrested by a writ of capias ad respondendum, and obtained his liberty by the execution of a bailbond in which the appellants joined him; almost immediately afterwards Lafonta came to New Orleans, where they obtained, on the production of the bail-piece, from the Commercial Court of this city, an order to the sheriff to arrest him and deliver him to them, in order that they might be enabled to surrender him as their principal in the court of the State of Massachusetts, which had issued the writ on which they became bail. The petitioner, having been arrested by the sheriff on this order, obtained from the court of the first judicial district a writ of habeas corpus, on which he was discharged; the District Court being of opinion that the petitioner was arrested and confined in a case where the law does not allow the issuing of orders of arrest and imprisonment, and that the Commercial Court of New Orleans had exceeded its jurisdiction as defined by law in ordering said arrest.

Martin, J. "If the appellants had been bail for Lafonta in a suit depending in any of the courts of this state, there is no doubt he could not be retained by them since the abolition of imprisonment for debt; because the act abolishing it relieved them from all the obligations they incurred by becoming his bail, and consequently deprived them of any right over him. * * * The decision of the Superior Court of the late territory, in the case of *Henderson* v. *Lynd*, 2 *Mart.*, 57, goes the whole length in support of the right of the bail to arrest his principal even out of the state in which bail was given, and after the latter has obtained a stay of proceedings." The code of Massachusetts showing that imprisonment for debt there was, *before* the arrest by the principal in that state, authorized by the laws there, the court held that they could not presume a repeal of them, on the grounds of the abolition of imprisonment for debt in Louisiana, and proceeded: "The right of the bail to seize his principal being admitted, it follows as a corollary that to avoid resistance and to prevent the appearance of a breach of the peace, he may on the production of his bail-piece, obtain the assistance of the sheriff or constable, and also if necessary the order of a court of justice or magistrate.

"Judgment of District Court reversed and ordered that appellee remain in custody of appellants, to be surrendered, &c."

In Virginia the question is not considered settled. "However competent it might be," says Mr. Robinson, in his valuable work on practice, 1 *Rob. Pr.*, 55, "to the federal legislature, or that of the states, to give operation to the laws of one state within the bounds of others, Judge Robertson was very doubtful of the power of the judiciary tribunals to act upon that principle in the absence of such legislation. His opinion was, that no construction of the constitutional provision could be admitted which would give to the laws of another state an extra-territorial operation, propria vigore. Nor did he think an argument in favor of the bail could be founded on the circumstance that a bail-piece is not technically considered as process. 'If,' said he, 'the regular process of law in one state cannot be legally served or executed in another by regular officers, under the sanction of official oaths and official responsibility, still less can a summary arrest and deputation by individuals acting under no such sanction be admitted.'

Waiving, however, any express adjudication of the doctrine in reference to bail, he held that a similar right was not by analogy to be extended to sureties in a ne exeat bond, executed in New York, notwithstanding it was argued that by the laws of that state such sureties or bail may in person, or by agent or deputy, take and surrender their principal.

In a case in which such sureties or bail had, by an agent empowered under their hands and seals, taken the principal in Virginia, with the intention of carrying him to New York and there surrendering him, Judge Robertson, on a petition by the principal, representing that he was a citizen and resident of Virginia, entitled to the security afforded by her laws, awarded a habeas corpus, and after argument ordered that he be discharged. Upon petition, the supreme Court of Appeals awarded a writ of error to this judgment; but the case was never heard in the appellate court. By an arrangement of the bail with the principal, he voluntarily returned to New York; and the writ of error was dismissed.

CHAPTER IV.

CONSTITUTIONAL AND STATUTORY GUARANTEES OF THE RIGHT OF PERSONAL LIBERTY IN ENGLAND.

At what time the right of personal liberty first became a special subject of political concern in England, in what manner it was entrenched in enduring constitutional enactments, with what spirit and success it was defended when assailed by arbitrary princes, and how it was finally secured by increasing the efficiency of the writ of habeas corpus, are inquiries full of interest and instruction to the American student, whose colonial ancestors claimed as their "birth-right" and finally defended with their lives, "the rights, liberties and immunities of Englishmen."

These inquiries lead to the subjects considered in the following sections:

SECTION I. MAGNA CARTA.

II. THE PETITION OF RIGHT.

III. THE BILL OF RIGHTS.

IV. THE HABEAS CORPUS ACT, 31 CAR. 2, C. 2.

SECTION I.

MAGNA CARTA.

In the month of June, A. D. 1215, the Barons of England with their retainers, "a numerous host, were encamped upon the grassy plain of Runingmede," to demand of their sovereign, and, if necessary, to enforce by the sword, an acknowledgment of their rights and liberties and a covenant to protect them. Unwilling to concede what was demanded, yet unable to resist, King John finally signed, and sealed, and swore faithfully to observe, the *Great Charter*.

This celebrated instrument, although in form a grant of certain rights and privileges by the sovereign, was essentially a solemn acknowledgment of those rights and privileges; and an agreement that for the future they should be maintained "*bona fide* and without evil subtilty."

It has always been regarded as a fundamental law. "It was for the most part," says Coke, "declaratory of the principal grounds of the fundamental laws of England; and for the residue it is additional to supply some defects of the common law." 2 *Inst., proeme, and pp.* 65, 77, 78, 108.

"This famous deed," says Hume, "either granted or secured very important liberties and privileges to every order of men in the kingdom; to the clergy, to the barons and to the people. The former articles of it contain such mitigations and explanations of the feudal law as are reasonable and equitable; and the latter involve all the chief outlines of a legal government, and provide for the equal distribution of justice and free enjoyment of property; the great objects for which political society was at first founded by men, which the people have a perpetual and inalienable right to recall, and which no time, nor precedent, nor statute, nor positive institution, ought to deter them from keeping ever uppermost in their thoughts and attention." 1 *Hist. Eng.*, 219.

"The great constitutional enactments of Magna Carta have, from the very earliest times, been regarded in that light, and treated not as temporary regulations, but as the fundamental institutions of our government and laws. Their confirmation was repeatedly exacted from the reigning sovereign by our parliaments, not because the Great Charter was supposed to become invalid without such ratification, but in order to impress more solemnly on impatient princes and profligate statesmen their duty of respecting the great constitutional ordinances of the realm." *Creasy, Const.*, 225.

"As this was," says Hallam, "the first effort towards a legal government, so it is beyond comparison the most important event in our history, except that revolution without which its benefits would rapidly have been annihilated. The constitution of England has indeed no single date from which its duration is to be reckoned. The institutions of positive law, the far more important changes which time has wrought in the order of society during six hundred years subsequent to the Great Charter, have undoubtedly lessened its direct application to our present circumstances; but it is still the keystone of English liberty." 2 *Mid. Ages,* 341.

Sir James Mackintosh says of it: "It was a peculiar advantage that the consequences of its principles were, if we may so speak, only discovered gradually and slowly. It gave out on each occasion only as much of the spirit of liberty and reformation as the circumstances of succeeding generations required, and as their character would safely bear. For almost five centuries it was appealed to as the decisive authority on behalf of the people, though commonly so far only as the necessities of each case demanded. Its effect in these contests was not altogether unlike the grand process by which nature employs snows and frosts to cover her delicate germs, and to hinder them from rising above the earth till the atmosphere has acquired the mild and equal temperature which insures them against blights.

"On the English nation, undoubtedly, the Charter has contributed to bestow the union of establishment with improvement. To all mankind it set the first example of the progress of a great people, for centuries, in blending their tumultuary democracy and haughty nobility with a fluctuating and vaguely limited monarchy, so as at length to form from these discordant materials the only form of free government which experience had shown to be reconcilable with widely extended dominions. Whoever in any future age or yet unborn nation may admire the felicity of the expedient which converted the power of taxation into the shield of liberty, by which discretionary and secret imprisonment was rendered impracticable, and portions of the people were trained to exercise a larger share of judicial power than ever was allotted to them in any other civilized state, in such a manner as to secure, instead of endangering public tranquillity; whoever exults at the spectacle of enlightened and independent assemblies, which under the eye of a well informed nation, discuss and determine the laws and policy likely to make communities great and happy; whoever is capable of comprehending all the effects of such institutions with all their possible improvements upon the mind and genius of a people, is sacredly bound to speak with reverential gratitude of the authors of the Great Charter. To have produced it, to have preserved it, to have matured it, constitute the immortal claim of England upon the esteem of mankind. Her Bacons and Shakespeares, her Miltons and Newtons, with all the truth which they have revealed, and all the generous virtue which they have inspired, are of inferior value when compared with the subjection of men and their rulers to the principles of justice, if, indeed it be not more true that these mighty spirits could not have been formed except under equal laws, nor roused to full activity without the influence of that spirit which the Great Charter breathed over their forefathers."

The "crowning glories" of Magna Carta are those "essential clauses which protect the personal liberty and property of all freemen, by giving security from arbitrary imprisonment and arbitrary spoliation."

39. Nullus liber homo capiatur, vel imprisonetur, aut dissaisiatur aut utlagetur, aut aliquo modo destrua-

tur; nec super eum ibimus, nec super eum mittemus, nisi per legale judicium parium suorum, vel per legem terre.

40. Nulli vendemus, nulli negabimus, aut differemus, rectum aut justiciam.

39. No freeman shall be taken or imprisoned, or disseized, or outlawed, or banished, or anyways destroyed, nor will we pass upon him, nor will we send him, unless by the lawful judgment of his peers, or by the law of the land.

40. We will sell to no man, we will not deny to any man, either justice or right.

To the unlettered barons whose practical wisdom approved these plain but most comprehensive words, and whose courage secured and defended them, the great commoner, in his speech in the House of Peers, on the 9th January, 1770, paid the following noble tribute: "It is to your ancestors, my lords, it is to the English barons that we are indebted for the laws and constitution we possess. Their virtues were rude and uncultivated, but they were great and sincere. Their understandings were as little polished as their manners, but they had hearts to distinguish right from wrong; they had heads to distinguish truth from falsehood; they understood the rights of humanity, and they had spirit to maintain them.

"My lords, I think that history has not done justice to their conduct; when they obtained from their sovereign that great acknowledgment of national rights contained in Magna Carta, they did not confine it to themselves alone, but delivered it as a common blessing to the whole people.

"They did not say, these are the rights of the great barons, or these are the rights of the great prelates. No, my lords; they said in the simple Latin of the times, *nullus liber homo*, and provided as carefully for the meanest subject as for the greatest. These are uncouth words, and sound but poorly in the ears of scholars; neither are they addressed to the criticism of scholars, but to the hearts of free men. These three words, *nullus liber homo*, have a meaning which interests us all; they deserve to be remembered, they deserve to be inculcated in our minds, *they are worth all the classics.*"

Mr. Hallam, commenting upon these words of the charter, says: "It is obvious that these words interpreted by any honest court of law, convey an ample security for the two main rights of civil society. From the era, therefore, of King John's charter, it must have been a clear principle of our constitution, that no man can be detained in prison without trial. *Whether courts of justice framed the writ of* HABEAS CORPUS *in conformity to the spirit of this clause, or found it already in their register, it became from that era the right of every subject to demand it.*" 2 *Hist. Mid. Ages*, 342.

Though the King seemed to submit passively to the regulations of the charter, he only dissembled till he should find a favorable opportunity for annulling all his concessions. He dispatched a messenger to Rome, in order to lay before the Pope the Great Charter, which he had been compelled to sign, and to complain, before that tribunal, of the violence which had been imposed upon him.

The Pope issued a bull, in which, from the plenitude of his apostolic power, and from the authority which God had committed to him, to build and destroy kingdoms, to plant and overthrow, he annulled and abrogated the whole charter as unjust in itself, as obtained by compulsion and as derogatory to the dignity of the apostolic see. He prohibited the barons from exacting the observance of it; he even prohibited the King himself from paying any regard to it; he absolved him and his subjects from all oaths which they had been constrained to take to that purpose; and he pronounced a general sentence of excommunication against every one who should persevere in maintaining such treasonable and iniquitous pretensions.

But the bull of the Pope was ineffectual. John still found that his nobility and people, and even his clergy, adhered to the defence of their liberties, and to their combination against him; the sword of his foreign mercenaries was all he had to trust for restoring his authority. The ravenous and barbarous mercenaries, incited by a cruel and enraged prince, were let loose against the estates, tenants, manors, houses, parks of the barons, and spread devastation over the face of the kingdom. Nothing was to be seen but the flames of villages and castles reduced to ashes, the consternation and misery of the inhabitants, tortures exercised by the soldiery to make them reveal their concealed treasures, and reprisals no less barbarous committed by the barons and their partisans on the royal demesnes, and on the estates of such as still adhered to the crown. 1*st Hume Hist. Eng.*, 222.

The event proved that although the perfidious king had power to excite civil war and desolate his dominions with the torch and sword of foreign mercenaries, he could no more suppress, even with the aid of the spiritual arm of the Roman Pontiff, the rising tide of liberty, or eradicate from the English Constitution the simple but all-pervading political truths declared in the Great Charter, than the vain-glorious Canute could by his royal word arrest the advancing billows of the sea, or extract from them, had he tried, the salt which conserves them.

The king died. The Great Charter still lives.

At the time of the king's death the Earl of Pembroke, the Ulysses of the camp at Runingmede, was mareschal of England, and by his office at the head of the armies—and, *flagrante bello*, of the government. His first act as Protector of the kingdom, was to renew the Great Charter, though with some changes.

It was granted again the next year, "and was again renewed by Henry in the ninth year of his reign, at which time the Charter of the Forest was granted. The two Charters were five times renewed between this period and Henry's death. At some of these renewals temporary variations were introduced; but it is in the form in which it was promulgated in the ninth year of Henry's reign that the Great Charter was solemnly confirmed by his successor, and in that form it appears at the head of our statute book." *Creasy, Constitution*, 166.

In the charter as thus confirmed, the "essential clauses" are in these words: chap. 29. "Nullus liber homo capiatur, vel imprisonetur, aut disseisietur de aliquo libero tenemento suo vel libertatibus vel liberis consuetudinibus suis, aut utlagetur, aut exulet, aut aliquo alio modo destruatur, nec super eum ibimus, nec super eum mittemus nisi per legale judicium parium suorum vel per legem terræ. Nulli vendemus, nulli negabimus, aut differemus rectum aut justitiam."

This chapter is translated in the common edition of the English Statutes, as follows: "No freeman shall be taken or imprisoned, or be disseized of his freehold, or liberties, or free customs, or be outlawed or exiled, or any otherwise destroyed, nor will we pass upon him, nor condemn him, but by lawful judgment of his peers, or by the law of the land. We will sell to no man, we will not deny or defer to any man, either justice or right." The precise import of the words "nec super eum ibimus, nec super eum mittemus," has been the subject of question and some diversity of opinion. 3 *Lingard*, 47 *n.*

By some they have been translated, "nor will we pass upon him, nor condemn him;" by others, "nor will we pass upon him, nor commit him to prison;" and Coke's exposition is different from all others: "No man shall be condemned at the King's suit, either before the King in his bench, where pleas are *coram rege* (before the King), (and so are the words *nec super ibimus*, to be understood), nor before any other commissioner or judge whatsoever, and so are the words "*nec super mittemus*," to be understood, but by the judgment of his peers, that is equals, or according to the law of the land." 2 *Coke Inst.*, 46.

Mr. Spooner, in his Essay on the Trial by Jury, after an elaborate examination, critical and historical, of the question, states the legal import of the chapter as follows:

"No freeman shall be arrested, or imprisoned, or deprived of his freehold, or his liberties, or free customs, or be outlawed or exiled, or in any manner destroyed (harmed), *nor will we* (the King) *proceed against him, nor send any one against him, by force or arms,* unless according to (that is, in execution of) the sentence of his peers, *and* (or, *or* as the case may require) the Common Law of England (as it was at the time of Magna Carta, in 1215). *Spooner's Trial by Jury*, 49.

To secure the observance of the Charters, the nobles and great officers were required to be sworn to support them. *Coke, proem,* 2 *Inst.* And every British sovereign at his coronation is still sworn to maintain them. *Wester. Comm.*, 142.

Earnest efforts were also made to make the Great Charter familiarly known throughout the land by all, as the common birthright of all; and the most stringent measures of law were devised to insure the prompt punishment of any who should dare to violate it. The Great Charter and the Charter of the Forest were required by law to be kept in every parish—to be sent to all cathedral churches throughout the realm, there to remain, and to be read to the people twice a year—to be sent as well to the justices of the forest as to others, to all sheriffs and other officers, and to all the cities in the realm—to be read by the sheriffs four times a year, before the people of the shire in open county court.

It was also provided in the confirmation of 25 *Ed. I.*, "that all archbishops and bishops shall pronounce the sentence of excommunication against all those that by word, deed, or council, do contrary to the foresaid Charters, or that in any point break or undo them; and that the said curses be twice a year denounced and published by the prelates aforesaid."

The following is a copy of the famous curse:

"THE CURSE.

"In the name of the Father, the Son and the Holy Ghost, *Amen*. Whereas our Sovereign Lord, the King, to the honour of God, and of Holy Church, and for the common profit of the realm, hath granted for him and his heirs for ever, these articles above written; Robert, Archbishop of Canterbury, primate of all England, admonisheth all his province, once, twice, and thrice: Because that shortness will not suffer so much delay, as to give knowledge to all the people of England of these presents in writing: We therefore enjoyn all persons, of what estate soever they may be, that they and every of them, as much as in them is, shall uphold and maintain these articles granted by our Sovereign the King in all points. And all those that in any point do resist or break, or in any manner hereafter procure, counsel, or any ways assent to resist or break those ordinances, or go about it, by word or deed, openly or privily, by any manner of pretence, or color, We the foresaid archbishop by our authority in this writing expressed, do excommunicate and accurse, and from the body of our Lord Jesus Christ, and from all the company of heaven, and from all the sacraments of Holy Church do sequester and exclude."

SECTION II.

THE PETITION OF RIGHT.

After the lapse of four hundred years, during which time the Great Charter not only remained unrepealed, but was more than thirty times solemnly ratified, 2 *Hallam's Middle Ages*, 343, and its essential principles known to all the people, and recognized in all courts, though sometimes most unjustly evaded by them—the power of the people peaceably to maintain them against the encroachments of an artful, grasping and faithless king was brought to the test.

In the year 1627, Hampden, Darnel, Corbet, Earl and Heveningham having with others been committed to prison by the Privy Council for refusing obedience to the forced loans demanded of them without authority of Parliament, applied to the court of King's Bench for the writ of habeas corpus.

"The writ was granted; but the warden of the fleet made return that they were detained by a warrant from the Privy Council, informing him of no particular cause of imprisonment, but that they were committed by the special command of his Majesty. This gave rise to a most important question whether such a return was sufficient in law to justify the court in remitting the parties to custody. The fundamental immunity of English subjects from arbitrary detention had never before been so fully canvassed; and it is to the discussion which arose out of the case of these five gentlemen that we owe its continual assertion by Parliament, and its ultimate establishment in full practical efficacy by the statute of Charles II. It was argued with great ability by Noy, Selden, and other eminent lawyers, on behalf of the claimants, and by the Attorney-General Heath for the crown." 1 *Hallam's Const. Hist.*, 383.

The prisoners based their demand for liberty upon Magna Carta, "the fundamental laws and statutes of the realm." But the court was deaf to their plea. Seizing upon an obscure precedent more than a hundred years old, they held that "the special command of the King or the authority of the Privy Council as a body, was such sufficient warrant for commitment as to require no further cause to be expressed;" and remanded the prisoners to jail.

But the nation could not be diverted from its cardinal faith in its own prescriptive franchises by measures of illegal severity towards the uncompliant. Another Parliament became indispensable.

It assembled in 1628; Coke, Selden, Glanvil, Pynne, Elliott, famous for their sturdy independence and their zeal in the cause of popular rights, were members.

The decision in the case of Hampden and others was made the subject of special inquiry and animadversion. The judges were summoned to give an account of their judgment. They answered contrary to the record, "that the prisoners were only remanded that the court might be further advised. 7 *St. Tr.*, 183. The investigation proceeded. "What is this," said Coke, speaking of the decision, "but to declare, upon record, that any subject by such absolute command may be detained in prison forever? What doth this tend to but the utter subversion of the choice, liberty and right belonging to every free born subject in this kingdom?"

Resolutions were proposed and carried.

"I. That no freeman ought to be committed or detained in prison or otherwise restrained by command of the King, or the Privy Council or any other, unless some cause of the commitment, detainer or restraint be expressed, for which by law he ought to be committed, detained or restrained.

"II. That the writ of habeas corpus cannot be denied, but ought to be granted to every man that is committed or detained in prison or otherwise restrained by command of the King, the Privy Council or any other."

Not content with resolutions, they proceeded to the more efficient work of a declaratory statute, commonly called the PETITION OF RIGHT, by which it was designed to subject the King to the power of the law and to bring the right of personal liberty explicitly under its protection. The King, after attempting to evade giving his consent, was at length—but not until after the "*auricular taking of the judges' opinions*"—compelled to accede to the petition. In the petition it was, amongst other things, recited and declared as follows:

"III. And whereas, also, by the statute called 'The Great Charter of the Liberties of England,' it is declared and enacted, that no freeman may be taken or imprisoned, or be disseized of his freehold or liberties, or his free customs, or be outlawed or exiled, or in any manner destroyed, but by the lawful judgment of his peers, or by the law of the land.

"IV. And in the eight-and-twentieth year of the reign of King Edward III., it was declared and enacted by authority of Parliament, that no man, of what estate or condition that he be, should be put out of his land or tenements, nor taken, nor imprisoned, nor disinherited, nor put to death without being brought to answer by due process of law.

"V. Nevertheless, against the tenor of said statutes and other the good laws and statutes of your realm to that end provided, divers of your subjects have of late been imprisoned without any cause shewed; and when for their deliverance they were brought before your justices by your Majesty's writs of habeas corpus, there to undergo and receive as the court should order, and their keepers commanded to certify the causes of their detainer, no cause was certified, but that they were detained by your Majesty's special command, signified by the lords of your Privy Council and yet were returned back to several prisons, without being charged with anything to which they might make answer according to law."

In the subsequent sections the King was petitioned to declare that, "as their rights and liberties according to the laws and statutes of this realm," — "no freeman, in any such manner as is before mentioned, be imprisoned or detained," &c., &c.

The King having privately obtained from the judges a construction of the Petition to suit his wishes, granted it. It was then supposed that the people were effectually protected against illegal exactions, arbitrary commitments, quartering of soldiers or sailors, and infliction of punishment by martial law.

"Bonfires were kindled all over London, and the whole nation was thrown into a transport of joy." But the Parliament was soon after dissolved by the

King who was incensed at the conduct of those advocates of popular rights, by whose "disobedient and seditious carriage," he said, "we and our regal authority and commandment have been so highly contemned as our kingly office cannot bear, nor any former age can parallel." 1 *Hallam Const. Hist.*, 390.

Prerogative then reigned. The obnoxious members of the late Parliament were seized and imprisoned for words spoken in debate. The writ of habeas corpus was rendered powerless even to liberate them on bail by the servile *procrastination* of the court who dared not expressly to *deny* the right. And finally JOHN ELLIOTT, the most distinguished leader of the popular party, doomed to imprisonment and loaded with fines by a court usurping jurisdiction, died in the Tower — a martyr to parliamentary freedom of speech.

Denzil Holles, one of his associates in the royal persecution afterwards, being then a peer, brought the record of this judgment in the King's Bench by writ of error before the House of Lords, by whom it was reversed — thus establishing the great principle of free speech in parliament and exclusive jurisdiction of the House over its members for alleged contempts therein. 1 *Hallam Const. Hist.*, 424.

SECTION III.

THE BILL OF RIGHTS.

Mention ought to be made, in this connection, of the Bill of Rights, another fundamental statute passed in 1689, which, with the Petition of Right and the Great Charter, constitute, according to Lord Chatham, "*the Bible of the English Constitution*," to which appeal is to be made on every grave political question."

The Bill of Rights, in some respects the archetype of our own Declaration of Independence, recites the injuries and usurpations of the late King James II., by which he "did endeavor to subvert and extirpate the Protestant religion, and the laws and liberties of this kingdom," and then "for the vindicating their ancient rights and liberties," "as their ancestors in like case have usually done," declares:

"1. That the pretended power of suspending laws, or the execution of laws, by regal authority, without consent of Parliament, is illegal.

"2. That the pretended power of dispensing with laws, or the execution of laws, by regal authority, as it hath been assumed and exercised of late, is illegal.

"3. That the commission for creating the late Court of Commissioners for ecclesiastical causes, and all other commissions and courts of like nature, are illegal and pernicious.

"4. That levying money for or to the use of the crown, by pretence and prerogative, without grant of Parliament, for longer time or in other manner than the same is or shall be granted, is illegal.

"5. That it is the right of the subjects to petition the King, and all commitments and prosecutions for such petitioning are illegal.

"6. That the raising or keeping a standing army within the kingdom in time of peace, unless it be with consent of Parliament, is against law.

"7. That the subjects which are Protestants, may have arms for their defence suitable to their conditions, and as allowed by law.

"8. That election of members of Parliament ought to be free.

"9. That the freedom of speech, and debates or proceedings in Parliament, ought not to be impeached or questioned in any court or place out of Parliament.

"10. That excessive bail ought not to be required, nor excessive fines imposed; nor cruel and unusual punishments inflicted.

"11. That jurors ought to be duly empanelled and returned, and jurors which pass upon men in trials for high treason ought to be freeholders.

"12. That all grants and promises of fines and forfeitures of particular persons before conviction, are illegal and void.

"13. That for redress of all grievances, and for the amending, strengthening and preserving of the laws, Parliaments ought to be held frequently."

Macauley sees in this instrument an inexhaustible stock of statute-germs, adequate for all the wants of posterity.

"The Declaration of Right," says he, "though it made nothing law which had not been law before, *contained the germ* of the law which gave religious freedom to the Dissenter, of the law which secured the independence of the judges, of the law which limited the duration of Parliaments, of the law which placed the liberty of the press under the protection of juries, of the law which prohibited the slave trade, of the law which abolished the sacramental test, of the law which relieved the Roman Catholics from civil disabilities, of the law which reformed the representative system — *of every good law which has been passed during a hundred and sixty years, of every good law which may hereafter, in the course of ages, be found to promote the public weal, and to satisfy the demands of public opinion.*" *Macauley Hist. Eng.*, 394.

SECTION IV.

THE HABEAS CORPUS ACTS, 31 CAR. II., AND 56 GEO. III.

Although the writ of habeas corpus was greatly prized, and gradually superseded all other common law writs devised to relieve in cases of illegal imprisonment, it became in lapse of time the subject of great abuses. Delays, scarcely less grievous than denial, were frequently practiced by the courts in granting it; and, when granted, tardy execution too frequently tolerated. Some evasions were remedied by the statute of 16 Car. I, c. 10, § 8, which provided that if any person be committed by the King himself in person, or by his Privy Council, or by any of the members thereof, he shall have granted unto him, without any delay upon any pretence whatsoever, a writ of habeas corpus, upon demand or motion made to the Court of King's Bench or Common Pleas; who shall thereupon, within three court days after the return is made, examine and determine the legality of the commitment and do what to justice shall appertain, in delivering, bailing or remanding such prisoner.

Still "other abuses had also crept into daily practice, which had in some measure defeated the benefit of this great constitutional remedy. The party imprisoning was at liberty to delay his obedience to the first writ, and might wait till a second and third, called an *alias* and a *pluries*, were issued before he produced the party; and many other vexatious shifts were practiced to detain state prisoners in custody." 3 *Bl. Com.*, 135. Greater promptitude and a livelier sense of official responsibility were required to render the writ efficacious. The subject was accordingly brought forward in Parliament in 1668, and renewed from time to time until 1679, when the celebrated habeas corpus act of 31 Car. II. was passed.

The passage of this act has been made the theme of the highest praise and congratulation by British authors, and is even said to have "extinguished all the resources of oppression." *Western Com.*, 219.

The immediate occasion of this act has generally been said to be the oppression of an "obscure individual" by the name of Jenks; and the circumstance has been dwelt upon with pride "for the just idea it conveys of that readiness of all orders of men to unite in defence of common liberty, which is a characteristic circumstance in the English government." *Western's Com.*, 368. The case of Jenks was this: "He was a citizen of London, on the popular or factious side; having been committed by the King in council for a mutinous speech in Guildhall, the justices at quarter sessions refused to admit him to bail, on pretence that he had been committed by a superior court; or to try him, because he was not entered in the calendar of prisoners. The Chancellor, on application for a habeas corpus, declined to issue it during the vacation; and the Chief Justice of the King's Bench, to whom, in the next place, the friends of Jenks had recourse, made so many difficulties that he lay in prison for several weeks."

Mr. Hallam, however, does not concur in the common opinion, and states his reasons as follows: "The arbitrary proceedings of Lord Clarendon were what really gave rise to it. A bill to prevent the refusal of the writ of habeas corpus, was brought into the House on April 10, 1668, but did not pass the committee in that session. But another to the same purpose, probably more remedial, was sent up to the Lords in March, 1669–70. It failed of success in the upper house; but the Commons continued their struggle for this important measure, and in the session of 1673–4, passed two bills, one to prevent the imprisonment of the subject in gaols beyond seas, another to give a more expeditious use of the writ of habeas corpus in criminal matters. The same or similar bills appear to have gone up to the Lords in 1675. It was not till 1676, that the delay in Jenks's habeas corpus took place. And this affair seems to have had so trifling an influence that these bills were not revived for the next two years, notwithstanding the tempests that agitated the House during that period. But in the short Parliament of 1679, they appear to have been consolidated into one;

that, having met with better success among the Lords, passed into a statute, and is generally denominated the habeas corpus act." 2 *Hallam's Const. Hist.*, 176.

The same author proceeds to notice further, the subject of habeas corpus, and the more recent legislation in regard to it. "It is a very common mistake," he continues, "and that not only among foreigners, but many from whom some knowledge of our constitutional laws might be expected, to suppose that this statute of Charles II. enlarged in a great degree our liberties, and forms a sort of epoch in our history. But though a very beneficial enactment, and eminently remedial in many cases of illegal imprisonment, it introduced no new principle, nor conferred any right upon the subject. From the earliest records of the English law, no freeman could be detained in prison except upon a criminal charge or conviction, or for a civil debt. In the former case, it was always in his power to demand of the Court of King's Bench a writ of habeas corpus ad subjiciendum, directed to the person detaining him in custody, by which he was enjoined to bring up the body of the prisoner, with the warrant of commitment, that the court might judge of its sufficiency, and remand the party, admit him to bail, or discharge him, according to the nature of the charge. This writ issued of right and could not be refused by the court. It was not to bestow an immunity from arbitrary imprisonment, which is abundantly provided in Magna Carta (if indeed it is not much more ancient), that the statute of Charles II. was enacted; but to cut off the abuses by which the government's lust of power, and the servile subtlety of crown lawyers, had impaired so fundamental a privilege.

There had been some doubts whether the Court of Common Pleas could issue this writ; and the Court of Exchequer seems never to have done so. It was also a question, and one of more importance, as we have seen in the case of Jenks, whether a single judge of the Court of King's Bench could issue it during the vacation. The statute therefore enacts that where any person, other than persons convicted, or in execution upon legal process, stands committed for any crime except for treason or felony plainly expressed in the warrant of commitment, he may during vacation complain to the chancellor or any of the twelve judges; who, upon sight of a copy of the warrant, or an affidavit that a copy is denied, shall award a habeas corpus, directed to the officer in whose custody the party shall be, commanding him to bring up the body of his prisoner within a time limited according to the distance, but in no case exceeding twenty days, who shall discharge the party from imprisonment, taking surety for his appearance in the court wherein his offence is cognizable.

A gaoler refusing a copy of the warrant of commitment or not obeying the writ, is subjected to a penalty of £100; and even the judge denying a habeas corpus, when required, according to this act, is made liable to a penalty of £500, at the suit of the injured party. The Court of King's Bench had already been accustomed to send out their writ of habeas corpus into all places of peculiar and privileged jurisdiction, where this ordinary process does not run, and even to the Island of Jersey, beyond the strict limits of the kingdom of England; and this power, which might admit of some question, is sanctioned by a declaratory clause of the present statute. Another section enacts, that "no subject of this realm, that now is or hereafter shall be an inhabitant or resident of this kingdom of England, dominion of Wales, or town of Berwick-upon-Tweed, shall be sent prisoner into Scotland, Ireland, Jersey, Guernsey, Tangier, or into parts, garrisons, islands or places beyond the seas, which are, or at any time hereafter shall be, within or without the dominions of his Majesty, his heirs or successors, under penalties of the heaviest nature, short of death, which the law then knew, and an incapacity of receiving the King's pardon. The great rank of those who were likely to offend against this part of the statute was doubtless the cause of this unusual severity.

But as it might still be practicable to evade these remedial provisions by expressing some matter of treason or felony in the warrant of commitment, the judges not being empowered to inquire into the truth of the facts stated in it, a further security against any protracted detention of an innocent man is afforded by a provision of great importance; that every person committed for treason or felony, plainly and specially expressed in the warrant, may, unless he shall be indicted in the next term, or at the next sessions of general gaol delivery after his commitment, be, on prayer to the court, released upon bail, unless it shall appear that the crown's witnesses could not be produced at that time; and if he shall not be indicted and tried in the second term or sessions of gaol delivery, he shall be discharged.

The remedies of the habeas corpus act are so effectual that no man can possibly endure any long imprisonment on a criminal charge, nor would any minister venture to exercise a sort of oppression so dangerous to himself. But it should be observed that, as the statute is only applicable to cases of commitment on such charge, every other species of restraint on personal liberty is left to the ordinary remedy as it subsisted before this enactment. Thus a party detained without any warrant must sue out his habeas corpus at common law; and this is at present the more usual occurrence. But the judges of the King's Bench, since the statute, have been accustomed to issue this writ during the vacation in all cases whatsoever.

A sensible difficulty has, however, been sometimes felt, from their incompetency to judge of the truth of a return made to a writ. For, though in cases within the statute, the prisoner may always look to his legal discharge at the next sessions of gaol delivery, the same redress might not always be obtained when he is not in custody of a common gaoler. If the person therefore who detains any one in custody should think fit to make a return to the writ of habeas corpus, alleging matter sufficient to justify the party's restraint, yet false in fact, there would be no means, at least by this summary process, of obtaining relief. An attempt was made in 1757, after an examination of the judges, by the House of Lords, as to the extent and efficiency of the habeas corpus at common law, to render their jurisdiction more remedial.

It failed, however, for the time, of success; but a statute has recently been enacted, 56 *Geo.* III., *c.* 100, which not only extends the power of issuing the writ during the vacation, in cases not within the Act of Charles II. to all the judges, but enables the judge, before whom the writ is returned, to inquire into the truth of the facts alleged therein, and in case they shall seem to him doubtful, to release the party in custody, on giving surety to appear in the court to which such judge shall belong, on some day in the ensuing term, when the court may examine by affidavit into the truth of the facts alleged in the return, and either remand or discharge the party, according to their discretion. It is also declared that a writ of habeas corpus shall run to any harbour or road on the coast of England, though out of the body of any county; in order, I presume, to obviate doubts as to the effects of this remedy in a kind of illegal detention, more likely perhaps than any other to occur in modern times, on board of vessels upon the coast. Except a few of this description, it is very rare for a habeas corpus to be required in any case where the government has an interest." 2 *Hallam Const. Hist.*, 177 - 180.

An elegant and philosophical writer, referring to the habeas corpus act, says: "We must admire, as the keystone of civil liberty, the statute which forces the secrets of every prison to be revealed, the cause of every commitment to be declared, and the person of the accused to be produced, that he may claim his enlargement, or his trial within a limited time. No wiser form was ever opposed to the abuses of power. But it requires a fabric no less than the whole political constitution of Great Britain, a spirit no less than the refractory and turbulent zeal of this fortunate people, to secure its effects." *Ferguson's Essay on Civil Society*, 302.

The French philosopher, M. De La Croix, also, in his Review of the Constitutions of the Principal States of Europe, in 1792, concedes to England the highest meed of praise in the career of civil liberty, and acknowledges the writ of habeas corpus to be a peculiar characteristic of her laws, and the habeas corpus *act of* 31 *Car*. 2, an admirable and not unenvied security of personal liberty. After copying the act, he says: "Such is the spirit of this law, so important to England, *and which France has so long envied her rival*." 2 *Vol*., 290.

The attempt made in 1757, to improve the law relating to habeas corpus, deserves more particular notice. The bill was introduced by Mr. Pratt, afterwards Lord Camden, who in 1766 in the House of Lords, reasoned upon American affairs, and the rights and liberties of the Colonists, in a strain of eloquence which Pitt called divine. 2 *Campbell's Lives Ch. Jus*., 453; 5 *Bancroft*, 404.

The occasion and object of it are thus stated in 3 *Bac. Abr., Hab. Corp., B*., 13, *note*: "A gentleman having been impressed under a pressing-act, passed in the preceding session, and confined in the Savoy, his friends made application for a writ of habeas corpus, which produced some hesitation and difficulty; for according to the above statute (31 *Car*. 2) the privilege relates only to persons committed for criminal or supposed criminal matter; and this gentleman did not stand in that predicament. Before the question could be determined, he was discharged in consequence of an application to the Secretary at War; but the nature of the case seeming to point out a defect in the act, a bill for giving a more speedy remedy to the subject upon the writ of habeas corpus, was prepared and presented to the House of Commons. It imported, that the several provisions made in the above act of 31 *Car.* 2, for the awarding of writs of habeas corpus in cases of commitment, or detainer for any criminal or supposed criminal matter, should in like manner extend to all cases where any person, not being committed or detained for any criminal or supposed criminal matter, should be confined or restrained of his or their liberty under any color or pretence whatsoever; that upon oath made by such person so confined or restrained, or by any other person on his behalf, of any actual confinement or restraint, and that such confinement or restraint, to the best of the knowledge and belief of the person so applying, was not by virtue of any commitment or detainer for any criminal or supposed criminal matter: an habeas corpus, directed to the person or persons so confining or restraining the party, should be granted in the same manner as is directed, and under the same penalties as are provided by the said act in case of persons committed or detained for any criminal or supposed criminal matter; that the person before whom the party should be brought by virtue of an habeas corpus, granted in vacation-time under the authority of this act, might and should within three days after the return made, proceed to examine into the facts contained in such return, and into the cause of such confinement and restraint, and thereupon either discharge, or bail, or remand the party so brought, as the case should require, and as to justice should appertain. The rest of the bill related to the return of the writ in three days, and the penalties upon those who should neglect or refuse to make the return, or to comply with any other clause of this regulation. See the bill and the arguments for and against it, in the Appendix to Vol. 7, Debrett's Debates, from 1743 to 1774. The bill was soon passed by the Commons; but in the House of Lords, it was thrown out at the second reading, and the judges were ordered to prepare a bill to extend the power of granting writs of habeas corpus ad subjiciendum in vacation-time, in cases not within the statute of 31 *Car.* 2, to all the judges of his majesty's courts at Westminster, and to provide for the issuing of process in vacation-time to compel obedience to such writs; and that in preparing such bill they take into consideration, whether in any, and in what cases, it may be proper to make provision that the truth of the facts contained in the return to a writ of habeas corpus may be controverted by affidavits or traverse, and so far as it shall appear to be proper, that clauses be inserted for that purpose, and that they lay such bill before the House in the beginning of the next session of Parliament. The matter however was never resumed."

The bill was opposed by Lord Mansfield in the House of Lords. He contended that it was wholly unnecessary; that the remedy by habeas corpus at common law was ample in all such cases.

Horace Walpole says, "he spoke two hours and a half," and according to a report of his speech by Dr. Birch, he said, "that people supported it from the groundless imagination that liberty was concerned in it; whereas it had as little to do with liberty as the navigation laws, or the act for the encouragement of madder; that ignorance on subjects of this nature was extremely pardonable, since the knowledge of laws required a particular study of them; that the greatest genius, without such study, could no more become master of them than of Japanese literature, without understanding the language of the country; and that the writ of habeas corpus at common law was a sufficient remedy against all those abuses this bill was supposed to rectify." 2 *Campbell's Lives Ch. Jus.*, 453.

The "examination of the judges" during the pendency of the bill in the House of Lords, consisted in propounding to them ten questions which will be noticed hereafter. They relate to interesting questions of practice under the writ of habeas corpus. A majority of the judges declared in favor of the exercise of the powers which had been doubted.

We have now glanced at those famous laws of England, constitutional and statutory, which have been said to procure and complete to every individual that sense of independence which is the noblest advantage attending liberty. To the lover of liberty, the "Bible of the English Constitution" will ever appear a volume above all price. History, indeed, shows us that for many centuries, while as yet only the first chapter, Magna Carta, was written, political irreligion was wofully prevalent in the land; but the vital principles which were proclaimed in that chapter were indestructible. Steadily, though slowly, they worked their silent way to the very heart of English jurisprudence. In process of time, new chapters were added, expounding, applying and extending the principles of the first, until at last a consistent and comprehensive creed was given to civil liberty in England.

But this political bible, as well as THE BIBLE from which it drew its inspiration, was to shed the light of its pages upon another land and to nourish the spirit of liberty in the hearts of another people.

CHAPTER V.

CONSTITUTIONAL AND STATUTORY GUARANTEES OF THE RIGHT OF PERSONAL LIBERTY IN AMERICA.

SECTION I.

LIBERTIES IN THE COLONIES.

1. *Magna carta.*
2. *The writ of habeas corpus.*

1. *Magna Carta.* The American colonists always claimed to possess "all the rights, liberties and immunities of free and natural-born subjects within the realm of England." This claim was not founded so much upon their charters as upon the fact that they were Englishmen, and as such, inherited the laws of their country.

This idea of a birth-right in the laws, was always a favorite one in England. "In *Edw. VI.*, *fol.* 36, the laws are called the great inheritance of every subject, and the inheritance of inheritances, without which inheritance we have no inheritance," 8 *St. Tr.*, 117; and it is very justly observed by Chalmers, 1 *Annals*, 677, that "the customs of a free people are a part of their liberty."

It was, indeed, expressly declared in all the charters under which the colonies were settled, except that to

William Penn, that all subjects and their children inhabiting the colonies, should be deemed natural-born subjects, and entitled to all the liberties and immunities thereof.

The omission, however, in the charter to Penn, was never supposed to deprive the Pennsylvania colonist of his rights as an Englishman. On the contrary, it seems to have been thought "that the clause was wholly unnecessary, as the allegiance to the crown was reserved; and the common law thence inferred, that all the inhabitants were subjects, and of course were entitled to all the privileges of Englishmen." 1 *Chal. Annals*, 639, 658; 1 *Story's Const.*, § 122.

"It was," says Story, "under the consciousness of the full possession of the rights, liberties and immunities of British subjects, that the colonists in almost all the early legislation of their respective assemblies, insisted upon a declaratory act, acknowledging and confirming them." 1 *Story Const.*, § 165. Some of them were content with reaffirming the Great Charter; others added to its provisions.

In Maryland, in 1638, by the 4th sec. of the "Act ordaining certain laws for the government of this province," it was provided that "The inhabitants shall have their rights and liberties according to the Great Charter of England."

In Connecticut, in 1650, it was enacted that "No man's life shall be taken away, no man's honor or good name shall be stained, no man's person shall be arrested, restrained, banished, dismembered nor any ways punished; no man shall be deprived of his wife or children, no man's goods or estate shall be taken away from him, nor any ways indamaged under color of law or countenance of authority, unless it be by virtue or equity of some express law of the country, warranting the same, established by a general court and sufficiently published, or in case of the defect of a law in any particular case, by the word of God." 1 *Col. Rec. of Conn.*, 509.

In later times, when those rights and liberties were threatened, they were reasserted from time to time, by the colonies severally, and, as the danger increased, collectively.

The Congress of the Nine Colonies, in 1765, assembled at New York, declared that the colonists were "entitled to all the inherent right and liberties of his (the King's) natural-born subjects, within the kingdom of Great Britain." *Hutch. Hist. Mass. Bay, Appendix F.*

And the Continental Congress of 1774, composed of delegates from twelve colonies (Georgia did not unite with them until the next year), in their Declaration of Rights, amongst other things declared:

"That the inhabitants of the English colonies in North America, by the immutable laws of nature, the principles of the English Constitution, and the several charters or compacts, have the following RIGHTS.

"*Resolved*, 1. That they are entitled to life, liberty and property; and that they have never ceded to any sovereign power whatever a right to dispose of either without their consent.

"*Resolved*, 2. That our ancestors, who first settled these colonies, were, at the time of their emigration from the mother county, entitled to all the rights, liberties and immunities of free and natural-born subjects within the realm of England.

"*Resolved*, 3. That by such emigration they by no means forfeited, surrendered or lost any of their rights, but that they were, and their descendants now are, entitled to the exercise and enjoyment of all such of them, as their local and other circumstances enable them to exercise and enjoy." 1 *Am. Archives*, 911.

These views were not without advocates in Parliament. The Great Commoner, who "drew his ideas of freedom from the vital powers of the British Constitution," in his argument in the House of Lords against the doctrine of taxation without representation, in 1766, said: "The colonies are equally entitled with yourselves to all the natural rights of mankind and the peculiar privileges of Englishmen; equally bound by the laws, and equally participating of the constitution of this free country. The Americans are the sons, not the bastards of England."

To the journal published by the order of the Congress of 1774 and verified by the autograph of their secretary is prefixed in the title page a medallion, representing Magna Carta as the pedestal on which was raised the column and cap of liberty, supported by twelve hands and containing the words "Hanc Tuemur, Hac Nitimur."

The great popularity of the doctrine that the colonists were "co-heirs of liberty" with their brethren residing in England, may be inferred from the complaint of the royal Governor of New York in 1697, who thought it intolerable that not only the English emigrant but the Dutch also should be "big with the privileges of Englishmen and Magna Carta." 3 *Bancroft*, 56.

2. *The writ of habeas corpus.* It is said by Chalmers, speaking of the rights of the colonists, that "They had a right to possess every immunity which Englishmen, within a distant and subordinate territory of the empire, can possibly enjoy. They were entitled to *personal security*, to *private property*, and, what is of most importance of all, to *personal liberty;* though the foregoing annals demonstrate that the two first they enjoyed previously, the last they possessed not at all, since the effectual remedy, the writ of habeas corpus, they did not happily know." 1 *Chal. Annals*, 677. Again he says: "There is no circumstance in the history of colonial jurisprudence better established than the fact that the habeas corpus act was not extended to the plantations till the reign of Anne." 1 *Chal. Annals*, 74.

The writ may not have been and doubtless was not so efficient in the colonies as in England; but that it was unknown or undervalued, or that the habeas corpus act was considered inapplicable until expressly extended to the plantations, are propositions which are not sustained by the history of the times.

Mr. Washburn, in his "Judicial History of Massachusetts," p. 195, says: "Among other writs in use during the period of the provincial charter, was the writ of habeas corpus. It seems to have been adopted at first as a common law remedy. In 1689 application for such a writ was made to Judge Dudley by Mr. Wise, but the application was arbitrarily refused. In 1706 an application was made to Chief Justice Sewall for a writ of habeas corpus, and although it was refused for satisfactory reasons, there is nothing to indicate that the court regarded it as a novel application; I have, however, found none of a similar kind made at an earlier period of the Provincial Government."

After the Revolution (1688, 9), Judge Dudley was sued for refusing to allow the writ to Wise, "which shows that the right to this writ was regarded as one of the existing privileges of the colonists."

The Rev. John Wise, who applied for the writ above mentioned, was arrested with others, inhabitants of the town of Ipswich, for refusing to grant money, which they believed was illegally assessed by the Governor and Council.

"Being denied the writ of habeas corpus, the mittimus only showing that they were committed 'for contempts and high misdemeanor,' they were after a tedious and harassing delay put upon their trial. They claimed the privileges secured to them as Englishmen by the Magna Çarta and the laws of England. The Chief Justice, however, informed them that they must not expect that the laws of England would follow them to the ends of the earth, and concluded by telling them that they had no more privileges left them than to be sold as slaves. He charged the jury, and stated that the court 'expected a good verdict from them, seeing the matter had been so sufficiently proved against the criminals.' A verdict was accordingly rendered against them, and a severe punishment thereupon inflicted, because the town in which they resided declined yielding to an arbitrary and illegal act." *Washburn's Judicial Hist. Mass.*, 116.

The denial of the writ of habeas corpus was alleged as one of the grievances of the people, in a pamphlet published in April, 1689, entitled, "An Account of the late Revolution in New England, together with the Declaration of the gentlemen, merchants and inhabitants of Boston and the country adjacent." *IV. Force's Hist. Tracts.*

The Assembly of Massachusetts, in 1692, adopted the habeas corpus act of 31 *Car.* 2, but this was disallowed in 1695, by the authorities in England, who held a veto power over the legislation of the colony.

In South Carolina the writ was given a peculiar efficacy. The occasion of adopting the act of 31 *Car.* 2 is thus stated by Dr. Hewitt, in his *History of S. Carolina, p.* 116: "About this time (1692) forty men arrived in a privateer, called the Royal Jamaica, who had been engaged in a course of piracy and brought into the country treasures of Spanish gold and silver. These men were allowed to enter into a recognizance for their peaceable and good behavior for one year, with securities, till the Governor should hear whether the proprietors would grant them a general indemnity. At another time a vessel was shipwrecked on the coast, the crew of which openly and boldly confessed they had been on the Red Sea plundering the dominions of the Great Mogul. * * * The proprietors instructed Governor Ludwell to change the form of electing juries, and required that all pirates should be tried and punished by the laws of England made for the suppression of piracy.

"Before such instructions reached Carolina, the pirates, by their money and freedom of intercourse with the people, had so ingratiated themselves into the public favor, that it was become no easy matter to bring them to trial, and dangerous to punish them as they deserved. The courts of law became scenes of altercation, discord and confusion. Bold and seditious speeches were made from the bar in contempt of the proprietors and their government.

"Since no pardons could be obtained but such as they had authorized the Governor to grant, the Assembly took the matter under deliberation and fell into hot debates among themselves about a bill of indemnity. When they found the Governor disposed to refuse his assent to such a bill, they made a law impowering magistrates and judges to put in force the habeas corpus act made in England.

"Hence it happened that several of those pirates escaped, purchased lands from the colonists and took up their residence in the country. While money flowed into the colony, in this channel, the authority of the government was too feeble to stem the tide and prevent such illegal practices. At length the proprietors, to gratify the people, granted an indemnity to all the pirates, excepting those who had been plundering the Great Mogul, most of whom found means of making their escape out of the country."

This law, adopting the habeas corpus act, continued in force until 1712, when it was repealed and another passed, which has been continued since.

It is further stated by Chalmers, 1 *Annals*, 74, that "The ancient colonists being destitute of personal security, were in fact most grievously oppressed. Edward Randolph, the Surveyor-General of the Plantations during the reign of William, represented their lamentable condition to the Board of Trade in March, 1700; and among other beneficial regulations, and recommended "That, it being the practice for governors to imprison the subjects without bail, the habeas corpus act should be extended as fully to the colonies as it is in England." It was accordingly soon after conferred on Virginia, by Anne; whereupon, both houses of Assembly expressed their thanks for her "Majesty's late favor to this country in allowing us the benefit of the habeas corpus act, and in appointing courts of oyer and terminer for the more speedy execution of justice and relief from long imprisonment."

It does not follow because the habeas corpus act, 31 *Car.* 2, was not expressly adopted by the Provincial Assemblies, or expressly extended to them by Parliament or the royal authority, that therefore it was held to be wholly inoperative in the colonies. There was in some of the colonies a practical adoption of it and long use, by which it was held to have acquired the force of law—at least as to the mode of procedure.

In Maryland there was no provincial act upon the subject, and yet it was recognized and practically adopted. Chancellor Kilty, in his report, in 1810, to the Assembly on the subject, "of the English Statutes which existed at the time of the first emigration of the people of Maryland, and which, by experience, have been found applicable to their local and other circumstances, *and of such others as have since been made in England or Great Britain, and have been introduced, used and practiced* by the courts, &c.," speaking of the *Act*, 31 *Car.* 2, says: "It is to be presumed that this statute, which has been so highly eulogized and valued in England, and which was termed by Blackstone, the famous habeas corpus act, was held in equal estimation by the people of the province; and there cannot be a stronger proof of the love of power manifested by the governmental party, than is to be found in the speech of the Governor for the proprietor in 1725. 'Many debates,' he says, 'if I am rightly informed, have been in former assemblies, whether the statutes of England did extend to you or no, without either house coming to resolutions thereon, and the most common received opinions of the best lawyers of England have been against it, and several adjudged cases support these opinions, as in particular, the habeas corpus act has been often adjudged by all the judges not to extend either to Ireland or the plantations, which is as strong a case as can be mentioned, as it is in favor of liberty and the terms of the act as general as can be.'

"These opinions, however, were not acquiesced in by the people; and there were several proceedings which would show, if it was necessary, the adoption of this statute; in one of which it was defended in the upper house, as the birthright of the inhabitants."

In New Jersey, in 1710, the Assembly denounced one of the judges, William Pinhorne, for having corruptly refused the writ of habeas corpus to Thomas Gordon, which they said was "the undoubted right and great privilege of the subject." *Field's Colonial Courts, N. J.*, 76.

In New York, in January, 1707, Francis Makemie and John Hampton, two Presbyterian ministers, were arrested on the warrant of the Governor, Cornbury, for preaching without license; and on refusal to give bond and security that they would preach no more in that government, they were committed to prison under the Governor's warrant, which read as follows:

"You are hereby required and commanded to take into your custody the bodies of Francis Makemie and John Hampton, and them safely keep till further orders; and for so doing, this shall be your warrant.

"Given under my hand and seal this 23d day of
[L. S.] January, 1706–7,

"CORNBURY.

"To EBENEZER WILSON, *High Sheriff of New York.*"

Application was made to Ch. J. Mompesson for a writ of habeas corpus, which he allowed on the 8th of March. The Chief Jurtice was said to be the best lawyer in America. He was also the warm personal friend of the Governor. The mittimus was fatally defective in not specifying any offence. The writ of habeas corpus was placed in the sheriff's hands on Saturday, but was not executed until Monday, at which time the sheriff was furnished with another mittimus containing a statement of the offence. The prisoners were admitted to bail under the new mittimus; and Makemie only being indicted, was tried and acquitted. An interesting pamphlet containing a full account of the trial was immediately published and will be found in *IV. Force's Hist. Tracts.*

A search among the judicial records of the colonies would doubtless be rewarded, as was intimated by Chancellor Kilty, with the discovery of many cases in which the writ of habeas corpus was employed as a familiar remedy.

In Pennsylvania, for example, although the Council exercised the power of discharging from illegal imprisonment upon petition, 1 *Col. Laws, &c.*, 327, yet they sometimes referred such applications to the county courts as the appropriate tribunals to afford relief. An instance is mentioned in 1 *Col. Records,* 24, in 1683. The record is in these words: "Wm. Shute's petition concerning his son, detained by Dennis Rocheford, was read; he is referred to the County Court."

A court possessing common law powers, invoked to protect an admitted common law right, may reasonably be supposed to have employed the well known common law remedy.

General study of political rights in the colonies. There is abundant reason to believe that the colonists were fully instructed in the rights which were claimed in England to be the "inheritance of the free-born subject." The arguments in the celebrated case of Darnell, in 1627, when the right to the writ of habeas corpus was more thoroughly discussed than ever before, and on an occasion of public concern, were printed in pamphlet form and circulated amongst the people.

In 1647, the Governor and Assistants of Massachusetts ordered the importation of two copies of Coke on Littleton; two copies of Dalton's Jus.

Peace; two copies of Coke's Reports, *and two copies of Coke on Magna Carta. Sullivan's Address*, 23 *Law Intel.*, 229. The 5th ed. of Care's book, entitled, "English Liberties; or the Free-born Subject's Inheritance," containing Magna Carta, the Habeas Corpus Act and other statutes, with comments on each of them, was published in Boston in 1721. *Marvin's Legal Bibliography, tit. Care, Henry.*

As the time for revolution drew nigh, the colonists fully comprehended the magnitude of the questions at stake. Gage, writing from Boston to the British secretary in 1768, discourages measures of oppression towards a "country where every man studies law."

This addiction of the colonists to study and discuss their political rights, and the effects of such habits, were pressed upon the attention of the House of Commons by Burke in 1774, in his celebrated speech on Taxation of America, in the following terms:

"Permit me, Sir, to add another circumstance in our colonies, which contributes no mean part towards the growth and effect of this untractable spirit. I mean their education. In no country perhaps in the world is the law so general a study. The profession itself is numerous and powerful; and in most provinces it takes the lead. The greater number of the deputies sent to the congress were lawyers. But all who read, and most do read, endeavor to obtain some smattering of that science. I have been told by an eminent bookseller, that in no branch of his business, after tracts of popular devotion, were so many books as those on the law exported to the plantations. The colonies have now fallen into the way of printing them for their own use. I hear they have sold nearly as many of Blackstone's Commentaries in America as in England. General Gage marks out this disposition very particularly in a letter on your table. He states that all the people in his government are lawyers, or smatterers in law; and that in Boston they have been enabled, by successful chicane, wholly to evade many parts of your capital penal constitutions. The smartness of debate will say, that this knowledge ought to teach them more clearly the rights of legislature, their obligations to obedience, and the penalties of rebellion. All this is mighty well. But my honorable and learned friend (the Attorney-General) on the floor, who condescends to mark what I say for animadversion, will disdain that ground. He has heard, as well as I, that when great honors and great emoluments do not win over this knowledge to the service of the state, it is a formidable adversary to government.

"If the spirit be not tamed and broken by these happy methods, it is stubborn and litigious. *Abeunt studia in mores.* This study renders men acute, inquisitive, dexterous, prompt in attack, ready in defence, full of resources. In other countries, the people, more simple and of a less mercurial cast, judge of an ill principle in government only by an actual grievance; here they anticipate the evil, and judge of the pressure of the grievance by the badness of the principle. They augur misgovernment from a distance, and snuff the approach of tyranny in every tainted breeze." 2 *Burke's Works*, 38.

The last observation was verified in the sudden and general alarm which was excited in the colonies in 1774 by the passage of the "Quebec Bill," which "decreed an arbitrary rule over the vast region which included, besides Canada, the area of the present States of Ohio, Michigan, Indiana, Illinois and Wisconsin." 6 *Bancroft*, 527.

The acquisitions of Quebec and Florida, by the treaty of peace concluded at Paris, February 10, 1763, had been from the 7th October, 1763, governed under the proclamation of the King, which promised that "all persons inhabiting in or resorting to our said colonies, may confide in our royal protection for the enjoyment of the benefit of the laws of our realm of England."

The bill entitled "An act making more effectual provision for the government of the Province of Quebec in North America," was presented to the House of Lords on 2d May, 1774. It passed that House on the 17th, and was read the first time on the next day in the House of Commons.

It was opposed in the House of Commons because it left the inhabitants under the civil law of France, denying them the right of *Trial by Jury*, the *Writ of Habeas Corpus*, and, also, left them exposed to the French process, *Lettre de cachet*, more odious than general search warrants. The opposition was vain. The proposition to extend to the inhabitants the benefit of the English law of habeas corpus was defeated by a vote of 76 to 21; and the bill was soon passed by a large majority. 1 *Am. Archives, 4th series,* 170.

The passage of the bill was an augury of misgovernment to the other colonies. The writ of habeas corpus was regarded as one of the "dearest birthrights of Britons." They called the habeas corpus act the "great bulwark and palladium of English liberty;" and the denial of the benefit of it to a sister colony indicated to them the sure approach of tyranny towards the rest.

The act was immediately denounced in the journals of the colonies, and was made a special ground of complaint by the Continental Congress which assembled in September of the same year, 1774. 1 *Am. Archives,* 4 *ed.,* 920, 931. And it was finally regarded as manifesting so clearly the general spirit of tyranny of the British government towards the colonies, that it was included in that short catalogue of insupportable wrongs which was embodied in the Declaration of Independence.

SECTION II.

CONSTITUTIONAL AND STATUTORY GUARANTEES IN THE UNITED STATES.

1. *The provisions in the constitution of the United States.*
2. *The provisions in the constitutions of the several states.*
3. *Suspension of the privilege of the writ.*
4. *Statutory enactments relating to the writ of habeas corpus.*

1. *The provisions in the constitution of the United States.* The essential principles of civil liberty for which the colonists waged the war of independence, are declared in the Constitution of the United States,

and effectually secured by that instrument to the people, against the power of the federal government.

Those provisions relating more particularly to the right of personal liberty are contained in the fourth, fifth, sixth and eighth articles of the Amendments, and in the second clause of the ninth section of the first article of the Constitution, and are as follows:

"ART. IV. The right of the people to be secure in their persons, houses, papers and effects, against unreasonable searches and seizures, shall not be violated, and no warrants shall issue, but upon probable cause, supported by oath or affirmation, and particularly describing the place to be searched, and the persons or things to be seized.

"ART. V. No person shall be held to answer for a capital or otherwise infamous crime, unless on a presentment or indictment of a grand jury, except in cases arising in the land or naval forces, or in the militia, when in actual service in time of war or public danger; nor shall any person be subject for the same offence to be twice put in jeopardy of life or limb; nor shall he be compelled in any criminal case to be a witness against himself, nor be deprived of life, liberty or property without due process of law; nor shall private property be taken for public use without just compensation.

"ART. VI. In all criminal prosecutions, the accused shall enjoy the right to a speedy and public trial, by an impartial jury of the state and district wherein the crime shall have been committed, which district shall have been previously ascertained by law, and to be informed of the nature and cause of the accusation; to be confronted with the witnesses against him; to have compulsory process for obtaining witnesses in his favor, and to have the assistance of counsel for his defence.

"ART. VIII. Excessive bail shall not be required, nor excessive fines imposed, nor cruel and unusual punishments inflicted.

"ART. I., *sec.* 9, *clause* 2. The privilege of the writ of habeas corpus shall not be suspended, unless when, in cases of rebellion or invasion, the public safety may require it."

There will be occasion hereafter to notice particularly the provisions in Articles IV., V., VI. and VIII. of the Amendments. The clause in Sec. 9, of Art. I., relating to the writ of habeas corpus, deserves attention here.

There was no provision relating to the writ of habeas corpus in the Articles of Confederation. The article which was introduced into the Constitution of the United States demonstrates how highly the privilege of the writ was valued, and how thoroughly it was supposed to be incorporated in the jurisprudence of the colonies. It assumes the existence of the privilege, and provides against its infringement, even by the highest power in the state.

The Articles of Confederation having been found inadequate to secure the objects anticipated, a convention was finally convened at Philadelphia for the purpose of revising them. The result of the labor of that convention was our present Constitution. It assembled on the second Monday of May, 1787.

On the 29th of May, Mr. Charles Pinkney, of South Carolina, laid before the House a draft of a plan of a Federal Constitution, the VI. Art. of which provided * * *

"The legislature of the United States shall pass no law on the subject of religion; nor touching or abridging the liberty of the press; *nor shall the privilege of the writ of habeas corpus ever be suspended, except in case of rebellion or invasion.*"

The authenticity of this paper is questioned in some particulars, *Appendix* 2 *to* 5 *Elliott's Debates;* but the above article may well be supposed to be genuine, for it consists with Mr. Pinkney's subsequent course in the convention.

On the 6th of August, the "Committee of Detail," consisting of Rutledge, Randolph, Gorham, Ellsworth and Wilson, reported a "Draft of a Constitution," but it contained no provision on the subject of the writ of habeas corpus.

On the 20th August, Mr. Pinkney submitted to the House, in order to be referred to the Committee of Detail, the following proposition amongst others:

"The privileges and benefit of the writ of habeas corpus shall be enjoyed in this government in the most expeditious and ample manner; and shall not be suspended by the legislature, except upon the most urgent and pressing occasions, and for a limited time, not exceeding — months."

On the 28th of the same month Mr. Pinkney, urging the propriety of securing the benefit of the habeas corpus in the most ample manner, moved that it should not be suspended but on the most urgent occasions, and then only for a limited time, not exceeding twelve months.

Mr. Rutledge was for declaring the habeas corpus inviolate. He did not conceive that a suspension could ever be necessary at the same time through all the states.

Mr. Gouverneur Morris moved that "the privilege of the writ of habeas corpus shall not be suspended, unless when, in cases of rebellion or invasion, the public safety may require it."

Mr. Wilson doubted whether in any case a suspension could be necessary, as the discretion now exists with judges in most important cases, to keep in gaol or admit to bail.

The first part of Mr. Gouverneur Morris's motion, to the word "unless," was agreed to, *nem. con.*

On the remaining part the vote stood:

Aye. New Hampshire, Massachusetts, Connecticut, Pennsylvania, Delaware, Maryland and Virginia, 7.

Nay. North Carolina, South Carolina, Georgia, 3.

The article was then adopted as it now stands in the Constitution, in the following words: "The privilege of the writ of habeas corpus shall not be suspended, unless when, in cases of rebellion or invasion, the public safety may require it."

The State of Maryland is reported as voting in the affirmative; but the delegation was not unanimous. Luther Martin voted in the negative, and assigned his reasons therefor, in his letter to the Speaker of the House of Delegates of Maryland, January 27, 1788, in the following terms:

"By the next paragraph, the general government is to have a power of suspending the habeas corpus act in cases of rebellion or invasion.

"As the state governments have a power of suspending the habeas corpus act in those cases, it was said there could be no reason for giving such a power to the general government, since, whenever the

State which is invaded, or in which an insurrection takes place, finds its safety requires it, it will make use of that power; and it was urged that, if we gave this power to the general government, it would be an engine of oppression in its hands, since, whenever a state should oppose its views, however arbitrary and unconstitutional, and refuse submission to them, the general government may declare it an act of rebellion, and suspending the habeas corpus act, may seize upon the persons of those advocates of freedom who have had virtue and resolution enough to excite the opposition, and may imprison them during its pleasure, in the remotest parts of the Union, so that a citizen of Georgia might be *bastiled* in the farthest part of New Hampshire; or a citizen of New Hampshire in the farthest extreme of the South—cut off from their family, their friends and their every connection.

These considerations induced me, sir, to give my negative also to this clause." 1 *Elliott's Debates*, 375.

The debate on this article in the Massachusetts' Convention, called to determine whether the Constitution should be ratified or not, is too interesting to be overlooked.

On the 26th January, 1788, the clause relating to the writ of habeas corpus being read:

Gen. Thompson asked the president to please to proceed. We have, said he, read the book often enough; it is a consistent piece of inconsistency.

Mr. Adams, in answer to an inquiry by Hon. Mr. Taylor, said: That this power given to the general government to suspend this privilege in cases of rebellion and invasion, did not take away the power of the several states to suspend it, if they shall see fit.

Dr. Taylor asked why this darling privilege was not expressed in the same manner as in the Constitution of Massachusetts. * * He remarked on the difference of expression, and asked why the time was not limited?

Judge Dana said: The answer, in part, to the honorable gentleman, must be, that the same men did not make both constitutions; that he did not see the necessity or great benefit of limiting the *time*. Supposing it had been, as in our constitution "not exceeding twelve months," yet, as our own legislature can, so might congress continue the suspension of the writ from year to year. The safest and best restriction therefore arises from the nature of the cases in which congress are authorized to exercise that power at all, namely, in those of rebellion nor invasion. These are clear and certain terms, facts of public notoriety, and whenever these shall cease to exist, the suspension of the writ must necessarily cease also. He thought the citizen had a better security for his privilege of the writ of habeas corpus under the federal than under the state constitution; for our legislature may suspend the writ as often as they judge "the most urgent and pressing occasions" call for it.

Judge Sumner said: That this was a restriction on congress, that the writ of habeas corpus should not be suspended, except in cases of rebellion or invasion. The learned judge then explained the nature of the writ. * * * The privilege, he said, is essential to freedom, and therefore the power to suspend it is restricted. On the other hand, the state, he said, might be involved in danger; the worst enemy may lay plans to destroy us, and so artfully as to prevent any evidence against him, and might ruin the country, without the power to suspend the writ was thus given: "Congress have only power to suspend the privilege to persons committed by their authority. A person committed under the authority of the states will still have a right to the writ." 2 *Elliott's Debates*, 108.

2. *The provisions of the constitutions of the several states.* Most of the state constitutions contain provisions relating to personal liberty, similar to those quoted from the Constitution of the United States.

The provisions relating to the subject of bail will be cited more fitly under that head. Those relating to the suspension of the privilege of the writ of habeas corpus, are in substance the same as that contained in the federal Constitution. In Virginia and Vermont, however, it is provided that the privilege of the writ shall in no case be suspended, and in Massachusetts the suspension cannot exceed twelve months, nor can it exceed three months in New Hampshire. In Maryland, North Carolina and South Carolina, the writ is not mentioned,

These constitutional clauses do not in any case confer the right nor do they operate as grants of jurisdiction over the writ of habeas corpus. They recognize the existence of the right, and declare that the benefit of it shall not be taken away, "unless when, in cases of rebellion or invasion, the public safety may require it." *Ex parte Bollman and*

Swartwout, 4 *Cr.*, 75; *Ex parte Hickey*, 4 *S. & M.*, 749.

The provisions relating to warrants, have some shades of difference which it may be important to notice when the validity of such process comes to be considered. They are interesting also as tending to show, by the attempted amendments of the clause in the federal constitution, the anxious concern of the people of the several states for the protection of the right of personal liberty.

MAINE. The people shall be secure in their persons, houses, papers and possessions from unreasonable searches and seizures; and no warrant to search any place, or seize any person or thing, shall issue without a special designation of the place to be searched, and the person or thing to be seized, nor without probable cause, supported by oath or affirmation.

MASSACHUSETTS. Every person has a right to be secure from all unreasonable searches and seizures of his person, his house, his papers and all his possessions. All warrants, therefore, are contrary to this right, if the cause or foundation of them be not previously supported by oath or affirmation; and if the order, in a warrant to a civil officer, to make search in all suspected places, or to arrest one or more suspected persons, or to seize their property, be not accompanied with a special designation of the persons or objects of search, arrest or seizure. And no warrant ought to be issued but in such cases, and with the formalities prescribed by the laws.

NEW HAMPSHIRE. Every person hath a right to be secure from all unreasonable searches and seizures of his person, his house, his papers, and all his possessions. Therefore, all warrants to search suspected places, or arrest a person for examination or trial, in prosecution for criminal matters, are contrary to this right, if the cause or foundation of them be not previously supported by oath or affirmation; and if the order, in the warrant of a civil officer, to make search in suspected places, or to arrest one or more suspected persons, or to seize their property, be not accompanied with a special designation of the persons or objects of search, arrest or seizure; and no warrant ought to be issued but in cases, and with the formalities, prescribed by law.

VERMONT. That the people have a right to hold themselves, their houses, papers and possessions, free from search or seizure; and, therefore, warrants without oath or affirmation first made, affording sufficient foundation for them, and whereby any officer or messenger may be commanded or required to search suspected places, or to seize any person or persons, his, her or their property, not particularly described, are contrary to that right, and ought not to be granted.

RHODE ISLAND. The right of the people to be secure in their persons, papers and possessions, against unreasonable searches and seizures, shall not be violated; and no warrant shall issue, but on complaint in writing, upon probable cause, supported by oath or affirmation, and describing, as nearly as may be, the place to be searched and the persons or things to be seized.

CONNECTICUT, PENNSYLVANIA, KENTUCKY, ALABAMA, TEXAS. The people shall be secure in their persons, houses, papers and possessions, from unreasonable searches or seizures; and no warrant to search any place, or to seize any person or things, shall issue, without describing them as nearly as may be, nor without probable cause, supported by oath or affirmation.

MARYLAND. All warrants, without oath or affirmation, to search suspected places, or to seize any person or property, are grievous and oppressive; and all general warrants to search suspected places, or to apprehend suspected persons, without naming or describing the place or the person in special, are illegal, and ought not to be granted.

VIRGINIA. General warrants, whereby an officer or messenger may be commanded to search suspected places, without evidence of a fact committed, or to seize a person or persons not named, or whose offence is not particularly described and supported by evidence, are grievous and oppressive, and ought not to be granted.

NORTH CAROLINA. General warrants, whereby any officer or messenger may be commanded to search suspected places, without evidence of the fact committed, or to seize any person or persons not named, whose offences are not particularly described and supported by evidence, are dangerous to liberty and ought not to be granted.

NEW JERSEY, OHIO, INDIANA, IOWA, WISCONSIN, CALIFORNIA. The right of the people to be secure in their persons, houses, papers and effects, against unreasonable searches and seizures shall not be violated; and no warrant shall issue but upon probable cause, supported by oath or affirmation, and particularly describing the place to be searched, and the papers and things to be seized.

DELAWARE. The people shall be secure in their persons, houses, papers and possessions, from unreasonable searches or seizures; and no warrant to search any place, or to seize any person or things, shall issue without describing them as particularly as may be, nor then, unless there be probable cause, supported by oath or affirmation.

TENNESSEE, ILLINOIS. That the people shall be secure in their persons, houses, papers and possessions, from unreasonable searches and seizures; and that general warrants, whereby an officer may be commanded to search suspected places, without evidence of the fact committed, or to seize any person or persons not named, whose offences are not particularly described and supported by evidence, are dangerous to liberty and ought not to be granted.

MISSISSIPPI, FLORIDA. That the people shall be secure in their persons, houses, papers and possessions, from unreasonable seizures and searches; and that no warrant to search any place, or to seize any person or thing, shall issue without describing the place to be searched, and the person or thing to be seized, as nearly as may be, nor without probable cause, supported by oath or affirmation.

MISSOURI. That the people ought to be secure in their persons, papers, houses and effects, from unreasonable searches and seizures; and no warrant to search any place, or seize any person or thing, can issue without describing the place to be searched, and the person or thing to be seized, as nearly as may be, nor without probable cause, supported by oath or affirmation.

MICHIGAN. The persons, houses, papers and possessions of every person shall be secure from unreasonable searches and seizures. No warrant to seize any person or things shall issue without describing them, nor without probable cause, supported by oath or affirmation.

ARKANSAS. That the people shall be secure in their persons, houses, papers and possessions from unreasonable searches and seizures; and that general warrants, whereby any officer may be commanded to search suspected places, without evidence of the fact committed, or to seize any person or persons not named, whose offences are not particularly described and supported by evidence, are dangerous to liberty, and shall not be granted.

It will be observed that the states of New York, Georgia, South Carolina and Louisiana are not included in the foregoing list. The constitutions of these states contain no provisions limiting the power to issue general warrants.

In New York, however, they have a *statutory* Bill of Rights, wherein amongst other things, it is declared that;

The right of the people to be secure in their persons, houses, papers and effects, against unreasonable searches, and seizures, ought not to be violated; and no warrants can issue but upon probable cause supported by oath or affirmation, and particularly describing the place to be searched, and the persons or things to be seized.

If this provision were only a declaration of a great principle of civil liberty, incapable of practical application or enforcement, it would perhaps be as secure in a statute as in a constitution. But it is more than that when embodied in a constitution. It operates there as a limitation upon legislative power, and consequently is, in that instrument, a more complete security of the right of personal liberty, unless, indeed, constitutions are to be reformed more frequently than statutes.

3. *Suspension of the privilege of the writ.* The power of suspending the privilege of the writ of habeas corpus, is, by the federal constitution and by those of the several states, limited to those occasions in which the public safety is threatened by rebellion or invasion; and, by fair construction, is limited also to offences endangering the public safety.

The Federal Convention, when acting upon this clause, undoubtedly had in view the British act of 1777, by which the writ of habeas corpus was denied, for a definite period, to persons taken in the act of high treason, committed in any of the colonies or on the high seas; or in the act of piracy, or who were charged with or suspected of any of those crimes. This act is often referred to as an instance of the suspension of the habeas corpus act, as if it were nothing more than that; and Mr. Martin, in his letter above cited, speaks of the clause in the Constitution as if it authorized a suspension of the "habeas corpus act." But in the United States there was no habeas corpus act, to which the clause could refer; and, besides, such a power would cover only half the ground. For there would remain after the suspension of the *act*, the common law right to the writ in term-time and probably in vacation. The clause in the Constitution expresses accurately the restriction imposed and the power which it necessarily implies, viz: the power to suspend the *privilege* of the writ, when in cases of rebellion or invasion the public safety may require it—and then only.

Rebellion and invasion are eminently matters of national concern; and charged as Congress is, with the duty of preserving the United States from both these evils, it is fit that it should possess the power to make effectual such measures as it may deem expedient to adopt for their suppression.

In the discharge of this duty, it may provide for the arrest and imprisonment of offenders or of suspected persons, and forbid their release, while the exigency lasts, by either state or federal courts.

Mr. Rawle, in his "View of the Constitution," page 117, expresses the opinion that the restriction imposed by this clause in the Constitution extends to the states as well as to the United States. But it is a settled rule of construction of that instrument that the limitations of power contained in it, where they are expressed in general terms, apply only to the government created by it. And, although this clause has not been the subject of express adjudication, there is no doubt that its construction is governed by this rule, and consequently the restriction does not extend to the states. *Barron* v. *The Mayor and City of Baltimore*, 7 *Peters*, 243; *James* v. *Commonwealth*, 12 *S. & R.*, 220; *Barker* v. *The People*, 3 *Cow.*, 701; *Reed* v. *Rice*, 2 *J. J. Marsh.*, 45; *Colt & another* v. *Eves*, 12 *Conn.*, 243,

This power has never been exercised by Congress. The Senate, indeed, on the occasion of the supposed treasonable conspiracy of Aaron Burr, as if panic-stricken, took hasty action in that direction.

On the 22d of January, 1807, the President sent to Congress a special message on the subject of Burr's alleged conspiracy, in which among other things he informed them that one of the "principal emissaries of Mr. Burr," whom General Wilkinson had caused to be apprehended, had been liberated by habeas corpus.

On the next day the Senate appointed a committee to inquire whether it was expedient to suspend the writ of habeas corpus and referred to it the President's message and accompanying documents. The committee immediately reported a bill to suspend the privilege of the writ for three months in certain cases; and the bill being read three times by unanimous consent, and amended, was passed the same day. The passage of the bill was communicated "in confidence," to the House on the 26th of January, and their concurrence therein requested as speedily as the emergency of the case should in their judgment require.

The House acted with equal promptness and almost equal unanimity; but adversely. It received the Senate's message and bill in secret session, but on learning their nature immediately resolved, by the very decisive vote of 123 to 3, that they ought not to be kept secret; and, accordingly opened its doors.

A motion was then made to reject the bill, which is regarded as a motion of indignity, importing that the bill is unworthy of consideration. After a short but interesting debate touching the state of public affairs, and the nature and value of the writ of habeas corpus, the motion to reject prevailed by a vote of 113 to 19. 3 *Benton's Abr. Debates*, 490, 504, 515.

The bill, as it passed the Senate, was as follows:

A bill suspending the writ of habeas corpus for three months, in certain cases:

"*Be it enacted, by the Senate and House of Representatives of the United States of America, in Congress assembled,* That in all cases, where any person or persons, charged on oath with treason, or other high crime or misdemeanor, endangering the peace, safety or neutrality of the United States, have been or shall be arrested or imprisoned, by virtue of any warrant or authority of the President of the United States, or from the Chief Executive Magistrate of any State or Territorial Government, or from any person acting under the direction or authority of the President of the United States, the privilege of the writ of habeas corpus shall be, and the same hereby is suspended for and during the term of three months from and after the passage of this act, and no longer."

The attempt to pass this measure did not escape the animadversion of Col. Burr. 1 *Burr's Trial*, 78.

No state, it is believed, has ever suspended the privilege of the writ of habeas corpus except Massachusetts, which on the occasion of "Shay's Rebellion" passed a law suspending it from November, 1786, to July, 1787. *Minot*, 64, 69.

The policy of such a step was urged upon the attention of the Legislature of Louisiana in 1814, when impending invasion threatened her metropolis; but General Jackson, impatient of the delay consequent upon their divided counsels, at length laid the city under martial law and practically suspended the privilege of the writ.

He ordered the arrest of Louallier, a member of the Legislature, for an alleged act of mutiny. The prisoner applied to Judge Hall, of the United States Court, for a writ of habeas corpus which was granted. The General, deeming this an interference with his jurisdiction under martial law, ordered the arrest of the judge and removed him from the city.

After the revocation of martial law the court resumed its peaceful sway and summoned the General to answer for the contempt of arresting the judge. The General was fined a thousand dollars, which he paid before leaving the court.

Congress many years afterwards refunded the fine.

4. *Statutory enactments relating to the writ of habeas corpus.* In the Judiciary Act of Sep. 24, 1789, Congress prescribed the jurisdiction of the federal courts and justices under the writ of habeas corpus, so that this great constitutional privilege "might receive life and activity."

Some of the states had not waited until the adoption of the federal constitution.

Virginia passed an act in 1784, to which additions were subsequently made. They were revised in 1818, and again in 1849, when their present clear, concise and comprehensive statute was passed.

Pennsylvania, in 1785, adopted the act of 31 *Car.*, 2, extending its provisions, however, to all cases of detainer other than those for criminal or supposed criminal matter. This statute survived two constitutions of the state and is still in force.

New York, in 1787, adopted, almost literally, the act, 31 *Car.*, 2, which continued without material alteration, until 1818, when important changes were introduced. By the act of 1818, authority was given to the officers before whom the writ was returned, to revise the commitment, and examine into the truth of the facts alleged in the return.

In 1828, still further changes were introduced, to clear the proceeding of doubts which had been started, and increase its efficiency. These modifications were adopted on the recommendation of the distinguished and able commissioners to whom the legislature had committed the very important charge of revising, for their use, the laws of the state. The act as then passed, though revised since, is substantially the same as that now in force.

In 1795, the statute of 31 *Car.*, 2, was in substance re-enacted in New Jersey, and is still the law of the state.

In South Carolina and Georgia, the Act of 31 *Car.*, 2, was adopted before the revolution, and remains in force with only slight changes.

The new states have quite generally passed laws defining the jurisdiction and regulating the practice under the writ. In Tennessee, however, they have no statute on the subject, other than that of 1823, which merely provided for the subpœnaing of witnesses on behalf of either party in order that justice may be duly administered on the trial.

The new states have, in many instances, copied their acts relating to this writ from those of some of the older states; and the act of 31 *Car.*, 2, may be said to be "the basis of all the American statutes on the subject." 1 *Kent*, 642. There are some differences in the mode of procedure, but there are no such material departures in the statutes of any of the states from the established principles by which the practice was governed at common law, as to render the general rules of the common law procedure wholly inapplicable.

It would be impracticable to give in detail the provisions of the statutes of all the states on this subject, within the limits proposed for this work. The same spirit pervades them all, and the inquiries which remain to be considered cannot be uninteresting nor unimportant in any of the states.

BOOK II.

THE WRIT OF HABEAS CORPUS.

THE WRIT OF HABEAS CORPUS.

CHAPTER I.

NATURE OF THE WRIT OF HABEAS CORPUS, AND SOURCES AND EXTENT OF JURISDICTION OVER IT.

SECTION I.

GENERAL NATURE OF THE WRIT OF HABEAS CORPUS.

The writ of habeas corpus is that legal process which is employed for the summary vindication of the right of personal liberty when illegally restrained. It takes its name from the emphatic words which it contained when it was written in Latin. The same words were, however, used in a variety of writs which had for their object the production of a person before a court or judge. These writs were distinguished from each other, at common law, by the terms which denoted the particular purpose for which they were issued; as, *ad respondendum; ad faciendum et recipiendum; ad prosequendum; ad satisfaciendum; ad testificandum*, and *ad subjiciendum et recipiendum.*

It was the last of these only, which was designed to procure liberation from illegal confinement. It was directed to the person detaining another, and commanded him to produce the body of the prisoner or person detained, together with the day and cause of his caption and detention, to submit to and receive whatsoever the court or judge awarding the writ might consider in that behalf.

Employed to vindicate the right of personal liberty by whatever power infringed, it became inseparably associated with that right; and in proportion as the right was valued, so was the writ by which it was defended. It was its grateful office which commended this species of the writ to the favorable regard of the people, and finally dignified it as, *The* writ of habeas corpus.

There were, indeed, other writs, at common law, viz: *de atiȯ et atia, de homine replegiando*, which in particular cases, were used to obtain a similar object; but being more limited in their application and more complicated and slow in their operation, they gradually fell into disuse.

The date of the origin of the writ of habeas corpus is unknown. It is supposed to have been in use before the date of the Magna Carta. But a diligent inquirer, having access to the best sources of information, states the result of his investigation into the origin of the writ as follows: "The writ of habeas corpus is found in operation at a remote period of the English law. The earliest reign in which I have been able to trace its frequent appearance, is that of Henry VI. At that period it seems to have been familiar to and well understood by the judges. *Vine's Case*, 34 *H.* 6.

"After this period the existence of the writ of habeas corpus is distinctly observed, and its progress can be effectually traced. But before the reign of Henry VI., I find myself obscured by a cloud. In the Year Book, 48 Ed. III., 22, there is a case upon this writ, or as it was then called, corpus cum causa.

"The research for a higher origin than the time of Henry VI., is unnecessary. The investigation may answer antiquarians; it cannot materially assist a constitutional lawyer." *Hill's Report Canadian Prisoner's Case*, 6.

In its early history it appears to have been used as a means of relief from private restraint. The earliest precedents where it was used *against the crown* are in the reign of Henry VII. Afterwards the use of it became more frequent, and in the time of Charles I., it was held an admitted constitutional remedy.

Though the writ of habeas corpus originated in the common law of England, the leading idea of it—deliverance by summary legal process from illegal confinement—may be traced in the laws of other countries which derived none of their principles of jurisprudence or rules of procedure from English law.

The interdict, *de homine libero exhibendo*, of the civil law, was a remedy in some important particulars similar to the writ of habeas corpus. When a *freeman* was restrained by another in bad faith, the prætor ordered his interdict that such person should be brought before him in public that he might be liberated. *Dig.*, 43, *tit.* 29.

And the process of the Spanish law, called "Manifestation," appears to have resembled the writ of habeas corpus. Mr. Hallam cites a remarkable instance of its use and efficiency against the sovereign, "not only in order to illustrate the privilege of *manifestation*, but as exhibiting an instance of judicial firmness and integrity, to which, in the fourteenth century no country in Europe could offer a parallel." *Hallam's Mid. Ages*, 222.

But the writ of habeas corpus in England and America has not only been rendered a more complete and efficacious remedy for illegal imprisonment in all cases, than any similar process in any other country; but it has also been raised to the importance and clothed with the power of a political principle, so that while and because it is an invaluable and incomparable protection for personal liberty, it is also in turn protected by the highest power in the State, constitutional and legislative, as a cherished popular right and safeguard of civil liberty.

In the further examination of the subject of the writ of habeas corpus, it is proposed to consider the sources and extent of the jurisdiction over it; the general principles of practice under it; the law of imprisonment under legal process; the law of bail; the law of private restraint; the law of extradition of fugitives; the subjects of writs of error and of recommitment after discharge under the writ.

SECTION II.

JURISDICTION IN ENGLAND.

1. *Jurisdiction at Common Law.*
2. *Statutory Jurisdiction.*

1. *The common law jurisdiction.* The origin of this jurisdiction as has been seen cannot now be ascertained. It is supposed to have been exercised before Magna Carta. *Hallam Middle Ages*, 342. It extended to all cases of illegal imprisonment whether claimed under public or private authority. 2 *Inst.*, 55; *Rex.* v. *Mead*, 1 *Burr.* 542; 3 *Bl. Com.*, 133.

It was exercised by the Courts of Chancery, King's Bench and Common Pleas, and in a case of privilege by the Exchequer. *Bac. Abr. Hab. Corp., B.* 1. The chancellor or a judge of the Court of King's Bench might grant the writ in vacation, returnable immediate at chambers. *Watson's Case*, 36 *Eng. C. L.*, 254.

2. *Statutory jurisdiction.* By the statute 31 *Car.*, 2, the Court of Exchequer, in cases of imprisonment for "criminal or supposed criminal matters," was authorized to grant the writ in term time as well as the Courts of Chancery, King's Bench and Common Pleas: and upon a proper application it was made the duty of "lord chancellor, lord keeper, or any of his majesty's justices, either of the one bench or of the other, or the barons of the exchequer of the degree of the coif," to grant the writ in vacation.

By the act of 56 *Geo.* 3, *c.* 100, similar jurisdiction in cases of imprisonment or restraint of liberty, other than those provided for in 31 *Car.* 2, was conferred upon any baron of the exchequer, or any judge of either bench in England or Ireland, in vacation time.

SECTION III.

JURISDICTION OF THE FEDERAL COURTS OF THE UNITED STATES.

The constitutional provisions bearing upon the subject are found in *Art.* I, *sec.* 9, § 2.

"The privilege of the writ of habeas corpus shall not be suspended, unless when in cases of rebellion, or invasion the public safety may require it;" and in *Art.* III, *sec.* 1, 2.

"The judicial power of the United States shall be vested in one supreme court, and in such inferior courts as the congress may from time to time ordain and establish. The judicial power shall extend to all cases in law and equity arising under this constitution, the laws of the United States and treaties made or which shall be made under their authority; to all cases affecting ambassadors, other public ministers and consuls; to all cases of admiralty and maratime jurisdiction; to controversies between two or more states, between a state and citizens of another state, between citizens of different states, between citizens of the same state claiming lands under grants of different states, and between a state or the citizens thereof and foreign states, citizens or subjects."

"In all cases affecting ambassadors, other public ministers and consuls, and those in which a state shall be a party, the supreme court shall have original jurisdiction. In all the other cases before mentioned, the supreme court shall have appellate jurisdiction, both as to law and fact, with such exceptions and under such regulations as the congress shall make."

The provision relating to the writ of habeas corpus limits the legislative power, but confers no definite practical jurisdiction upon the courts.

It remained for Congress "to provide efficient means by which this great constitutional privilege should receive life and activity; for if the means be not in existence the privilege itself would be lost, although no law for its suppression should be enacted." *Marshall, C. J., Ex parte, Bollman*, 4 *Cranch*, 75.

The courts of the United States not having their origin in the common law, but being the creatures of the written law, must look to the written law for their jurisdiction. Their jurisdiction in habeas corpus was first prescribed in the 14th sec. of the Judiciary Act of Sep. 24, 1789. 1 *U. S. Stat. at Large*, 81, which section provides:

"That all the before-mentioned courts of the United States," (Supreme Court, Circuit Court and District Court,) "shall have power to issue writs of scire facias, habeas corpus, and all other writs not specially provided for by statute, which may be necessary for the exercise of their respective jurisdictions, and agreeable to the principles and usages of law. And that either of the justices of the Supreme Court as well as judges of the District Courts, shall have power to grant writs of habeas corpus for the purpose of an inquiry into the cause of commitment: *Provided*, that writs of habeas corpus shall in no case extend to prisoners in gaol, unless where they are in custody, under or by color of the authority of the United States, or are committed for trial before some court of the same, or are necessary to be brought into court to testify."

The nature and extent of the jurisdiction in habeas corpus granted in the foregoing section, have frequently been considered by the Supreme Court, and many questions arising upon it have been determined by that court.

The term habeas corpus, although a generic one comprehending several species of writ, is nevertheless used in this section and in the constitution without addition or qualification, to denote the highest species of the writ—*habeas corpus ad subjiciendum*—the great writ of liberty.

"No law of the United States prescribes the cases in which this great writ shall be issued, nor the power of the court over the party brought up by it. The term used in the constitution is well understood; and the judicial act authorizes the courts of the United States and the judges thereof, to issue the writ 'for the purpose of inquiring into the cause of commitment.'" *Ex parte Watkins*, 3 *Peters*, 201.

Whether the power to grant the writ is confined to cases where prisoners "are in custody under or by color of the authority of the United States, or are committed for trial before some court of the same, or are necessary to be brought into court to testify;" whether the term "commitment" as used in the statute is to be construed as equivalent to "imprisonment in gaol," under legal process, or as comprehending every kind of restraint, are questions which have not been decided by the Supreme Court. They were fully and ably discussed in the case of

Barry v. *Mercien*, 5 *How.*, 103; but were not decided, as the court held they had no jurisdiction of the writ of error under the act of 1789, *ch.* 20, § 22.

In that case it appeared that the petitioner, John A. Barry, in the summer of 1844, presented a petition to the Circuit Court for the Southern District of New York, praying that a writ of habeas corpus ad subjiciendum might issue directing Eliza Ann Barry, the wife of petitioner, and Mary Mercien her mother, to bring up the person of an infant child, the daughter of the petitioner and the said Eliza Ann his wife, and alleged to be in the custody of the said Mary Mercien and Eliza Ann Barry. In the application to the Circuit Court, in order to bring himself within the provisions of the constitution and laws of the United States, the petitioner set forth that he was a natural-born subject of the Queen of Great Britain, and alleged that the child though born in the State of New York, was also a British subject and allegiant to the British crown.

Judge Betts, in an elaborate and able opinion, refused the application, holding:

1st. That a Circuit Court of the United States could not exercise the common law functions of parens patriæ; and had no common law jurisdiction over the matter set forth in the petition.

2d. That that court had not judicial cognizance of the matter by virtue of any statute of the United States.

As to the last proposition, if the jurisdiction in such cases is to be sought for in that clause of the Act of 1789, which provides that the writ may issue "for the purpose of inquiring into the cause of commitment," as the Supreme Court has intimated, there would seem to be no serious difficulty; for the term "commitment" has a technical signification, importing a detainer under legal process, and that it is used in that sense in that section, appears from the proviso which follows.

As to the first point decided above, the opinion of the judge will probably be held eventually to express the true view of the law.

The common law power denied by the court was, indeed, exercised previously in the case of the *United States* v. *Green*, 3 *Mason*, 482, but the question of jurisdiction was not raised. It is difficult to see how such jurisdiction can be conferred upon a court of the United States without a material modification of the common law idea of the writ; for it was neither designed for, nor is it now adapted to the litigation of controverted matters between private parties. Questions of that character do, it is true, sometimes arise in the course of the proceeding, but strictly speaking, they arise only collaterally.

It was well said by the judge: "A procedure by habeas corpus can in no legal sense be regarded as a suit or controversy between private parties. It is an inquisition by the government, at the suggestion and instance of an individual, most probably, but still in the name and capacity of the sovereign."

"Jurisdiction in habeas corpus, is in its nature appellate and therefore belongs to the Supreme Court. The question brought forward on a habeas corpus, where the commitment is under legal process, is always distinct from that which is involved in the cause itself. The question whether the individual shall be imprisoned is always distinct from the question whether he shall be convicted or acquitted of the charge on which he is to be tried, and therefore these questions are separated, and may be decided in different courts. The decision that the individual shall be imprisoned must always precede the application for a writ of habeas corpus, and this writ must always be for the purpose of revising that decision, and therefore appellate in its nature." *Ex parte Bollman & Swartwout*, 4 *Cr.*, 75.

In the exercise of its appellate jurisdiction it will grant the writ wherever that jurisdiction extends. It will not grant the writ at the instance of the subject of a foreign government, to obtain the custody of a minor child, detained by a citizen of one of the states; for that would be the exercise of original jurisdiction. *Ex parte Barry*, 2 *How.*, 65.

It will grant the writ on the application of one committed for trial in the Circuit Court on a criminal charge. *Ex parte Bollman & Swartwout*, 4 *Cr.*, 75; *Ex parte Hamilton*, 3 *Dall.*, 17.

It will grant it where the petitioner is committed on an insufficient warrant. *Ex parte Burford*, 3 *Cranch*, 448.

And where the petitioner is detained by the marshal on a *capias ad satisfaciendum*, after the return-day of the writ. *Ex parte Watkins*, 7 *Peters*, 568.

But it will not grant the writ after conviction to relieve the petitioner from imprisonment under the sentence, although the record should show that the party was indicted for an act not criminal; for the law does not confer upon that court appellate jurisdiction in *criminal* cases. *Ex parte Watkins*, 3 *Peters*, 193.

Nor will it grant it to relieve from a commitment for contempt; for that is equivalent to, is in fact, a conviction. *Ex parte Kearney*, 7 *Wheat.*, 38.

None of the courts of the United States have authority to grant the writ for the purpose of inquiring into the cause of commitment, where the prisoner is imprisoned under process issued from the state courts.

It was refused by the Supreme Court, where the party, for whose benefit the application was made, had been convicted in a state court of levying war against a state. *Ex parte Dorr*, 3 *How.*, 103.

It was refused by the Circuit Court, where the petitioner, a secretary attached to the Spanish legation, was confined under criminal process issued under the authority of the state of Pennsylvania. *Ex parte Cabrera*, *Wash. C. C.*, 232.

Also where the petitioner, a British seaman, was arrested under the authority of an act of the legislature of the state of South Carolina, which was held to conflict with the Constitution of the United States. *Ex parte Elkinson*, 2 *Wheeler Cr. Cas.*, 56.

It will be granted, however, where the imprisonment although by a state officer, is under or by color of the authority of the United States as where the prisoner was arrested under a governor's warrant, as a fugitive from justice of another state, requisition for him having been regularly made. *Ex parte Joseph Smith*, 3 *McLean*, 121.

Neither the Supreme or Circuit Court will grant the writ where the petitioner is in conviction or execution of a sentence of a court having jurisdiction. *Ex parte Kearney*, 7 *Wheat.*, 38; *Johnson* v *United States*, 3 *McLean*, 89.

The Supreme Court once doubted whether habeas corpus was the proper remedy in the case of arrest under civil process. *Ex parte Wilson*, 6 *Cranch*, 52; but the doubt was soon abandoned. *Ex parte Randolph*, 2 *Brock.*, 447; *Nelson & Graydon* v. *Cutter & Tyrrell*, 3 *McLean*, 326.

The jurisdiction of the Supreme Court being appellate, it must be shown to the court that they have power to award the writ before it will be granted. *Ex parte Wilburn*, 9 *Peters*, 704.

By the 7th section of the "Act further to provide for the collection of duties on imports," passed March 2, 1833, 4 *U. S. Stat. at Large*, 634, it is enacted:

"That either of the justices of the Supreme Court or a judge of any District Court of the United States, in addition to the authority already conferred by law, shall have power to grant writs of habeas corpus, in all cases of a prisoner or prisoners in jail or confinement, where he or they shall be committed or confined, on or by any authority or law, for any act done or omitted to be done, in pursuance of a law of the United States, or any order, process, or decree of any judge or court thereof, anything in any act of Congress to the contrary notwithstanding. And if any person or persons to whom such writ of habeas corpus may be directed, shall refuse to obey the same, or shall neglect or refuse to make return, or shall make a false return thereto, in addition to the remedies already given by law, he or they shall be deemed and taken to be guilty of a misdemeanor, and shall on conviction before any court of competent jurisdiction, be punished by fine, not exceeding one thousand dollars, and by imprisonment not exceeding six months, or either, according to the nature and aggravation of the case."

The immediate occasion of the passage of the act containing the foregoing section, was the rebellious attitude of South Carolina on the tariff laws.

It having been demonstrated in the matter of Alexander McLeod, that further legislation on the part of Congress was necessary to enable the government of the United States to discharge its duty to foreign governments under the law of nations, in certain cases; by the "Act to provide further remedial justice in the courts of the United States," passed August 29, 1842, 5 *U. S. Stat. at Large*, 539, power was given to the justices of the Supreme Court and judges of the District Courts to "grant writs of habeas corpus in all cases of any prisoner or prisoners in jail or confinement, when he, she or they, being subjects or citizens of a foreign state, and domiciled therein, shall be committed or confined, or in custody, under or by any authority or law, or process founded thereon, of the United States, or of any of them, for or on account of any act done or omitted under any alleged right, title, authority, privilege, protection or exemption, set up or claimed under the commission or order, or sanction of any foreign state or sovereignty, the validity and effect whereof depend upon the law of nations, or under color thereof," &c.

By the 3d section of the "Act for the government and regulation of seamen in the merchant service" passed July 20, 1790, 1 *U. S. Stat. at Large*, 131, it is provided that refractory seamen in certain cases shall not be discharged on "habeas corpus or otherwise."

We have now adverted to all the acts of Congress relating to the writ of habeas corpus.

An interesting class of cases has lately arisen under the fugitive slave act of 1850, involving the question of power vested in the "justices of the Supreme Court and judges of the District Courts," of the United States under the 7th section of the act of Congress of March 2, 1833, above cited. These cases present some of the most serious and exciting questions which have ever arisen in the judicial history of the country; serious, because they involve the constitutional powers of Congress, and exciting, because they are connected with the prominent political topics of the day.

The leading case in the United States Courts on the construction of the 7th section of the act of March 22, 1833, is *Ex parte Jenkins*, 2 *Wal.*, 521, decided in the Circuit Court of the Eastern District of Pennsylvania, at the October Term, 1853. The relators were deputy marshals of the United States, who, in attempting to execute a warrant to arrest William Thomas, a fugitive slave, had a "violent and bloody encounter" with him at Wilkes-Barrè, in which the negro was successful, and afterwards escaped.

1*st Case*. The marshals were arrested on a warrant of a justice of the peace, charged with an assault and battery with intent to kill Thomas. The acts of violence complained of were those committed in the encounter above mentioned. They were discharged on habeas corpus by the Circuit Court.

2*d Case.* Soon after their discharge they were again arrested on a *capias ad respondendum* at the suit of Thomas, brought in the Supreme Court of Pennsylvania, the same acts of violence being the predicate of the action. They were also discharged on habeas corpus on this arrest by the same court.

3*d Case.* Soon after their second discharge they were again arrested under a bench warrant of outlawry from the Court of Quarter Sessions of Luzerne county, based on an indictment found there by the grand jury, charging them with riot, assault and battery, and assault with intent to kill; but not setting forth that the parties indicted were officers of the United States, nor that the alleged crimes had been committed while they were acting or professing to act in pusuance of a law of the United States, or under some order, process or decree of some judge or court thereof.

They were again discharged by the same court. Mr. Justice Grier being absent on the hearing of the last two cases they were decided by Judge Kane.

In all the cases it was held that the returns to the writs of habeas corpus were not conclusive, and that evidence would be received of the actual state of the facts complained of in the prosecutions in the criminal cases and relied on in the civil action; that it was the imperative and peculiar duty of that court under the 7th section of the act, March 2d 1833, to determine under the writ of habeas corpus the *matter of fact* whether the acts complained of were done in pursuance of a law of the United States or any order, process or decree of any judge or court thereof; and that in committing the acts complained of the marshals "did not exceed the exigency of the process under which they acted."

A remarkable instance of the use of the writ of habeas corpus and of the power claimed and exercised under the acts of Congress of 1833 and 1850, occurred before the judge of the District Court for the Southern District of Ohio, in April, 1856, in the matter of Gaines' slaves.

One of the slaves just before she was arrested in Cincinnati, under the warrant of the U. S. commissioner, murdered one of her children, also a slave, to prevent its capture, as she was reported to have said. Being brought before the commissioner of the Circuit Court, he decided in favor of Gaines, the claimant, and granted his certificate thereof. She was indicted in the Court of Common Pleas of Hamilton county, for the murder of her child, and while in the custody of the marshal under the warrant of the commissioner, was arrested by the sheriff of the county under process of the state court, issued upon the indictment and taken out of the custody of the marshal.

The marshal petitioned for a writ of habeas corpus, which was granted by the judge of the U. S. District Court. The points determined by him are thus stated in his letter to A. Harlon and others, April, 26, 1856: "The only point raised for my decision was on the return to a writ of habeas corpus, granted on the petition of the marshal for the Southern District of Ohio, in which it was set forth under oath, that the fugitives were lawfully in the custody of that officer, under a warrant from the commissioner, and while so in custody were seized by the sheriff of Hamilton county, by process from a state court, on an indictment charging them with crime. The question was whether the fugitives, while thus held by the marshal, could be taken, forcibly or otherwise, from his custody. I held that, the process being first served by that officer under a law of the United States, which made him responsible for the safe keeping of the fugitives, and which expressly prohibited state interference in any manner or under any circumstances, the sheriff could not take them from his custody by any state process."

The United States District Court of Wisconsin also adopted and applied the doctrine of the case, Ex parte Jenkins in the case of the *United States ex rel. Garland* v. *Morris*, *Am. Law Reg.*, *Apl.* 1854, 348.

And so did the Circuit Court, for the Southern District of Ohio, in the case, *Ex parte H. H. Robinson*, 6 *McLean*, 355, where a marshal of the United States was discharged, on habeas corpus, from imprisonment commanded by a state judge for contempt in rearresting a slave discharged from his custody which he held under a warrant from a U. S. commissioner; the complaint for which the warrant issued, being, at the time of the issuing of the habeas corpus and the order of discharge by the state judge, pending, and undetermined by the commissioner.

The Supreme Court of Pennsylvania, however, has taken strong ground against the construction given to the 7th section of the Act of March 22, 1833, by the U. S. Circuit Court in Ex parte Jenkins.

After the lapse of nine months from the time of the discharge of Jenkins and others, on habeas corpus, from the custody of the sheriff of Philadelphia county, under the capias ad respondendum in the civil action brought by Thomas against them, in the Supreme Court of Pennsylvania, stated *ante*, a motion was made in said court at nisi prius for an attachment against the sheriff, on the ground of an insufficient return, he having returned that the defendants were discharged out of his hands, and for a failure to bring in the bodies of the defendants.

The motion was heard before Ch. J. Lewis, and Woodward and Knox, JJ., and is reported, *Thomas* v. *Crossin et al.*, 3 *Am. Law Reg.*, 207. Ch. J. Lewis, in an elaborate opinion controverting the doctrine held in the case of *Jenkins*, 2 *Wallace*, 521, the other judges concurring, holds that,

"The seventh section of the Act of Congress of 2d March, 1833, commonly called 'The Force Bill,' which authorizes the writ of habeas corpus to be issued by the courts of the United States, under certain circumstances, for the protection of officers, and others acting with them, in execution of the laws of the United States, is to be confined in its application to cases where there has been an avowed purpose, by some authority or law *of a state*, to disregard an Act of Congress, and to imprison or otherwise punish the officers of the United States for enforcing it; and operates moreover, only in cases where such purpose appears on the face of the proceedings.

"Where a habeas corpus has been issued in pursuance of the statute, by a United States court, it has no right to go behind the return to the writ; and if it does, and discharges the relator upon evidence taken at the hearing, such discharge is inoperative and will be disregarded by a state court. But though the discharge was invalid, yet as the plaintiff had unnecessarily delayed his application for the attachment, and there was no reason to suspect the sheriff of a willful contempt, the attachment should be denied.

Territorial limitation of jurisdiction. The jurisdiction of the circuit and district courts is limited to their respective geographical divisions. In *Ex parte Graham*, 4 *Wash. C. C.*, 211, the defendant was arrested in Pennsylvania, on process issued from the Circuit Court of Rhode Island. He was discharged on habeas corpus, the court saying: "The division and appointment of particular courts for each district necessarily confines the jurisdiction of these local tribunals within the limits of the respective districts within which they are directed to be holden. Were it otherwise and the court of one district could send compulsory process into any other, so as to draw to itself a jurisdiction over persons and things without the limits of its district, there would result a clashing of jurisdiction between the different courts not easily to be adjusted, and an oppression upon suitors too intolerable to be endured."

SECTION IV.

JURISDICTION OF THE STATE COURTS.

The several states, in their character of sovereign political communities, possess all the judicial power appertaining to independent nations, except what they have committed to the Federal Government.

They establish courts, and create, apportion, regulate and enforce their jurisdiction in such manner as in their judgment the just ends of government require.

The principles of jurisdiction in habeas corpus proceedings being essentially the same in all the states, it does not fall within the plan of this work to inquire in detail to what courts or officers it has been committed in the several states.

This is to be sought in the statutes of the states, for although there are provisions in the constitutions of all the states, except Maryland, North Carolina and South Carolina, against the suspension of the privilege of the writ, there are express grants of jurisdiction over it in only twelve, Virginia, Florida, Alabama, Louisiana, Ohio, Illinois, Missouri, Michigan, Arkansas, Texas, Wisconsin and California.

SECTION V.

CONCURRENT JURISDICTION OF THE FEDERAL AND STATE COURTS.

The constitutional provision that "the judicial power of the United States shall extend to all cases, in law and equity arising under this Constitution, the laws of the United States, and treaties made or which shall be made under their authority," has never been held to prohibit the exercise of judicial power by the state courts in such cases, though it has been said that Congress have power to make the jurisdiction of the federal courts exclusive in all cases to which the judicial power of the United States is extended by the Constitution. *Martin* v. *Hunter's Lessee*, 1 *Wheat.*, 337.

Congress not having undertaken (if indeed it has the power) to make *original* jurisdiction in such cases exclusive in the federal courts, the state courts have hitherto exercised it concurrently with the federal courts, subject only to the final *appellate* jurisdiction of the Supreme Court of the United States, as provided by the Judiciary Act of Congress.

Jurisdiction in habeas corpus, as we have seen, is granted to the federal courts and judges only in certain cases; but it is not by the Constitution or the act of Congress declared to be exclusive in them. Accordingly the state tribunals, exercising a judicial power which they possess independent of national authority, and of which they have not been divested by the Constitution, or any law of the United States, have always exercised in these cases a concurrent jurisdiction with the federal courts. The fact that under the present law of Congress, no appeal lies to the Supreme Court from a decision of a state court in a habeas corpus proceeding, involving questions which affect the Constitution or laws of the United States, does not deprive the state courts of their jurisdiction since it is supposed to be competent for Congress to extend the appellate jurisdiction of the Supreme Court to such a decision. *Sug. Com.*, 287.

Whether the judges of a state court have power to issue a writ of habeas corpus in cases of commitment, or detainer under the authority of the United States, and, if so, under what circumstances, and how far they may decide as to the validity of such commitment or detainer, are questions which have been frequently determined in many of the state and some of the federal courts; but they have not been decided by the Supreme Court.

In Georgia the power was, at first, disclaimed.

In Massachusetts its existence was thought too clear to require argument.

In Maryland it was maintained, but not upon the most satisfactory grounds.

In New-York, in 1812, the question was waived by the Supreme Court. *Kent, Ch. J.*, alone disclaiming the power.

In Pennsylvania and New Jersey, it was asserted and maintained by arguments which have never been refuted.

In South Carolina, in 1819, it was disclaimed.

In Virginia, it was asserted and exercised in 1821.

In some of the inferior courts of the United States, the power has been denied; but in most of them where the question has arisen, the power to issue the writ has been conceded, but the jurisdiction under it has been claimed by them to be more circumscribed than the state courts have held it to be.

It may be considered settled that state courts may grant the writ in all cases of illegal confinement under the authority of the United States.

And the weight of authority clearly is that they may decide as to the legality of the imprisonment; and discharge the prisoner if his detention be illegal, though the determination may involve questions of the constitutionality of acts of Congress, or of the jurisdiction of a court of the United States. Their right to proceed to the extent of declaring an act of Congress unconstitutional, or of pronouncing a judicial act of a court of the United States void for want of jurisdiction, has been denied by some of the district and circuit courts of the United States; but the denial does not appear to be supported by satisfactory reasons or authority.

An act of Congress made in pursuance of the Constitution of the United States, is binding alike upon the state and federal judges, as a part of the supreme law of the land. But when its validity is questioned, in a suit or proceeding in a state court, over which it has jurisdiction, it becomes, not a privilege but the unavoidable duty of the court to decide the question. And where in a like suit or proceeding a question arises upon a judgment or act of a court of the United States, in regard, not to its regularity merely but its validity for want of jurisdiction over the subject matter or the parties, it is as much the duty of the court to decide the question as it would be if it arose upon a judgment or act of a state court.

These principles have been repeatedly advanced and enforced by the highest courts, state and federal, and ought to be considered settled.

1st. *Of void laws.* "The right of all courts," says Mr. Justice Story, "state as well as national, to declare unconstitutional laws void, seems settled beyond the reach of judicial controversy." 2 *Story's Com.*, § 1842; 1 *Kent's Com.*, 494, 8*th ed.*; *Serg. Com.*, *ch.* 34; *Marbury* v. *Madison*, 1 *Cranch*, 173.

2d. *Of void judgments.* The law on this point is clearly stated by the Supreme Court of the United States, in the case of *Williamson* v. *Berry*, 8 *How.*, 540: "It is a well settled rule in jurisprudence, that the jurisdiction of any court exercising authority over a subject may be inquired into in every other court, where the proceedings in the former are relied upon, and brought before the latter by a party claiming the benefit of such proceedings. The rule prevails, whether the decree or judgment has been given in a court of admiralty, chancery, ecclesiastical court, or court of common law, or whether the point ruled has arisen under the laws of nations, the practice in chancery, or the municipal laws of states. This court applied it as early as the year 1794, in the case of *Glass et al.* v. *Sloop Betsey*, 3 *Dall.*, 7; again, in 1808, in the case of *Rose* v. *Himely*, 4 *Cranch*, 241; afterwards, in 1828, in *Elliott* v. *Piersol,* a case of ejectment, 1 *Peters,* 328, 340. This is the language of the court in that case, not stronger though than it was in the preceding cases: "It is argued that the Circuit Court of the United States had no authority to question the jurisdiction of the County Court of Woodford county, and that its proceedings were conclusive upon the matter whether erroneous or not. We agree, if the County Court had jurisdiction, its decision would be conclusive. But we cannot yield assent to the proposition, that the jurisdiction of the County Court could be questioned, when its proceedings were brought collaterally before the Circuit Court. Where a court has jurisdiction, it has a right to decide every question which occurs in the cause, and whether its decision be correct or otherwise, its judgment, until reversed, is regarded as binding in every other court. But if it act without authority, its judgments and orders are nullities; they are not voidable, but simply void, and form no bar to a recovery sought even prior to a reversal, in opposition to them; they constitute no justification, and all persons concerned in executing such judgments, or sentences, are considered in law as trespassers."

The same principle was announced and applied in *Wilcox* v. *Jackson,* 13 *Peters,* 499; *Shriver's Lessee* v. *Lynn and others,* 2 *How.,* 59; *Lessee of Hickey* v. *Stewart et al.,* 3 *How.,* 750.

The reports of the state courts abound in decisions recognizing and enforcing the same principles.

A short review of the cases in the state and federal courts where these questions have been determined or discussed in habeas corpus proceedings, will serve to show more satisfactorily the ground upon which these general principles rest as also the circumstances in which they have been applied. The first case reported, where the question as to the power of the state courts to issue the writ of habeas corpus and decide as to the validity of a commitment under the authority of the United States, appears to have been noticed, was in Georgia, in 1807. *The State* v. *Phine and Vessel, T. U. P. Charl.*, 142. By the return to the habeas corpus, it appeared the prisoners, two seamen, had been committed for desertion from their respective vessels, by a justice of the peace, pursuant to the act of congress. A motion was made for their discharge upon some objections to the formality of the warrant of commitment.

The Court said: "The proceedings of the justice appear to be regular under this act; and though this court hath not denied the benefit of the writ of habeas corpus, yet it is conceived that it possesses no jurisdiction in the present case. The powers given to the justice and master are derived from the law of the United States, and whether exercised properly or improperly, by the one or the other, is not a subject for the investigation of *this court*."

The next year, however, it seems that this disclaimer was recalled in the case of *The State* v. *Wederstrandt, T. U. P. Charl.*, 213.

That was a case of habeas corpus for seamen detained as witnesses in an admiralty suit.

Charlton, J., said: "For the purpose of testimony, a seaman is a component part of his ship, and until an adjudication is had he is in the custody of the captors, unless the admiralty take some other method of obtaining his testimony. The seaman may at any moment apply to that jurisdiction and solicit the taking of his deposition, after which the restraint imposed upon him by the captors will necessarily cease; or he may stipulate for his appearance.

"When these privileges are refused him I should always be happy to extend to that valuable class of our citizens the benefit of the writ of habeas corpus, *for in resisting any violation upon the personal liberty of a citizen, I cannot be supposed to combat with any other jurisdiction.*"

The next case was probably that of *Emanuel Roberts* in Maryland, March, 1809, 2 *Hall Law Jour.*, 192.

Nicholson, C. J., said: "The petition upon which the habeas corpus issued in this case, contained a statement of facts verified upon oath, extremely different from those which have appeared in evidence. The petition stated that *Emanuel Roberts*, the son of the petitioner, had been seized and forcibly carried on board the brig Syren, commanded by Captain Gordon, and lying in the basin of Baltimore, where he had been detained since the 10th of April. The statement contained so gross a violation of law, and intimated to the court something so extremely like impressment, that no hesitation was felt in granting a writ which every citizen illegally held in custody has a right to demand. If the facts as stated in the petition had been supported by evidence, the party detained must have been discharged, whether the detention had been by officers of the United States or others, and I would most certainly have held them to bail to answer upon a criminal prosecution. But it appears as well by the return of the habeas corpus, as by the testimony adduced, that Emanuel Roberts had voluntarily enlisted in the service of the United States, and had received from the recruiting officers three months' pay in advance; the question therefore necessarily arises, how far this court can take cognizance of the case. No man is more anxious to preserve, nor will more steadily persevere in the support of the state authorities than myself. I consider the well adjusted balance between the general and state governments to be essential to the preservation of the blessings of each, and as in the exercise of my public functions, I will never suffer the general government or its officers to infringe such of the state rights as are trusted to me, so I hold it to be my duty not to interfere with the rights of the general government.

"The Constitution gives the United States the power of raising and maintaining a navy; Congress have by law directed the President to enlist for the service of the navy, a certain number of men, and the brig Syren has been sent to Baltimore for the purpose of completing her crew. The whole of the evidence shows, nor indeed is the fact now pretended to be denied, that the party whose release is applied for, had enlisted in the service of the United States. It is, therefore, a proceeding under the authority of the United States. This court, however, is called upon to go further, and to inquire into the regularity of the enlistment, it being alleged that the party is only sixteen years of age, and was drunk when enlisted.

"The power of the court to examine into the regularity of the proceeding, is only contended for on the ground that the citizens of the state are entitled to its protection; that the writ of habeas corpus is all important to secure the liberty of the citizen, and that every man may claim relief under it. These positions cannot be denied, and might apply very forcibly to the case under consideration, if there was no contract or agreement to service in question. To this contract the United States is one party, and an individual the other. Emanuel Roberts, by an agreement in writing signed by himself, has contracted to serve the United

States for two years at a stipulated price, and has received a part of his wages. I know of no law by which the United States can be made a party in a state court, except only where special acts of Congress have given the state courts jurisdiction, and if the United States cannot appear in a state court to prosecute a suit in their own behalf, unless in cases specially provided for, how can we call them before us to inquire into the nature of their contracts with individuals, if in our judgment they shall appear to have been irregularly made, or to be oppressive to either party? An extreme case has been supposed, in which I acknowledge that I would interfere without hesitation. It is asked if a child of eight or ten years of age had been enlisted, would the court refuse to discharge him. I answer no; I would discharge him because of his incapacity to make a contract, not an incapacity arising from the general principle that he who has not attained the age of twenty-one years, is incapable of binding himself, but from an actual imbecility of mind owing to his tender years. If in such a case I should exceed the technical limits of my authority, I should have the approbation of all good men for resisting oppression under the color of law. Emanuel Roberts is not of this description, and if he be only sixteen years of age, is remarkably well grown. Although it is a general rule that a person under twenty-one years of age cannot bind himself by contract, yet I am far from saying that this rule will apply in its unlimited extent, to prevent young men from enlisting in the service of their country, or to authorize their discharge upon an application to the courts of the United States. The history of our own times has taught us that young men under twenty-one years of age, if not the best, are certainly not inferior to any other soldiers in the world.

"This case differs very widely from that of Adair and Ogden, in which I did interfere and discharged the parties.

They stated, in their petition, that they were confined in Fort McHenry without the authority of law, and prayed for a habeas corpus, which was granted them. It appeared on the return of the writ that they had been arrested by General Wilkinson at New Orleans on a suspicion of their being connected with Burr in certain treasonable practices, and had been transported by sea to this place to wait the order of the secretary at war. They were private citizens, not subject to military authority, and as there was not a shadow of proof against them I was bound to discharge them from arrest. Whatever might have been my private opinion of their guilt I was not at liberty to remand them into custody without some evidence furnishing a probable cause of suspicion against them. Presuming that some such testimony might possibly be in possession of the President, I wrote immediately to him informing him what had taken place, and requesting him to send on any proof that he might have, upon the receipt of which I would issue a warrant and have them arrested. But I believe he had none. As General Wilkinson had no right to arrest them, his inferior officers of course could have none to detain them, and as there was no proof of their guilt before me, I had no power to commit them. The officers there acted without even the color of authority; but here the whole proceeding is under the constitution and laws of the United States. I am therefore decidedly of opinion that this court has no right to interfere in the present case; and if it had I am not very certain that I should discharge the party with a knowledge of the facts that have been found."

The Chief Justice of Pennsylvania felt the importance of the question, but met it with less hesitation and left it on firmer ground. The case *Ex parte Sergeant*, 8 *Hall's Law Jour.*, 206, reported also under the head of *Olmsted's Case*, *Brightley Rep.*, 9, occurred in April, 1809. In that a writ of habeas corpus was issued upon the petition of Mrs. Sergeant, directed to the U. S. marshal and returnable before the Chief Justice of Pennsylvania. The return showed that Mrs. Sergeant was held in custody by virtue of a writ of attachment issued from the District Court of the United States:

Tilghman, Ch. J., said: "If I order Mrs. Sergeant to be discharged, it must be because the court of the United States has proceeded in a case in which it had no jurisdiction. If it had jurisdiction, I have no right to inquire into its judgment or interfere with its process. But the counsel of Olmsted have brought forward a preliminary question, whether I have a right to discharge the prisoner even if I should be clearly of opinion that the District Court had no jurisdiction. I am aware of the magnitude of this question, and have given it the consideration it deserves. My opinion is, with great deference to those who may entertain different sentiments, that in the case supposed, I should have a right and it would be my duty to discharge the prisoner. This right flows from the nature of our federal Constitution, which leaves to the several states absolute supremacy in all cases in which it is not yielded to the United States. This sufficiently appears from the general scope and spirit of the instrument. The United States have no power, legislative or judicial, except what is derived from the Constitution. When these powers are clearly exceeded, the independence of the states, and the peace of the Union demand that the state courts should, in cases brought properly before them, give redress. There is no law which forbids it; their oath of office exacts it, and if they do not, what course is to be taken? We must be reduced to the miserable extremity of opposing force to force, and arraying citizen against citizen; for it is in vain to expect that the states will submit to manifest and flagrant usurpations of power by the United States, if (which God forbid), they should ever attempt them. If Congress should pass a bill of attainder or lay a tax or duty on articles exported from any state (from both which powers they are expressly excluded), such laws would be null and void, and all persons who acted under them would be subject to actions in the state courts. If a court of the United States should enter judgment against a state which refused to appear in an action brought against it by a citizen of another state, or of a foreign state, such judgment would be void, and all persons who act under it would be trespassers. These cases appear so plain that they will hardly be disputed; it is only in considering doubtful cases that our minds feel a difficulty in deciding; but if, in the plainest case which can be conceived, the state courts may declare a judgment void, the principle is established. But while I assert the power of state courts, I am deeply sensible of the necessity of exercising it with the greatest discretion. Wo to that judge who rashly or wantonly attempts to arrest the authority of the United States; let him reflect again and again before he declares that a law or a judgment has no validity. The counsel for Mrs. Sergeant have, with great candor and propriety, admitted that when there is reasonable cause for doubt, that doubt should be decisive in favor of the judgment in question. The same principle has been adopted by the judges of the Supreme Court of the United States and of our own state, when questions concerning the validity of laws have come before them, and it has my hearty approbation."

The judge then proceeded to consider the point of jurisdiction, and came to the conclusion that the District Court had jurisdiction of the subject of the suit and of the persons who were parties, and accordingly ordered that Mrs. Sergeant remain in the custody of the marshal.

In the case of the *Commonwealth* v. *Murray, 4th Binn.*, 487, occurring three years afterwards, the Supreme Court of the state acted upon the same principle. The writ of habeas corpus was directed to Commodore Murray, commander of the gun boats at Philadelphia, to bring up the body of John Lewis Conner. The return stated the act of Congress of 31 January, 1809, enlistment of Conner, &c. The boy was proved to be between seventeen and eighteen years of age. His father had been dead many years. He had no guardian and he entered into the service of the navy, not with but against his mother's consent. The court held the contract of enlistment to be binding upon him.

In August of the same year (1812), occurred the case of *Ferguson*, 9 *John.*, 239, which is remarkable as containing the only argument to be met with, by a judge, though he one of the ablest, of a state court against the power in question.

That case was an application to the Supreme Court of New York, for the allowance of a writ of habeas corpus directed to John Christie, a lieutenant-colonel in the army of the United States, to bring up the body of Jeremiah Ferguson. The application was founded on the affidavit of the father of Ferguson, in which he stated that Jeremiah Ferguson was an enlisted soldier in the 13th regiment of infantry, in the army of the United States, then under the command of John Christie, and that the said Jeremiah was an infant, under the age of twenty-one years, viz.: of the age of seventeen years and nine months; and that he enlisted without the consent of his father, and was desirous of being released and discharged.

Kent, Ch. J., said: "The cause of the detention of the prisoner being fully and distinctly detailed in the affidavit, an important question, arising upon the motion, is, whether this court has jurisdiction in the case.

"A similar application was made to this court, in July term, 1799, in the case of *Husted*, who was stated to be an enlisted soldier, 1 *John. Cas.*, 136, and the motion was denied; but the court gave no opinion on the question of jurisdiction. The only case I have met with, in which this question has been considered, is that of *Emanuel Roberts*, which arose in Maryland in 1809. 2 *Hall's Law Jour.*, 192. The habeas corpus was awarded in that case upon *affidavit* that the person had been seized and forcibly carried on board of a public vessel, belonging to the United States, then lying in the harbor of Baltimore, and where he was detained. By the return of the writ, it appeared that Roberts had voluntarily enlisted in the naval service of the United States; and the court declared it to be a proceeding under the authority of the United States and that they 'had no right to interfere,' although it was alleged that the party was only sixteen years of age and was drunk when enlisted.

"As far as the case goes, it is an authority against the jurisdiction of the state courts; and yet *Nicholson, Ch. J.*, in delivering the opinion of the court, seemed to consider that there might be cases in which it would be the duty of the state courts to interfere, even though the imprisonment was under color of the authority of the United States.

"As far as I have reflected upon the question, I have been led to conclude that our jurisdiction does not depend upon the greater or less degree of aggravation in the case, and that we have either no jurisdiction at all, or a completely concurrent jurisdiction, in granting relief upon habeas corpus, in all cases of unlawful imprisonment by an officer of the United States, under color or by pretext of the authority of the United States.

"The present case being one of an enlistment under color of the authority of the United States, and by an officer of that government, the federal courts have complete and perfect jurisdiction in the case; and there is no need of the jurisdiction or interference of the state courts; nor does it appear to me to be fit that the state courts should be inquiring into the abuse of the exercise of the authority of the general government. Numberless cases may be supposed of the abuse of power, by the civil and military officers of the government of the United States; but the courts of the United States have competent authority to correct all such abuses, and they are bound to exercise that authority. The responsibility is with them, not with us; and we have no reason to doubt of their readiness, as well as ability, to correct and punish every abuse of power under that government. The judicial power of the United States is commensurate with every case arising under the laws of the Union, and the act of Congress, *Laws of U. S., vol. I.*, 53, 55, gives to the federal courts, exclusively of the courts of the several states, cognizance of all crimes and offences cognizable under the authority of the United States. If the soldier, in the present case, be detained against his will, knowing him to be an infant, or if, though an adult, he has been compelled to enlist, by *duress*, or violence, it is a public offence, but an offence of which this court cannot take cognizance. An abuse of the authority of the United States is an offence against the United States, and exclusively cognizable in their courts. When the state courts have not jurisdiction over the whole subject matter of the imprisonment, and when the federal courts have such jurisdiction, by indictment as well as by habeas corpus, there appears to me to be a manifest want of jurisdiction in the case.

"The want of jurisdiction over the offence of unlawful imprisonment by indictment, seems equally to exclude the collateral remedy by habeas corpus, except where a jurisdiction in the latter case is specially conferred. The writ of habeas corpus, as applied to such purposes, is a prerogative writ, and the issuing of it in term-time rests in sound legal discretion. There appears to be an incongruity in such a maimed jurisdiction as this court would possess, of having a right to deliver from an illegal imprisonment, and yet no right to call to an account the authors of such illegality and oppression. The general principle is, that if a court has no jurisdiction of the principal question, it has none of its consequences and incidents. Thus it is laid down that a common law court has no cognizance of any question incidental to that of *prize*, because they are incompetent to embrace the whole subject matter. *Le Caux* v. *Eden*, *Doug.*, 594. It would be easy to state and multiply difficulties in the exercise of any jurisdiction in cases arising under the exercise of the authority of the government of the United States, or in drawing with precision any line between the cases in which we may, and in which we may not, interfere by habeas corpus. Suppose the marshal of the district were to detain a person in prison, under color of process, when it could be shown to this court that the process was void, or that the arrest was after the return day, would a state court undertake to deliver the party from the marshal's custody? I presume not, and yet I see no reason for any distinction, as to the question of jurisdiction, between that case and the present. The detention in each case is by an officer of the United States, under color of its authority.

"The civil remedy of the party by private suit in a state court, is a distinct question, not before us; and in cases of private suits, the state courts have, in most cases, by the act of Congress, a concurrent jurisdiction. My conclusion is, that it would not only be unfit for the court to interpose in this case so long as the courts and judges of the United States have ample and perfect jurisdiction over the whole subject matter, but that it would also be exercising power without any jurisdiction, and therefore I am of opinion that the writ ought to be denied."

Thompson, J., said: "I concur in refusing the allowance of the habeas corpus; but I think it unnecessary to disclaim having jurisdiction, in any case, where the imprisonment or restraint is under color of the authority of the United States. Questions of jurisdiction between the United States courts and the state courts are generally nice and delicate subjects. I should be unwilling to assume jurisdiction where we have it not. And I do not feel myself at liberty to renounce it, when it is given to this court. The case of *Emanuel Roberts*, referred to by the Chief Justice, seems to be the only one where this question has received a judicial decision; and although in that case the habeas corpus was denied, yet Nicholson, Ch. J., said there might be cases in which it would be the duty of the state courts to interfere. The immediate object of a habeas corpus is to liberate the party from an illegal restraint. The allowance of it does not necessarily draw after it an inquiry into any offence, committed either by the party imprisoned or by him who assumes the right of restraint. The criminal offence is still open to the cognizance of the proper tribunal. The state courts must have the power, in many cases, to determine upon the extent and operation of the laws of Congress. As in the case now before us, if a *civil* suit should be brought for *false imprisonment, the legality of the enlistment*, under the act of Congress, would probably be involved, and must be determined collaterally. And this is the only inquiry upon the habeas corpus. The objections, however, stated by the Chief Justice, against the jurisdiction of this court, are entitled to great consideration; and as the allowance of the writ, in term-time, rests in sound legal discretion, and as the party may have relief by application to one of the judges of the Supreme Court of the United States, or of the District Court for this district, whose jurisdiction in the case is unquestionable, I think the application ought to be denied." *Spencer, J., Van Ness, J., and Yates, J.*, concurred; expressly reserving themselves as to the question of jurisdiction, but agreeing, for the reasons assigned by *Thompson, J.*, that the application ought to be refused.

The views of the Chief Justice were not finally adopted by the Supreme Court of New York. The year following they enforced, by the most efficient means known to the law, attachment for contempt, obedience to a writ of habeas corpus allowed by a commissioner of the court, directed to Morgan Lewis, "General of division in the army of the United States," commander of the troops of the United States at Sackett's Harbor, commanding him to bring up the body of Samuel Stacy, "a natural-born citizen, born in the state," who it appeared from the affidavits upon which the motion for attachment was founded, had been arrested by Commodore Chauncey on a charge of treason, and by his authority delivered into the custody of General Lewis, who placed him in close confinement. In delivering the opinion of the court, directing an attachment to issue against General Lewis for making an evasive return to the writ, Kent, Ch. J., said: "This is a case which concerns the personal liberty of the citizen. Stacy is now suffering the rigor of confinement in close custody, at this unhealthy season of the year at a military camp and under military power. He is a natural-born citizen residing in this state. He has a numerous family dependent upon him for their support. He is in bad health, and the danger of a protracted confinement to his health, if not to his life, must be serious. The pretended charge of treason (for upon the facts before us we must consider it as a pretext), without being founded upon oath, and without any specification of the matters of which it might consist, and without any color of authority in any military tribunal to try a citizen for that crime, is only aggravation of the oppression of confinement. It is the indispensable duty of this court, and one to which every inferior consideration must be sacrificed, to act as a faithful guardian of the personal liberty of the citizen, and to give ready and effectual aid to the means provided by law for its security. One of the most valuable of those means is the writ of habeas corpus, which has justly been deemed the glory of the English law."

And in the case of *Carlton*, 7 *Cow.*, 471, occurring in 1827, the Supreme Court unanimously affirmed their right to discharge a minor who had enlisted in the United States army, alleging himself at the time to be over twenty-one; Savage, Ch. J., said: "By the act of Congress, the enlistment is void; and the soldier ought to be discharged if this court have jurisdiction. We have jurisdiction unless it has been expressly surrendered or taken away. Any person illegally detained has a right to be discharged, and it is the duty of this court to restore him to his liberty. No act of Congress or of this state has forbidden the exercise of this common law jurisdiction. We are of opinion that Carlton should be discharged by the recorder, whose power upon this writ is the same as ours."

It is supposed that this authority is exercised now without hesitation by the courts of New York. *United States* v. *Wyngall*, 5 *Hill*, 16.

The opinion of Kent, Ch. J., in the case of *Ferguson*, 9 *Johns.*, 239, was pressed upon the attention of the Supreme Court of Pennsylvania, in *Lockington's case*, *Brightley Rep.*, 269, occurring in 1813; and the right of the state courts to issue the writ was reëxamined and reaffirmed by all the judges.

Tilghman, Ch. J., addressing himself to the question with his wonted vigor, said: "It is to be observed that the authority of the state judges, in cases of habeas corpus, emanates from the several states, and not from the United States. In order to destroy their jurisdiction, therefore, it is necessary to show, not that the United States have given them jurisdiction, but that Congress possesses and have exercised the power of taking away that jurisdiction, which the states have vested in their own judges. Our act of Assembly directs that in all cases 'where any person, not being committed or detained for any criminal or supposed criminal matter, shall be confined or restrained of his liberty, under any color or pretence whatsoever,' he shall be entitled to a writ of habeas corpus. Now it is no answer to this law to say, that, being made before the present Constitution of the United States was established, it could not be intended to apply to cases arising under the Constitution. The people of Pennsylvania still remain citizens of the commonwealth, as well as of the United States; and it is of as much importance to them to be relieved from unlawful imprisonment, under color of authority derived from the United States, as from any other imprisonment. When the present federal Constitution was adopted, the people were not easy until they had obtained an amendment, declaring that the powers not delegated to the United States, by the Constitution, nor prohibited by it to the states, were reserved to the states respectively, or to the people. A writ of habeas corpus must, therefore, be issued in all cases where the right to issue it has not been given up to the United States. That this right has not been given up was my opinion, delivered in the case of *Olmsted*, where I assigned reasons which I shall not now repeat. But this not all. It is a principle well established, that even in cases where Congress might assume an exclusive jurisdiction, the authority of the states remains until such jurisdiction is assumed. There are many instances in which the powers of the United States lie dormant, such as the power of establishing uniform laws on the subject of bankruptcies; and while the power remains dormant, the several states regulate the subject. In subjects, also, within the jurisdiction of Congress, when they do legislate, the authority of the states is not taken away only so far as the law of the United States declares. This is exemplified in the act establishing the judicial courts of the United States, where it will be found that in some instances the courts of the United States are vested with an exclusive jurisdiction; but in many more they have jurisdiction concurrent with the courts of the several states. And although it is true that, by the terms of the act, the courts of the United States have only a concurrent jurisdiction, yet I apprehend the construction would be the same, if the express terms had been omitted. By the 14th section of the same act, power is given to the judges of the United States to grant writs of habeas corpus, for the 'purpose of an inquiry into the cause of commitment; provided that they shall in no case extend to prisoners in jail, unless where they are in custody under or by color of the authority of the United States, or committed for trial before some court of the same, or are necessary to be brought into court to testify.' Now, if it had been intended to exclude the state judges, this is the place in which we might expect to find evidence of such intention; for the subject was full in the mind of the legislature, as appears by the care with which they restrained their own judges from interfering with commitments not under the authority of the United States.

"The judicial power of the United States extends to all cases, in law or equity, arising under the Constitution, the laws of the United States and the treaties made under their authority. Supposing that Congress had the right to assume an exclusive jurisdiction in all cases founded immediately on these subjects, the exercise of it would be intolerably grievous, without a great increase of courts and judges; and even then, it would often happen that the state courts would have to decide on the Constitution, laws and treaties of the United States, on questions arising collaterally, in causes within their jurisdiction. Still the authority of the United States may be preserved, by retaining, as they have retained, an appeal to their own courts. But it seems to be the general opinion that from a decision on a habeas corpus no appeal or writ of error lies; and thus points of vital importance to the United States may be determined by state judges, without an opportunity of revision. This may certainly be a very serious evil, but it does not appear to be without remedy. For although, by the general principles of the law, an appeal or writ of error might not lie, yet the subject being within the power of Congress, they may regulate it as they please. As to an attempt to take away from the state courts altogether the right of issuing a writ of habeas corpus, in any case where a man pretends to justify an imprisonment under the authority of the United States, whenever the subject shall be brought before Congress, it will be found to be attended with very great if not insuperable difficulties.

"I have said thus much on the point of jurisdiction (although I consider it as having been long settled and acted upon by the Supreme Court of this state), because some persons of high standing in other states, for whose opinions I entertain the most sincere respect, have expressed doubts on the subject. It is a matter deserving the greatest consideration, in which the people of the different states are deeply interested. The inconvenience of clashing opinions between federal and state judges may sometimes be felt; but when I consider the situation of a Pennsylvanian, imprisoned unlawfully, by color of a pretended authority from the United States, on the banks of the Ohio, or the shore of Lake Erie, with only one federal judge to whom he can apply, and that judge in the city of Philadelphia, I feel as little inclination as I have right to surrender the authority of the Commonwealth."

It was held by the court in this case, that:

"The act of Congress, of July 6, 1798, authorized the President to direct the confinement of alien enemies, although such confinement or restraint was not for the purpose of removing them from the United States. The act having authorized the President to direct the confinement of alien enemies, necessarily conferred on him all the means to enforce his orders; and the marshals of the districts were the proper persons to execute such orders. It was not necessary that the judicial authority should be called in to enforce the regulations of the President in respect to alien enemies; and the marshal might act without such authority."

The prisoner was remanded.

Notwithstanding these express determinations and subsequent practice in conformity to them, the question was renewed in the Supreme Court in 1847, in the case of *The Commonwealth, ex rel. Webster*, v. *Fox*, 7 *Barr.*, 336, and *Ferguson's case*, 9 *Johns.*, 229, again presented when *Coulter, J.*, in delivering the opinion of the court, said:

"In Pennsylvania the jurisdiction of the state judges and state courts has not before been doubted; and from the case of *Commonwealth* v. *Murray*, 4 *Binn.*, 487, down to the present time, numerous cases have occurred in which it has been exercised, some of them reported and many more unreported. Our statute of 18th February, 1785, section 13, provides that the writ shall issue in all cases where any person, not committed or detained for any criminal or supposed criminal matter, shall be confined or restrained of his liberty, under any color or pretence whatsoever; and imposes the like penalties for not granting the writ as are imposed by the previous sections where the person is committed or detained for any criminal or supposed criminal matter. This is in accordance with the principles of the common law, by the provisions of which the writ of habeas corpus ad subjiciendum is the prerogative writ of the citizen, the safeguard of his person and the security of liberty. No matter how or where the chains of his captivity were forged, the power of the judiciary of this state is adequate to crumble them to dust if an individual is deprived of his liberty contrary to the law of the land."

In this case the relator was a minor, enlisted in the army; and although the return showed that he had subsequently deserted and was then in custody as a deserter, the court held the enlistment void under the act of Congress, and the desertion therefore immaterial and no justification of the restraint.

In 1819, in New Jersey, *Southard, J.*, delivering the opinion of the Supreme Court, in *The State* v. *Brearly and others*, 2 *South.*, 555, expressed himself upon this question in the following terms:

"It will require in me a great struggle both of feeling and judgment before I shall be prepared to deny the jurisdiction of the state, and say that she has surrendered her independence on questions like this; that her highest judicial tribunal, for such purposes, is incapable of inquiring into the imprisonment of her citizens, no matter how gross or illegal it may be, provided it be by agents of the United States and under color of their laws.

"There are, indeed, cases of daily occurrence in which the citizens of a state are parties, but of which we have not jurisdiction. They are those which originate from and depend altogether upon the nature and character and powers of the general government, and which would not have existed without its formation; such for example as relate to its revenue. These subjects belong in all respects exclusively to the United States. The state or its agents cannot judge concerning them, unless the power be expressly granted by the Constitution, to which the state has given its consent. There are other questions where the state and federal courts both have jurisdiction. They are such as existed and were the subjects of state cognizance and judicial notice before the formation of the general government, and are given to the United States, but altogether without words of exclusion used in application to the state. They are possessed by the federal courts because expressly given; they are retained by the state upon the impregnable ground that they have never been surrendered. The present appears to me to be a case where the right of jurisdiction did exist in this court in full, ample and complete extent, and it must therefore still exist unless surrendered by clear, explicit and indubitable grant.

"It is a right of judgment upon habeas corpus; it is a question of imprisonment or release of the citizen. Where and how were that right and question, the dearest to the citizen, relating to the highest duty of a government, to the proudest attribute of sovereignty, given up and surrendered?

"Have we lost the jurisdiction, because we cannot construe and determine the extent and operation of acts of Congress? We are often compelled to construe them; they are our supreme law, when made in conformity with the Constitution. Is it because the United States is a party? How does she become a party on such a question? Is she a party for the purpose of despotism, whenever a man who holds a commission from her shall, without legal authority, or in violation of her own statutes, injure, imprison and oppress the citizen? Surely not. Is it because the United States judges have jurisdiction? The jurisdiction of one does not exclude the other unless expressly and in words so ordained and ordered. To my mind, therefore, under its present impressions, there is no real difficulty on this part of the case. The power of this court, in rescuing the citizen from unlawful imprisonment, is without limit from any of these sources; and I do not see how it can be otherwise, so long as any portion of sovereignty remains in the states."

During the same year, 1819, the power was disclaimed in South Carolina in *Ex parte Andrew Rhodes*, 12 *Niles W. Reg.*, 264; 2 *Wheeler, Crim. Cas.*, 559; *S. C.*, cited, *Sergt. Const. Law*, 284.

"Where a prisoner was arrested by a warrant from a justice of the peace of the State of South Carolina, on a charge of counterfeiting protections of American seamen, an offence against the law of the United States, and brought up on habeas corpus before Judge Cheeves, and it was contended that the magistrate who committed him had no authority to commit for an offence against the United States, because the 33d section of the Judicial Act of September 24th, 1789, vesting such power, was unconstitutional, the judge held that he had no jurisdiction over the case; that the criminal jurisdiction under the laws of the United States was expressly exclusive, and that as a state court had no authority to take cognizance of the offence charged, so as to punish or acquit, it could not take jurisdiction under a habeas corpus, or declare an act of Congress unconstitutional and void."

But in Maryland, the same year, where a habeas corpus issued from a state court, directed to the marshal of that district, to bring up a citizen of the United States committed by a justice of the peace of that state, on a charge of piracy, the court, consisting of Judges Bland and Hanson, decided that the court had jurisdiction to issue the writ and decide upon it, unless it appeared by the return that the case had been constitutionally placed under the exclusive cognizance of the United States; and that if the authority of the officer committing were unconstitutional and void, the prisoner must be discharged; but to justify this decision the case should be a clear one. They proceeded to inquire into the authority of the committing magistate, and decided that he could not constitutionally commit for an offence against the United States, and discharged the prisoner. *Sergt. Const. Law*, 286; *Ex parte Joseph Almeida*, 2 *Wheeler Cr. Cas.*, 576.

Two years afterwards, 1821, it was held by the General Court of Virginia that the writ of habeas corpus may be issued by a state judge, on the application of any party who, by proper affidavit, shows probable cause that he is unlawfully restrained of his liberty; that the question whether the law authorizes his confinement, is to be decided by the laws of the state, considered as a member of the United States; and that the court is at liberty to consider all persons as lawfully restrained of their liberty who are confined in obedience to the constitutional laws of the state or United States. In the practical application of these principles, the state judges will not discharge a party, whose commitment is *regularly* made with a view to a prosecution in the courts of the United States, for an offence actually committed and cognizable therein; neither will the judges of the state courts, as such, admit the party to bail. Whether they will look beyond the warrant of commitment, when made by any other than a judge of the courts of the United States, and inquire into the fact, is a matter of sound discretion, to be regulated by the circumstances of the case. But the state courts and judges have concurrent jurisdiction with the courts and judges of the United States, in all cases of illegal confinement under color of the authority of the United States, when that confinement is not the consequence of a suit or prosecution pending in the courts of the United States, in which the allegation, upon which the commitment is made, will be tried. *Sergt. Const. Law*, 286; *Ex parte Pool and others, Nat. Intell., Nov.* 10, *and Dec.* 11, 1821.

These qualifications of the power were not at all enlarged in the *Case of J. H. Pleasants*, 11 *Am. Jurist*, 257, tried at Richmond, in 1834.

The Court said: "The applicant is in custody of the marshal for the eastern district of Virginia; and has petitioned for and obtained a habeas corpus, to relieve him from what he alleges to be an illegal detention. The marshal has made return to the writ, by which it appears that he arrested the prisoner under authority of an attachment issued from the Circuit Court of the District of Columbia, for the county of Alexandria, for a contempt by him committed, in not attending the said court as a witness after being thereunto legally summoned. The attachment itself and the previous proceedings, together with an affidavit of the attorney for the District of Columbia, are annexed to the return. By these papers it appears that the grand jury of that county have before them a bill of indictment charging Robert B. Randolph and others with a conspiracy to commit an assault on the President of the United States, in the said county, and that in the estimation of the said attorney, the said Pleasants may be a material witness in the said prosecution.

"It is objected that the court cannot take cognizance of the case, because the arrest of which the applicant complains has been made *by virtue of process of a court of the United States*, who alone can judge of the legality of the arrest. This is a delicate question, and is attended with difficulty. The provisions of the habeas corpus act are very general and comprehensive. In every case in which there is a detention without lawful authority, the court may relieve the party detained. It would seem that if the commitment be made by a court having jurisdiction to commit, this court ought not to discharge, although the judgment of the committing magistrate be erroneous. But if it be made by a court having no jurisdiction, then the discharge may be made.

"Without going into the controverted question of commitments made under unconstitutional and therefore void laws, there may be cases in which, under constitutional and valid laws, a Circuit Court of the United States may exceed its commission. It may exercise powers which the law will not warrant. By such unwarranted jurisdiction they may seriously encroach on the personal liberty of men whom the state courts are bound to protect.

"In the present case a *foreign* court, that is, a court sitting beyond the limits of Virginia and alleged to have only a local jurisdiction, has sent its process beyond its own territory and arrested an individual within the jurisdiction of this court. I find it to be a *general* principle that the courts of one state or county, cannot issue its process into another without the consent of that other; but the court of the county of Alexandria claims an exemption from that general principle and undertakes to arrest a citizen within our jurisdiction. I am of opinion I ought to entertain jurisdiction."

The prisoner was discharged.

In Massachusetts the question was made in 1814. *The Commonwealth* v. *Harrison*, 11 *Mass. Rep.*, 63. This was a writ of habeas corpus, granted at the instance of a master to bring up his apprentice, a minor, who had enlisted in the army. On the trial, counsel for the defendant cited the opinion of Kent, Ch. J., in *Ferguson's case*, 9 *Johns.*, 239, that the state courts have no jurisdiction in cases of this kind.

The court answered very briefly, but very emphatically:

"This court has authority, and it will not shun the exercise of it on proper occasions, to inquire into the circumstances under which any person brought before them by a writ of habeas corpus is confined or restrained of his liberty."

The prisoner was discharged.

The court exercised the same authority in the case of *The Commonwealth* v. *Cushing*, 11 *Mass.*, 67, during the same year. And subsequently, 1836, in the case of *The Commonwealth* v. *Downs*, 24 *Pick.*, 227.

In *Sims' case*, 7 *Cush.*, 285, which occurred in 1851, the court recognized the principle although they did not grant the writ. The petitioner was in custody of the United States marshal, by virtue of a warrant from a commissioner of the Circuit Court of the United States, for the Massachusetts district, charged with being a fugitive from labor and with having escaped from service in the State of Georgia. He alleged in his petition that he was free, and not a slave. The court directed the whole case to be argued on the application, and, after argument, held the "Act of Congress of 1850, c. 60, concerning fugitives from service, being substantially like the act of Congress of 1793, c. 7, the constitutionality of which has been settled by the decisions of the courts of the United States, must be deemed constitutional, and that the authority which it confers on commissioners of the Circuit Courts, and its making no provision for a trial by jury, do not make it unconstitutional." In the course of the opinion, Shaw, Ch. J., said:

"An obvious question occurs here, how far it is competent for this court, by a writ of habeas corpus to the marshal, to take a prisoner from the custody of another tribunal, court or magistrate, of which the marshal is the executive officer, and after the prisoner has by the execution and return of the warrant been placed under the control and direction of such court or magistrate, to be held, discharged, brought in or remanded. This point has not been noticed in the argument, and is not perhaps of much importance, and perhaps it might be avoided by an amendment of the petition. But we have thought it worthy of remark as one of those considerations which presented themselves to our minds after a similar petition had been submitted on a former occasion, indicating that apparently and on the face of the proceedings the petitioner was in regular and lawful custody. It is now argued that the whole proceeding, as it appears upon the warrant and return, is unconstitutional and void; because, although the act of Congress of 1850, c. 60, 9 *U. S. Stat. at Large*, 462, has provided for and directed this course of proceeding, yet that the statute itself is void, because Congress had no power, by the Constitution of the United States, to pass such a law and confer such an authority."

After reviewing the authorities and holding the question to be settled in favor of the constitutionality of the act of Congress, by a course of legal decisions which they were bound to respect, and which they regarded as binding and conclusive upon the court, the judge adds:

"We do not mean to say that this court will in no case issue a writ of habeas corpus to bring in a party, held under color of process from the courts of the United States, or whose services, and the custody of whose person, are claimed under authority derived from the laws of the United States. This is constantly done, in cases of soldiers and sailors, held by military and naval officers, under enlistments complained of as illegal and void. But it is manifest that this ought to be done only in a clear case, and in a case where it is necessary to the security of personal liberty from illegal restraint.

"It seems to us to be the less necessary to call into action the powers of the state judiciary, in a case like this, because it is quite competent for the judges of the United States courts to bring the petitioner before them by habeas corpus, and ascertain whether he is detained by an illegal and colorable authority of an officer claiming to act under the laws of the United States. This consideration is, perhaps, of no other importance than as showing that there is no necessary occasion for drawing the authority of the state and the United States judiciary into conflict with each other. Such a conflict can hardly arise, although it may often seem impending; because it must generally appear, upon a cool and deliberate examination of all the facts and circumstances, whether a subject to which a law of Congress relates is or is not within the jurisdiction of the general government; if it be so it is conclusive. All judges of all courts are obliged to act upon the same principles, and be governed by the same rules of duty; they are bound alike by oath to support the Constitution of the United States, which delares that the Constitution itself, and all laws made pursuant to it, shall be the supreme law of the land."

In reply to the objection to the act of 1850, because it made no provision for a trial by jury, the court said:

"We think that this cannot vary the result. The law of 1850 stands, in this respect, precisely on the same ground with that of 1793, and the same grounds of argument which tend to show the unconstitutionality of one apply with equal force to the other; and the same answer must be made to them.

"The principle of adhering to judicial precedent, especially that of the Supreme Court of the United States, in a case depending upon the Constitution and laws of the United States, and thus placed within their special and final jurisdiction, is absolutely necessary to the peace, union and harmonious action of the state and general governments. The preservation of both, with their full and entire powers, each in its proper sphere, was regarded by the framers of the Constitution, and has ever since been regarded, as essential to the peace, order and prosperity of all the United States.

"If this were a new question, now for the first time presented, we should desire to pause and take time for consideration. But though this act, the construction of which is now drawn in question, is recent, and this point, in the form in which it is now stated, is new, yet the solution of the question depends upon reasons and judicial decisions, upon legal principles and a long course of practice, which are familiar and which have often been the subject of discussion and deliberation. I have therefore to state in behalf of the court, under the weighty responsibility which rests upon us, and as the unanimous opinion of the court, that the writ of habeas corpus prayed for cannot be granted."

In New Hampshire, on the petition for habeas corpus by an enlisted soldier, the court said:

"If the laws of the United States justify the detention of the applicant, there is nothing illegal. If they do not, it is not a case arising under the laws of the United States, although it may be under color or pretence of authority by virtue of those laws. But a mere pretence of authority under the laws of the United States is no better than any other pretence. It neither confers an exclusive jurisdiction on the courts of the United States, nor ousts the ordinary jurisdiction of the courts of this state. Nor can it make any difference that the illegal imprisonment, if there be one, is by an officer of the United States army. The courts of the United States have no exclusive jurisdiction over their officers." *The State* v. *Dimick*, 12 *N. Hamp.*, 197.

As before intimated, some of the federal courts have denied the right of the state courts to exercise jurisdiction under the writ of habeas corpus to the extent claimed by them.

In the matter of Veremaitre and others, Am. Law Jour., 438, a District Court of the United States, in 1850, declared that "a state court has no jurisdiction on habeas corpus to discharge a soldier or sailor held under law of the United States."

And Mr. Justice Nelson of the Supreme Court, in his charge to the grand jury at the April Term, 1851, of the Circuit Court for the Southern District of New York, denied the right of a state court under the writ of habeas corpus to decide as to the constitutionality of a law of Congress, or the jurisdiction of a court or officer of the United States. He says:

"It is obvious that the existence of either power, on the part of the state tribunals, would be fatal to the constitution, laws and treaties of the general government. No government could maintain the administration or the execution of its laws, civil or criminal, if their constitutionality or the jurisdiction of its judicial tribunals were subject to the determination of another. I need not stop, however, to discuss this question, as it arose and was settled in the case of *The United States* v. *Peters*, 5 *Cranch*, 115, more familiarly known as *Olmsted's case*. The legislature of Pennsylvania had passed an act declaring that the jurisdiction claimed by the District Court of the United States was unconstitutional, and empowered the Governor to resist the execution of the judgment. Chief Justice Marshall, in delivering the opinion of the court, observed, that 'if the legislatures of the several states may, at will, annul the judgments of the courts of the United States and destroy the rights acquired under those judgments, the Constitution itself becomes a solemn mockery; and the nation is deprived of the means of enforcing its laws by the instrumentality of its own tribunals.' He further remarked, "if the ultimate right to determine the jurisdiction of the courts of the Union is placed by the Constitution in the several state legislatures, then this act concludes the subject; but if that power necessarily resides in the supreme judicial tribunal of the nation, then the jurisdiction of the District Court of Pennsylvania over the case in which that jurisdiction was exercised, ought to be most deliberately examined; and the act of Pennsylvania, with whatever respect it may be considered, cannot be permitted to prejudice the question.' "

The judge proceeds in his charge to define the limits of the jurisdiction of a state court:

"It is proper to say, in order to guard against misconstruction, that I do not claim that the mere fact of the commitment or detainer of a prisoner by an officer of the federal government bars the issuing of the writ, or the exercise of power under it. Far from that. Those officers may be guilty of illegal restraints of the liberty of the citizen, the same as others. The right of the state authorities to inquire into such restraints is not doubted; and it is the duty of the officer to obey the authority, by making a return. All that is claimed or contended for is, that when it is shown that the commitment or detainer is under the Constitution, or a law of the United States, or a treaty, the power of the state authority is at an end; and any further proceeding under the writ is *coram non judice*, and void. In such a case, that is, when the prisoner is in fact held under process issued from a federal tribunal, under the Constitution, or a law of the United States, or a treaty, it is the duty of the officer not to give him up, or allow him to pass from his hands in any stage of the proceedings. He should stand upon his process and authority, and, if resisted, maintain them with all the powers conferred upon him for that purpose. These views of the paramount authority of the laws of the federal government in no way endanger the liberty of the citizen. The writ of habeas corpus, secured to him under that government, affords the appropriate and effectual remedy for any illegality in the process or want of jurisdiction in the court, or for any unconstitutionality of the law."

In the case of *Norris* v. *Newton*, 5 *McLean*, 92, Mr. Justice McLean expressed himself in terms somewhat similar as to the extent of the jurisdiction of the state courts in such cases,

"I have no hesitation," says he, "in saying that the judicial officers of a state, under its own laws, in a case where an unlawful imprisonment is shown by one or more affidavits, may issue a writ of habeas corpus and inquire into the cause of the detention. But this is a special and limited jurisdiction. If the plaintiff, in the reception of his fugitive slaves, had proceeded under the act of Congress, and made proof of his claim before some judicial officer of Michigan, and procured the certificate which authorized him to take the fugitives to Kentucky, these facts being stated as the cause of detention would have terminated the jurisdiction of the judge under the writ. Thus it would appear that the negroes were held under federal authority, which in this respect is paramount to that of the state. The cause of detention being legal, no judge could arrest and reverse the remedial proceedings of the master. ** The return made by the plaintiff being clearly within the provisions of the Constitution, as decided in the case of *Priggs* v. *Pennsylvania*, and the facts of that return being admitted by the counsel by the negroes, the judge could exercise no further jurisdiction in the case. His power was at an end. The fugitives were in the legal custody of the master, a custody authorized by the Constitution and sanctioned by the Supreme Court of the Union. ** The legal custody of the fugitives by the master being admitted, as stated in the return on the habeas corpus, every step taken subsequently was against law and in violation of his rights."

Enough, perhaps, has already been said on the question of the power of the state courts to decide a law of Congress to be unconstitutional, or a judgment or process of a court of the United States to be void. Yet it may be added that for all useful purposes it would be quite as well to deny to the state courts all jurisdiction in cases of detainer under color of authority of the United States, as to limit it so narrowly as was done by Mr. Justice Nelson, in his charge above quoted.

A sovereign state has a right to be informed why any of her citizens are imprisoned, simply because it is her duty to set them free from all illegal imprisonment. To concede the power to issue the writ, and at the same time withhold the power to afford relief under it, when the party claiming the custody stands revealed, by his return, a trespasser without excuse, is to convert the great writ of liberty into a pitiful process of idle curiosity.

Did the learned judge in his charge mean to say, that if in obedience to the writ the marshal made a return, and from that it appeared that the imprisonment was for a supposed criminal matter over which no federal court or officer had any jurisdiction, or that the warrant relied on was palpably, fatally and incurably defective, he would advise the officer to disregard an order of discharge by the state court and "stand upon his process?" Or, if the return were by some military officer, and showed beyond all question that he had violated the law under which he assumed to act; as, that the party detained as an enlisted soldier was an infant or a female, he would advise the officer to "stand upon his authority," and maintain the custody of such person against the order of discharge?

Would not *such* process be somewhat dangerous ground for the officer to stand on? And would it be entirely safe in all cases for counsel to advise and encourage an officer to continue or repeat a grievous personal trespass, when it was well known it could neither be justified nor palliated?

It is not claimed that the writ of habeas corpus, in the hands of a state court, can be used to defeat the exercise of a jurisdiction already begun by a federal court or judicial officer and still pending; nor that the state courts have any power to exercise a corrective jurisdiction over any federal court or judicial officer.

But where the detainer is not under judicial process, a state court may discharge the person detained if the restraint be manifestly illegal. And where the detainer is under legal process of a federal court or officer, which is manifestly void for want of jurisdiction, and the question of jurisdiction has not been the subject of express adjudication in the particular case, a state court may discharge the prisoner, provided such discharge will not in any manner interfere with the right and duty of the federal court or officer to proceed to the final disposition of a pending case or investigation. The general subject, however, of the powers of courts, under the writ of habeas corpus, to inquire into the proceedings of other courts, will be considered more fully hereafter.

SECTION VI.

ULTIMATE JURISDICTION OF THE SUPREME COURT OF THE UNITED STATES.

Notwithstanding the right of the state courts to issue the writ of habeas corpus, where the detainer is under color of the authority of the United States, and to determine the legality of such detainer, and consequently in some cases to decide as to the validity of an act of Congress, or the jurisdiction of a federal court or officer, has been maintained with great unanimity by the state courts, it is not to be thence inferred that final authority is claimed for them, under this process, over those questions to which the judicial power of the United States is extended by the Constitution.

Such a doctrine is sometimes advocated, but it finds no support in the foregoing cases. The second section of Article III. of the Constitution of the United States, which contains the grant of judicial power, has been made the subject of much ingenious discussion; and the doctrine of the paramount authority of the Supreme Court of the United States over the cases and controversies enumerated in that section has been greatly deprecated, as furnishing a dangerous way for the usurpation, by the general government, of the unceded powers of the states.

But it is to be remembered, the question is not one of policy, as to the power which should be granted, but one of construction, as to the power which has been granted

And although in a matter of construction, the liability to abuse of the power questioned may be a legitimate, it is by no means a conclusive, nor is it always a very forcible argument against the existence of the power.

The watchful spirit of a just state pride has also tried the resource of strict verbal criticism, but without any very satisfactory results.

After all, the fact stands acknowledged, that a tribunal, in whose selection all the states are represented, is, if not indispensable to the peace and harmony of the Republic, at least the most fit arbiter of those important questions, arising under the federal Constitution and laws, in the decision of which the citizens of all the states have a common interest. And the argument deducible from this fact, that the Supreme Court of the United States was designed by the Constitution to be the common arbiter of all questions arising under it, and whose decision thereon should be final and paramount over all the states, has never yet been satisfactorily answered.

As before observed, the cases above cited, so far from asserting an authority for the state courts of equal conclusiveness with that of the Supreme Court of the United States, do, many of them expressly recognize the superior authority of the latter. The Chief Justice of Pennsylvania, in 1809 and 1813, in Olmsted's case and Lockington's case, as has been seen, claimed for the state court the right to decide upon the validity of an act of Congress, and also upon the jurisdiction of a District Court of the United States; yet he, at the same time, admitted the power of Congress to provide for an appeal to the Supreme Court in such cases; and afterwards, in 1815, in the case of *The Commonwealth* v. *Robinson*, 1 *Serg. & Rawle*, 352, made the difficulty of bringing a proceeding in habeas corpus in a state court under review in the Supreme Court of the United States, a ground of objection against allowing the writ when the validity of an act of Congress was questioned, saying: "It is understood that the validity of an act of Congress is to be brought in question. The subject is worthy of the most solemn discussion and mature deliberation. And above all, it is desirable that it should be brought on in such form as will admit of a removal to the Supreme Court of the United States, the tribunal in the last resort for deciding all questions arising out of the Constitution or laws of the United States."

The observations of Mr. Justice Washington, in the case of *The United States* v. *Bright and others*, 3 *Hall's Law Jour.*, 225; *S. C. Brightley's Rep.*, 26, tried in 1809, appear to have been called forth by the remarks of Chief Justice Tilghman, in the Olmsted case, which had then been recently before him on the application of Mrs. Sergeant, for discharge under a habeas corpus:

"Whether a state court," says the judge, "is competent to declare a judgment of a federal court void for want of jurisdiction, need not now be considered. It may, however, be observed, that admitting the right in the first instance, the ultimate decision of the question belongs to the supreme judicial tribunal of the nation, if that decision be required; for the judicial power extends to all cases arising under the Constitution, and the laws of the United States made in pursuance thereof; and the twenty-fifth section of the judiciary act, with a view to secure the national judiciary this important privilege, vests in the Supreme Court a power to review and affirm, or reverse, the decision of the highest court of law or equity in a state, where a question depending upon the construction of any clause in the Constitution, treaty or statute of the United States, had been decided against the title, &c., claimed under the Constitution, &c. It seems, however, that this power is considered as unsafely lodged in the national courts, because it may be abused for the purpose of drawing every case into the vortex of federal jurisdiction. Whence can arise this jealousy? Had the judges of those courts, or of any courts, an interest in extending the sphere of their jurisdiction? Quite otherwise: as the jurisdiction of the court is abridged, the labor of the judge is diminished. Is it a privilege which is claimed for the advantage of the court, or of the individuals who compose it? By no means. It is the privilege of the citizen; and as long as I have the honor of a seat on the bench, I will consider myself one of the guardians of this privilege (a very feeble one, I acknowledge), and with a steady and unvarying eye fixed upon the Constitution as my guide, I shall march forward, without entertaining the guilty wish to limit this privilege, where the citizen may fairly claim it, or the desire, not less criminal, to enlarge its boundaries, because it is claimed."

So long as any serious questions which arise affecting the subjects which are by the Constitution committed to the Supreme Court of the United States for final determination, yet over which the state courts exercise an original concurrent jurisdiction, remain undetermined by that court, a diversity of judicial opinion may be anticipated in the courts of the several states and an occasional collision between them and the inferior courts of the United States.

Instances have occcurred in the judicial history of the country, where the validity of acts of Congress have been questioned and variously decided, notwithstanding, as Chief Justice Shaw observes in *Sims' case*, 7 *Cush.*, 285, it ought to appear alike to all courts, "upon a cool and deliberate examination of all the facts and circumstances, whether a subject to which a law of Congress relates is or is not within the jurisdiction of the general government."

Such collisions are greatly to be deprecated and never to be incurred, except in defence of some vital principle of constitutional liberty. The writ of habeas corpus forms so important and material a part of our system of free government, that the judge who should refuse to exercise all the power which he might rightfully employ under the writ, would be held, in so far, to have betrayed Public Liberty. Rashness, however, is not a judicial virtue; and he who wantonly and without cause brings on such a collision, cannot escape public condemnation.

CHAPTER II.

PRACTICE IN PROCURING AND SERVING THE WRIT.

SECTION I.

PRELIMINARY OBSERVATIONS.

The common law writ of habeas corpus, as has been observed, was not taken away by the act of 31 *Car.* 2; but was left wholly untouched by it in all cases where the detainer was not for criminal or supposed criminal matter. The courts, however, when the writ was afterwards issued at common law, adopted in practice, so far as the same were applicable, the provisions of the habeas corpus act. *Opinions of the judges*, 1758, *Bac. Abr.*, *Hab. Corp.*

A similar course was pursued in this country. In the case of *U. S.* v. *Bollman & Swartwout*, 1 *Cranch, C. C., Dist. Col. R.*, 373, Cranch, Ch. J., says: "Since the statute of 31 *Car.* 2, the practice in cases not within it has been founded upon it, the judges having considered it as furnishing a rule of proceeding in all cases;" and in that case, which was not within the statute, an attachment was refused in accordance with the provisions of the statute, because three days had not elapsed from the service of the writ.

In the United States the statutory provisions relating to the writ are essentially the same in all the states. They differ sometimes in respect to the courts or officers to whom jurisdiction over it is committed; sometimes in respect to the form of procedure and sometimes in respect to the effect of it. But the general principles of practice are substantially the same as those prevailing at common law and under the statute, 31 *Car.* 2.

Where material alterations have been introduced in the principles or the form of procedure in any of the states, they will be noted so far as the limited access had to the necessary sources will allow.

SECTION II.

THE APPLICATION.

1. *In what cases it may be made.*
2. *By whom it may be made.*
3. *The mode of making it.*
4. *When it may be denied.*
5. *When it must be granted.*

1. *In what cases the application may be made.* All persons imprisoned or under actual restraint, except those who by the habeas corpus act are excluded, may apply to the proper court or judge for the writ. It is not necessary that the imprisonment or restraint should be close confinement to entitle a party to the writ.

Every restraint upon a man's liberty is, in the eye of the law, an imprisonment, wherever may be the place or whatever may be the manner in which the restraint is effected. 1 *Kent*, 631; 2 *Inst.*, 482, 589.

Words may constitute an imprisonment, if they impose a restraint upon the person, and he be accordingly restrained and submits. 1 *Kent*, 631, *note; Homer* v. *Battyn, Buller N. P.*, 62; *Pike* v. *Hanson*, 9 *N. H.*, 491. It may be on the high street and though the party be not put into any prison or house. *Per Thorpe Fitzhugh, Bar.*, 301, *Com Dig.*, "*Imprisonment, G.*"

"Whenever a person is deprived of the privilege of going when and where he pleases he is restrained of his liberty and has a right to inquire if that restraint be illegal and wrongful, whether it be by a jailor, constable or private individual. It is not necessary that the degradation of being incarcerated in a prison should be undergone to entitle any citizen, who may consider himself unjustly charged with a breach of the laws, to a hearing." *Commonwealth* v. *Ridgeway*, 2 *Ashm.*, 247. A mere moral restraint, however, is not such imprisonment as will entitle the party to the writ; as where he was committed on execution and admitted to the prison bounds under bond, according to law, held, he was under no such restraint as authorized a resort to the writ of habeas corpus. *Dodge's case*, 6 *Mart. Low. Rep.*, 569.

"Persons discharged on bail will not be considered as restrained of their liberty so as to be entitled to a writ of habeas corpus, directed to their bail." 1 *Bouv. Law Dic.*, 574; 3 *Yeates R.*, 263; 1 *Serg. and R.*, 356.

It is immaterial whether the imprisonment be under criminal or civil process; if it be illegal, the prisoner is entitled to the benefit of the writ of habeas corpus. *Hecker* v. *Jarrett*, 3 *Binn.*, 404. It was at one time doubted whether the writ of habeas corpus was a proper remedy in case of illegal imprisonment under a civil process. *Ex parte Wilson*, 6 *Cranch*, 52; *Cable* v. *Cooper*, 15 *Johns.*, 152.

The doubt originated in too limited a view of the jurisdiction of the British courts in habeas corpus, attending only to their statutory jurisdiction, which by its terms was confined to criminal cases. When their common law jurisdiction was considered, the doubt vanished. *Ex parte Randolph*, 2 *Brock.*, 447. *U. S. Bank* v. *Jenkins and others*, 18 *Johns.*, 305.

2. *By whom it may be made.* Although the person imprisoned has an undoubted right to make the application, it is not necessary that it should proceed directly from him. An agent or friend may make it in behalf of the prisoner; 14 *How. St. Tr.*, 814, 4*th Resolution*, 825; the wife in behalf of her husband.

In the case of *Cobbett* v. *Hudson*, *X Eng. Law & Eq.*, 318, Campbell, Ch. J., said, "The first day I sat here, Mrs. Cobbett desired to make a motion, on behalf of her husband, for a habeas corpus; and I heard her without the smallest scruple, as my illustrious predecessor, Hale, heard the wife of John Bunyan. On each of those occasions the liberty of the subject was in question; and in such a case great inconvenience might arise from refusing to hear the wife or any other person on behalf of the party who was under restraint.

The husband in behalf of the wife; *Anne Gregory's case*, 4 *Burr.*, 1991; *Rex* v. *Clarke*, 1 *Burr.*, 606.

But no legal relation is required to exist between the prisoner and the person making the application. It may be made by any one. *The State* v. *Philpot, Dudley Geo. Rep.*, 42; *The Hottentot Venus case*, 13 *East*, 195.

Where the application is by a third person it is supposed to be made in accordance with the wishes of the party restrained of his liberty; and is allowed to prevent delay, where the party is represented to be under any disability, or in any manner prevented from making the application in his own right.

But mere volunteers, who do not appear in behalf of the prisoner or show some right to represent him, will not be listened to. *Rex* v. *Clark*, 3 *Burr.*, 1363. In *Ex parte Child, XXIX. Eng. Law & Eq.*, 259 Jervis, Ch. J., said: "A mere stranger has no right to come to the court and ask that a party *who makes no affidavit, and who is not suggested to be so coerced as to be incapable of making one*, may be brought up by habeas corpus to be discharged from restraint. For anything that appears, Captain Child may be very well content to remain where he is." Rule discharged. And in *Linda* v. *Hudson*, 1 *Cush.*, 385, it was held that a person brought up on habeas corpus, without his request or authority, might maintain an action on the case against the party who procured the writ to issue.

It is not, however, required as a condition, without which the writ will be withheld, that the party suffering the imprisonment expressly authorized the application; for that would be in many cases to furnish a spur to closer and more rigorous confinement. It is enough that the application, by whomsoever presented, shows probable ground to suspect that the person on whose behalf it is made is suffering an involuntary and wrongful restraint or imprisonment.

Persons having a right to the custody of the prisoner may also make the application.

It may be granted at the instance of the parent for his child, *The People* v. *Mercein,* 3 *Hill,* 399, and cases cited; of the guardian for his ward, *Commonwealth* v. *Downs,* 24 *Pick.,* 227; *Commonwealth* v. *Hammond,* 10 *Pick.,* 274; *Hovey* v. *Morris,* 7 *Blackf.,* 559; *Ex parte Ralston, R. M. Charl.,* 119; *Hyde* v. *Jenkins,* 6 *La. (Curry),* 436; by the master for his apprentice, *The People* v. *Pillow,* 1 *Sandf. Sup. Ct. Rep.,* 672; see, *post* — and of the special bail for his principal, *Halsey* v. *Trevillo,* 6 *Watts,* 402; *Anon., Pennington's Rep.,* 284; *Bond* v. *Isaac,* 1 *Burr.,* 339.

The person on whose behalf the writ issues is usually called the *relator*, and his name appears in the statement of the proceedings, that the record may show jurisdiction to support any order or judgment for costs which may be rendered against him.

3. *The mode of making the application.*

In term-time at common law.

"To obtain the writ in term at common law, an application is made by the party's counsel, grounded on an affidavit of the circumstances, which must show some probable cause for the application to induce the court to grant the writ; but if a probable ground be shown that the party is imprisoned without just cause, and therefore hath a right to be delivered, the writ of habeas corpus is then a writ of right, and a rule will accordingly be granted for the writ to issue." *Hand's Pr.*, 73; 2 *Mod.*, 306; 1 *Ch. Cr. L.*, 124; 3 *Bl.*, 132.

In vacation and under the act 31 *Car.* 2.

By this act the mode of application was required to be by "request made in writing by such person or persons (imprisoned), or any on his, her or their behalf, attested and subscribed by two witnesses who were present at the delivery of the same."

The "request," it seems, was usually accompanied by an affidavit of the circumstances (though that does not appear to be required by the act), and a copy of the warrant or an affidavit that it had been denied. *Hand's Pr.*, 73.

In the courts of the United States the practice prevailing at common law, and at the time of the adoption of the Constitution, is still pursued, no law of Congress having been made to alter or regulate it. *Ex parte Bollman & Swartwout*, 4 *Cr.*, 75. In one case the analogy of the statute, 31 *Car.* 2, appears to have been carried so far as to require the application, when made to the court, to be by petition in writing. *Harrison's case*, 1 *Cr. C. C.*, 159.

It is customary in all cases to make the application in writing, which is usually called the petition.

In Pennsylvania, it is provided, *sec.* 1, *Stat.* 1785, that where the commitment is for any criminal or supposed criminal matter, the application "in vacation time and out of term, shall be by request in writing by the prisoner, or any person on his behalf, attested and subscribed by two witnesses who were present at the delivery of the same." *Sec.* 11 seems to require the same mode of procedure when the application is to the court in term-time.

In all other cases of confinement or restraint of liberty "under any color or petence whatsoever," the same provision applies, with the further provision that the application shall be supported by the oath or affirmation of the person confined, or some one in his or her behalf, that there is "actual confinement or restraint, and that such confinement or restraint, to the best of the knowledge and belief of the person so applying, is not by virtue of any commitment or detainer for any criminal or supposed criminal matter." *Sec.* 13.

Under this section it does not appear necessary to allege even that the restraint is unlawful. But it is necessary to allege that there is actual confinement or restraint. Accordingly, where there is no actual confinement or restraint, as in the case of an infant voluntarily leaving his parent and unwilling to return, no relief can be had by the parent under the statute of 1785, but must be by habeas corpus at common law, which the statute has not wholly superseded. *Commonwealth* v. *Robinson*, 1 *Serg. & Rawle*, 352.

In Ohio, it is provided by the act of 1811, *Swn. St.*, 450, *sec.* 1, that if any person, except, &c., shall be unlawfully deprived of his or her liberty, and shall make application either by him or herself, or any person on his or her behalf, to any one of the judges, &c., and does at the same time produce to such judge a copy of the commitment or cause of detention of such person; or if the person so imprisoned or detained is imprisoned or detained without any legal authority, upon making the same appear to such judge by oath or affirmation, it shall be his duty, &c.

This act does not by its terms extend to courts in session.

It does not appear to have been considered indispensable in Ohio or Pennsylvania, under their statutes, to state fully the circumstances of the imprisonment or restraint, constituting the ground upon which the applicant relies for relief.

In the case of *Commonwealth* v. *Tilghman*, on habeas corpus, before the Court of Common Pleas for Philadelphia county, decided in 1848, it was moved by the defendant's counsel that the writ be quashed, on the ground that the petition did not set forth with precision the nature of the alleged restraint. Judge King said, that

"The form of petition adopted in this case has been the form in existence and practice during his entire judicial recollection, which extends over twenty-four years. If the petition states that he has been restrained of his liberty for no criminal matter, and is sustained by oath, it has always been considered sufficient. Precedent has settled the practice into a principle which cannot now be disturbed.

"If the matter were now *de novo*, the form might be amended. Suppose the man is restrained without any cause being assigned, how could he then regain his liberty?

"The ground resides in the bosom of the party who restrains. The cause may be given, and the petitioner would be unable to make oath to the ground alleged. There is no hardship in this. If there is no restraint, the answer to the petitioner who says, 'You restrain me of my liberty,' is, 'I do not, you may go.'

"Where the party makes oath that he is restrained of his liberty, without any criminal charge, it puts the burden upon the other side, to show why he does so."

In several states the substance of the petition is prescribed by statute.

In MASSACHUSETTS it is provided that the "Application for such writ shall be made to the court or magistrate authorized to issue the same, by complaint in writing, signed by the party for whose relief it is intended, or by some person in his behalf, setting forth:

First, the person by whom and the place where the party is imprisoned or restrained, naming the prisoner and the person detaining him, if their names are known, and describing them if they are not known;

Secondly, the cause or pretence of such imprisonment or restraint, according to the knowledge and belief of the person applying;

Thirdly, if the imprisonment or restraint is by virtue of any warrant or other process, a copy thereof shall be annexed, or it shall be made to appear that a copy thereof has been demanded and refused, or that for some sufficient reason a demand of such copy could not be made; and,

Fourthly, the facts set forth in the complaint shall be verified by the oath of the person making the application, or by that of some other credible witness, which oath may be administered by the court or magistrate to whom the application is made or by any justice of the peace." *Rev. St.*, 1836, *p.* 656.

Similar provisions are found in the statutes of Indiana, Alabama, Arkansas, Missouri and Maine.

In KENTUCKY it is provided by the Rev. St., 1852, that the writ shall be granted "to any person who shall apply for the same by petition, showing by affidavit or other evience, probable cause to believe that he is detained without lawful authority or is imprisoned when by law he is entitled to bail."

Verification of the petition. Where the imprisonment is not for criminal or supposed criminal matter, as has been intimated, the petition was required to be verified by affidavit; but the affidavit was sometimes dispensed with. *Lady Leigh's case*, 3 *Keb.*, 433; *Bac. Abr.*, *Hab. Corp.*, 3; *Mary Heath's case*, 18 *How. St. Tr.*, 10, *per Lord Marlay, Ch. J. In the matter of Parker and others*, 5 *M. and W.*, 31, the court said: "Before granting a habeas corpus to remove a person in custody, we must ascertain that an affidavit is not reasonably to be expected from him," none being presented. "An affidavit is absolutely necessary, either from the party who claims the writ, or from some other person, so as to satisfy the court that he is so coerced as to be unable to make it."

In Georgia, where the common law practice had not been modified by statute, it was held in the case of *The State* v. *Philpot*, *Dudley Geo.*, *Rep.*, 46, that the omission of an affidavit to the petition did not invalidate the writ, nor constitute a sufficient reason for refusing obedience to it. The court said: "Regularly the facts stated in the petition for the writ ought to be supported by affidavit; but still the affidavit is not of the essence of the writ, and in cases of great emergency the writ will be allowed to issue without it, *in fact to enable the party to make it. Lady Leigh's case*, *Bac. Abr.* "At common law, and nearly a century ago, the judges of England gave it as their unanimous opinion that such a writ ought not to issue of course, but upon probable cause, supported by affidavit, which has been the regular practice since."

The want of the affidavit in that case was treated as a mere irregularity which might be and had been waived.

In the matter of Keeler, Hemp. Rep., 306, the application was made to the United States District Judge in Arkansas, by Lewis Keeler, to obtain the release of his son, alleged to be a minor, enlisted without his consent. The application was verified by the affidavit of the applicant, purporting to be sworn to before a justice of the peace in New York, but not otherwise authenticated, nor his official character otherwise proved; Held, that it did not sufficiently appear that the person administering the oath had proper authority. Petition denied but without prejudice to another application.

The prisoner may verify the petition, although a negro, and an incompetent witness against a white person. *De Lacy* v. *Antoine*, 7 *Leigh*, 438. The court in this case allowed the writ to stand, not as a matter of evidence, but simply as a foundation for subsequent proceedings. They remark that "a free negro as well as a free white man must be entitled to the benefit of the habeas corpus act, both according to its language which is broad and general, and still more according to its spirit which is yet more liberal and beneficent. If it were otherwise, that wretched class would be altogether without protec tion from the grossest outrages, and their liberty would be an unsubstantial shadow."

When the application may be denied. It may be denied in the cases excepted in the habeas corpus act or where no probable ground for relief is shown, unless it is otherwise directed by statute:

1. *Cases excepted in the habeas corpus act.* "The habeas corpus act, 31 *Car.*, 2, c. 2, § 10, excepts persons committed for felony or treason, plainly expressed in the warrant, as well as persons convicted or in execution by legal process, who are consequently not entitled to this writ, either in term-time or vacation." 1 *Ch. Cr. L.*, 126; *Com. Dig.*, *Hab. Corp.*, *C.*

In PENNSYLVANIA. "Persons committed or detained for treason or felony, the species whereof is plainly and fully set forth in the warrant of commitment."

In OHIO. "Persons convicted of some crime or offence for which they stand committed, or persons committed for treason or felony, the punishment whereof is capital, plainly and specially expressed in the warrant of commitment;" and "persons committed by any judge or justice, and charged as accessory before the fact to any felony, the punishment whereof is capital, which felony shall be plainly and specially charged in the warrant of commitment." *Swn. St.*, 450, 451.

In DELAWARE. "1st. Persons committed or detained on a charge of treason or felony, the species whereof is plainly and fully set forth in the commitment. 2d. Persons convicted of or charged with treason, felony or any offence in another state, who ought, by the Constitution of the United States, to be delivered to the executive of such state. 3d. Persons imprisoned by the authority of the United States."

In KENTUCKY. The habeas corpus act of this state, *Rev. St.*, 1852, *p.* 379, contains no exceptions; but the judge, &c., is required to grant it when "legally applied to."

In INDIANA. No exceptions are found in the habeas corpus act of this state, *Rev. Stat.*, 1843, *p.* 928, but the court or judge is required to grant it when a "proper application is made."

In GEORGIA. The act of 31 *Car.* 2 was adopted in this state in 1778, and continues in force. *Cobb's Digest, A. D.* 1851, *p.* 1131.

In ALABAMA. Writs may issue upon proper showing in all cases. *Sec.* 1, *Hab. Corp. Act, Clay's Digest,* 462, provides: "Every person, committed, confined or in any manner restrained of his liberty, for any matter, either criminal or supposed to be so, or under any pretence whatever may prosecute a writ of habeas corpus, according to the provisions of this chapter, to inquire into the cause of such commitment, confinement or restraint."

In NEW JERSEY. "Persons committed for treason, murder, manslaughter, sodomy, rape, arson, burglary, robbery, forgery or larceny, or for rescues of voluntary escapes in any such case, plainly and specially expressed in the warrant of commitment," and persons "convict, or in execution by legal process."

In FLORIDA. The writ issues in all cases, whether the party detained in custody be "charged with a criminal offence or not," upon it being shown by affidavit or evidence that there is probable cause to believe that he is detained without lawful authority.

In NEW YORK. 1st. "Persons committed or detained by virtue of any process issued by any court of the United States, or any judge thereof, in cases where such courts or judges have exclusive jurisdiction under the laws of the United States, or shall have acquired exclusive jurisdiction by the commencement of suits in such courts.

"2d. Persons committed or detained by virtue of the final judgment or decree of any competent tribunal of civil or criminal jurisdiction, or by virtue of any execution issued upon such judgment or decree; but no order of commitment for any alleged contempt, or upon proceedings as for contempt, to enforce the rights or remedies of any party, shall be deemed a judgment or decree within the meaning of this section; nor shall any attachment or other process, issued upon any such order, be deemed an execution within the meaning of this section."

2. *Where no probable cause is shown for relief.* Where the application was to the court in term-time, whether at common law or under the *Act*, 31 *Car.* 2, the writ was not granted "without showing some probable cause why the extraordinary power of the crown is called to the party's assistance. For, as was argued by Lord Chief Justice Vaughan, 'it is granted on motion, because it cannot be had of course, and there is therefore no necessity to grant it; for the court ought to be satisfied that the party hath a probable cause to be delivered.' And this seems the more reasonable, because (when once granted) the person to whom it is directed can return no satisfactory excuse for not bringing up the body of the prisoner. So that if it issued of mere course, without showing to the court or judge some reasonable ground for awarding it, a traitor or felon under sentence of death, a soldier or mariner in the king's service, a wife, a child, a relation or a domestic, confined for insanity or other prudential reasons, might obtain a temporary enlargement by suing out a habeas corpus, though sure to be remanded as soon as brought into court. And therefore, Sir Edward Coke, when Chief Justice, did not scruple in 13 *Jac.*, 1, to deny a habeas corpus to one confined by the Court of Admiralty for piracy, there appearing, upon his own showing, sufficient grounds to confine him." 3 *Black.*, 132; *Bushel's case*, 2 *Jon.*, 13; 3 *Bulstr.*, 27; 2 *Roll. Rep.*, 138.

Notwithstanding these authorities, the question as to the power of the court to withhold the writ in any case, has recently been brought under consideration of the courts, both in England and America. In a late case in Massachusetts, Chief Justice Shaw resolved it in the following terms:

"Before a writ of habeas corpus is granted, sufficient probable cause must be shown; but when it appears upon the party's own showing that there is no sufficient ground, prima facie, for his discharge, the court will not issue the writ. The ordinary course is for the court to grant a rule *nisi*, in the first instance, to show cause why the writ should not issue. Of course, if sufficient cause is not shown, it will be withheld. *Blake's case*, 2 *M. & S.*, 428; *The King* v. *Marsh*, *Bulstr.*, 27; and in *Hobhouse's case*, 3 *B. & Ald.*, 420, the question came before the court and was fully discussed. It was there considered that whether the writ of habeas corpus were claimed at common law or under the statute, a proper ground ought to be laid before the court, previously to granting the writ. It is not granted, as a matter of course; and the court will not grant the writ when they see that, in the result, they must remand the party. We think the same rule and practice have prevailed in this country. In *Watkins' case*, 3 *Pet.*, 201, Marshall, Ch. J., said: 'the writ ought not to be granted if the court is satisfied that the prisoner would be remanded.' Indeed, by necessary implication it is the fair result of the provisions of the habeas corpus act of this commonwealth. The *Rev. St.*, *c.* iii., § 3, require in all cases of an application for the writ of habeas corpus that the party imprisoned, or some person in his behalf, shall present a petition, and if held under legal process, or color or pretence of legal process, shall annex a copy of the process under which the respondent claims to hold and detain him, or make proof by affidavit that a copy of such a writ or warrant has been applied for and refused. But why annex a copy of the process, unless it be to enable the court to form an opinion whether the party is rightly held in custody or not; and why form an opinion in that stage of the proceeding, if it is to constitute no ground for judicial action?

"It is urged that this is a writ of right, and therefore grantable without inquiry. But it is not a writ of right in that narrow and technical sense; if it were, the issuing of it would be a mere ministerial act, and the party claiming it might go to the clerk and sue it out as he may a writ on a claim for land or money.

"Nor does this limit or restrain the full and beneficial operation of this writ, so essential to the protection of personal liberty. The same court must decide whether the imprisonment complained of is illegal; and whether the inquiry is had in the first instance on the application or subsequently on the return of the writ, or partly on the one and partly on the other, it must depend upon the same facts and principles and be governed by the same rule of law. It was upon these grounds that we said and we now repeat that when it appears from the party's own showing in the petition, that if brought before the court he would not be entitled to a discharge, the court will not issue the writ." *Sims' case*, 7 *Cush.*, 285.

The same general doctrine has been recognized in other cases. *Ex parte Kearney*, 7 *Wheat.*, 38; *Commonwealth* v. *Robinson*, 1 *Serg. & R.*, 353; *Ex parte Campbell*, 20 *Ala. R.*, 89: see also *Ex parte Pardy*, 1 *Lowndes, Maxwell & Pollock*, 16; *Ex parte Williamson*, 4 *Am. Law Reg.*, 27.

The same general rule, it is supposed, applies where the application is to a judge in vacation, unless the inquiry before him is restricted by statute, or he is subject to penalties for refusing it.

5. *When it must be granted.* 1st. It cannot be denied where "a probable ground is shown that the party is imprisoned without just cause, and therefore, hath a right to be delivered." for the writ then becomes a "writ of right, which may not be denied but ought to be granted to every man that is committed or detained in prison or otherwise restrained of his liberty, though it be by the command of the King, the Privy Council, or any other." 3 *Black.*, 132.

In Arkansas, where a judge of the Circuit Court denied the writ on the application of a guardian for his ward, under an erroneous opinion that he had no jurisdiction to grant it; the Supreme Court, on that being returned by the judge to an alternative mandamus as the ground of his denial, ordered a peremptory mandamus, requiring the judge to grant the writ, &c. *Wright* v. *Johnson*, 5 *Pike*, 687.

2d. It cannot be denied where the granting of it is made a matter of imperative duty by statute.

By the 10th section of the *Act*, 31 *Car.* 2, it was provided that:

"If the said lord chancellor or lord keeper, or any judge or judges, baron or barons, for the time being, of the degree of the coif of any of the courts aforesaid" (being the same officers who by the 3d section were required to grant the writ), in the vacation time, upon view of the copy or copies of the warrant or warrants of commitment or detainer, upon oath made that such copy or copies were denied as aforesaid, shall deny any writ of habeas corpus, by this act required to be granted, being moved for as aforesaid, they shall severally forfeit to the prisoner or party grieved the sum of £500, to be recovered in manner aforesaid."

In many of the states, also, a wrongful denial of the writ subjects the judge or officer authorized to grant it in vacation to a pecuniary penalty; and in some, the members of a court may incur the penalty for improperly denying the writ in open session. This extension of the penal provision of the English statute was first introduced in the statute of New York, in the Revised Statutes of 1830.

The provision on that subject, which is still in force, is as follows:

"If any court or officer, authorized by the provisions of this article to grant writs of habeas corpus or certiorari, shall refuse to grant such writ when legally applied for, every member of such court, who shall have assented to such refusal, and every such officer, shall severally forfeit to the party aggrieved one thousand dollars." 2 *Rev. St.*, 799, § 46.

Chancellor Kent, speaking of the extension of the penal provision to members of the court, says:

"The penalty for refusal to grant the writ was by the English statute confined to the default of the chancellor or judge in vacation time; whereas the penalty and suit for refusal to grant the writ applies, under the New York statute to the judges of the Supreme Court in term-time. This is the first instance in the history of the English law that the judges of the highest common law tribunal, sitting and acting not in a ministerial, but in a judicial capacity, are made responsible, in actions by private suitors, for the exercise of their discretion according to their judgment in term-time." 1 *Kent*, 634.

In the case of *Yates* v. *Lansing*, 5 *Johns. Rep.*, 282, the allowance of the writ by a judge in vacation was said not to be a judicial act, and that the judges were made responsible when they refused in a mere ministerial capacity to allow the writ. But the act under the statute is the same in both cases, and if the penalty is degrading when applied to a member of the court in term-time, it is no less so when applied to him in vacation.

It is plain that the penalty may be avoided in all cases. If the law requires the court or judge to examine the commitment, and grant or refuse the writ according as he finds treason or felony plainly expressed in it or not, and then punishes him for refusing it when he should have allowed it, the court or judge will be very apt to act upon the hint of the Chancellor of Delaware, in the case of *The State* v. *Munson*, *Hall's Jour. Juris.*, 257:

"If," said he, "the party is imprisoned for treason or felony, the species whereof is plainly and fully set forth in the warrant of commitment, he is not even entitled to the writ in vacation; *though it would not be prudent to refuse it, not knowing the opinions of those who might have to decide the question on a suit for the refusal.*"

In Arkansas and Missouri, the courts, as well as judges in vacation, are subject to penalties not only for refusing the writ, but also for unreasonably delaying to issue it. In Pennsylvania, Kentucky, New Jersey, North Carolina, South Carolina, Georgia, California, the penalty applies only to a refusal of the writ by a judge in vacation or at chambers.

In Ohio, Connecticut, Virginia, Texas, New Hampshire, the statutes are silent as to any penalties in any case of refusal of the writ.

SECTION III.

SECURITY FOR COSTS AND AGAINST ESCAPE.

By the act 31 *Car.* 2, the officer to whom the writ was directed was required to make return of it within three days after the service thereof, "upon payment or tender of the charges of bringing the said prisoner, to be ascertained by the judge or court that awarded the same, and endorsed upon the writ, not exceeding 12 pence per mile, and upon security given by his own bond to pay the charges of carrying back the prisoner, if he shall be remanded by the court or judge to which he shall be brought, according to the true intent of this present act, and that he will not make any escape by the way."

It was held, however, that the omission of the prisoner to tender the fees due to the gaoler was no excuse to him for not obeying the writ, though it was said the court would not discharge the prisoner when brought up till the fees were paid. *Bac. Abr., Hab. Corp., B., sec.* 8.

In Massachusetts, where the party is confined in a common jail or in the custody of any civil officer, the costs of bringing him from the place of confinement must be paid or tendered, or the officer is not bound to obey the writ.

In some states, however, a discretion is vested in the court or judge to exact security.

In Kentucky, by section 5 of the habeas corpus act, it is provided that the "officer granting the writ may previously require bond, with surety in sufficient penalty, payable to the commonwealth or to the person against whom the writ is directed, conditioned that the person detained shall not escape by the way, and for the payment of such costs and charges as may be awarded against him."

In Arkansas, "in order to render the service effectual," the court or judge allowing the writ may require "that the charges of bringing up the prisoner, and conveying him back if remanded, shall be paid by the petitioner; the amount, to be specified by the court on the writ, not to exceed ten cents per mile."

In Missouri, it is provided that the costs of bringing up the prisoner may be required to be paid by the petitioner, and if not paid, and bond given to pay the costs of returning him if remanded, it is declared that the service of the writ shall not be considered complete.

SECTION IV.

ALLOWANCE OF THE WRIT.

1. *Mode of allowance.*
2. *Notice of allowance.*

1. *Mode of allowance.* Where the writ is awarded by the court in term, the fact is shown by an entry upon its journal. When it is awarded by a judge in vacation, the fact is shown by an order under his hand, indorsed usually upon the petition.

The act of 31 *Car.* 2 provided that the writ, when granted according to its provisions, should "be marked in this manner: 'Per statutum, tricesimo primo Caroli secundi Regis,' and be signed by the person that awards the same, and to the intent that no sheriff, gaoler or other officer may pretend ignorance of the import of any such writ."

The Pennsylvania statute, 1785, still in force, contained the same provision; except the words "By act of Assembly, 1785," are substituted for the words "Per statutum tricesimo primo Caroli secundi Regis."

No such "marking" or indorsement of the writ is required in Ohio, The judge indorses his allowance upon the petition, but even that is not necessary. The order may be on a detached piece of paper.

The omission in England to make and sign the writ under the act 31 *Car.* 2, rendered it inoperative, *Rex* v. *Roddam*, *Cowp.*, 672, and probably would have the same effect in Pennsylvania under their statute.

2. *Notice of the allowance.* While it is a matter of great moment to the prisoner to be speedily released

from illegal imprisonment, it is also a matter of concern to the state that public offenders should not escape merited punishment, and one of interest to the citizen, that he should not be wrongfully deprived of any remedy, however severe, which the law may afford him. Hence it has been customary for the court in cases of habeas corpus to require notice of the application for or pendency of the writ to be served upon the public prosecutor where the imprisonment is under criminal process, and upon the creditor, or party interested in continuing the imprisonment, where it is under civil process. *The King* v. *Taylor*, 7 *Dowl. & Ryl.*, 622; *Ex parte Smith*, 3 *McLean*, 121; *Mr. Justice Foster's Letter*, 20 *How. St. Tr.*, 137, *sec.* 5; *Bromley's case*, 3 *Jac. & W.*, 453.

The want of such notice to the creditor was held to vitiate the discharge on habeas corpus of the debtor in execution, in the case of *Hecker* v. *Jarrett*, 3 *Binn.*, 404. Tilghman, Ch. J., said: "The power of discharging from an execution is a very important one, and should be exercised with great discretion. I will not say that the judge had no right to discharge from imprisonment in a case of this nature. I am of opinion, however, that granting his right to discharge, his proceedings were void for want of notice to the plaintiff in execution. It is contrary to the first principles of justice to deprive a man of his rights without a hearing or the opportunity of a hearing."

In New York, it has been made a statutory duty. *The People* v. *Pelham*, 14 *Wend.*, 48; 2 *Rev. Stat.*, 1852, 802, *secs.* 61, 62. So also in Indiana, notice is required in cases of imprisonment, "on any process under which any person has an interest in continuing his imprisonment or restraint," to be given to such interested party; and when the detainer is on a criminal charge, notice shall be given to the person, his agent or attorney, on whose complaint such party is held in custody." *Rev. Stat.*, 1843, *p.* 932, *secs.* 28, 29.

Also in Alabama, *Clay's Dig.*, 465, except in cases of confinement on a criminal charge, the notice shall be given to the solicitor or attorney-general, as well as the prosecutor.

SECTION V.

THE WRIT.

1. *The form of the writ.*
2. *In what name to issue.*
3. *To whom directed.*

1. *The form of the writ.* The writ, as has already been observed, took its name from the emphatic words it contained when it was used in the Latin tongue. The following was the usual form when it was addressed to an officer, in the singular number.

Rex vicecom. London salutem:

Præcipimus tibi, quod CORPUS A. B. in prisona nostra sub custodia tua detent. ut dicitur una cum causa detentionis suæ quocunque nomine idem A. B. censeatur in eadem HABEAS coram nobis apud Westm. die Jovis prox. post Octabis S. Martini *ad subjiciendum et recipiendum* ea quæ curia nostra de ea adtunc, et ibidem ordinari contigerit in hac parte et hoc nullatemus, omittatis periculo incumbente, et habeas ibi hoc breve. 2 *Inst.*, 53; *Trem. P. C.*, 354.

Sometimes, instead of naming a time for the production of the body, &c., the words were: "Immediate post receptionem hujus brevis." *Rex* v. *Gardner*, *Trem. P. C.*, 354.

Blackstone says the writ contained the words "ad faciendum" also, but they are not found in the form given by Coke nor in the writ copied in the case of *Rex* v. *Gardner*, *Trem. P. C.*, 354.

Whether the words "ad faciendum" were used or not, the great prerogative writ was always distinguished by the words "ad subjiciendum." These words have been rendered, "to submit to," *Black.*, 3, 131; "to undergo," *Hand's Pr.*, 520; "to perform," per Solicitor-General, *In re Belson*, 3 *Eng. Law and Eq.*, 56.

To the observation of Lord Campbell in the last case, that he did not see how the writ of "habeas corpus ad faciendum et recipiendum differed in substance from the writ of habeas corpus ad subjiciendum et recipiendum," it was answered: "The difference consists in the one being a writ of process, from which in case of error in the proceedings there would have been a rehearing before the Lord Chancellor and an appeal to the House of Lords; but can any one say there would have been an appeal if the Lord Chancellor had issued his fiat at once for the great prerogative writ of habeas corpus ad subjiciendum? The word subjiciendum would be omitted in the writ of habeas corpus cum causa."

The terms "to do, submit to and receive," are commonly used in the United States, where the form of the writ has not been prescribed by statute.

In the forms prescribed in Maine, Massachusetts, Ohio, the words "submit to" are omitted. They were omitted in the form prescribed in Massachusetts, as early as 1785. *Mass. Laws*, 1788, *p.* 150.

2. *In what name to issue.* The writ, as appears, always runs in the name of the state. *Commonwealth* v. *Briggs*, 16 *Pick.*, 203.

The state in all cases of wrongful detention is in legal presumption concerned in having justice done, and therefore must be a party to the proceeding to remove it. *Wade* v. *Judge*, 5 *Ala.*, 130. "It is a prerogative writ which the King may send to any place, he having a right to be informed of the state and condition of every prisoner, and for what reason he is confined." 1 *Ch. Cr. L.*, 119; *Bac. Abr.*, *tit.*, *Hab. Corp.*, 2.

The proceeding in habeas corpus "is an inquisition by the Government at the suggestion and instance of an individual, but still in the name and capacity of the sovereign." *Per Betts, cited in Barry* v. *Mercein*, 5 *How.*, 108.

3. *To whom directed.* Wherever a person is imprisoned by any person whatsoever, whether he be one concerned in the administration of justice, as a sheriff, gaoler, &c., or a private person, such as a doctor of physic, who confines a person under pretence of curing him of madness, &c., the habeas corpus must be directed to him. *Bac. Abr.*, *Hab. Corp.*, 6; *Commonwealth* v. *Ridgeway*, 2 *Ashm.*, 247.

But it should not be directed in the disjunctive; for example to the sheriff *or* the gaoler. "Where a party is taken by a warrant of the sheriff, the writ must be directed to him, for in contemplation of law the prisoner is in his custody, and the writ must be returned with the body; but where the prisoner has been immediately committed to the custody of the gaoler, as in all criminal cases, it must be directed to him." 1 *Ch. Cr. L.*, 126; *Bac. Abr.*, *Hab. Corp.*, 6.

It may also be directed to any one participating in the illegal detention, though he be not the immediate actor in the wrong. Where the father applied for the writ to obtain the custody of his infant child, the mother having it with her at her father's, where she was staying, the writ was held to be properly directed to the wife's father. *The People, ex rel. Barry* v. *Mercein*, 3 *Hill*, 406.

In Ohio, it is provided, *Swan Stat.*, 453, *sec.* 4., that:

"The person having the custody of the prisoner may in all writs of habeas corpus be designated by his name of office, if he have any, or by his own name; or, if both such names are unknown or uncertain, he may be described by an assumed appellation; and any one who is served with the writ shall be deemed the person intended thereby." Sec. 5. "The person to be produced shall be designated by his name, if known, and if that is unknown or uncertain, he may be described in any other way so as to make known who was intended."

It is also provided by the statute passed Feb. 8, 1847, sec. 1:

"That in case of confinement, imprisonment or detention by any person not a sheriff, deputy sheriff, coroner, jailor, constable, or marshal of this state, nor a marshal, deputy marshal or other like officer of the courts of the United States, the writ of habeas corpus shall be in the form following:

THE STATE OF OHIO, COUNTY, *ss.*

[L. S.] *To the Sheriffs of our several counties, greeting:*

We command you, that the body of of by of imprisoned and restrained of his liberty, as it is said, you take and have before , a judge of our court , or, in case of his absence or disability, before some other judge of the same court, at , forthwith, to do and receive what our said judge shall then and there consider concerning him in this behalf; and summon the said then and there to appear before our said judge to show the cause of the taking and detaining of the said , and have you there this writ, with your doings thereon. Witness, &c.

The common law direction of the writ in all cases of mere private restraint has been altered in this state. No penalty has been prescribed in cases of eloinment, and perhaps in such cases further legislation may be required to give the writ the efficiency which it had at common law.

The writ in Massachussetts and Maine is required to be directed in like manner; and in Kentucky, on good cause shown, the officer or person serving the writ may be directed to take the applicant into his custody, and produce him on return of the writ. So in Indiana, if it be made to appear in any case, by satisfactory proof by affidavit, that the applicant is illegally held in custody, confinement or restraint, and that there is good reason to believe that such person will be carried out of the jurisdiction of the court or judge where the application is made, or will suffer some irreparable injury before compliance with the writ of habeas corpus can be enforced, a warrant stating the facts may be issued to the sheriff to take the person, &c. And in Alabama, when the detention is in any other place than the penitentiary, or the common jail of the county, the writ commands the sheriff or coroner to take into his custody the person alleged to be illegally detained or confined, and forthwith to have him before the judge, &c.

In Maine, Massachusetts and Delaware, the concealing of the prisoner or changing his custody, with the intent to elude the service of the writ of habeas corpus, is prohibited under severe penalties; in the last, $3,600. In Indiana, Arkansas and Alabama, the act is declared a misdemeanor, and the offender subjected to fine and imprisonment.

SECTION VI.

SERVICE OF THE WRIT.

The writ at common law and under the statute 31 *Car.* 2, was not required to be served by an officer. The solicitor of the prisoner or any person in his behalf might deliver it to the person to whom it was directed. *Hand's Pr.*, 73.

Under the act 31 *Car.* 2, it might be delivered to the officer to whom it was directed, or "left at the gaol or prison with any of the under officers, under keepers or deputy of said officers or keepers"

In some of the United States, special provisions have been made in reference to the mode of service where an evasion of service is attempted. In Louisiana and Indiana, where the person or officer refuses to receive the writ it will be sufficient service to state to him the contents (and probably in any other state);

and, if the party conceal himself or refuse admittance, it may be posted up on his residence or the prison where the prisoner is confined.

The service may be proved by the oath of the party making it.

CHAPTER III.

THE RETURN.

SECTION I.

GENERAL NATURE OF THE RETURN, AND MODE OF ENFORCING IT.

1. *General nature of the return.*
2. *Must be made without delay.*
3. *May be enforced by attachment.*

1. *General nature of the return.* The answer in writing, signed by the party to whom the writ is addressed, stating the time and cause of the caption and detention of the prisoner and his production before the court or judge, or, if the prisoner be not produced, then the reasons for not producing him, constitutes the return.

2. *Must be made without delay.* It is of the very essence of the proceeding that the return be made without delay. It was the neglect of this duty which supplied the staple of the preamble to the act, 31 *Car.* 2: "Whereas great delays have been used by

sheriffs, gaolers and other officers, to whose custody any of the King's subjects have been committed, for criminal or supposed criminal matters, in making returns of writs of habeas corpus," &c.

Delays, for good cause shown, will be permitted; as, where the person confined is a lunatic, detained by relatives who are proceeding in good faith to obtain a commission of lunacy, the time for making the return will be enlarged. *Rex* v. *Clarke*, 3 *Burr.*, 1362.

It is not indispensable that the party to whom the writ is addressed should attend before the court or judge, in all cases, to make the return, unless so required by statute. If the prisoner is produced, the court may determine the legality of the imprisonment in the defendant's absence. *In re Hakewell*, 22 *Eng. Law and Eq.*, 395.

3. *May be enforced by attachment.* Prior to the act, 31 *Car.* 2, the mode of compelling a return to a habeas corpus was by taking out an alias habeas corpus and then a pluries, and if no return was made to that, an attachment issued of course. Sometimes the court made the rule on the officer to return his writ, and if disobeyed they might proceed against such disobedience in the same manner as they usually did against the disobedience of any other rule. *Bac. Abr.*, *Hab. Corp.*, 13, *sec.* 8.

This oppressive procrastination and shameful trifling with the writ was designed to be remedied by the act, 31 *Car.* 2.

By that act the return was required to be within three days after the service of the writ, "unless the commitment of the said party be in any place beyond the distance of twenty miles from the place or places where such court or person is or shall be residing, and if beyond the distance of twenty miles and not above one hundred miles, then within the space of ten days, and if beyond the distance of one hundred miles, then within the space of twenty days, after such delivery aforesaid and not longer."

It became the practice, soon after this act was passed, to require the return to be made to the first writ, and to enforce obedience by an attachment. *The King* v. *Winton*, 5 *T. R.*, 89.

One of the courts of the United States, although regarding this act as furnishing a reasonable rule of proceeding merely, refused to grant an attachment before the expiration of the three days allowed in the act for the return. *U. S.* v. *Collman & Swartwout*, 1 *Cr. C. Rep.*, 373

In the United States an attachment may issue at once upon default of the party to make return forthwith. But the court must be satisfied by proper evidence, usually the affidavit of the person who makes the service, that the writ has been served before they will grant an attachment. A certificate of service, although given by one who held the office of sheriff, was held insufficient. "A writ of habeas corpus was issued, directed to the defendant (Wm. Raborg), to bring up the bodies of Walter Wilson and others, persons of color. The sheriff of Somerset sent up a copy of the writ, with a certificate of service upon it. The defendant did not appear, nor return the writ, and it was suggested that he intended to depart the state, taking with him the persons named in the writ. It was, therefore, moved that an attachment issue; but it was refused because the return and evidence were not sufficient.

At a subsequent day the affidavit of William Hoagland was read, proving the service of the habeas corpus; and it appearing that the said writ had not been returned by the said Raborg, it was on motion ordered that an attachment do forthwith issue against him for contempt of the court in disobeying the said writ of habeas corpus. *The State* v. *Raborg*, 2 *South.*, 545; see also *Rex.* v. *Wright*, *Str.*, 915.

The court, however, will not grant the attachment unless the circumstances are such as to excite a suspicion of a willful disobedience.

Where the writ was only served the preceding day, although returnable immediately, the court, on application for attachment, refused it, there being no ground for supposing that a return would not be made. *Stockdale* v. *Hansard*, 8 *Dowl.*, 474. In several of the states this matter is regulated by statute.

SECTION II.

FORM OF THE RETURN.

The return is required to be in writing and signed by the party. It should properly be addressed to the court or officer to whom the writ is returnable; but a mistake in the address or direction will not be deemed material. It was moved in *Brass Crosby case*, 2 *W. Bl.*, 754, to discharge the prisoner, on the ground that there was no legal return to the writ because it was directed to the chief justice only, and not to the other judges of the court. But the court held the direction to be surplusage and that the return might be good without any direction at all.

SECTION III.

GENERAL REQUISITES OF THE RETURN.

The command of the writ is twofold, the production of the body and a statement of the cause of the caption and detention.

The requisites of the return may be considered under the following heads:

1st. The non-production of the body, with the reasons therefor.

2d. The production of the body, and the cause of the caption and detention.

SECTION IV.

NON-PRODUCTION OF THE BODY AND THE REASONS THEREFOR.

1. *Importance of the production of the body.*
2. *Disability from want of possession, custody or power.*
3. *Disability from sickness of prisoner.*

1. *Importance of the production of the body.* The production of the body constitutes an essential element of this proceeding. It is called a summary proceeding. It is one of applied justice. It is nerved with all the energy of the law. It begins with a power which belongs only to the final process

of other proceedings, which is said to be the "life of the law." It deals with present restraints upon the living corporeal man, and it demands his presence before the court face to face with his jailor.

Without the production of the body, said the Supreme Court of Massachusetts, the writ is without effect; the case has no status, and the court will hear no evidence upon the question of the validity of the imprisonment. *Commonwealth* v. *Chandler*, 11 *Mass. Rep.*, 83.

They will, however, inquire with great caution into the reasons assigned for not producing the body. There are several reasons which are accepted as sufficient.

2. *Disability from want of possession, custody or power.* The strictness of the law upon this point, and the consequences of an evasive return, are fully exemplified and the policy of the rule ably vindicated in the leading case of *Rex.* v. *Winton*, 5 *T. R.*, 89, which was heard upon a rule to show cause why an attachment should not issue against the defendant. The affidavit of J. Greygoose, on which the writ in that case issued, stated that his wife was, in June 1790, seduced by the defendant, with whom she continued to live until the month of May last, when she returned to her husband; that about three days afterwards, in consequence of a letter written by the defendant, threatening to publish her conduct in case of a refusal to go back to him, she was induced to go back to the defendant, who, as the deponent believed, detained her by threats, and with whom she was now living in a state of adultery, but that she was desirous of returning to her husband. The

return was: "I had not at the time of receiving this writ, nor have I since had, the body of the within named M. Greygoose detained in my custody, so that I could not have her before the within named W. H. Ashurst, as within I am commanded."

BULLER, J. "I will first dispose of the last objection against the attachment, because it is of more general consequence than the two others. Notwithstanding what is to be found in some of the old books on this subject, it has long been settled that the court will require a return to be made to the first writ of habeas corpus; and it is of infinite importance to every individual in the kingdom that we should insist on a return being made to that writ without issuing an alias or pluries. If the first writ be not obeyed an attachment must issue immediately. Then it was argued, on the authority of a case in 2 *Lev.*, that this is a sufficient return; but I am of opinion that that case is by no means an authority to support this return. There the words were widely different from those used in this case. There Sir R. Viner returned that 'he had no such person in his custody, nor had he on the day of issuing that (pluries) writ, or afterwards.' Here the return is, 'I had not at the time of receiving this writ, &c., nor have I since had the body, &c., detained in my custody, &c.' This is an equivocal return; the defendant does not deny having the party, he only denies the detaining of her; but we must inquire when she is brought up whether she is detained or not."

GROSE, J., said: "The court always look with a watchful eye at the returns to writs of habeas corpus. The liberty of the subject so essentially depends on a ready compliance with the requisitions of this writ that we are jealous whenever an attempt is made to deviate from the usual form of the return. The general form is, 'that the party has not the person in his possession, custody or power;' that has not been adopted in this case, but another, and that an equivocal one, adopted in its place, 'detained,' &c., omitting the words 'power and possession.' What the defendant means by the word 'detained,' I know not; but it does not satisfy me that the woman is not under the defendant's control." Rule absolute.

In *Elizabeth Warman's case*, 1 *W. Bl.*, 1204, a writ of habeas corpus was directed to Sir David Murray, Baronet, commanding him to produce the body of Elizabeth, wife of Edward Warman, with the causes of her taking and detaining; and upon affidavit that he detained her by force from her husband for unlawful and suspicious purposes, he returned that he did not detain and never had detained her. The court thought this was no answer to the taking, and gave leave to amend his return, which he did, &c.

The same doctrine was held and applied in the case of *Samuel Stacy, Jr.*, 10 *Johns.*, 328, where it was also held that an attachment, where the return was evasive, would not in all cases be delayed until a rule to show cause why it should not issue had been served. In that case the writ was directed to Morgan Lewis, as commander of the troops of the United States at Sackett's Harbor, and under his title of "General of Division in the army of the United States." He returned "that the within named Samuel Stacy, Jr., is not in my custody."

KENT, CH. J. "This was evidently an evasive return. He ought to have stated, if he meant to excuse himself for the non-production of the body of the party, that Stacy was not in his 'possession or power.'

"The only question that can be made is whether the motion for an attachment shall be granted, or whether there shall be only a rule upon the party offending to show cause, by the first day of next term, why an attachment should not issue. It is the indispensable duty of this court, and one to which every inferior consideration must be sacrificed, to act as a faithful guardian of the personal liberty of the citizen, and to give ready and effectual aid to the means provided by law for its security. One of the most valuable of those means is this writ of habeas corpus, which has justly been deemed the glory of the English law.

"On ordinary occasions the attachment does not issue until after a rule to show cause, but whether it shall not issue in the first instance must depend upon the sound discretion of the court, under the circumstances of the particular case. It may and it often does issue in the first instance, without a rule to show cause, if the case be urgent or the contempt flagrant." *Rex* v. *Jones*, *Str.*, 185; *Davies ex dem. Powers* v. *Doe*, 2 *Bl. Rep.*, 892; *Rex* v. *Earl Ferrers*, 1 *Burr.*, 631.

The court granted the attachment, regarding the case as urgent, but gave it an alternative form, indicating thereby that they did not regard the contempt as flagrant. The following is a copy of the order:

"Ordered, that an attachment in this cause issue against General Morgan Lewis, but that the same be accompanied with a copy of this rule, which is to operate as instructions to the sheriff not to serve the same, if General Morgan Lewis shall forthwith, upon service of a copy of this rule upon him, discharge the said Samuel Stacy, Jr., or shall cause him to be brought before Nathan Williams, Esq., commissioner, &c., in obedience to the habeas corpus heretofore issued by him in this cause."

It was formerly held that the return should show that the defendant had not the party in his possession, custody or power, not only at the time of the return, but also at the time of granting the writ. "Habeas corpus" are always returned in the preter-perfect tense." *Sid.*, 273; *The King* v. *Wagstaff and others, Viner Abr., Hab. Corp., F.* Upon a pluries habeas corpus, the return was, "I have no such person in my custody, nor had I on the day of the obtaining of this writ, nor at any time since." The return was held bad, for it did not appear that he had not the custody on the day of the obtaining of the first writ. 2 *Lev.*, 128; *The King* v. *Sir Robt. Viner, Viner Abr., Guardian and Ward, p.* 4, *marginal note.*

There is no doubt that it ought to show at least that he had not the person in his "possession, custody or power," at the time of the service of the writ or at any time after. In the case of *The State* v. *Philpot, Dudley Geo. Rep.*, 46, this point was fully discussed. The defendant had been imprisoned for contempt in making an evasive return. It was objected that "the order of imprisonment was illegal in this, that it was impossible for him to perform, and because the court was not authorized to require the production of the boy as the condition of his purging his contempt if any were committed."

The court answered: "As has been repeatedly said the attachment was for an evasion and disobedience of the writ, and the only condition imposed on him was obedience. His obedience was not made to depend upon the arbitrary will of the judge, but upon his own will if that will should lead to action. That such an order is not illegal must be manifest to any one who considers the order and allows to the court the power of enforcing its own process. Such orders are of common occurrence and are absolutely necessary for the attainment of justice. They are issued and enforced against sheriffs, justices of the peace and constables who collect money and neglect or refuse to pay it over when ordered to do so; to compel the production of personal chattels under a warrant of restitution, and in a variety of instances of small importance compared with personal liberty; and it would be a very singular defect of power in the court not to possess the same means of enforcing the writ of habeas corpus. If the court had the right to issue the writ it had the right to compel the production of the boy, and to use the only means adequate to that end. Senator Clinton's opinion in the case of *Yates*, 6 *Johns.*, 507, contends that the commitment to be legal must be definite, and terminable either by the efflux of time, or on the doing of some act by the prisoner. We are of opinion that Philpot ought to remain attached until he produce the boy James, or shows that it is impossible to produce him." The evidence showed that after the service of the habeas corpus Philpot had had possession of the boy and sold him, and that he had been taken away west. "*If Philpot's return had shown that neither at the service of the writ nor at any time since had the boy been in his possession, custody, power or control, it would have been full and perfect; but he evades a part and will not swear that at the service of the writ the boy was not in his power or control. Had Philpot, however, sworn that the boy was not in his possession, power or custody, still if, looking into the facts stated in the return, the conscience of the court should not be satisfied that all the material facts were disclosed, it was not bound to discharge him.*"

It seems also that the return will be considered evasive although sufficient on its face, if the evidence shows that the party restrained was removed to avoid the process after notice that it would be applied for.

The case of the *United States* v. *Thomas N. Davis*, 5 *Cr. C. C. Rep.*, 622, *A. D.* 1840, is an interesting one, showing the favorable action of this doctrine.

That was a proceeding in habeas corpus. The writ was directed to Thomas N. Davis, commanding him to have before the court the bodies of Israel Brinkley, Emanuel Price and Maria Course, persons of color, with the cause of their detention.

The return of the writ by Davis stated upon oath, that he purchased the negroes publicly in the bar-room of Lloyd's tavern in the city of Washington, as slaves for life, from one Joseph Woodall, on the 31st December, 1839, and took from him a bill of sale warranting the title to the negroes, and that they were slaves for life; which bill of sale he produces as part of his return; that he paid for them the sum of $1,200, which he avers to be a reasonable price for them; that he never had any reason to doubt that they were slaves for life as they were warranted to be. It was also averred by Davis in the return, that the said individuals were removed, as he believed, beyond the District of Columbia, before the service of the said writ of habeas corpus, and before he heard of the existence of such process, and that they were now beyond his control and out of his custody, and, as he believed, beyond the District of Columbia.

A number of witnesses were sworn and examined, whose testimony tended to show that Davis had removed the negroes because he suspected they would apply for a writ of habeas corpus.

Mr. Key, for the prisoners, moved for an attachment, and contended that the return was evasive, because it did not deny that the prisoners were in his power, or that he was unable to produce them; also, that the sending the prisoners away with intent to avoid the expected process of the court was itself an obstruction of justice and a contempt of the court.

The court made the following order:

"The court having examined and considered the return of the said Thomas N. Davis to the writs of habeas corpus aforesaid, and having heard counsel thereupon, do adjudge the said answer to be evasive and insufficient, and that the said Davis is bound to produce the bodies of the said negroes, mentioned in the said writs, before the court; and the said Davis being now present in court and refusing to produce the said negroes, it is therefore, this 16th day of January, 1840, ordered that the said Davis be committed to the custody of the marshal, until he shall produce the said negroes, or be otherwise discharged in due course of law." It appearing to the court afterwards, that the negro Israel Brinkley had run away, and had been taken up and lodged in jail in Baltimore, they modified, on the 18th of January, the order of commitment so as to relate only to the cases of the other two. On the 20th of January, being the last day of the term, Davis caused these to be brought into court, who subsequently, under a petition for freedom, filed in accordance with the laws of Maryland, of 1796, established their right to freedom and were discharged.

The allegation in the return, that the party is not in the possession, power or custody of the defendant, will not entitle the defendant to be discharged if there is any reason to suspect that he has not stated the whole truth. In *United States* v. *Green*, 3 *Mason*, 482, Story, J., said: "The court will look into all the facts stated in the return, and will not discharge the defendant simply because he declares the infant not to be in his possession, power or custody, if the conscience of the court is not satisfied that all the material facts are disclosed."

In some of the foregoing cases, it appears that the court heard proofs, and by them determined the return to be evasive; and in the case of *Leonard Watson*, 36 *Eng. C. L.*, 254, the court received an affidavit to the falsity of the return as a predicate for a rule upon the defendant to show cause why he should not be attached for contempt.

The identical words "possession, custody and power" are not essential, though the court regards any deviation from them with jealousy, per Grose, J., *Rex* v. *Winton*, 5 *T. R.*, 89; but where the facts stated, not being controverted, satisfy the judgment of the court, the return will be sufficient, as in the case of *Rex* v. *Wright*, *Str.*, 915, the habeas corpus being directed to the defendant, a doctor, to bring up a woman under his care for lunacy, he returned "that before the delivery of the writ he had delivered the woman to her husband, and that he does not know where she is, nor can he produce her." The court held the answer sufficient.

So if the return be that before the coming of the writ, the prisoner was discharged out of defendant's custody by competent legal authority. *Rex* v. *Bethuen*, *Andr.*, 281. Also it is a good return that, before the coming of the writ, the party "had by force and arms broke the said prison, and out of my custody, without any leave and against my will, escaped and fled to places to me unknown, and is not yet brought back or retaken." *Impey's Sheriff*, 530.

2. *Disability from sickness of prisoner.* It is a good return by the defendant to the writ that the party is sick and languishing, so that he could not have the body without danger and peril of his life. *Lib. Intr.*, 190; *Kitch.*, 258; *Dalt.*, 250; *Impey's Sheriff*, 527.

But regularly, in such case the return should be accompanied and sustained by medical opinion. In the case *Ex parte Bryant*, 2 *Tyler Rep.*, 269, the sheriff to whom the writ was directed returned "that the prisoner was in his custody, but sick and languishing, so that he could not be removed without endangering his life, and he therefore prayed to be in mercy for not obeying the writ." This return was objected to, and a rule upon the sheriff moved for for a contempt, but the court refused it, saying: "The return is satisfactory to the court. If the prisoner be dangerously sick, it is a sufficient reason why he should not have been removed; but a return of this nature, it is expected, will in future be accompanied with affidavits of physicians, that the court may judge whether the bodily indisposition of the prisoner be so great as to justify the sheriff in his disobedience to the writ."

It was held at common law, when it was the prevailing opinion that a return could not be contradicted, "that if a gaoler return one *languidus* when the party himself brings his habeas corpus, and is in good health, an attachment shall issue against him; otherwise, if the habeas corpus was brought by another." *Bac. Abr.*, *Hab. Corp.*, 8.

If the person confined is too weak or too much deranged to be brought into court, they will make a rule that certain persons have access to him, *Rex* v.

Wright, 2 *Burr. Rep.*, 1099; *Rex* v. *Turlington*, 3 *Burr.*, 1115, but will not give that liberty unless to persons who have some pretensions to demand it. *Rex* v. *Clark*, 3 *Burr.*, 1362.

It has been observed that on the application it was made the duty of the court or judge to examine the commitment where a copy was produced to see whether it was "for treason or felony, plainly and especially expressed," or whether the prisoner was "convict or in execution by legal process." Yet if the writ be issued this question may be again presented for more complete consideration and determination; and this appears to have been allowed without the production of the body under the implication arising upon a clause in the 1st section of the act of 31 *Car.* 2.

In a case cited in 10 *Pet. C. L.*, 199, *n.*, it is said that, "although the body of the prisoner is usually returned with the writ, the reasons of the prisoner's detention are, however, sometimes returned without actually bringing up the applicant; as where he is charged with treason or felony, clearly expressed in the warrant of commitment, or imprisoned for any civil cause of action, or in execution; and in either case the return must distinctly show by whom and for what cause the prisoner was committed."

This, however, is not only an exception to the general rule but should be regarded as a particular indulgence, for if the officer had a right to stand upon his construction of the warrant of commitment, there would have been but little gained by the act of 31 *Car.* 2.

SECTION V.

PRODUCTION OF THE BODY AND STATEMENT OF THE DAY AND CAUSE OF THE CAPTION AND DETENTION.

1. *Statement of the cause of caption.*
2. *Statement of the cause of detention.*

1. *Statement of the cause of caption.* The writ requires not only that the cause of the detention should be shown; but also the day and cause of the caption. The supposition of the writ is that the detention is by the same authority under which the caption was made, and the aim and effect of the writ is to require the defendant to show the cause of the imprisonment and when it commenced. For the object of the proceeding in habeas corpus, is to set the prisoner free from present illegal restraint, and he is entitled to it although the original taking was lawful. 4 *Inst.*, 290.

And if at the time of the return the defendant shows a legal cause for restraint then imposed, the prisoner will not be discharged notwithstanding the original taking may have been without any legal authority. *Dow's Case*, 18 *Penn. Rep.*, 37.

And though the original warrant of commitment be irregular, yet, if a regular warrant of detainer for the same offence, issued subsequently to the writ of habeas corpus, be returned, the court will remand the prisoner. *Rex* v. *Gordon*, 1 *Barn. & Ald.*, 572, *n.*

The cause of the caption appears not to be material, only as it stands connected with continuing restraint, or the good faith of the defendant in not complying with the command of the writ to produce the body.

It is not to be prosecuted as an independent inquiry in this proceeding, for it furnishes no remedy for false imprisonment already overpast.

2. *Statement of the cause of detention.* The production of the body does not satisfy the demand of the writ. If the party having brought the body into court, refuses to return the cause of the caption and detention, he is subject to be proceeded against for contempt; and may, by attachment, be compelled to make the return. *Newman's case*, 2 *West. Law Jour.*

To justify the detention, the return must show it to be founded on sufficient authority, either public or private. Detention by public authority may be by commitment in writing, as by special warrant, or by process of law not in writing, as by an order of court or by authority of law.

Detention by private authority must be founded upon some right, growing out of the domestic or civil relations.

1st. Where there is a warrant in writing it must be returned, for otherwise it would be in the power of the jailor to alter the case of the prisoner and make it either better or worse than it is upon the warrant, and if he may take upon himself to return what he will, he makes himself judge; whereas the judge ought to judge and that upon the warrant itself. *Bac. Abr.*, *Hab. Corp.*, *B.*, *sec.* 9; *Semb.*, 5 *Mod.*, 159; 1 *Salk.*, 349.

The whole commitment must be set out. *Matter of Power*, 2 *Russ.*, 583.

The return in such cases need not be confined to the particular warrant placed in the hands of the officer. If it contains recitals or references to other papers, documents or proceedings relating to the authority to commit, they may be embodied in the return.

Where, however, a written warrant is not material to the legality of the imprisonment, it may be omitted from the return, although it exists; and if attempted to be set forth, the general return will not be vitiated by great mistakes in setting it out. *Leonard Watson's case*, 36 *E. C. L.*, 254.

2d. Where the commitment is not under any warrant in writing, or the restraint is by private authority, the return must set forth all the facts which are relied on, to justify the imprisonment or restraint.

Where the commitment is in court to a proper officer there present, there is no warrant of commitment, and therefore there can be no return of a warrant in hæc verba, but the officer must return the truth of the whole matter. *Rex* v. *Clark*, 1 *Salk.*, 349.

Where an officer holding a prisoner thus committed by a court of record, is called on to show the cause of detention he must produce a copy of the record of the commitment as the cause.

"A commitment for legal cause of any man present in court, by an order of a competent court entered of record, is still a legal commitment and the sheriff is bound to obey the order. The prisoner knows for what cause and by whom he is committed; and he may at any time have a copy of the record. And the sheriff, if called upon to justify the imprisonment, or to certify the cause of it, may have access to the same record, a copy of which the clerk will give him, ex officio. Where a prisoner comes into court on recognizance, and after conviction is sentenced to imprisonment, the sheriff is obliged immediately to obey the order of the court, and to commit the prisoner in execution; and on application to the clerk, he may have a copy after sentence." *Randall* v. *Bridge*, 2 *Mass.*, 549.

In such cases the return need not be confined to the simple copy of the order of commitment but may include copies of any other orders or proceedings referred to in the order of commitment, showing the grounds of the commitment.

Where the sheriff returned that he held the prisoner by order of the Court of Chancery, which order referred to a former attachment setting forth the grounds of commitment and from which the prisoner had been discharged by a judge of the Supreme Court in vacation, on another habeas corpus, and the sheriff also returned the attachment and proceedings prior to the last order of commitment; held that the sheriff could not return the true cause of the caption without also stating the original attachment and subsequent orders; and that the whole might be received and examined by the court. *Yates' case*, 4 *Johns.*, 317.

In *Indiana* the officer or person upon whom the writ is served is required to state in his return,

"Plainly and unequivocally: 1. Whether he have or have not the party in custody or under his power or restraint. 2. If he have the party in his custody or power or under his restraint, he shall state the authority and the cause of such imprisonment or restraint, setting forth the same at large. 3. If the party be detained by virtue of any writ, warrant, or other written authority, a copy thereof shall be annexed to the return, and the original shall be produced and exhibited to the court or judge, on the hearing of such return. 4. If the officer or person upon whom such writ shall have been served shall have had the party in his power or custody or under restraint at any time prior or subsequent to the date of the writ of habeas corpus, but such officer or person has transferred such custody or restraint to another, the return shall state particularly to whom, at what time and place, for what cause, and by what authority, such transfer took place."

If from sickness or infirmity the prisoner cannot be produced without danger, that fact may be returned under oath, and the court, if satisfied of the truth of it, may proceed as if the party was produced, or adjourn the hearing until he can be produced.

Somewhat similar provisions are contained in the laws of Alabama, Arkansas, Maine, Massachusetts and Ohio.

SECTION VI.

CERTAINTY REQUIRED IN THE RETURN.

The same strictness has never been applied to the return to a habeas corpus which was applied to pleadings in civil actions. In an early case, *City of London case*, 8 *Co.*, 127, *b*, 128, *a*; 2 *Roll. Rep.*, 158, it was said, "It was objected that the said return consists much in recital, which ought to have been directly and certainly alleged. To which it was answered and resolved, that this is not on a demurrer in law, but a return on a writ of privilege, upon which no issue can be taken or demurrer joined; neither upon our award herein doth any writ of error lie, and therefore the return is no other but to inform the court of the truth of the matter in which such a precise certainty is not required as in pleading." It will be seen that this "resolution" of the court fell far short of settling the law, even in England, in respect to some of the propositions or recitals contained in it. It shows, however, that the same certainty was not required in the return which was required in pleading, yet some certainty was required, and precisely what that was, it would be difficult to define. In the case of *Rex* v. *Horne*, *Cowp.*, 672, Lord Chief Justice De Gray speaking upon the general rule of certainty in pleading, observed: "Though the law requires certainty, we have no precise idea of the signification of the word, which is as indefinite in itself as any word that can be used." We have, however, a statement of the rule and the reasons of it in the case of *The King* v. *Lyme Regis*, *Doug. Rep.*, 150, with as much precision as, perhaps, can elsewhere be found. Buller, Justice, speaking of returns to mandamus, in which he said the same certainty was required as in returns to writs of habeas corpus, says: "It is one of the first principles of pleading that you have only occasion to state facts; which must be done for the purpose of informing the court whose duty it is to declare the law arising upon those facts, and to apprise the opposite party of what is meant to be proved in order to give him an opportunity to answer or traverse it."

"Lord Coke has distinguished certainty in pleading into three sorts:

1st. Certainty to a common intent, which is sufficient in a plea in bar.

"2d. Certainty to a certain intent in general, as in counts, replications, &c., and so in indictments.

"3d. Certainty to a certain intent in every particular, which is necessary in estoppels.

"The second of those sorts is all that is requisite here; and I take it to mean, what upon a fair and reasonable construction, may be called certain, without recurring to possible facts which do not appear."

In *Watson's case*, 9 *Ad. & E.*, 371; 36 *E. C. L.*, 254, the subject was particularly considered, and the court held that: The return does not require minute correctness, if the substance of the facts is stated.

If the return alludes to documents which are not material to the validity of the imprisonment, they need not be specially set forth.

If, however, in attempting to set out such documents, the defendant intentionally misstate them, neither their immateriality nor the circumstance that the prisoner had not been injured by the falsehood, will protect him from an attachment for contempt.

A return stating a capital conviction for high treason and felony and a commutation of the sentence, is sufficient without specifying the treason or felony.

"Minute correctness" is not required; but the facts necessary to warrant the detention must in substance be alleged. They will not be presumed. Where the habeas corpus was brought for the discharge of an apprentice above the age of twenty-one, a return stating the custom of London, that every citizen and freeman of the city may take as an apprentice any person above the age of fourteen and under twenty-one, to serve for seven years or more, must show that the apprentice was within those ages when he bound himself apprentice; for the court will not intend that from matter dehors the return. *Eden's case*, 2 *M. & S.*, 226.

SECTION VII.

AMENDMENT OF THE RETURN.

In England it seems that before the return be filed any defect in form, or the want of an averment of a matter of fact may be amended; but this must be at the peril of the officer in the same manner as if the return were originally what it is after amendment. After the return is filed it becomes a record of the court and cannot be amended. 1 *Mod.*, 102, 103. So the omission of the words in which the contempt consists. *Cro. Car.*, 133. In like manner the writ may be amended before it is returned and filed, but not afterwards. 2 *Lib. Abr.*, 2.

It was held, however, in *Leonard Watson's case*, 36 *Eng. C. L.*, 254, that the return might be amended after return filed. It has been customary in the United States to allow amendments to be made at any time before the decision of the case, where it appeared to the court to be necessary to the ends of justice.

In Pennsylvania, the Act of 1785, section 1, provides that "the return by leave of the judge may be amended before or after it is filed." So in Delaware, *Rev. Stat.*, 1852, *p.* 412, *sec.* 5.

Undoubtedly anywhere in the United States it is competent for the court to permit an amendment at any time before the final disposition of the case.

SECTION VIII.

VERIFICATION OF THE RETURN.

At common law no affidavit was required to the return. *Leonard Watson's case*, 36 *Eng. C. L.*, 285. But in many of the states it is required that the return shall be under oath.

In Ohio, *Swn. St.*, 454, *sec.* 7, it is required that the return or statement shall be signed by the person making it; and shall be sworn to by him, unless he is a sworn public officer, and makes the return in his official capacity. So in Indiana, *Rev. St.*, 1843, 929, *sec.* 5; and in New York, 2 *Rev. St.*, 1852, 800, *sec.* 47.

SECTION IX.

EFFECT OF THE RETURN AT COMMON LAW.

In 2 *Hawk. P. C.*, *ch.* 15, *sec.* 78, it is said:

"It seems to be agreed that no one can in any case controvert the truth of the return to a habeas corpus, or plead or suggest any matter repugnant to it."

In the examination of the judges before the House of Lords, in 1758, the following question was addressed to them:

"Whether in all cases whatsoever, the judges are so bound by the facts set forth in the return to the writ of habeas corpus, that they cannot discharge the person brought up before them, although it should appear most manifestly to the judges, by the clearest and most undoubted proof, that such return is false in fact, and that the person so brought up is restrained of his liberty by the most unwarrantable means, and in direct violation of law and justice?"

The answers of the several judges, though disagreeing in some particulars, are nevertheless curious and instructive. They show at least that the proposition above quoted from *Hawkins' P. C.*, was not, in its absolute form, the law.

Lord Ch. J. Willes, Justices Noel, Bathurst, Clive and Baron Legge, answered categorically in the negative.

Mr. Justice Foster, who was absent, subsequently concurred with them. He also addressed a letter to Ch. Baron Parker expressing his views at length, which is cited *post*.

The other judges gave qualified answers.

Mr. Baron Smythe: "The judges were so bound by the facts set forth in the return to the writ of habeas corpus, that they cannot enter into proof by affidavits to controvert them; the facts set forth in the return can be controverted or contradicted only by the verdict of a jury."

Mr. Baron Adams: "If an action should be brought for a false return made to an habeas corpus, and therein the return should be falsified by judgment upon verdict, demurrer or otherwise, the judges might thereupon issue an alias habeas corpus, and upon that discharge the party; but that, in all cases whatsoever, when the matter comes before the court, singly upon the return made to the habeas corpus, if that return contains a sufficient and justifiable cause of restraint, the judges must determine upon the cause as it there appears, and cannot hear any proof in contradiction to it, but are so bound by the facts set forth therein, that though they be false in fact, and the party in truth restrained of his liberty by the most unwarrantable means, and in direct violation of law and justice, they cannot discharge him, but he is driven to his action."

Mr. JUSTICE DENNISON. "In all cases whatsoever where the return consists of facts justifying the taking and detaining by law, the judges are so bound by the facts set forth in the return to the writ of habeas corpus, that they cannot discharge the person brought up before them upon affidavits to be read in that proceeding contradicting the facts contained in the return; but if it should appear most manifestly to the court, by the clearest and most undoubted proof, either in action or some collateral proceeding, that such return is false in fact, and that the person so brought up is restrained of his liberty by unwarrantable means, and in direct violation of law and justice, the prisoner may be discharged."

Mr. JUSTICE WILMOT. "I am of opinion that 'in no case whatsoever, the judges are so bound by the facts set forth in the return to the writ of habeas corpus, that they cannot discharge the person brought up before them, if it shall most manifestly appear to the judges, by the clearest and most undoubted proof that such return is false in fact; and that the person so brought up is restrained of his liberty by the most unwarrantable means and in direct violation of law and justice;' but by the clearest and most undoubted proof, I mean the verdict of a jury, or judgment on demurrer or otherwise, in an action for a false return; and in case the facts averred in a return to a writ of habeas corpus are sufficient in point of law to justify restraint, I am of opinion that the court or judge before whom such writ is returnable cannot try the facts averred in such return by affidavits in any proceeding grafted upon the return to such writ of habeas corpus."

It deserves to be noticed in this connection that while this learned judge argued strenuously against receiving affidavits to controvert the facts stated in the return, he was willing, in some cases, to allow them that effect indirectly. As where the affidavits tended to show the commission of a crime in the matter of the imprisonment or that the return was false, he would suspend further action under the writ of habeas corpus to enable the party brought up to appeal to the court in the exercise of its summary criminal jurisdiction to grant an information against the person making the return, *and then, by imposing severe terms in the matter of bail, compel him to grant immediate relief to the person imprisoned! Wilmot's Opinions*, 106.

Mr. Justice Foster, in his letter found in 20 *How. St. Tr.*, 1375, says:

"As I always considered the case of a barely wrongful detention as not within the habeas corpus act, but merely at common law, I thought a legal, sound discretion ought to be used, and generally expected an affidavit on behalf of the party applying for the writ setting forth some probable ground for relief on the merits of his case. This method I constantly observed in the case of men pressed into the service, and that the public service might not suffer by an abuse of the writ, I ordered notice to be given to the proper officers of the crown of the time at which the party was to be brought before me, with copies of the affidavits. * * * From the notes of cases I have, I find the court hath not granted the writ as of course and within the habeas corpus act, but hath required affidavits on behalf of the party applying for it, setting forth the merits of his case; *and, on the other hand, though proper returns in point of form may have been made, the court hath not given entire credit to them, and put the party complaining to his action for a false return, but* *hath constantly entered into the merits of the case upon affidavits, and either discharged or remanded the party as the case hath appeared.*"

In his letter to Lord Chief Baron Parker, 20 *How. St. Tr.*, 1378, he says:

"I agree with your lordship in the truth of the general doctrine, that a return to a writ of habeas corpus is conclusive in point of fact. It cannot be traversed; the court is bound by it, and the injured party is driven to his action. This I admit is the general rule, but I think that it is not universally true. Cases may be put which are exceptions to it; and the exceptions do not, as your lordship well knows, destroy but rather establish a general rule. The case of persons pressed into the service is, I conceive, one of them, for this plain reason, that if the party cannot controvert the truth of the facts set forth in the return, he is absolutely without remedy. An inadequate, ineffectual remedy is no remedy; it is a rope thrown out to a drowning man which cannot reach him, or will not bear his weight. It is the offering of baubles to the children of one's family, when they are crying for bread. In common cases, in every case where the general rule is laid down, the injured party must wait with patience till he can falsify the return in a proper action. This, it must be confessed, is a great misfortune, but till the day of his deliverance comes, he continues at home in the custody of the law and under its protection. This your lordship knows is not the case of a man pressed into the service by land or sea, supposing him to be no object of the law. * * * The principle is that though in common cases the return is conclusive in point of fact, yet there are special cases as they come not within the general reason of the law are not within the general rule. The parties are without remedy if they are not to controvert the truth of the return in a summary way, and therefore they shall do it."

Mr. Justice Foster does not undertake to enumerate all the exceptions to the general rule, and we have no means of determining at this day to what extent exceptions were allowed in practice.

Some additional light is thrown upon the subject by the researches of Mr. Hill, shown in his argument in *Watson's case*, 9 *Ad. & E.*, 731; 36 *Eng. C. L.*, 254, and from which the following extracts are taken:

"In *De Vine's case* (cited in *Hutchins* v. *Player*, *O. Bridg.*, 288, from a Register book of the city of London, called Liber Dunthorne; see *O. Bridg.*, p. 305, also pp. 276, 295, 308), in 34 *H.* 6, a prisoner pleaded to the return, and the party returning replied to the plea, upon which the prisoner was remanded. It appears that the judges, among whom was Fortescue, Ch. J., were the advisers of the Lord Chancellor in the matter."

In *Sir William Chancey's case*, 12 *Rep.*, 82, it appears that the return to a habeas corpus was held bad for a reason, among others, which would appear on looking out of the return; namely that the high commission, under which the parties acted, could not be executed by four, which was the number of the commissioners making the warrant under which the imprisonment was justified.

In *Hutchins* v. *Player*, *O. Bridg.*, 272, the court looked into numerous matters extrinsic to the return, to see whether the custom set out in the return was good.

In *Swallow* v. *The City of London*, 1 *Sid.*, 287, there seems to have been a discussion whether the prisoner should be allowed the benefit of a fact not pleaded, but the court gave him the benefit of it.

In *Dodson's Life of Foster*, 53 (see also 20 *How. St. Tr.*, 1376, appendix), is an account of *Rex* v. *White*, which was a case of impressment under *Stat.* 18 *Geo.* 3, *c.* 10. The court there allowed affidavits to be read on each side, though they said it was not usual; for that the prisoner had no other remedy; and the prisoner was discharged, though the return was good on the face of it.

In *Goldswain's case*, 2 *W. Black.*, 1207, the court took into consideration the affidavits on which the habeas corpus was obtained, and Gould, J., said: "I do not conceive that either the court or the party are concluded by the return of a habeas corpus, but may plead to it any special matter necessary to regain his liberty."

"In the case of *Rex* v. *Gardner*, *Cro. Eliz.*, 821; *S. C.*, *Tr. P. C.*, 354; the return to the habeas corpus showed that the prisoner was committed under a warrant of a justice of the peace, on a conviction before him, for carrying a hand-gun charged with powder, contrary to law, &c.

"The prisoner craved oyer of the writ, and return, which being granted, he pleaded, in justification, that he carried the hand-gun in defence of himself and another sheriff's bailiff in the execution of a warrant upon a fieri facias.

"The Queen's coroner and attorney confessed the plea and the prisoner was discharged."

In *Watson's case*, cited *ante*, the court of King's Bench left the question undecided. Lord Denman, Ch. J., however, said:

"As to the question, how far the truth of this return might be canvassed, I neither assent to or dissent from the propositions which have been laid down. I am not prepared to say that if Watson (the prisoner) had pledged his oath to the falsity of any statement of fact on the return, we might or might not make that the foundation of a proceeding to quash the return."

In the case of *The King* v. *Hawkins*, *Fort.*, 272, Parker, Ch. J., said: "As to the truth of the facts, the return of the officer is the same as a special verdict."

Return may be confessed and avoided.

It is added to the above proposition, quoted from 2 *Hawk. P. C., ch.* 15, *sec.* 78:

"That a man may confess and avoid such a return, by admitting the truth of the matters contained in it, and suggesting others, not repugnant, which take off the effect of them.

"And upon this ground, where one Swallow, a citizen of London, was committed for refusing to accept the office of an alderman of the said city, to which he had been elected, and the custom of the city justifying a commitment for such a refusal, and the election and refusal were set forth in the return to the habeas corpus; he filed a suggestion in the Crown office, that he was an officer of the King's mint, and that all such officers were exempted from all city offices, both by prescription and by the King's charter: and therefore the patent of the grant of his office, and also the patent of the exemption, being inrolled in the court, he was discharged."

Where the return shows that the prisoner is legally detained on a civil process, he may, by affidavit, show that he is privileged from arrest. *Ex parte Dakins*, 39 *Law and Eq.*, 331; or that he was arrested on a privileged day, as on Sunday. *Ex parte Eggington*, 24 *Law and Eq.*, 146.

It does not admit of question, that it was by its use in criminal cases, and especially in state prosecutions, that the writ of habeas corpus acquired its notoriety, and became an object of jealous regard on the part of the people of England. It was in the struggles for political power, in resisting the encroachments of the crown, upon popular rights, that it became conspicuous, not only as an invaluable personal shield against oppression, but also as a noble bulwark of civil liberty. But for this, it, no more than the subpœna in Chancery, would have been dignified with a place in the British constitution.

It is no less certain that it was never looked to as a *means of escaping trial.* The genius of English law rebukes the thought of trying contested facts going to the merits, in a criminal case, without the intervention of a jury. There was a firmness and vigor, and not unfrequently a severity, in the administration of punitive justice, wholly inconsistent with the notion of a recognized right in the prisoner to a preliminary judicial experiment, on *ex parte* evidence, where the guilty might be acquitted, but could never be convicted.

It was the hateful oppressiveness of long and close confinement, and not the dread of a *trial by his peers,* which made the suffering prisoner of state exclaim: "The *writ of habeas corpus* is the water of life to revive from the death of imprisonment."

When the *Habeas Corpus Act of* 31 *Car.* 2 was passed, it was the common opinion and the boast of the English nation that the personal liberty of the subject was thereby forever *secured,* that is, that the right which the subject had before was now established and guarded by a most beneficent statute, fit to be called a second Magna Carta.

And what is the sum and substance, the very essence of that statute? Simply this, *that persons committed for criminal or supposed criminal matters, in such cases where by law they were bailable, should be* LET TO BAIL SPEEDILY.

The idea of an absolute discharge is nowhere suggested in it, except in the 7th section, and there it is confined to two cases—first, where the prisoner had not been indicted and tried the second term after his commitment, and second, where upon his trial he had been acquitted. In all other cases, by the clear terms of the act, the prisoner was to be discharged on giving satisfactory bail, or remanded.

It is indeed said, in *Bac. Abr., Hab. Corp., B.* 1, that "By the *Habeas Corpus Act*, 31 *Car.* 2, any of the said courts in term-time, and any judge, &c., in the vacation, may award a habeas corpus for *any prisoner whatever*, and on return thereof discharge him, if it shall clearly appear that the commitment was against law, as being made by one who had no jurisdiction of the cause, or for a matter for which no man ought by law to be punished."

This passage, sometimes cited to prove that the truth of the return might be controverted, admits of three observations.

1st. It is not true that by virtue of the statute the writ could be awarded for any prisoner whatever, for first, it was limited to that class of prisoners who were committed for criminal or supposed criminal matters; and second, it excepted out of that class, all who were convict or in execution by legal process, or who were committed for felony or treason, plainly expressed in the warrant.

2d. It proves what could be done under the writ rather than what was required or authorized to be done by the statute.

3d. It does not really touch the question whether the facts stated in the return could be controverted, but is confined to the question of jurisdiction, and proves, that for the want of that, whether shown upon the face of the return or aliunde, the prisoner might be discharged.

It is obvious, moreover, as well from the nature of the question and answers of the judges in 1758, as from the occasion which elicited their examination, that their attention was particularly directed to cases of habeas corpus not within the habeas corpus act, to cases where the petitioner was expected to show, before the writ would be granted, some probable ground for relief upon the merits of his case; and where, of course, the return would be expected to show the facts and circumstances relied on to justify the imprisonment. In a vast majority of such cases the hearing upon habeas corpus would be the first judicial hearing of the parties upon the questions involved. In such cases, and especially in all cases of private restraint, there would seem to be, if not a clear necessity for it, at least a peculiar fitness in admitting evidence of all the facts important to be known to enable the court to determine whether the imprisonment was illegal.

The following reasons may also be suggested why it is probable returns in such cases would more readily be allowed to be controverted than in cases within the habeas corpus act:

1st. They had not the same official sanction.

2d. The commitment for a "criminal or supposed criminal matter," implied some previous judicial investigation.

In the following case, decided in 1825, the court concede that where the commitment was under the act, 31 *Car.* 2, the return could not be controverted.

In *Ex parte Beeching and others*, 6 *Dowl. & Ryl.*, 209, writs of habeas corpus were issued to bring up prisoners, alleged to have been taken into custody at sea, under the provisions of the Customs Acts, and carried to the city of Rochester, and detained an unreasonable length of time for the purpose of being examined before a justice of that city, contrary to the provisions of the 57 *Geo.* 3, *c.* 87, *sec.* 6, which enacts that persons arrested under the authority of that statute, shall be conveyed before one or more justices of the peace, residing *near to the place where such persons shall be so taken or arrested.*

The return alleged, amongst other things, that the prisoners had been carried to Rochester with their own consent, and were there detained for the purpose of being examined on a charge of smuggling, whereupon affidavits were tendered on behalf of the prisoners, for the purpose of contradicting the facts stated in the return.

The court at first doubted its authority to inquire into the truth of the return, but finally heard the affidavits.

ABBOTT, Ch. J. "If no decision has taken place upon this statute, it is probable that the point was never made before. The object of the habeas corpus act, 31 *Car.* 2, *c.* 2, was to provide against delays in bringing to trial such subjects of the king as are committed to custody for criminal or supposed criminal matters. The person making this return is not an officer to whose custody these persons have been committed, but he is a person who by the authority given him has taken them into custody. It seems to me, therefore, that the writs of habeas corpus in this instance are not to be considered as writs issuing under the statute, 31 *Car.* 2, but as writs issuing at common law, under the general authority of the court, and consequently that the discussion of the truth of the return is left open by virtue of the 56 *Geo.* 3, *c.* 100, *sec.* 4.

"This is not the case of a committal to a jailor, or an officer of the court, for an offence known as a crime, and the only question is whether this is a criminal matter. The object of the 56 *Geo.* 3, was to give the party a summary remedy, by controverting the truth of a return, instead of putting him to bring an action for a false return.

"There is very good reason for not permitting the truth of a return to be traversed where the party is charged with a crime, for that would be trying him upon affidavits; but here we are not called to try whether these persons have committed an offence, or that which may be called an offence. The objection to the proceeding against these persons is that they have been carried a distance of one hundred and forty miles from the place where they were originally arrested. Part of the allegation of the return is, that they were taken to Rochester with their own consent. Now, I think, the truth of the return in that respect may be controverted. The 56 *Geo.* 3, was passed in furtherance of the liberty of the subject, and therefore ought not to receive a restrained construction."

The merits of the case were then discussed on affidavits, and the prisoners were remanded.

How far a court in the exercise of *appellate* jurisdiction over another *made subordinate to it*, having power by the writ of certiorari to compel the production of the record of the inferior court and also the depositions and examination upon which the commitment was founded, may review the grounds upon which the inferior court acted, and receive additional evidence with a view to discharge absolutely or let to bail, are questions which will more properly be considered hereafter.

Upon the whole it may be concluded:

1st. That in commitments for criminal or supposed criminal matters, the truth of the facts stated in the return upon which the commitment was founded could not either at common law or under the habeas corpus act, 31 *Car.* 2, be controverted with a view to the absolute discharge of the prisoner.

With a view to bail, however, extrinsic evidence might be received, 2 *Hawk. P. C.*, *ch.* 15, § 79, though it was sometimes rejected. 1 *Chitty Cr. L.*, 130.

There are occasional exceptions, as we have seen, to be met with to the rule as above stated, but they rest upon no well defined principle. But how far particular instances of departure are to be regarded as indefensible anomalies, must depend upon the obligatory force of a general rule in a proceeding so summary, and in many respects so discretionary as that in habeas corpus.

2d. That in cases of imprisonment or restraint, other than for criminal or supposed criminal matters, the truth of the facts set forth in the return could not as a general rule be controverted.

But this rule was subject to exceptions. One, clearly established, was that of impressment. This, however, was governed by a principle sufficiently comprehensive to include most other cases, to very many of which it was undoubtedly in the discretion of the court extended in practice, viz., that the prisoner had no other effectual remedy. The result is that in cases of commitments for criminal or supposed criminal matters, it is impossible to specify those in which the truth of the return could be controverted, and in all other cases it is impossible to specify those in which it could not.

SECTION X.

EFFECT OF THE RETURN IN THE UNITED STATES.

In the United States, the doctrine of the incontrovertibility of the return has often been recognized as the rule of the common law; though its qualifications do not appear to have been, at any time, very critically considered.

1. *In the Federal Courts.* Congress never having provided any particular rules of procedure under the writ of habeas corpus, the federal courts look to the common law as their guide. What that was may be seen by reference to the preceding pages.

The Supreme Court of the United States have pronounced no opinion upon the point, but it has recently been under examination in some of the Circuit and District Courts.

In the case *Ex parte Jenkins et al.*, 2 *Wallace Rep.*, 521, the Circuit Court, Grier of the Supreme Court and Kane district judge, held: That in the case of an arrest on state process, whether issued in a criminal prosecution or a civil action, of an officer of the United States, for an alleged abuse of his powers, this court, acting under the act of Congress, of 2d March, 1833, will not only hear evidence to disprove the truth of the affidavits, upon which the state authorities proceeded, but will independently of such proof consider the affidavits; and if in the judgment of this court those affidavits do not contain a prima facie ground for arrest, will discharge the federal officer. Also, if an officer of the United States has been arrested to answer an indictment found by a state court for riot, assault and battery and assault with intent to kill, the indictment not showing that the alleged offences were committed while the officer was professing to act under a law of the United States, or under some order, process or decree of some judge or court thereof, this court, on a habeas corpus, where the petition of the officer denies the offence and avers that what is alleged as offence was done in proper execution of an order, process or decree of a federal court, will go outside the indictment, and hear evidence to show the truth of the facts set forth by the officer.

Mr. Justice Grier conceded that, if they were acting upon a habeas corpus issued under the Judiciary Act of 1789, the return of the warrant of commitment, under the proviso to the 14th section, would be conclusive. *Ib.* 527.

In the case of *Nelson & Graydon* v. *Cutter & Tyrrell*, 3 *McLean*, 326, the defendants being arrested on a *capias ad respondendum*, were brought up on a writ of habeas corpus, and discharged because of a defect in the affidavit upon which the writ issued. It was objected, on the hearing, that the return of the capias was conclusive; but the court said that the writ could not lawfully issue without an affidavit, and that they would not presume against personal liberty the existence of a sufficient affidavit, and so required it to be read. The affidavit was held defective because the indebtedness was sworn to only upon the "information and belief of the affiant." He was the agent of the plaintiffs.

In *Ex parte Smith*, 3 *McLean*, 121, the prisoner was in custody under a warrant of extradition. On habeas corpus he offered affidavits to show an *alibi* at the time of the committing of alleged offence. It was objected that the return could not be controverted, and the court declined to decide the question, as there were other sufficient grounds for discharging the prisoner.

It has been seen that the bill to render the jurisdiction in habeas corpus more remedial in cases not within the *Act* 31 *Car.* 2, which was before the House of Lords in 1758, was lost in consequence of the earnest opposition of Lord Mansfield. In the debate upon the bill he contended that the courts and judges possessed at common law all the jurisdiction in such cases which was proposed to be given by the bill. In his subsequent administration of the law in habeas corpus in such cases he seems to have acted upon that conviction; and it is perhaps owing to the liberal practice which he adopted that the rejected bill was suffered to sleep for more than half a century.

2. *In the State Courts*. The seeds, however, which had been sown in the discussion upon the bill, sprang

up and yielded appropriate fruits in American law long before the passage of the statute of 56 Geo. III.

Pennsylvania. In 1785 the legislature of Pennsylvania, in the 13th section of their habeas corpus act, adopted the proposed amendment of 1758, and in the words of the rejected bill. By the 1st section of this act, it is provided that when the prisoner stands committed or detained for any criminal or supposed criminal matter, the court or judge before whom he shall be brought on habeas corpus, shall, within two days, discharge him from imprisonment, taking his recognizance, with sureties for his appearance at the next court of Oyer and Terminer, &c., "unless it shall appear to the said judge or justice, that the party so committed is detained upon legal process, order or warrant, for such matter or offence, for which by the law the said prisoner is not bailable." So far it follows substantially the *act* 31 *Car.* 2, but it proceeds to add new and important provisions, "*and that the said judge or justice may, according to the intent and meaning of this act, be enabled by investigating the truth of the circumstances of the case, to determine whether, according to law, the said prisoner ought to be bailed, remanded or discharged, the return may before or after it is filed, by leave of the said judge or justice, be amended, and also suggestions made against it, that thereby material facts may be ascertained.*"

By the 13th section it is provided that where the detainer is not for criminal or supposed criminal matter, "the court, judge or justice before whom the party so confined or restrained shall be brought, shall, after the return made, *proceed in the same manner as is hereinbefore prescribed, to examine into the facts relating to the case, and into the cause of such confinement or restraint, and thereupon either bail, remand or discharge the party so brought, as to justice shall appertain."*

The power conferred by this act upon the "court, judge or justice" is quite sufficient to enable them to hear "suggestions" and evidence, not only in strict contradiction to the precise allegations of the return, which, in cases of imprisonment under legal process, would be to limit the right to controvert the truth of the return very narrowly, but also in disproof of the merits of the cause of detainer.

The courts of the state, however, have found, in the nature of the proceeding, the general spirit and policy of the law in relation to the trial of litigated facts and the necessity of preserving other jurisdictions, indispensable to the administration of justice, uncrippled, certain limitations of their powers under the writ of habeas corpus.

"On a habeas corpus the court is called on 'to examine into the facts relating to the case,' and therefore must necessarily determine contested facts. If it were doubtful whether the true person was arrested, they consider themselves as necessarily bound to submit the matter to the decision of a jury; but where there was a plain mistake they would not do what 'appertains to justice,' unless they interposed for the immediate relief of the confined party." *Respublica* v. *The Gaoler of Philadelphia*, 2 *Yeates*, 258.

They will not grant the writ for error or irregularity merely in the judgments or process of other courts in civil or criminal cases. 2 *Yeates'* 349; 4 *Sergt. & R.*, 149; 1 *Watts*, 66; 7 *Watts & Sergt.*, 108.

They will look beyond the commitment in a criminal case, and hear extrinsic evidence, and go into an examination of the facts, in order to ascertain whether or not there is sufficient cause of suspicion against the prisoner, and will commit or bail him when there appears to be, on such examination, probable cause for suspecting him of an indictable offence, and will discharge him when there does not. 2 *Par. Sel. Cas.*, 317; *Vaux Rep.*, 40, *n*, *id.* 206; *Commonwealth* v. *Ridgway*, 2 *Ashm.*, 247.

In *Com. ex rel. Chew*, v. *Carlisle*, *Bright.*, 36, the relators, who were "master ladies' shoemakers," were committed on a charge of conspiring not to employ any journeyman who would not consent to work at reduced wages.

On the motion to discharge,

GIBSON, J., said: "Unless it clearly appears that a prisoner brought up on habeas corpus is entirely innocent, the judge is bound to bail or remand. But difficulty or hesitation as to the law, arising from facts indisputably established is not that kind of doubt of guilt which justifies in refusing to discharge, where the mind inclines, after full consideration, to pronounce in favor of innocence. On all questions of law arising in the course of the investigation the prisoner is entitled to the benefit of the judge's decision, and although he may regret the necessity of encountering an unsettled principle without the assistance of his brethren, yet, being legally competent, he is bound to meet all questions of law; for he trifles with the rights of the prisoner and the liberties of the citizen, as secured by the habeas corpus act, when, from timidity, he delegates his functions to another tribunal, and refuses to decide on the only ground on which the prisoner rests his claim to be discharged.

"The argument, then, that I am bound to remand if I have the least doubt, holds only as to doubt of the truth of the facts in evidence, with respect to which the commonwealth, as well as the prisoner, has a right to go before a grand jury, who are the constitutional judges in that particular."

After adverting to the evidence upon which the prosecution was founded, he proceeds:

"It would be an assumption of the question to say it is criminal to do a lawful act by unlawful means, when the object must determine the character of the means. It must therefore be obvious that the point in this case is, whether the relators have been actuated by an improper motive; *and that being a question purely of fact, I am bound to refer its decision to a jury, the constitutional triers of it.*"

This decision was made in 1821. Mr. Vaux, in his "Remarks on the Writ of Habeas Corpus," published in 1846, represents the Courts of Common Pleas in Philadelphia as practicing upon a somewhat broader construction of the statute. *Vaux Rep.*, 206.

Most of the other states have also removed by statute all doubts as to the power of the court to hear allegations and evidence in contradiction to the return; so that this haze resting upon the practice at common law may be considered as cleared away, at least in most of the state courts. The provisions on this subject in several states are as follows:

OHIO. By the habeas corpus act of 1811, *sec.* 3, *Swn. St.*, 451, it is provided: "That when the said judge shall have examined into the cause of caption and detention of the person so brought before him, and shall be satisfied that the person is unlawfully imprisoned or detained, he shall forthwith discharge such prisoner from said confinement."

By the amendatory act of 1847, *Ib.*, 454, it is provided in sec. 8: "That upon the return of any writ of habeas corpus, issued as aforesaid, if it shall appear that the person detained or imprisoned is in custody under any warrant or commitment in pursuance of law, the commitment shall be considered as prima facie evidence of the cause of detention; but if the person so imprisoned or detained is restrained of liberty by any alleged private authority, the return of said writ shall be considered only as a plea of the facts therein set forth, and the party claiming the custody shall be held to make proof of such facts."

ALABAMA, *Code*, 1852, *p.* 654: "The party imprisoned or restrained may deny any of the facts stated in the return, and may allege other facts which may be material in the case; and the court, chancellor or judge may, in a summary way, examine into the cause of the imprisonment or restraint, and hear the evidence produced and dispose of the party as the rules of law may require; and if no legal cause for the imprisonment or restraint be shown he must discharge the party therefrom."

VIRGINIA. By the *Revised Code of* 1849, *p.* 614, *sec.* 6, it is provided that "The court or judge before whom the petitioner is brought, after hearing the matter both upon the return and any other evidence, shall either discharge or remand him, or admit him to bail, as may be proper, and adjudge the costs of the proceeding, including the charge for transporting the prisoner, to be paid as shall seem to be right."

FLORIDA. *Thompson's Dig.*, 529: "The return made to such writ shall not be taken to be conclusive as to the facts stated therein; but it shall be competent for the judge or court before whom such return is made, to receive evidence in contradiction thereof, and to determine the same, as the very truth of the case shall require.

"If it shall be inconvenient to procure the attendance of a witness, his affidavit, taken upon reasonable notice to the adverse party, may be received in evidence."

MASSACHUSETTS. *Rev. St.*, 1836, *p.* 658, *sec.* 21: "The party imprisoned or restrained may deny any of the facts set forth in the return or statement, and may allege any other facts that may be material in the case; and the court or judge shall proceed in a summary way to examine the cause of the imprisonment or restraint, and to hear the evidence that may be produced by any person interested or authorized to appear, both in support of such imprisonment or restraint and against it, and thereupon to dispose of the party as law and justice shall require."

MISSISSIPPI. *Hutch. Code*, 1848, *p.* 1001, *sec.* 5: "The return made to such writ shall not hereafter be taken to be conclusive as to the facts stated therein; but it shall be competent for the judge or court, before whom such return is made, to receive evidence in contradiction thereof, and to determine the same, as the very truth of the case shall require."

DELAWARE. *Rev. St.*, 1852, *p.* 412, *sec.* 5: "The return may be contradicted and may also be amended."

MISSOURI. *Rev. St.*, 1845, *p.* 562, *sec.* 2: "The party brought before any court or magistrate, by virtue of any writ of habeas corpus, may deny the material facts set forth in the return, or allege any fact to show either that his detention or imprisonment is unlawful, or that he is entitled to his discharge, which allegations or denials shall be on oath."

ARKANSAS. *Eng. Dig.*, 575, *sec.* 2: The provision is similar to that in Missouri.

NEW JERSEY. The habeas corpus act of this state, passed 1795, contains no provisions upon this point. It is in substance a copy of the *Act* 31 *Car.* 2.

MAINE. *Rev. St.*, 1857, *p.* 596, *sec.* 16: "The party imprisoned or restrained may deny facts stated in the return or statement, and may allege other material facts; and the court or justice may in a summary way examine the cause of imprisonment or restraint; hear evidence produced on either side, and if no legal cause is shown for such imprisonment or restraint, the court or justice shall discharge him; except as provided in section nine."

Sec. 9. "If it appears that he is imprisoned on mesne process for want of bail, and the court or justice thinks excessive bail is demanded, reasonable bail shall be fixed, and on giving it to the plaintiff he shall be discharged."

KENTUCKY. The habeas corpus act of this state, passed in 1796, also copied from the *Act* 31 *Car.* 2, contained no provision on the point. But by the act now in force, *Rev. St.*, 1852, *p.* 380, *sec.* 12, it is provided that "At the discretion of the officer or court before whom the writ is returned, the affidavits of witnesses, taken by either party on reasonable notice to his agent or attorney, may be used as evidence on the trial of the return;" and by sec. 11, that after the matter shall be heard, "both upon the return and any other evidence," the court or judge shall either discharge or remand the petitioner.

INDIANA. *Rev. St.*, 1843, *p.* 930, *sec.* 15. The party brought before the court or judge, on the return of the writ, may deny or controvert any of the material facts or matters set forth in the return, or except to the sufficiency thereof, or allege any facts, to show either that his imprisonment or detention is unlawful or that he is entitled to his discharge; which allegations, except in cases of commitments on a criminal charge by a justice of the peace, shall be on oath or affirmation; the petition, return, pleadings, and allegations of the parties may be amended in form or substance, without any delay or continuance of the hearing

NEW YORK. In New York the first habeas corpus act was substantially a transcript of the *Act* 31 *Car.* 2. It was not until 1813 that its provisions were extended to persons detained on civil process.

In 1818, in the case of *Cable* v. *Cooper*, 15 *Johns.*, 152, the Supreme Court denied to an officer or judge acting upon a habeas corpus out of term the power of looking beyond the return. *Spencer J.*, dissented. The legislature immediately passed an act, April 21, 1818, reciting that "Whereas doubts are entertained whether returns made to writs of habeas corpus issued under said act (1813) are traversable or examinable by facts dehors the returns," and enacting that the officer before whom a prisoner is brought shall examine into the facts contained in the return, *and into the cause of the imprisonment,* and remand, bail or discharge, as the case shall require and to justice shall appertain. *Laws of* 1818, *ch.* 277, *p.* 298.

In the next revision of the statutes the provision upon this subject was contained in secs. 40, 41, 45 and 50, 2 R. S., 469. Secs. 40 and 41 required the court to examine the facts contained in the return and into the cause of the confinement of the prisoner, and, if no legal cause be shown for its continuation, to discharge him. The 45th sec. provided for bailing him. The 50th sec. provided that:

"The party brought before such court or officer, on the return of any writ of habeas corpus, may deny any of the material facts set forth in the return, or allege any fact to show either that his imprisonment or detention is unlawful, or that he is entitled to his discharge, which allegations or denials shall be on oath; and thereupon such court or officer shall proceed in a summary way to hear such allegations and proofs as may be produced in support of such imprisonment or detention, or against the same, and to dispose of such party as the justice of the case may require."

These provisions are retained in the last revision of the statutes. 2 *Rev. St.*, 1852, 802, *sec.* 64.

It was the opinion of Mr. Justice Cowen, in the case of *The People* v. *McLeod*, 1 *Hill*, 377, that the words above quoted "are satisfied by being limited to the lawfulness of the authority under which the prisoner is detained, without being extended to the force of the evidence upon which the authority was exerted, or which it may be in the prisoner's power to adduce at the trial." The same view is maintained in *Mr. Hill's note* 30, 3 *Hill*, 658.

In the cases, however, of *The People* v. *Tompkins*, 1 *Parker Cr. Rep.*, 224, and *The People* v. *Martin*, *ib.*, 187, the question was very fully examined and the authorities reviewed by Mr. Justice Edmonds, of the Supreme Court, who held that the Supreme Court, in the exercise of its common law appellate jurisdiction in criminal matters, and any member of it out of court, under the statute might, where the commitment was by an examining magistrate before trial, not only review the grounds of commitment upon which the magistrate acted, but hear new proofs, and bail, discharge or remand the prisoner as the justice of the case might require.

But the judge admitted that the power was subject to important qualifications.

"In thus asserting and defending," said he, "the high prerogative of administering relief against unjust imprisonment, as existing in this court at common law and in its members out of court, under the statute, I must not be understood as maintaining that the appellate power thus conferred can or will be exercised in a wild or loose or arbitrary manner, or that an appeal exists as a matter of course in every case of a commitment, with a right to demand a review of the grounds of the commitment.

"Where the party is in custody, by virtue of a final judgment of a court of competent jurisdiction, he must be immediately remanded. 2 *R. S.*, 567, *sec.* 40. If the party is in custody on an indictment found for felony not bailable, there being no means of ascertaining the grounds on which the indictment is predicated, he will be remanded. *McLeod's case*, 25 *Wend.*

"If in custody on process merely irregular, he will be remanded on habeas corpus, and be remitted to the proper court to correct and remedy the formal defects in its own process. *People* v. *Nevins*, 1 *Hill*, 154; *Bank of U. S.* v. *Jenkins*, 18 *Johns.*, 305.

"If detained on civil process, regular and valid on its face, the examination will be confined to the jurisdiction of the power which issued it, and to the inquiry whether some event has not since occurred to entitle the prisoner to his discharge. *Ibid.*

"If in custody on criminal process before indictment, the prisoner has an absolute right to demand that the original depositions be looked into, to see whether any crime is in fact imputed to him, and the inquiry will by no means be confined to the return. Facts out of the return may be gone into to ascertain whether the committing magistrate may not have arrived at an illogical conclusion, upon the evidence given before him; whether he may not have been governed by malice, or have exceeded his jurisdiction; and whether he may not have mistaken the law, or, in the language of Lord Ellenborough, in the case of Sir Francis Burdett against the Speaker of the House of Commons, 14

East, 1, to ascertain whether the commitment was not palpably and evidently arbitrary, unjust and contrary to every principle of positive law or rational justice. Confined within these limits, the inquiry can be effectual for the protection of personal liberty against oppression under color of legal process. Extended beyond it, it might be eminently mischievous in retarding the due administration of justice, and therefore, though the power of exceeding those limits is clearly conferred, no discreet judge will step over them, unless for some palpable and overpowering cause."

CHAPTER IV.

THE ISSUE.

SECTION I.

ISSUE OF LAW.

The issue may be one of law simply, as where the facts stated in the return are not controverted.

Mr. Justice Wilmot, although he maintained that the nature and quality of the fact with which the party is charged and the jurisdiction which has taken cognizance of it are the only matters to be considered on the return, and that the existence of the facts stated in it could not be controverted, correctly described the issue of law.

"The writ," said he, "is not framed or adapted to litigating facts; it is a summary, short way of taking the opinion of the court upon a matter of law, where the facts are disclosed and admitted; it puts the case exactly in the same situation as if an action of false imprisonment had been brought, and the defendant had set forth the facts to justify the imprisonment and the plaintiff had demurred to the plea." *Wilmot's Opinions*, 106.

Motion to discharge. This issue may be made and usually is on motion, though in the case of *Hovey and wife* v. *Morris*, 7 *Blackf.*, 559, a demurrer to the reply was allowed. Where it is desired to test the sufficiency of the return in law, it may be done on a motion to discharge the prisoner, which has the effect of a demurrer. On this motion the return is conceded to be true. "The return," said Lord Denman, in *Watson's case*, 36 *Eng. C. L.*, 237, "must necessarily be received as true in all particulars that appear upon it in the present stage, in which its sufficiency alone is examined. We are sitting as on a demurrer, or a writ of error on the judgment of another court."

SECTION II.

ISSUES OF FACT AND LAW.

The issue may be one of fact and law, where the facts stated in the return are either controverted or confessed and avoided.

It has been seen that the facts stated in the return may be controverted; but the issue to be raised must have a necessary connection with the question of the legality of the imprisonment. It has sometimes been attempted to bring into consideration other matters, as will be seen hereafter, but they have been uniformly rejected. It is important, therefore, to note the class of facts which may properly be put in issue. The field of inquiry on this point of practice has not been accurately defined, and some obscurity has been occasioned, perhaps, by not sufficiently attending to the true nature of the writ and the questions which it necessarily involves.

The following rule, it is believed, correctly describes the nature of the facts which may be controverted. Where the commitment is under express legal process, those facts may be put in issue which, on a question arising only collaterally, are necessary to warrant the imprisonment; and where the restraint is claimed under private authority those facts may be put in issue which are legally necessary to justify the detention.

As before remarked and as there will be occasion to repeat, the object of the writ is to liberate from *illegal* restraint. The vital question in all cases of habeas corpus, is: Is the party complaining illegally deprived of his liberty? and it is the only material question except in cases of infants or persons accused of crimes where, in certain contingencies to be hereafter noticed, relating to the disposing of the prisoner or infant, certain additional inquiries are instituted.

It is important also to observe that only such questions as are necessarily involved will be determined. It is, indeed, frequently said that the right of guardianship, for instance, will not be determined on habeas corpus. But that depends entirely on whether restraint by the guardian is made the ground of complaint. If it is, the right must be passed upon. Thus if the ward be the relator seeking to be released from the custody of his guardian the guardian may stand upon his right of guardianship; the ward may dispute the right, and the court must say whether the guardian's custody is wrongful or not.

If, however, the guardian seek by the writ of habeas corpus to obtain or recover the custody of his ward, or not being a party to the writ issued at the instance of another, seek such custody by a motion on the hearing, his right of guardianship, if controverted in good faith, will not, as a general thing, be adjudicated; for in one case it is a perversion of the writ of habeas corpus to employ it simply as a process of recaption, and in the other it is not necessarily involved under the writ.

This issue may be made on the return by a reply which should be a succinct statement of the facts which are relied on by the prisoner to show the imprisonment to be illegal. It may consist of a mere denial of the facts alleged in the return or of new facts, legally admissible, to avoid their effect.

The following cases will serve to show what controverted facts and rights the courts have declined to adjudicate under the writ:

In *Rex* v. *Smith*, 2 *Str.*, 982; *S. C.*, *Ridgway Cases*, 149, the father sued out the writ for his son, aged fourteen years, who was living with his aunt. The court having a bad opinion of the father's design, refused to deliver the child to the father, and assigned as a reason that they could not determine the right of guardianship in so summary a way.

In the case of *Rex* v. *Johnson*, 1 *Str.*, 579; *S. C.*, 2 *Ld. Raym.*, 1333, the writ was sued out by the guardian for the child only six years old. The right of guardianship was not disputed, and the child was delivered into his custody, not on the ground that he had a legal right to demand it under that writ, but because the court in the exercise of its discretion thought it for the interest of the child so to dispose of it. *Rex* v. *Delaval*, 3 *Burr.*, 1436.

The reason assigned by Lord Hardwicke, in *Rex* v. *Smith*, for not determining the right of guardianship on habeas corpus was that the party would be disabled from taking the opinion of a superior court on a writ of error. *Ex parte Hopkins*, 3 *P. Wms.*, 151, *n.*; *Ridgway Cases*, 149.

In *The King* v. *Edgar*, *Ridgway Cases*, 152, the writ was sued out by the wife, directed to her husband and his three sons. She relied upon articles of separation showing a renunciation of his right to her custody. He admitted the execution of the articles; but claimed they were not binding because other articles were to be executed, which had not been done, and offered to show this by affidavits. The court declined to hear them, saying they had heard enough to proceed to liberate her.

In *Rex* v. *Clarkson*, 1 *Str.*, 447, the writ was sued out by the pretended husband for his alleged wife, directed to her guardians. She denied him to be her husband, and the court refused to hear any proof on the question of marriage, declaring that she was at her liberty to go where she pleased.

In Pennsylvania, on a habeas corpus, issued under the act of 1785, the court would not try the question of property in a master to an apprentice who had voluntarily enlisted in the United States army, under the act of Congress of December 10, 1814, and was satisfied to remain. The master, it was said, should resort to his action against him who harbored the apprentice. *Commonwealth* v. *Robinson*, 1 *S. & R.*, 353.

In Georgia it was held that a question of property could not be tried on a writ of habeas corpus. And where it appeared that the prisoner was imprisoned at her own request, to protect her from a person claiming her as his slave, and there was no objection to the discharge, the court granted the discharge, but refused to go further and adjudicate the question whether she was a slave or not. *The State* v. *Fraser*, *Dudley*, *Geo.*, 42.

The same doctrine has been applied in other states. The right of guardianship will not be determined in this proceeding. *Commonwealth* v. *Hammond*, 10 *Pick.*, 274; *The People ex rel. Barry*, v. *Mercein*, 8 *Paige*, 47; *Commonwealth* v. *Hamilton*, 6 *Mass.*, 273.

"In cases of habeas corpus the technical legal rights of the parties do not govern. A guardian, whether appointed by the parent or the court, has his ordinary civil remedy if any of his legal rights are violated. But in this summary proceeding these rights cannot be redressed; no damages can be assessed, no restoration of property can be decreed, except in cases of slaves, under our statutes." *Foster and wife* v. *Alston*, 6 *How. Miss. Rep.*, 406.

The contest about the right in all these cases should be real, not merely colorable.

In Virginia, if upon the return of the writ it appears that the applicant is a person of color, and there seems to be a real ground for litigation between the applicant and the person claiming him as a slave, the court will not determine the question of freedom upon the habeas corpus, but the applicant will be admitted to bring his suit for freedom as the statute prescribes, in forma pauperis. If, however, there seems to be no real ground of litigation as to the right of freedom, the court may discharge the applicant on the writ, without putting him to his suit.

A claim of the vice-consul of a foreign state that the applicants are slaves, supported by his own affidavit that he believes them to be so, but with an admission that the owners are to him unknown, does not afford sufficient ground for putting the applicants to their suit. *De Lacy* v. *Antoine*, 7 *Leigh*, 438.

This point was again under consideration before the same court in the case of *Ruddle's Excutors* v. *Ben*, 10 *Leigh*, 468.

PARKER, J., said: "A preliminary question arises, can the matters in controversy between these parties be properly tried on a writ of habeas corpus?

"If the issue was one of slavery or no slavery, and the right of the defendant in error to freedom was the litigated point, presenting some real and not merely colorable ground for controversy, I should concede that it ought not to be determined upon habeas corpus for the reasons assigned in the case of *De Lacy* v. *Antoine*, 7 *Leigh*, 438.

"But it appears here that the matter in question is not the right to freedom but the right to levy an execution on one who has been duly emancipated by an acknowledged owner. The real question is whether Ben is illegally confined in custody; and the solution of that question depends not upon the inquiry whether he was duly and properly emancipated, but whether, being emancipated, he is not liable to a charge which, if allowed, may or may not reduce him to his original state of slavery.

"Although the inquiry thus presented may be complicated and difficult, involving questions of fact as well as law, yet that is no reason for denying to the petitioners the benefit of the great and salutary writ of habeas corpus. It often happens that a judge is forced to decide the most embarrassing and delicate questions on the return to that writ. The writ itself applies to all cases of illegal detention of the person except that which grows out of the relation of master and slave, and it would apply to that also but that another remedy is provided, which seems virtually to exclude a resort to the writ of habeas corpus."

In the matter of Wakker, 3 *Barb. Sup. Ct. Rep.*, 162, it was held that where the warrant on which the prisoner was arrested was issued by a person who was acting as a police justice de facto, under color of an election in pursuance of an act of the legislature, that was sufficient on habeas corpus to detain him; and that the writ of habeas corpus could not be converted into a quo warranto in order to determine whether he was a police justice de jure.

CHAPTER V.

THE HEARING.

SECTION I.

THE MODE OF TRIAL.

The trial has always been to the court or judge and hence is commonly called the *hearing*. Although the trial of questions of fact under the writ by the court has been deprecated as infringing the right of trial by jury, *Wilmot's Opinions*, 106, yet the inconvenience and delay consequent upon the jury trial; the desire of prisoners to obtain and of the judges to afford instant relief in cases of wrongful imprisonment, to which, perhaps, should be added the common opinion that an order in habeas corpus had not the force and effect of a final judgment, have overcome all objections, and the practice has long been settled in England and America of submitting all questions arising under the writ to the determination of the court.

The provisions in the Constitution of the United States and of the several states, for the inviolability of the right of trial by jury, do not extend to proceedings in habeas corpus as it has sometimes been claimed. It is not provided in the Constitution of any state that all issues of fact shall be tried by a jury. The provision in all is that the right of jury trial shall not be violated; that is, the right as it was understood and enjoyed at the time of the adoption of the Constitution. And as such trial was not then demandable as a matter of right in a habeas corpus proceeding, any more than it was in a proceeding in equity, it is not now. It is, however, within the power of the court, perhaps, in the exercise of its discretion, to direct an issue of fact under the writ to be tried by a jury. This has sometimes been done but the practice has not met with general favor.

The mode of trial has been the subject of observation in several cases.

In the matter of Hakewell, xxii. *Eng. Law and Eq.*, 395, there is an intimation that a jury in some cases might be employed. That was a habeas corpus by the mother to obtain possession of her children from their father, and consequently was conducted under the provisions of the *act* 56 *Geo.* 3, *c.* 100, which enacts, section 3, "That in all cases provided for by this act, although the return to any writ of habeas corpus shall be good and sufficient in law, it shall be lawful for the justice or baron, before whom such writ may be returnable, to proceed to examine into the truth of the facts set forth in the return by affidavit, &c., and do therein as to justice shall appertain." Jervis, Ch. J., alluding to the doubt expressed in the case of *Watson*, 36 *Eng. C. L.*, whether there be any mode, other than by action, of impeaching the truth of such return or of introducing new matter, says: "I must confess I should have thought it was competent to the party, at whose suit the writ is obtained, to impeach the return upon affidavit, or to traverse it and go to a jury, or to argue upon the return that it does not justify the detention."

In New Jersey, an application to the court to empannel a jury to ascertain the facts in a case of habeas corpus, was refused as early as 1782. In the case of *The State* v. *Farlee*, *Coxe*, 41, the application was renewed in the year 1790, when it was again refused. The court said: "We have no power in such a case to order a jury. * * * The writ is a writ of right, intended for the protection of individuals against arbitrary and illegal detention; and we are to decide upon it in our own constitutional capacity, sitting here to superintend the liberty of the citizen, and to protect it from violation." To the same effect is the case of *The State* v. *Beaver et al.*, *Coxe* 80, in the year following.

In Pennsylvania, however, in 1798, it was said by the court in the case of *Respublica* v. *The Gaoler, &c.*, 2 *Yeates*, 258, that "We are called on to examine into the facts relating to the case (2 *Dall. St Laws*, 246, *sec.* 13), and must, in some instances, necessarily determine contested facts. If we had any doubt whether the true person was arrested, we should hold ourselves bound to submit the matter to a decision by a jury."

In the case of *Graham* v. *Graham*, 1 *Serg. and Rawle*, 331, in 1815, on a habeas corpus pending in the court of Common Pleas of Philadelphia county, the court ordered an issue to try whether a certain Edward Simmons had a right to hold Shephard Graham by virtue of an indenture of apprenticeship, whereby the said Shephard was bound to the said Simmons until he attained the age of fifteen years, to be instructed in the art of chimney sweeper. A verdict was given in favor of Simmons, which was set aside and a new trial ordered. On a second trial the jury found against Simmons, but a bill of exceptions was taken.

In the Supreme Court,

TILGHMAN, Ch. J., said: "The habeas corpus act (1785), authorizes the court to decide both fact and law; but it has been the practice in the Common Pleas to direct an issue for trial of facts in doubtful cases. The right to order an issue is not denied, but it is said that when an issue is ordered, the court have parted with all their power over the facts. It is true they have so far parted with their power that they cannot themselves decide the fact. But they still retain the superintending authority over the verdict. This authority is incident to the trial by jury by the principles of the common law, where the trial is in a court of record of general jurisdiction, such as the court of common pleas."

In Vermont, *Ex parte Davis*, 18 *Vt.*, 401, it was said that where a debtor, who has been imprisoned, grounds his claim to be discharged upon certain papers or documents prescribed by statute, he may enforce his right by habeas corpus; but where he grounds it upon matter *in pais*, upon which an issue to a jury might be expected to arise, he should be put to his *audita querela*.

SECTION II.

THE EVIDENCE.

1. *General observations.* The general nature and principles of evidence, the means or instruments by which it is conveyed, and the rules which govern its production in courts of justice, afford the most attractive, if not the most important field of inquiry in the whole domain of legal science; and it has been thoroughly cultivated by skillful hands. The treatises of Starkie, Gresley and Greenleaf, and Cowen and Hill's Notes, with a treatise by Phillips, leave but little room for further research in this department of the law.

If the various rules collected and expounded by these authors, whose works are within the reach of all, were of uniform application in all judicial proceedings, there would be no occasion, and, perhaps, no excuse for doing more than to refer to them. But these rules are not applied with equal strictness in all cases. They admit of some relaxation in summary proceedings, especially where the inquiry is addressed to the discretion of the court.

The proceeding in habeas corpus is summary in its nature. The common opinion has been that the order pronounced in it was not subject to review on error as a final judgment; and for this reason, perhaps, as well as from the fact that the trial was always to the court without the intervention of a jury, the same modification of the rules of evidence has been allowed in practice under this writ as has obtained in other summary proceedings addressed to the discretion of the court.

It is not, indeed, a settled question that an order in habeas corpus is not, in some instances, on common law principles, subject to review for error. It is probable that the common impression to the contrary will be found to be unsupported by the just analogies of the proceeding and order. The tendencies of the judicial mind, as will be seen hereafter, are certainly in this direction. But it is not probable that the rules of evidence applicable to the proceeding will undergo any change on that account.

2. *Evidence in summary proceedings.* There are numerous applications to the court, in civil and criminal cases, which are addressed to the discretion of the court, upon the hearing of which some departure from the rules of evidence as applied in trials to the jury is permitted. The ground of such practice is thus stated by *Tilghman, Ch. J.*, in *Shortz* v. *Quigley*, 1 *Binn.*, 222: "The motion to open the judgment was an appeal to the court to exercise a summary jurisdiction on principles of equity. In hearing these motions courts are not tied down to those strict rules of evidence which govern them in trials by jury; because it is presumed that their knowledge of the law prevents their being carried away by the weight of testimony not strictly legal."

In the case of *The State* v. *Lyon*, *Coxe*, 403, parol evidence being offered to support the claim to freedom it was objected to but allowed by the court, which said:

"It has been the constant practice of the court in cases of this kind, to hear *viva voce* testimony when offered. The general principle in the admission of evidence, is not that courts are restricted by narrower rules in receiving testimony than juries are; but that being able to discriminate between that which ought to be listened to, and that which should be disregarded, are not prohibited from hearing any evidence which they may think calculated to illustrate the subject before them."

An instance of the application of this doctrine is found in *The Matter of Heywood*, 1 *Sandf. Sup. Ct.*, 701. In that case the validity of the process under which the prisoner was detained by the police justice being in question, the justice and clerk who happened to be present were called as witnesses by the prisoner, to prove upon what complaint or other papers the prisoner was arrested and committed, and the clerk having with him the original complaint, that was offered. It was objected that this evidence was not the best, that the complaint was a record of the police court and could not be produced and carried about the city, neither was it proper to call the police justice to prove his judicial acts or omissions. But the court, Sandford, J., said:

"The inquiry before me is, on what documents did the justice issue his warrant against the prisoner. This inquiry is by the statute made summary; and if these gentlemen were not present, or if they were here without the complaint, I should feel bound to receive the best evidence that was at hand, or which a prisoner with reasonable diligence might procure, both as to what writings were the ground of the proceeding against him, and what those writings contained; without regard to the ordinary rules of evidence. The clerk is here, and as he states has the complaint, I think he should produce it. As to the justice, he is not to be asked about his reasons or his judgment in the matter. It is simply this, on what affidavit and papers did this warrant issue. Neither the justice nor the clerk interpose any objection to being sworn, and can have no feeling on the subject.

"It is in no respect *infra dignitatem* for the judge to appear as a witness in this mode.

"In the habeas corpus case of Prime, Ward & Co., Judge Edmonds of the Supreme Court whose warrant was under review came voluntarily and was examined as a witness, And Judge Betts of the U. S. District Court as I am informed, appeared in the same manner before Judge Edmonds in the extradition case of Metzger."

3. *Competency of witnesses.* In the case of the *Commonwealth* v. *Harrison*, 11 *Mass.*, 63, it was held that the relator, the person on whose application the writ issued, was an incompetent witness.

In the case of the *Commonwealth* v. *Cushing*, 11 *Mass.*, 67, before the same court, the party for whose benefit the writ issued, was allowed to give evidence. No objection appears to have been made, and it does not expressly appear that the writ issued on his application, though that seems to be a fair inference.

In the case of the *United States* v. *Wyngall*, 5 *Hill*, 16, it was intimated by the Supreme Court of New York, that the relator was not a competent witness, though the admission of his evidence by the court below was an error which could not, under their statute, be reviewed.

In the case of *The People ex rel. Ordonaux*, v. *Chegaray & Condert*, 18 *Wend.*, 637, it was doubted whether the relator claiming the custody of children which her husband, their father, had placed under the care of the defendant for instruction, was a competent witness, the controversy being essentially between the wife and husband. But her affidavit was read.

In the case of *The People, ex rel. Barry*, v. *Mercein*, 8 *Paige*, 47, the controversy relating to the custody of a child of the relator and his wife, the defendant's daughter, the Chancellor said: "the wife is a competent witness for the defendant to prove acts of cruelty committed by her husband on her, to justify her separation from him and her refusal to return to his house; but she cannot testify to his general character or as to any misconduct of his in any other respect."

In the matter of Belt, 1 *Parker Cr. Rep.*, 169, it was held that the claimant of a fugitive slave on a habeas corpus, sued out by the fugitive, was an incompetent witness.

4. *Evidence by affidavit.* It was not provided by statute in England until the passage of the act, 56 *Geo. III.*, *c.* 100, *sec.* 3, that the truth of the facts set forth in the return in cases other than commitments for criminal or supposed criminal matter, might be examined into by affidavit; but it was nevertheless the practice to do so, long before that period. *Foster's letter*, 20 *How. St. Tr.*, 1376; *Rex* v. *Delaval*, 3 *Burr.*, 1434; *S. C.*, 1 *Wm. Bl.*, 412; *The State* v. *Lyon*, *Coxe.*, 403.

And the same practice prevailed in other summary proceedings; such as interlocutory appplications in chancery, *Danl. Ch. Pr.*, 1769; and various motions in actions at law, to set aside judgments, to obtain attachments, to enter satisfaction, &c., *Tidd's Pr.*, 440; and in criminal proceedings, for leave to file a criminal information, 1 *Ch. Cr. Law*, 697; and after conviction of misdemeanor, for leave to show matter in aggravation by the prosecutor, or in mitigation by the defendant. 1 *Ch. Cr. Law*, 564.

But the summary proceedings having the closest analogy to the proceeding in habeas corpus, are motions for rules to show cause why the applicant should not be discharged from an alleged wrongful imprisonment, as where the defendant was arrested in a civil action on Sunday, *Atkinson* v. *Jameson*, 5 *T. R.*, 25; *The King* v. *Myers*, 1 *T. R.*, 265; and in cases of impressed soldiers, *Rex* v. *Dawes*, 1 *Burr.*, 636; *Rex* v. *Kessel*, 1 *Burr.*, 637; in which cases the merits were fully heard upon affidavits.

Other instances of summary applications on affidavits, for discharge from illegal imprisonment may be found mentioned in *Bagley's Chamber Practice*, 55, 110, 121.

This species of evidence is, certainly, liable to the objection that it is *ex parte*, and does not admit of the application of that invaluable test of truthfulness, a cross-examination. And, in some cases, the affidavits have been rejected where an opportunity to cross-examine had not been afforded. In the case of *The State* v. *Lyon*, *Coxe*, 403, which was in habeas corpus, the only evidence offered in behalf of the defendant, was an affidavit taken *ex parte* without notice to any one interested for the prosecution, and without being entitled as of any cause in court. The affidavit was objected to, and the court excluded it, saying, "The party adducing it is bound to show that the testimony is legal, and taken in a mode conformable to law. We are not satisfied that there exists any reason to take it out of the general rule."

On the argument in this case, it was conceded that the English cases showed that cases in habeas corpus were examined upon affidavits; but it was claimed that they did not show that they were taken without notice. They do not, indeed, show expressly that no notice was given, but they do not show that any notice was ever given or required, or that a cross-examination was ever had; many of them, however, do show that affidavits were taken under circumstances which preclude the idea of any notice or opportunity to cross-examine. Moreover, it is manifest that in summary proceedings generally, such as motions for interlocutory orders, or decrees in suits at law and in chancery, affidavits were used without any notice to the adverse party of the taking of them. 3 *Danl. Ch. Pr.*, 1780.

Besides, the fact that they were so taken, that no cross-examination could be had, was urged as an objection against extending the use of them. *Wilmot's Opinions*, 106.

The English practice was doubtless as stated by counsel, in the case of *The State* v. *Lyon*, above cited, viz.: "To read the affidavits with which the party was prepared at the opening of the case, and where it was requisite a day was given to the adverse party to answer them."

A similar practice has been allowed in New York. *The People ex rel. Ordonaux*, v. *Chegaray*, 18 *Wend.*, 637.

In the D'Hautville case in the court of General Sessions of the City and County of Philadelphia, in 1840, *ex parte* affidavits taken before the writ of habeas corpus was sued out were rejected by the court, which thought the "admission of such evidence would be a dangerous precedent." The court, however, admitted that it was within their discretion to receive the affidavits. They held that the party offering them could not insist upon their reception as a matter of right; and that under the circumstances of the case,—the conduct of the relator in giving notice of the taking of other evidence subsequent to the date of the writ and the lapse of time, affording ample opportunity to take the evidence contained in the affidavits objected to on like notice—they ought not to be received.

Some important questions relating to the admissibility and value of affidavits as evidence under the writ of habeas corpus, were considered by the Supreme Court of the United States, in the case of *Ex parte Bollman & Swartwout*, 4 *Cr.*, 75.

Bollman and Swartwout had been committed by the Circuit Court for the district of Columbia, on a charge of treason. The Supreme Court having granted a habeas corpus and certiorari proceeded to examine the evidence on which the commitment was grounded, that they might do that which the court below ought to have done. On this examination an affidavit of General Wilkinson, made prior to the arrest of the defendants but as a predicate for their arrest, was offered in evidence and objected to.

The court had difficulty upon two points:

1. Whether the affidavit of General Wilkinson was evidence, admissible in that stage of the prosecution.

2. Whether, if admissible, his statement of the contents of the substance of a letter, when the original was in his possession, was such evidence as the court ought to notice.

The first point involved the question whether an affidavit made before a magistrate to obtain a warrant of arrest, being necessarily ex parte, could be used as evidence on the motion to commit, after the accused was taken, and whether he was not entitled to demand that the evidence against him should be given *viva voce* and in his presence. The court held the affidavit admissible on the ground that the examination to determine whether the accused should be discharged or held to trial was not, strictly speaking, a prosecution; but merely an inquiry which, without deciding upon guilt, preceded the institution of a prosecution; and that before the accused was put upon his trial all the proceedings were ex parte. They also held that an affidavit made before competent authority, as the foundation of a commitment, was not extra-judicial, though not made before the committing magistrate, and that the affiant would be as liable to a prosecution for perjury as if the warrant of commitment had been issued by the magistrate before whom the affidavit was made.

On the second point the court was equally divided. How they were divided is not stated; but it is sufficiently plain that the Chief Justice was against the admissibility of that portion of the affidavit. In delivering the opinion of the court he says, on this point:

"Two judges are of opinion that as such testimony delivered in the presence of the prisoner on his trial would be totally inadmissible, neither can it be considered as a foundation for a commitment. Although in making a commitment the magistrate does not decide on the guilt of the prisoner, yet he does decide, on the probable cause, and a long and painful imprisonment may be the consequence of his decision. This probable cause, therefore, ought to be proved by testimony in itself legal, and which, though from the nature of the case it must be ex parte, ought in most other respects to be such as a court and jury might hear.

"Two judges are of opinion that in this incipient stage of the prosecution an affidavit stating the general purport of a letter may be read, particularly where the person in possession of it is at too great a distance to admit of its being obtained, and that a commitment may be founded on it."

A few months after the decision of this case the same question was presented to the Circuit Court of the United States, sitting at Richmond, in the case of Aaron Burr. The constitutional right of the accused "to enjoy the right to be confronted with the witnesses against him," was earnestly pressed upon the court as a ground for excluding the affidavits, made before the arrest of the prisoner, and then as the learned counsel claimed "obsolete and evaporated"—but the court, Chief Justice Marshall presiding, considered the question settled in favor of the admissibility of such evidence by the decision in *Ex parte Bollman & Swartwout.*

"That a magistrate," said the court, "may commit upon affidavits has been decided in the Supreme Court of the United States, though not without hesitation. The presence of the witnesses to be examined by the committing justice, confronted with the accused, is certainly to be desired; and ought to be obtained, unless considerable inconvenience and difficulty exist in procuring his attendance. An *ex parte* affidavit, shaped perhaps, by the person pressing the prosecution, will always be viewed with some suspicion, and acted upon with some caution; but the court thought it would be going too far to reject it altogether. If it was obvious, that the attendance of the witness was easily attainable, but that he was intentionally kept out of the way, the question might be otherwise decided." 1 *Burr Tr.*, 97.

Another important question, that of the proper authentication of the affidavit, was determined by the court in Burr's case. The affidavit of Jacob Dunbaugh was offered which was taken on the 15th of April, 1807, before B. Cenas, a justice of the peace, "to which was subjoined a certificate of Governor William C. C. Claiborne, dated 'at New Orleans, the 16th of April, 1807,'" stating "that B. Cenas was a justice of the peace for the county of New Orleans."

To the reading of this affidavit it was among other things, objected: 1st. That though the Governor of New Orleans had certified that B. Cenas was a justice of the peace yet he had not said, that it was the same B. Cenas before whom that affidavit was taken. 2d. That B: Cenas had not stated in the caption of his certificate or elsewhere, that the affidavit was taken "at New Orleans," so as to show, that he was acting within his jurisdiction.

The learned Chief Justice delivered the opinion of the court.

"The exception," said he, "is that the paper is not so authenticated as to be introduced as testimony on a question which concerns the liberty of a citizen. This objection is founded on two omissions in the certificate. The first is that the place at which the affidavit was taken does not appear. The second, that the certificate of the governor does not state the person who administered the oath to be a magistrate; but goes no farther than to say that a person of that name was a magistrate. That, for aught appearing to the court, this oath may or may not, in point of fact, have been legally administered must be conceded. The place where the oath was administered not having been stated, it may have been administered where the magistrate had no jurisdiction, and yet the certificate be perfectly true. Of consequence there is no evidence before the court that the magistrate had power to administer the oath, and was acting in his judicial capacity.

"The effect of testimony may often be doubtful and courts must exercise their best judgment in the case; but of the verity of a paper there ought never to be a doubt. No paper writing ought to gain admittance into a court of justice, as testimony, unless it possesses those solemnities which the law requires. Its authentication must not rest upon probability, but must be as complete as the nature of the case admits of; this is believed to be a clear and legal principle. In conformity with it is, as the court conceives, the practice of England and of this country, as is attested by the books of forms; and no case is recollected in which a contrary principle has been recognized. This principle is, in some degree, illustrated by the doctrine with respect to all courts of limited jurisdiction.

"Their proceedings are erroneous, if their jurisdiction be not conclusively shown. They derive no validity from the strongest probability that they had jurisdiction in the case; none, certainly, from the presumption that being a court, an usurpation of jurisdiction will not be presumed. The reasoning applies in full force to the actings of a magistrate whose jurisdiction is local. Thus, in the case of a warrant, it is expressly declared that the place where it was made ought to appear.

"The attempt to remedy this defect, by comparing the date of the certificate given by the magistrate with that given by the governor, cannot succeed. The answer given at bar to this argument, is conclusive; the certificate wants those circumstances, which would make it testimony, and without them, no part of it can be regarded.

"The second objection is equally fatal. The governor has certified, that a man of the same name, with the person who has administered the oath is a magistrate; but not that the person who has administered it, is a magistrate. It is too obvious to be controverted, that there may be two or more persons of the same name, and, consequently, to produce that certainty which the case readily admits of, the certificate of the governor ought to have applied to the individual who administered the oath. The propriety of this certainty and precision in a certificate, which is to authenticate any affidavit to be introduced into a court of justice, is so generally admitted, that I do not recollect a single instance in which the principle has been departed from. It has been said that it ought to appear that there are two persons of the same name, or the court will not presume such to be the fact. The court presumes nothing. It may or may not be the fact, and the court cannot presume that it is not. The argument proceeds upon the idea that an instrument is to be disproved by him who objects to it, and not that it is to be proved by him who offers it. Nothing can be more repugnant to the established usage of courts. How is it to be proved that there are two persons of the name of Cenas in the territory of Orleans? If, with a knowledge of several weeks, perhaps months, that this prosecution was to be carried on, the executive ought not to be required, with the notice of a few hours, to prove that two persons of the same name reside in New Orleans?

"It has been repeatedly urged that a difference exists between the strictness of law, which would be applicable to a trial in chief, and that which is applicable to a motion to commit for trial. Of the reality of this distinction, the present controversy affords conclusive proof. At a trial in chief, the accused possesses the valuable privilege of being confronted with his accuser. But there must be some limit to this relaxation, and it appears not to have extended so far as to the admission of a paper not purporting to be an affidavit, and not shown to be one.

"When it is asked whether every man does not believe that this affidavit was really taken before a magistrate? it is at once answered that this cannot affect the case. Should a man of probity declare a certain fact within his own knowledge, he would be credited by all who knew him; but his declaration could not be received as testimony by the judge who firmly believed him. So a man might be believed to be guilty of a crime, but a jury could not convict him, unless the testimony proved him to be guilty of it. This judicial disbelief of a probable circumstance does not establish a wide interval between common law and common sense. It is believed in this respect to show their intimate union.

"The argument goes to this, that the paper shall be received and acted upon as an affidavit, not because the oath appears to have been administered according to law, but because it is probable that it was so administered.

"This point seems to have been decided by the Constitution: 'The right of the people,' says that instrument, 'to be secure in their persons, houses, papers and effects against unreasonable searches and seizures, shall not be violated; and no warrants shall issue but upon probable cause, supported by oath or affirmation, and particularly describing the places to be searched, and the persons or things to be seized.' The cause of seizure is not to be supported by a probable oath, or an oath that was probably taken, but by oath absolutely taken. This oath must be a legal oath; and if it must be a legal oath, it must legally appear to the court to be so. This provision is not made for final trial; it is made for the very case now under consideration.

"In the cool and temperate moments of reflection, undisturbed by that whirlwind of passion with which, in those party conflicts which most generally produce acts or accusations of treason, the human judgment is sometimes overthrown; the people of America have believed the power even of commitment to be capable of too much oppression, in its execution, to be placed, without restriction, even in the hands of the national legislature. Shall a judge disregard those barriers which the nation has deemed it proper to erect?"

It has, probably, been a general impression that the provision in the Constitution of the United States, and which is found in the constitutions of most of the states in the same terms, that "In all criminal prosecutions the accused shall enjoy the right to be confronted with the witnesses against him," applied as well to the preliminary examination instituted to determine whether the accused should be discharged or held to trial, as to the trial itself.

No decisions of the state courts have been met with on this point of constitutional construction, and it would suffice, perhaps, to leave the matter on the decision in *Ex parte Bollman & Swartwout.* Yet, inasmuch as this provision is sometimes cited as the ground of the right of the accused to meet the witnesses against him face to face in a preliminary examination, 1 *McKinney Jus.*, 236; 2 *Hale P. C.*, 120, *Am. ed.*, *n.* 5, it may not be improper to suggest, in addition to what was said by the court in that case, that all that is contained in the Constitution of the United States on procedure in criminal cases, is found in Articles IV., V. and VI. of the Amendments. The provision in question is found in the last. This article, considered alone, appears to contemplate that stage of the prosecution which is to be decisive of the prisoner's guilt or innocence. The nature of the rights secured by this article being those which are of vital importance to the prisoner upon his trial, and the order of enumeration being that in which they naturally arise at the trial, favor the idea that it was the trial only which was had in view in the formation of the article.

It secures first the right to a speedy and public trial by an impartial jury; next the right to be informed of the nature and cause of the accusation; next the right to be confronted with the witnesses against him; next the right to have compulsory process for obtaining witnesses in his favor, and finally, to complete the security of all these, the right to have the assistance of counsel for his defence.

Again, the gradation of the three articles is not unworthy of notice. They are all designed to secure certain rights of the prisoner, but not the same rights.

They also observe a consecutive, technical order. First the warrant, then the indictment and last the trial. Article IV. treats of the warrant and secures the rights deemed essential in the first stage of the prosecution. The warrant shall not issue but upon probable cause supported by oath or affirmation and particularly describing the person to be seized. Article V. treats of the formal institution of the prosecution which the prisoner may demand before he can be called upon to answer: "No person shall be held to answer for a capital or otherwise infamous crime, unless on a presentment or indictment of a grand jury."

Article IV., as before observed, advances to the trial and secures the rights most important to the prisoner in the last stage of his prosecution.

It is also worthy of suggestion that the adoption in article V., without any qualification, of the common law procedure, by indictment of a grand jury, before whom the accused was never suffered to appear or adduce any witnesses in his favor, tends strongly, if not conclusively, to show that the provision in article VI., "In all criminal prosecutions," &c., was not designed to extend to every stage of the prosecution where testimony should be given; for it will hardly be claimed that it was intended by this provision to throw open the doors of the grand-jury room to the accused, his witnesses and counsel.

Besides, the universality of the words "all criminal prosecutions," may be satisfied by referring them to the trial in every prosecution, without extending them to every preliminary step taken in them.

Finally, if these words extend to the preliminary examination by reason of their generality, then they must include every step of the prosecution grounded on the testimony of witnesses; and so would exclude the use of affidavits against the prisoner on motions, whether preferred by the prosecution or the defendant.

Although the constitutional guaranty of the right of the accused to be "confronted with the witnesses against him," extends only to the trial; yet in many of the states there are statutory provisions requiring the preliminary examination to be conducted in the presence of the accused and of his counsel; and in one, Connecticut, he is admitted to the grand jury room and permitted to cross-examine the witnesses against him. But this is by sufferance of the grand jury. The accused has no constitutional or statutory right to be present. *The State v. Wolcott*, 21 *Conn.*, 272.

The weakness of this kind of evidence, its liability to abuse, and the propriety of prompt action of the court when an imposition is suspected, are well illustrated in the case of *Mary Heath*, 18 *How. St. Tr.*, 10.

During the progress of her trial, a motion was made for a writ of habeas corpus to be directed to John Blakney, to bring up the body of Sarah Weedon. The motion was founded on two affidavits made by her two sons, stating positively that their mother was detained against her will, &c.

The proceeding on this motion, is reported as follows:

"Mr. THOMAS BLAKNEY, attorney, offered to falsify those affidavits by affidavits, and asked the motion to be laid over to next day, which was done. On the next day he produced affidavits tending to show Mrs. Weedon was not detained against her will. The affidavits of the sons of Mrs. Weedon were *signed with a mark.*

"THE COURT: Here is affidavit against affidavit. We are imposed on by one affidavit or the other. The honor of the court is concerned. Therefore, before we do anything we will hear what John Weedon has to say. Call John Weedon!

"Mr. HARWARD objects: If this person is to be examined, I do apprehend it must be on the footing of some supposed transgression that he hath committed.

"THE COURT: No sir. It is to discover the truth. We will have no concealing of the truth in this court. Swear him.

"The court then proceeded to examine both of the sons, from which it appeared that their mother was not really detained by Blakney against her will. The matter was then debated by counsel.

"LORD CH. J. MARLAY. We are of opinion in the first place, that no habeas corpus can be granted in this case. A habeas corpus for the liberty of the subject is, a writ of right and may be applied for without an affidavit of the party, as was done in the case of my Lord Leigh, Sir Robert Viner and Sir Robert Howard. In the case of Sir Robert Viner an habeas corpus was sued for to obtain the liberty of a woman detained in his house. The woman said she was not confined by him, but chose to stay with him. But this does not appear to us at all to be the case here, that there is the least restraint upon Sarah Weedon; but on the contrary, that she is at her full liberty; for notwithstanding these affidavits of these men, it does appear so. Edward Weedon of the Gravelly Hill, in the county of Carlow, maketh oath, that Sarah Weedon is now detained (sworn 8th Nov.) by Col. John Blakney at Abbort, near Castle Blakney, in the county of Galway. John Weedon of the city of Dublin, maketh oath, that Sarah Weedon is now detained against her will, and without any legal process at law or warrant against her, at the house &c., '*in terminis terminantibus*,' the same. Both illiterate persons, and yet both make these positive affidavits of her being under restraint when it appears she was at full liberty, not only before but after these affidavits were made. These affidavits were made by marksmen, and therefore, the court sent for the person that drew the affidavits to know why he drew them in the manner they appear to us, for upon the table, these men have declared that they do not know, nay, they cannot say they believe, that she is restrained of her liberty. Can we then, when they have declared that their affidavits are not true, grant the habeas corpus? By no means.

"The next point to be considered is, whether these men could be attached for falsifying their affidavits. I am amazed to hear it said there are no precedents of persons being attached for prevarication and imposing on the court. May be not in this case, but in most great causes which have been long depending, such things have happened. Suppose a man in an affidavit to put off a trial should swear that such a bond was perfected, and he explains himself when he comes to be examined that he heard such a one say so. Is not he guilty in conscience of perjury and ought he not to be punished for prevarication and imposition? I can give instances where persons have endeavored by artful affidavits to extort exorbitant bail, for which they have been committed by the court. Now as to these two persons, they have sworn in the most express terms in their affidavits, everything which is necessary to induce the court to grant an habeas corpus! I think they ought to be committed.

"WARD, J. The only thing to excuse them is their ignorance. But as the matter now stands it is plain that the person who drew the affidavits knew they were false; knew that these men swore to a fact they did not know to be true. Really a man of business must know the practice in drawing affidavits, and what kind of affidavits will serve the end proposed by them; but these men swear further and say that they told him the same story they did now. If that be true, he drew these affidavits most falsely. He led them into perjury, and is as guilty as they are, and should as certainly be punished if we had him; but I find on inquiry he is not here, therefore as we have nobody else to punish but these men who have thus prevaricated and imposed upon the court.

"Lord Ch. J. MARLAY: It is a most wicked, profligate thing in an agent to make an illiterate man swear an affidavit he knows to be false. Whether that be Goostry's case or no I will not say, because he is not here to clear himself, but it looks very like it."

In the case of *Moore* v. *Ewing*, *Coxe*, 144, the court animadverted on affidavits drawn up by counsel and sworn to in the same words.

In the absence of any statutory provisions prescribing the mode and means of proof in habeas corpus cases, the following conclusions are believed to be warranted by the practice:

1. Affidavits, if taken before competent authority and properly authenticated, though taken without notice to the adverse party, may be received.

2. The question of their reception is addressed to the sound discretion of the court, to be exercised upon the circumstances of each case.

3. In examinations relating to criminal charges, the personal attendance of the witnesses will be required, unless it be shown that it could not be obtained by the exercise of reasonable diligence.

4. This species of evidence is of the lowest admissible grade, and therefore is to be received cautiously and scrutinized closely.

In Kentucky, *Rev. Stat.*, 1852, *p.* 379, the court at its discretion may hear affidavits taken by either party on reasonable notice to the adverse party, and they may summon witnesses.

So in Florida; and witnesses may be summoned and their attendance enforced in Alabama and Arkansas.

SECTION III.

CUSTODY PENDING THE HEARING.

Pending the examination or hearing, the prisoner, in all cases on the return of the writ, is detained, not on the original warrant, but under the authority of the writ of habeas corpus. He may be bailed on the return *de die in diem*, or be remanded to the same jail whence he came, or to any other place of safe-keeping under the control of the court or officer issuing the writ, and by its order brought up from time to time till the court or officer determines whether it is proper to discharge or remand him absolutely.

The King's. Bench may, pending the hearing, remand to the same prison or to their own, the Marshalsea. The efficacy of the original commitment is superseded by this writ while the proceedings under it are pending, and the safe-keeping of the prisoner is entirely under the authority and direction of the court issuing it, or to which the return is made. *Per Nelson, J.*, *In re Kaine*, 14 *How.*, 134; *Bac. Abr.*, *tit. Hab. Corp.*, *B.* 13; *The King* v. *Bethel*, 5 *Mod.*, 22; 1 *Vent.*, 330–346; *Fort.*, 242.

In several of the states it is provided by statute that the court may make such order for the safe-keeping of the prisoner, pending the hearing, as they may judge expedient.

SECTION IV.

ATTACHMENT FOR CONTEMPT.

At common law, when the writ of habeas corpus was returnable before the court, any disobedience was subject to be punished as a contempt by attachment. This, as has been seen, was not generally issued, prior to the 31st Car. 2, until after the third default. But subsequently it was granted upon the first. It would appear, from the answers of the judges in 1758 to the sixth question propounded to them, that although a judge of the Court of King's Bench might grant the writ in vacation, and make it returnable immediately, before himself, he had no power to enforce obedience to it in time of vacation, if the party served therewith should neglect or refuse to obey the same; though, by the answers of Mr. Baron Smythe and Mr. Justice Dennison, it would seem that the Court of King's Bench in the next term might proceed against the person committing the contempt, and enforce obedience to the writ by attachment.

In the Act of 31 Car. 2 there was no provision authorizing a judge of the court to proceed against an officer for neglecting or refusing to obey the writ by attachment for the contempt, the provision on that subject prescribing only that the officer should be subject to a penalty of £100 for the first offence and £200 for the second, "to be recovered by the prisoner or party aggrieved, by an action of debt, suit, bill, plaint or information in any of the King's courts at Westminster," and should also by such act be made "incapable to hold or execute his said office;" and, accordingly, Mr. Justice Wilmot, in his answer to the said sixth question, says that a judge in vacation had no power to enforce obedience to writs of habeas corpus, "whether they issue in cases within the 31 Car. 2, or in cases out of that act."

By the 2d section of the *Act* 56 *Geo.* 3, *c.* 100, power is given to the justice or baron issuing the writ in vacation, in cases other than those "for criminal or supposed criminal matter," to issue his warrant for the apprehension of the party disobeying the writ, and to require him to enter into recognizance with two sufficient sureties to appear in the court of which such justice or baron is a judge, at the ensuing term, to answer the matter of contempt.

It is not proposed to pursue this inquiry here fully, as it belongs more properly to the criminal jurisdiction of the courts. Where the writ is granted by, or is properly made returnable before, a court exercising a common law jurisdiction, there is no doubt of its power, in the absence of statutory provisions regulating its procedure on the subject, to punish as a contempt a corrupt or willful neglect or refusal to obey the writ, and also, by the process of attachment, to compel obedience to it promptly and completely.

What powers are conferred upon judges or other officers, to whom jurisdiction is given over the writ in vacation, in the several states for enforcing obedience to the writ, must of course be sought for in their statutes.

In some of the states, as ample power has been vested in the judge in vacation, as is possessed by the court in term-time.

In Virginia, *Code*, 1849, *p*. 614, *sec*. 9, it is provided that: "The judge issuing any such writ in vacation, or the judge before whom it is tried, shall have the same power to enforce obedience to the writ, to compel the attendance of witnesses, or to punish contempts of his authority as a court has."

In Alabama, *Code*, 1852, *sec*. 3751, it is provided that: "Any person to whom a writ of habeas corpus is directed, who refuses to receive the same, or neglects to obey and execute it according to the provisions of this chapter, unless sufficient excuse is shown for such refusal or neglect, the court, judge or chancellor, before whom the writ is returnable, must forthwith proceed by process of attachment, as for contempt, to compel obedience to the writ, and punish the person guilty of such contempt; and such person is also guilty of a misdemeanor, and, on conviction, must be fined not less than fifty or more than five hundred dollars; and is also responsible in damages to the party aggrieved."

In Maine, *Rev. St.*, 1857, *p*. 597, *sec*. 26, it is provided that: "If any person or officer, to whom such writ is directed, refuses to receive it or neglects to obey and execute it, as hereby required, and no sufficient cause is shown therefor, he shall forfeit to the aggrieved party four hundred dollars; and the court or judge, before whom the writ was returnable, shall proceed forthwith by attachment, as for a contempt, to compel obedience to the writ and to punish for the contempt."

In Mississippi, *Hutch. Code*, 1000, it is provided that the prisoner may recover a penalty of three hundred dollars of the delinquent party; and also that the "court or judge, respectively, may further punish every disobedience to such writ as a contempt, and compel obedience thereto by process of attachment."

In Missouri, *Rev. St.*, 1845, *p.* 560, *secs.* 10, 11, 12, it is provided that, in case of refusal or neglect to obey the writ, without sufficient cause being shown, the court or officer before whom the writ is returnable, shall issue an attachment and commit the delinquent to close custody in jail, "until he shall comply with the writ and obey any order that may be made by such court or officer, in relation to the person for whose relief such writ shall have issued."

CHAPTER VI.

JURISDICTION IN RESPECT TO THE VALIDITY OF LEGAL PROCESS WHEN ASSERTED AS CAUSE OF DETENTION.

When legal process is shown by the return as the cause of detention, the legality of the imprisonment is determined by the existence and validity of the process, except in certain cases which will be noticed as we proceed. And as the validity of process may be questioned on many grounds, it becomes necessary to examine the subject with attention to ascertain, as far as practicable, what defects will so far invalidate the process as to entitle the prisoner to his discharge. This examination will involve inquiries relating to the nature and extent of the jurisdiction under the writ of habeas corpus in cases of imprisonment under legal process, as well as the nature and requisites of the process. The first inquiry will be considered in this chapter under the heads of the following sections:

Section I. General nature of this jurisdiction.

II. Extent of the jurisdiction.

III. Corrective jurisdiction.

IV. The writ of certiorari as ancillary to the habeas corpus.

V. The certiorari in connection with the habeas corpus as a writ of error.

SECTION I.

GENERAL NATURE OF THIS JURISDICTION.

In a general sense this jurisdiction is appellate in its nature. The expression "appellate jurisdiction," has been defined to be "the power of one tribunal to review the proceedings of another." *Federalist, No.* 81.

"The decision that the individual shall be imprisoned must always precede the application for a writ of habeas corpus; and this writ must always be for the purpose of revising that decision, and therefore appellate in its nature." *Ex parte Bollman and Swartwout*, 4 *Cr. Rep.*, 75; *The People* v. *Martin*, 1 *Parker Cr. Rep.*, 187; *The People* v. *Tompkins*, *Ib.*, 225.

The phrase "appellate jurisdiction" does not however, necessarily import a subordination of one court or officer to another, although that is its more usual signification. It may signify the power to act judicially upon a question or right, *notwithstanding* a supposed conclusion against it, resulting from an alleged judgment. And this is its true signification as applied to the writ of habeas corpus.

It is not, strictly speaking, a power of revision, which includes properly the power to affirm or reverse the judgment or order and so establish or destroy it; but a power to arrest the execution of a void judgment or order. It acts directly on the effect of the judgment, to wit, the imprisonment; but only collaterally on the judgment itself.

The jurisdiction, therefore, under the writ of habeas corpus over the judgment or order relied on to justify the imprisonment, is only collaterally appellate.

SECTION II.

THE EXTENT OF THE JURISDICTION.

1. *Limited grounds of inquiry.*
2. *Defects cognizable under the habeas corpus.*
3. *Limitations resulting from the superior rights of other acting judicial tribunals.*

1. *Limited grounds of inquiry.* The practice in the Court of King's Bench at common law, is thus stated in *Wilmot's Opinions, p.* 106 :

"In imprisonment for criminal offences the court can act upon it only in one of three manners :

"1. If it appears clearly that the fact for which the party committed is no crime; or that it is a crime, but he is committed for it by a person who has no jurisdiction, the court discharges.

"2. If doubtful whether a crime or not, or whether the party be committed by a competent jurisdiction; or if it appears to be a crime, but a bailable one, the court bails him.

"3. If an offence not bailable, and committed by a competent jurisdiction, the court remands or commits him."

It is to be observed that these were the rules of a court possessing a general appellate or supervisory jurisdiction over all inferior courts and officers, and may not be applicable in every particular to courts of a more limited jurisdiction.

The following rule has been proposed and in several cases recognized as comprehending the whole ground of inquiry, viz.: "Where the return shows a detainer on process, the existence and validity of the process are the only facts upon which issue can be taken." 3 *Hill*, 368, *note*, § 30; *The People* v. *Cassels*,

5 *Hill*, 164; *Benace* v. *The People*, 4 *Barb. Sup. Ct. Rep.*, 31; *The State* v. *Buzine*, 4 *Harring.*, 575.

But this rule does not accurately define the extent of the jurisdiction. It does not include the case of valid process rendered inoperative by subsequent events, *The People* v. *McLeod*, 25 *Wend.*, 483; and it seems to exclude the idea of a revisory power over the facts in criminal matters by courts of legitimate appellate jurisdiction. *The People* v. *Tompkins*, 1 *Parker Cr. Rep.*, 224.

The following is submitted as a more complete definition:

Where the return shows a detainer under legal process, the only proper points for examination are the existence, validity and present legal force of the process; except where, in commitments for criminal or supposed criminal matters, the court or officer hearing the habeas corpus is invested with a revisory or corrective jurisdiction over the court or officer commanding the imprisonment, and with jurisdiction also over the offence or subject matter of the commitment, in which case the facts constituting the grounds of the commitment may be reviewed.

2. *Defects cognizable under the habeas corpus.* The jurisdiction over the process being only *collaterally* appellate, the habeas corpus, as before intimated, cannot have the force and operation of a writ of error or a certiorari; nor is it designed as a substitute for either. It does not, like them, deal with errors or irregularities which render a proceeding voidable only; but with those radical defects which render it absolutely void.

Hale, in his *Pleas of the Crown*, 584, says that the habeas corpus is in nature of a writ of right or of error to determine whether the imprisonment be good or erroneous. But in the case of *Hammond* v. *Howell*, 1 *Mod.*, 119, he expressed himself more accurately as follows: "A certiorari and an habeas corpus, whereby the body and proceedings are removed hither are in the nature of a writ of error."

A proceeding defective for irregularity and one void for illegality may be reversed upon error or certiorari; but it is the latter defect only which gives authority to discharge on habeas corpus.

An *irregularity* is defined to be the want of adherence to some prescribed rule or mode of proceeding; and it consists either in omitting to do something that is necessary for the due and orderly conducting of a suit, or doing it in an unreasonable time or improper manner," *Tidd's Pr.*, 434: "It is the technical term for every defect in practical proceedings or the mode of conducting an action or defence as distinguishable from defects in pleadings." 3 *Chit. Gen. Pr.*, 509.

Illegality is, properly, predicable of radical defects only, and signifies that which is contrary to the principles of law, as distinguished from mere rules of procedure. It denotes a "complete defect in the proceedings." *Tidd's Pr.*, 435.

It would be *irregular* to sentence a man to imprisonment in his absence, where the absence was occasioned by the order of the court pronouncing the sentence. It would be *illegal* to sentence him to imprisonment for a crime which was punishable by a pecuniary fine only.

Wise rules of procedure established for the regulation of other judicial proceedings are not to be disregarded in that of habeas corpus, when they are applicable. One of these rules is that when a record or process is only *collaterally* brought into question, it cannot be invalidated for error or irregularity. *Ex parte Kellogg*, 6 *Verm.*, 509; *Olmsted* v. *Hoyt*, 4 *Day*, 436, 441; *Pigot* v. *Davis*, 3 *Hawks.*, 25; *Walbridge* v. *Hall*, 3 *Verm.*, 114; *Cox* v. *White*, 2 *Mills Lou. Rep.*, 422; *Keen* v. *McDonough*, 8 *Lou. (Curry)*, 185; *Andrus* v. *Harman*, 2 *Mills Lou. Rep.*, 587; *The People* v. *Cavanagh*, 2 *Park. Cr. R.*, 650; *The People* v. *Nevins*, 1 *Hill*, 154; *Baker's case*, 11 *How. Pr. Rep.*, 418; *Rex* v. *Carlisle*, 4 *Car. & P.*, 415.

It matters not how flagrant the error is. As where a defendant on trial for vagrancy, was not allowed to cross-examine the prosecuting witnesses, nor to produce witnesses in her own behalf, the court upon habeas corpus could not release the prisoner. *Stewart's case*, 1 *Abbott Pr. Cas.*, 210. And where a prisoner was sentenced to the penitentiary, on conviction for horse-stealing, for one year, the law requiring a sentence for such offence for a period not less than three years, the error was held to afford no ground for discharge on habeas corpus. *Ex parte Shaw*, 7 *O. S. Rep.*

Where, however, a justice of the peace having power to fine, or imprison for a limited time, adjudged the defendant to pay a fine and stand committed until paid, the judgment was held void. The imprisonment being indefinite, was beyond the jurisdiction of the justice. *Howard* v. *The People*, 3 *Mich.*, 207;

Robinson v. *Spearman*, 3 *Barn. & Cress.*, 493; *Gurney* v. *Tufts*, 37 *Maine*, 130.

And where the act under which the prisoner was convicted, required the imprisonment to be for three months, and the commitment was, "until he should be discharged by due course of law," he was discharged by the Court of King's Bench. The court said he was committed in execution, and the exact time ought to be specified. *The Queen* v. *Green*, *Fort.*, 274.

3. *Limitations resulting from the superior rights of other acting judicial tribunals.* It is a rule essential to the efficient administration of justice, that where a court is vested with jurisdiction over the subject-matter upon which it assumes to act, and regularly obtains jurisdiction of the person, it becomes its right and duty to determine every question which may arise in the cause, without interference from any other tribunal. *Evans* v. *Perciful*, 5 *Pike*, 424; *Beaty* v. *Ross*, 1 *Branch*, 198; *Merrill* v. *Lake & others*, 16, *O*, 405; *Brooks* v. *Delaplaine*, 1 *Md. Ch. Decis.*, 351; *Winn* v. *Albert*, 2 *Md. Ch. Decis.*, 42; *Gould* v. *Hays*, 19 *Ala.*, 438; *Smith* v. *McIver*, 9 *Wheat.*, 532; *Thompson* v. *Hill*, 3 *Yerg.*, 167; *Brevoort* v. *McJimsey*, 1 *Edw. Ch.*, 551; *Waples* v. *Waples*, 1 *Harring.*, 392; *Hall* v. *Dana*, 2 *Aik.*, 381; *Green* v. *Robinson*, 5 *How. Miss.*, 80; *Eaton* v. *Patterson*, 2 *Stew. & Port.*, 9; *Mallet* v. *Dexter*, 1 *Curtis Ct. Ct.*, 178.

This rule is not without exception. A corrective jurisdiction may sometimes be exercised by a superior court, while the cause is still pending in the inferior court. In England, the Court of King's

Bench having a general superintendency over all the courts of inferior criminal jurisdiction, may remove the proceedings from any of them, except some particular statute or charter invest them with absolute judicature; and this may be done at any stage of the proceeding, but is generally refused after issue is joined. But this supervisory jurisdiction is exercised under the writ of certiorari, not that of habeas corpus. 1 *Chit. Cr. Law*, 305, 310; *Bac. Abr.*, *Certiorari, A.*

The writ of habeas corpus is designed as a searching and inquisitorial process and, undoubtedly, may be issued by a court of appellate jurisdiction, on sufficient showing, at any period of the prisoner's confinement. But when the cause of commitment is shown and the prisoner is found in custody of a court of competent jurisdiction, not illegally asserted, the writ has fulfilled its office and the prisoner should be remanded.

Where, also, it is discovered that it will interfere unnecessarily with another competent and acting jurisdiction, it will be denied as an inappropriate remedy, for it was never designed to be used to frustrate or interrupt the due course of justice, nor to intermeddle with other judicial proceedings while a ready redress may be had by application to the tribunal, whose action may be the subject of complaint.

The following cases will serve to illustrate these principles:

In the case of *Peltier* v. *Pennington and others*, 2 *Green*, 312, it appeared that the prisoner had been arrested on a capias ad respondendum out of the Supreme Court, at the suit of the plaintiffs, for the sum of $23,342.52; and on the 4th of March the court ordered his discharge on filing common bail, for material defects in the affidavit; after that order was made on the same day the plaintiffs moved for leave to discontinue, which was granted on payment of costs, with permission to enter the same at any time within twenty days, if they thought proper to do so. The court adjourned for the term on the same day. On the next day the plaintiffs sued out of the Common Pleas of Bergen a capias ad respondendum, for a different cause of action, and delivered it to the sheriff. The prisoner being in custody of the sheriff at that time as well on criminal process as on the capias issued out of the Supreme Court, gave bail at the suit of the state and demanded his enlargement in pursuance of the order of the Supreme Court. The sheriff thereupon told him he was discharged out of custody at the suit of the plaintiffs on that writ, but that he must (and he according did without liberating him at all) detain him in custody on the second writ, above mentioned. It also appeared that the Washington Banking Company, for which the plaintiffs had since been appointed receivers, had sued out an attachment against the property of the defendant as a non-resident debtor, for the same debt or cause of action for which the suit in the Common Pleas had been brought by the receivers; which attachment suit was still pending. Afterwards, and while the prisoner was detained in custody on the second capias, to wit, on the 7th of March, the plaintiffs filed a new affidavit for bail in the Supreme Court for the same cause of action mentioned in the first affidavit, and on the same day entered in the minutes a discontinuance of the original suit, but did not make the payment of costs a part of the rule, though they paid to the clerk of the court as taxed by him the defendant's costs. Whereupon the plaintiffs sued out of the Supreme Court on the next day, 8th March, and while the prisoner was in custody as aforesaid, delivered it to the sheriff and by virtue of which last mentioned writ the defendant was imprisoned at the suing out and return of the writ of habeas corpus."

Upon these facts it was moved to discharge the prisoner on the ground that his arrest and imprisonment were illegal.

HORNBLOWER, Ch. J., said: "If a judge at chambers, upon a habeas corpus, is to inquire into and decide upon the right of a plaintiff to arrest a defendant, and hold him to bail, where shall he stop? Shall he limit himself to the inquiry whether the proceedings are technically correct; or may he go further and inquire into the merits of the case, the honesty and justice of the plaintiff's demand? A defendant may be as unjustly and oppressively arrested on a regular as on an irregular writ. So there may be a regular arrest without a just cause of action. In either case the defendant is, in a general sense of the term, unlawfully arrested.

"The writ on which the defendant is detained is, *in itself*, a legal and proper one; the court out of which it issued is of competent jurisdiction. The matter in dispute is the regularity of the process, and the validity of the arrest. These are points that must and ought to be debated at bar before the court in which the cause is pending. They ought not, by means of a habeas corpus, to be drawn into discussion before a single judge at chambers. They are matters in the cause, upon which the parties have a right to be heard before, and to have the opinion of all the judges composing the court.

"If a contrary doctrine were established, every man conceiving himself improperly arrested upon mesne or final process, or entitled to his discharge upon the ground of some supposed mistake, irregularity or laches of the adverse attorney, would at once sue out a habeas corpus for his enlargement. In short it would lead to utter confusion in the prosecution of suits, and bring into conflict the different tribunals and officers of justice. I do not wish to restrict the use of this valuable writ, but we must not suffer our partiality for a proceeding so justly dear to freemen as is the writ of habeas corpus, to beguile us into an abuse of it. It is true the defendant is restrained of his liberty, and it may be that he is improperly restrained. But in this case it is not by force or violence; nor yet by mere pretence or color of law.

"It is upon process, by which and for a cause of action for which, all other matters being right, he may lawfully be imprisoned. The only questions are whether the writ issued with legal and technical regularity; and whether the defendant, under all the circumstances of the case, was properly arrested; questions, the court out of which the writ issued, is perfectly competent to decide, and which, the legal presumption is, it will decide, when called upon to do so, according to law.

"I am not a little strengthened in my opinion against entertaining this application by the singular and striking fact that not a single case has been cited, which either upon fact or principle, sustains the doctrine contended for."

Prisoner remanded.

In South Carolina it was held in the case, *Ex parte Gilchrist*, 4 *McCord*, 233, where the defendant was in custody on a writ of ne exeat, that the court could not, on habeas corpus, look into the bill to see whether it made a case upon which a court of equity had the power to order a writ of ne exeat. In the course of his opinion, Johnson, J., says:

"I should deprecate even more than the repeal of the habeas corpus act, that state of things in which tribunals, without the forms of law, would be permitted to review and control the judgment of each other, ad libitum. The habeas corpus act certainly confers no such power. Its object was to secure the citizen from illegal and arbitrary imprisonment; and the wildest speculations have never yet carried it so far as to subvert all law and order. For even in the case of *Yates* v. *Lansing*, 4 *John.*, 317; 5 *do.*, 282; 6 *do.*, 337, than which no case perhaps was ever more warmly contested, the bone of contention was whether the chancellor had jurisdiction over the subject matter for which he caused the defendant to be attached.

"Here the commissioner had power to issue the writ of ne exeat, and he is confined and imprisoned according to the strict forms of law; and the presiding judge had no more power to discharge him than the commissioner would have had to discharge a culprit committed for execution by a court of sessions."

The subject was fully examined in the case of *The Commonwealth* v. *Leckey*, 1 *Watts*, 66. The relator, Thos. B. Davis, being brought before the court on habeas corpus, objected to the legality of his arrest on a capias ad satisfaciendum, returned for the cause of his detention, that it was made *after the execution had been superseded by a writ of error*.

GIBSON, Ch. J. "The habeas corpus is undoubtedly an immediate remedy for every illegal imprisonment. But no imprisonment is illegal where the process is a justification to the officer; and process, whether by writ or warrant, is legal whenever it is not defective in the frame of it, and has issued in the ordinary course of justice from a court or magistrate having jurisdiction of the subject matter, though there have been error or irregularity in the proceedings previous to the issuing of it. *Mackalley case*, 9 *Co.*, 68 *a*; 1 *Hale P. C.*, 488.

"In *Cable* v. *Cooper*, 16 *Johns.*, 155, it was accurately said by the judge who delivered the opinion of the court, that whether the judgment or execution be voidable, is a point which the sheriff is never permitted to raise; and that having arrested the party he is bound to keep him till he is discharged by due course of law. To the same effect is *Cameron* v. *Lightfoot*, 2 *Bl. Rep.*, 1190; 2 *Saund.*, 101 *y*, *note* 2, where the authorities are collected.

"If, then, the officer cannot allege error in the process how can the prisoner do so consistently with the common law principle that the proceedings of a court of competent jurisdiction are not to be reversed or set aside by a collateral proceeding, where redress may be had by appeal, writ of error or any other direct means of review? That this principle is applicable in all its force to the habeas corpus is sustained by an abundance of authority. In *Barnes' case*, 2 *Roll. Rep.*, 157, a return that the prisoner had been commited in execution by the court of admiralty to the warden of the cinque ports till he should restore an anchor carried away by him, or pay the warden forty pounds, was held sufficient though the proceedings were irregular. So in *Bethel's case*, 1 *Salk.*, 348, it was held that if a commitment in execution be wrong in *form* only, the defendant may not be discharged, but is to be put to his writ of error. *S. C.*, 5 *Mod.* 19; and the case of the *King* v. *Elwell*, 2 *Stra.*, 794, is a still more signal instance. On motion to discharge the prisoner on exceptions to the commitment, which was conviction of forcible entry and detainer, the King's Bench refused to enter into any consideration of them till the conviction was regularly before them; and the proceedings having been removed by certiorari into that court at a subsequent term were first quashed, and the prisoner, who had been bailed in the mean time, was then discharged.

"The same principle appears to have been recognized by our own court in *Respub.* v. *Gaoler, &c.*, 2 *Yeates*, 349, where it was determined that the Supreme Court cannot discharge a party arrested on process from the Com. Pleas; and in *Commonwealth* v. *Hambright*, 4 *Serg. and R.*, 149, we refused to consider objections to an arrest upon similar process, urged on the ground of privilege.

"It must be admitted that the reasons on which the court proceeded in those two cases are not very fully unfolded; but the decisions are entirely consistent with the rule as I have stated it, and I know of none else on which they can be sustained. They may, I presume, be considered as in point, for that the arrest was on mesne instead of final process can scarce be thought a material difference. *Hecker* v. *Jarret*, 3 *Binn.*, 409, which was supposed to bear the other way, was distinctly decided on another ground; and though the power to discharge from an execution seems to have been recognized by the Chief Justice, there is no reason to think he had in view an execution merely *voidable*. Of the power to discharge from a void execution no one ever doubted; and his remark is in fairness applicable to no other. There are, I believe, few decisions on the point in our sister states. In New York it seems to be doubted whether their habeas corpus act extends to arrests on civil process; and their judges have for that reason, as well as on general principles, refused to discharge in some instances on exceptions to its regularity; as in *Cable* v. *Cooper*, already cited. But in *The Bank of the U. S.* v. *Jenkins*, 18 *Johns.*, 308, though it was held that the habeas corpus act did not extend to the Supreme Court in term-time, yet no doubt was entertained of the common law power of the court to relieve from all illegal imprisonments, whether in civil or in criminal cases; and it was expressly determined that a habeas corpus is not the remedy for a defendant imprisoned on a capias ad satisfaciendum, issued irregularly; the proper course being an application to the court from which it has issued. After this explicit recognition of the principle in a case exactly like the one before us, it is scarce necessary to refer to *Yates' case*, 4 *Johns.*, 318, in which it was determined that the Supreme Court of that state cannot discharge from a commitment by the chancellor for a contempt.

"Any other rule would present some very curious judicial phenomena.

"By an inversion of their functions, a single judge in vacation, and of perhaps an inferior court, would be legally competent to rejudge the judgments of the highest tribunals in the land; and the Supreme Court of the state, instead of proceeding systematically in the correction of errors, would be called upon to produce its results by a new and shorter process, while in the guise of writs of habeas corpus it would be flooded with appeals from the decisions of other courts on questions of bail. The rule is therefore absolutely necessary to prevent judicial proceedings from running into a state of incurable disorder; and an application of it to the relator's case is fatal to relief in this particular way.

"Every court is the proper tribunal to judge of the regularity or abuse of its process; and the remedy of the alleged irregularity here is an application to the court from which the process issued."

The observation in the foregoing case that "no imprisonment is illegal where the process is a justification to the officer" has sometimes been quoted as furnishing a test of the legality of imprisonment when raised in a proceeding on habeas corpus. But the proposition is not sustained by the more recent authorities, nor does it, standing alone, express the full idea of the court as will be seen by referring to the context. The weight of authority appears to be that an executive officer is protected by process, *legal on its face*, notwithstanding it may be shown that it was void by reason of a want of jurisdiction, unknown to him, in the court from which it emanates. *Savacool* v. *Boughton*, 5 *Wend.*, 170; *Jones* v. *Hughes*, 5 *Serg. & Rawle*, 299; *Paul* v. *Van Kirk*, 6 *Binn.*, 123; *Taylor* v. *Alexander and others*, 6 *O. R.*, 147.

But though the process be legal on its face, and therefore a justification to the officer in an action for false imprisonment, the court would nevertheless discharge the prisoner on habeas corpus if it appeared that the process was void, and that, upon the ground that the imprisonment was illegal.

In the case of *The Commonwealth* v. *Norton and others*, 8 *Serg. and Rawle*, 71, the relators had been tried in the Mayor's Court for forgery, on an indictment containing sixteen counts. The jury found them not guilty on nine, and said nothing of the rest. The court, without entering any judgment on the verdict, committed the defendants to take their trial on the other seven counts.

On return to a habeas corpus it was moved to discharge the defendants on the ground that an acquittal on the nine counts was an acquittal on the whole indictment. The court refused the motion, saying:

"It appears that Roosevelt and Eddy are in custody by order of the Mayor's Court, and that an indictment is still depending in that court. No judgment has been given on the verdict, nor do we know what judgment will be given. But we know that the Mayor's Court has jurisdiction over the offence with which the prisoners stand charged, and if they should give an erroneous judgment, remedy may be had by writ of error which will bring the case properly before us. We are of opinion that it would be improper to discharge the prisoners under the present circumstances, and therefore they are remanded to the keeper of the prison."

In Indiana, in the case of *Wright* v. *The State*, 5 *Ind. R.*, 290, the jury had been improperly discharged before verdict, so that the defendant could not be subjected to another trial; yet the court refused to discharge him on habeas corpus, and said he must apply to the court in which the indictment was pending for relief.

The Supreme Court of Pennsylvania intimated that they would carry the doctrine of non-interference with other jurisdictions, when in the regular exercise of judicial power, so far as to refuse to discharge a prisoner on a habeas corpus while under arrest on a charge of desertion, which was to be tried by a court-martial.

In the case of *The Commonwealth* v. *Gamble*, 11 *Serg. & Rawle*, 93, where the return showed that the relator enlisted in the marine corps of the United States, and was detained under arrest upon a charge of desertion, the court refused to discharge him, although he was proved to be a minor, *first*, because the enlistment of an infant at common law was good, and there was no act of Congress forbidding the enlistment of amin or in the *marine corps*, and *second*, because to discharge him would interfere with his trial before the court-martial; for, said *Gibson, J.:*

"It appears by the return to the writ of habeas corpus that he is in confinement on a charge of desertion from his post; and the law is clear, that he must abide the sentence of a court-martial before he can contest the validity of the enlistment. There would be an end of all safety if a minor could insinuate himself into an army, and after perhaps jeoparded its very existence, by betraying its secrets to the enemy, escape military punishment by claiming the privileges of infancy."

The refusal to discharge was, however, placed more particularly on the first ground. It was intimated in the case of *The Commonwealth* v. *Fox*, 7 *Barr.*, 336, that the foregoing observations relating to the second ground of discharge, were perhaps only applicable to an enlistment in the naval service, where the contract of a minor was not prohibited, but authorized.

In the case, *Ex parte H. H. Robinson, Marshal of the United States*, 6 *McLean*, 355, it appeared that a colored girl, Rosetta, was taken by a habeas corpus at Columbus, in Ohio, while passing through the state with the agent of her master, before a judge of probate, who decided that she was free, and at the same time appointed Van Slyke her guardian. That afterwards on the 24th of March, 1855, she was arrested as a fugitive from labor by the relator H. H. Robinson, under a warrant issued by John L. Pendery, commissioner of the Circuit Court of the United States. That while the matter was pending before the commissioner, the court of Common Pleas of Hamilton county, issued a habeas corpus at the instance of Van Slyke, the guardian, upon the hearing of which, the court ordered the girl to be discharged. That immediately after, she was seized by the marshal under the same warrant, whereupon the court attached the marshal for contempt and committed him, to be relieved from which, he applied to Mr. Justice McLean for a writ of habeas corpus, which was granted under the 7th section of the act of Congress, 2d March, 1833.

The court held that a writ of habeas corpus may issue to relieve an officer of the federal government, who has been imprisoned under state authority, for an act done while in the performance of his duty.

Where concurrent jurisdiction may be exercised by the federal and state authorities, the court which first takes jurisdiction can be interfered with by no other court, state or federal. It is a subversion of the judicial power to take a case from a court having jurisdiction, before its final decision is given.

The court concluded its opinion as follows:

"That the Commissioner had jurisdiction in the case is clear. While duly engaged in the investigation of the matter, the honorable judge of the Common Pleas, whose motives I by no means question, by a habeas corpus took from the custody of the marshal the body of the fugitive, which left the Commissioner without a case. It wrested from him without any authority of law, the subject of his jurisdiction. This, so far as I know, is without precedent. Had any commissioner or federal judge interposed, and by the same means disregarded and disturbed the jurisdiction of a state court, I should have felt not less concern than the eloquent counsel.

"A sense of duty compels me to say, that the proceedings of the honorable judge were not only without the authority of law, but against law, and that the proceedings are void, and I am bound to treat them as a nullity. The marshal is discharged from custody."

The same principle was applied by the Circuit Court of the United States for the Southern District of New York, where its own process was set aside, because it conflicted improperly with the jurisdiction of a state officer which had previously attached.

In the matter of Martin, 2 *Paine C. R. Rep.*, 348, *Thompson, J.*, said:

"This is a motion to quash the writs *de homine replegiando*, issued out of and made returnable in this court, by which the marshal is commanded that he cause to be replevied Peter Martin, otherwise called Lewis Martin, a citizen of the state of New York (whom John Enders and John Grace, citizens of the state of Virginia, have taken and do keep, &c.). From the affidavits upon which this motion is founded, it appears that Peter was claimed as the slave of John Enders, and owed labor and service to him at the city of Richmond, in the state of Virginia, from whence he escaped. Upon satisfactory proof of these facts being given to the Recorder of New York, he allowed a habeas corpus, upon which Peter was taken and brought before him. But before the Recorder had decided upon the case, the writs of *homine replegiando* were issued to the marshal of this district, and the custody of Peter was transferred from the sheriff to the marshal. Certain proceedings were afterwards had in the Supreme Court of the State, which it is not material here to notice. At a subsequent day, to wit, on the 20th of October last, Peter was brought before the Recorder, who after having heard the proofs and allegations of the parties, granted a certificate according to the provisions of the act of Congress, of February, 1793.

"It is not material to examine whether or not the Recorder had authority to allow a habeas corpus to bring before him the party examined as a slave. Admitting he had no authority to allow it, yet when the party was brought before him he acquired jurisdiction of the case, unless the act of Congress is unconstitutional and void. The claimant had a right to arrest the fugitive without any process, and that right is not taken away or relinquished by having such process.

"The Recorder, therefore, had jurisdiction of the case, and authority to proceed in the inquiry whether the person so seized and brought before him, doth under the laws of the state from which he fled, owe service or labor to the person claiming him.

"This inquiry may take up some time and require some delay for the purpose of procuring testimony; and whilst such examination is pending, the party must be deemed in the custody of the law, and the magistrate must necessarily have authority to imprison him for safe keeping.

"When, therefore, the writs of *homine replegiando* were served, the fugitive was taken out of the custody of the law; and this was an illegal execution of those writs whether the habeas corpus was void or not.

"If it was valid, the fugitive was in the custody of the sheriff of the city and county of New York, a state officer. And to permit the marshal, a United States officer, under a process issuing out of this court to take a party from the custody of the State officer, would be sanctioning a conflict that might be very serious in its consequences, and cannot be justified or excused.

"But if the habeas corpus was void, the execution of the writs of *homine replegiando* was illegal, for the fugitive was either in the custody of the law under the order of the recorder, or was in the custody of the complainant. If in the custody of the law, it was irregular to execute the writs pending the examination before the recorder; and if in custody of the claimant, a penalty of five hundred dollars is incurred by any person who shall knowingly and willingly obstruct the claimant in seizing such fugitive, or shall rescue such fugitive from such claimant when so arrested."

After considering the objections to the constitutionality of the act of Congress, of February 12,

1793, the judge concludes, "We are of opinion that the act of Congress, under which the certificate of the recorder was given is a valid and constitutional law; and that the writs of *homine replegiando* were irregularly issued, and must be set aside."

In the *Commonwealth* v. *Whitney*, 10 *Pick.*, 434, which was a habeas corpus directed to the deputy jailer, it appeared that the prisoner had been seized and committed to prison on a judgment after the death of the plaintiff. *Shaw Ch. J.*, said:

"The court are not prepared to say that the imprisonment was unlawful, so as to entitle the prisoner to his discharge forthwith, as a matter of right, but if it was, he has his remedy by writ of *audita querela*, in which the facts could be put in issue, and the rights of the parties more regularly settled. *Lovejoy* v. *Webber*, 10 *Mass. R.*, 101. But it is readily perceived that it might be a case of great hardship, should an unreasonable time elapse after the death of a creditor, and no administrator be appointed, and may require an extraordinary remedy.

"The writ of habeas corpus is a summary process; the power given by it, is to be exercised under a sound discretion, and with reference to all the circumstances of the case. The proceeding at present is of necessity *ex parte*. No unreasonable time has yet elapsed (about a month) since the death of the creditor, for the appointment and qualification of an administrator. Whatever claims the prisoner might have to the extraordinary interposition of the power of the court for his relief under other circumstances, we do not at present perceive sufficient ground upon which to discharge him from his imprisonment, on this process."

Instances have occurred however, where relief against irregular commitments on civil process, has been granted on habeas corpus, notwithstanding it might have been obtained, though not so speedily, on motion to the court from which it issued. In *Ex parte Beatty*, 12 *Wend.*, 229, the Supreme Court discharged a man irregularly committed by process from the court of chancery. In *Jones* v. *Kelley*, 17 *Mass.*, 116, the court relieved against excessive bail, which had been required in a civil action. In *Nelson & Graydon* v. *Cutler & Tyrrell*, 3 *McLean*, 326, the court discharged the defendants on habeas corpus, on the ground that the affidavit was insufficient, upon which the *capias ad respondendum* issued.

It would appear therefore, and it was conceded in *The Bank of U. S.* v. *Jenkins*, 18 *John.*, 305, that relief might be afforded by either mode.

It deserves to be noticed, however, that in all these instances the power to interfere was exercised or asserted by a court not only superior to the court, or officer under whose process the imprisonment was claimed, but having by its constitution an appellate jurisdiction over such court or officer.

SECTION III.

CORRECTIVE JURISDICTION.

A superior court, in the exercise of its revisory jurisdiction, may discharge a prisoner held under criminal process, where the commitment is voidable only, or where the grounds of commitment are insufficient; but to justify this it must have, by its constitution, appellate jurisdiction in the given case, and should exert its corrective power through process designed to bring under review the errors complained of, or the grounds of commitment.

1st. The court issuing the writ in such cases must be clothed with a supervisory power in the given case.

It is not enough that it is a court of more extensive jurisdiction or of higher dignity; it must have the power of revision in the particular case; the power to correct or reverse the action of the inferior court.

Thus, *In re Dimes*, 68 *Eng. C. L.*, 554, it was held that where a commitment was by a court over which the court issuing the writ of habeas corpus had no appellate jurisdiction, the grounds of the commitment could not be inquired into.

And the King's Bench would not on habeas corpus examine into the correctness of decision of a commissioner in bankruptcy remanding the prisoner, because it had not appellate power in such a case. *Ex parte Partington*, 51 *Eng. C. L.*, 648.

Nor will the writ be granted where the party is held under a commitment of a coördinate court, on the ground of fraud on the court or collusion with the officer. *Ex parte Cobbett*, 53 *Eng. C. L.*, 185.

2d. The court should exercise its corrective power by means of process calculated to bring under review the errors complained of, or the grounds of commitment. The process commonly employed for this purpose is the writ of certiorari. This writ is used in connection with the writ of habeas corpus—sometimes merely as ancillary to it, and sometimes as a writ of error.

SECTION IV.

THE WRIT OF CERTIORARI AS ANCILLARY TO THE HABEAS CORPUS.

In England, the evidence given before the magistrate, upon a criminal charge, is required to be reduced to writing and certified to the court to which the party accused may be recognized or required to appear. In case of commitment, these depositions or examinations do not accompany the warrant of commitment.

The command of the writ of habeas corpus does not extend to them. That is satisfied with the production of the body of the prisoner and a return of the warrant of commitment under which the prisoner is held. There has always been a willingness to go so far back of the commitment in such cases as to examine the depositions; for "even though the commitment be regular, the court will examine the proceedings, and if the evidence appear altogether insufficient, will admit him to bail; for the court will rather look to the depositions which contain the evidence, than to the commitment in which the justice may have come to a false conclusión." 1 *Ch. Cr. L.*, 129; 2 *Str.*, 911, *n.* 1.

To obtain these depositions resort is had to the writ of certiorari, which is usually issued at the same time with the habeas corpus, directed to the committing magistrate, requiring him to bring up the examinations or depositions, not for the purpose of being acted upon separately under the certiorari, but "in order that the court may be furnished with the means of judging in what way they should dispose of the prisoner." 1 *Ch. Cr. Law*, 127.

The case is then heard upon the habeas corpus and the depositions brought up by the certiorari. *The King* v. *Marks*, 3 *East*, 157.

The depositions being verified by affidavits have sometimes been allowed to be read, though not brought up by a certiorari, which was, however, said to be the proper course. *Van Boven's case*, 9 *Ad. & E.*, 676, *N. S.*

In some of the United States it is made the duty of the examining officer to reduce the evidence in such cases to writing. In those states where the power to issue the certiorari is vested in the court or officer granting the habeas corpus, there has been no difficulty in following the English practice of examining the depositions. But in many of the states it has never been required of the magistrate to reduce the evidence to writing, and, in such, a doubt has been felt whether the court, on habeas corpus, could look beyond the commitment at all, and, if so, how far.

There has been a decided repugnance against making the writ less remedial than it was at common law, and the tendency has been in such cases to give the hearing on habeas corpus the character of an original examination. See *post*.

The Circuit Court of the District of Columbia, in 1825, felt this difficulty and proposed to solve it by adopting the following rules of practice:

"Upon the return of the habeas corpus, if the commitment be in all respects regular and formal, and for an offence for which the committing magistrate had authority to commit, the court will, upon the request of the prisoner, issue a certiorari to certify the informations, examinations and depositions taken by and remaining with the committing magistrate in relation to such commitment; and if none such shall have been taken, will summon him to appear and state upon oath the evidence upon which he granted the warrant of commitment; and upon ascertaining such evidence will consider the same, and thereupon proceed to discharge, bail or remand the prisoner, as the magistrate ought to have done; *unless the prisoner shall require that the witnesses shall be reëxamined by the court*, in which case they will order the witnesses to be summoned, and remand the prisoner until such witnesses can be had." *Ex parte Bennett*, 2 *Cranch C. C. Dist. Col. Rep.*, 612, *n.*

In New York, where the evidence is required to be reduced to writing, it is provided by statute that the magistrate shall send up the depositions on a mere requisition of the officer allowing the habeas corpus.

SECTION V.

THE CERTIORARI, IN CONNECTION WITH THE HABEAS CORPUS, AS A WRIT OF ERROR.

In England "the Court of King's Bench hath a superintendency over all courts of an inferior criminal jurisdiction, and may, by the plenitude of its power, award a certiorari to have any indictment removed and brought before itself," to determine the validity of it, and to quash or affirm it. *Bac. Abr., Certiorari, A.*

It may be awarded to remove the proceeding from any inferior courts, to examine and affirm or reverse the proceedings and judgments given by inferior judges. *Ib.*

The use of the writ in this sense, in connection with the writ of habeas corpus, is thus explained *Bac. Abr., Hab. Corp., B.* 3: "As the certiorari alone removes not the body, so the habeas corpus alone removes not the record itself, but only the prisoner, with the cause of his commitment; and therefore, although upon the habeas corpus, and the return thereof, the court can judge of the sufficiency or insufficiency of the return and commitment, and bail and discharge, or remand the prisoner, as the case appears upon the return; yet they cannot, upon the bare return of the habeas corpus, give any judgment, or proceed upon the record of indictment, order or judgment, without the record itself be removed by certiorari; but the same stands in the same force it did, though the return should be adjudged insufficient, and the party discharged thereupon of his imprisonment; and the court below may issue new process upon the indictment."

In cases where the commitment was in execution upon a conviction, the court has refused to discharge for an imperfection in the commitment, unless the record of the conviction was brought before them by certiorari.

In the case of *The King* v. *Taylor and others*, 7 *Dowl. & Ryl.*, 622, the court was moved for writs of habeas corpus to bring up the bodies of the defendants, for the purpose of being discharged upon an objection applicable to all the warrants of commitment, viz.: that they did not show on the face of them that the magistrate had any jurisdiction over the offence imputed to the defendants.

BAILEY, J., said: "There is an old case in Fortescue which decided that if there is a conviction independently of the commitment, the court will not discharge on any defect in the warrant of commitment, unless the conviction is before them."

ABBOTT, Ch. J., said: "And this is very reasonable, for otherwise there must be as much certainty and length in the commitment as in the conviction, which would be productive of great inconvenience. We must suppose, until the contrary is shown, that there is a legal conviction to support the commitment. We must have the conviction brought up before we can take any notice of any defect in the warrant. For this purpose you may have a certiorari to bring up the record, and writs of habeas corpus to bring up the defendants." See *The King* v. *Rogers*, 1 *Dowl. & Ryl.*, 156; *In re Allison*, 28 *Eng. Law and Eq.*, 281.

The case of *The King* v. *Taylor and others*, above cited, is not however to be considered as a decision that the court will in no case discharge upon a defect in the commitment where there is a conviction. Its proper weight as an authority is noted in the case of *Regina* v. *Chancy*, 6 *Dowl. Pr. Cas.*, 281.

That was the case of a defective commitment. The writ of certiorari had been taken away in that class of cases from the defendant by statute, and the crown, having the power, had not brought up the record on certiorari. There were two questions:

1st. Whether, the commitment being bad, the court would presume the conviction to be good; the Crown, the only party interested in sustaining it, and the only party empowered to apply for the certiorari in the case, having omitted to bring up the record of conviction.

2d. Whether the record should be received on the hearing, it not having been brought up regularly by writ.

PATTERSON, J., said: "I have considered this case attentively, and have looked at the case of *The King* v. *Taylor and others;* and without at all meaning to say that what is there decided is not good law, yet it is not an authority binding upon me, because the court merely said there, that they would not look at defects in a commitment until they had before them the conviction itself, and when it was brought before them it appeared to be as defective as the commitment, and therefore the defendants were discharged. It is not therefore an authority to show that a party cannot be discharged on the ground of an error in the commitment. The case of *Wicks* v. *Clutterbuck*, 2 *Bing.*, 483, was a commitment for fishing in a pond, the commitment not stating it to be an inclosed pond. If the pond were not inclosed, fishing in it would only amount to a trespass, and would not be within the prohibition of the 5 *Geo.* 3, *c.* 14. The court there do not seem to regard whether the conviction was right or wrong. They said this commitment either pursues the conviction or it does not. If it follows the conviction, the conviction is defective; if it does not, then there is no conviction to warrant it, and accordingly decided that an action would lie against the magistrate who issued it.

"Here the certiorari is taken away, and therefore it is not in the power of the defendant to bring before the court the conviction itself, but it was in the power of the prosecutor to do so.

"It is true that on the part of the crown it was offered, in the course of the argument, to produce the conviction; but I cannot look at it, because it ought to be brought here regularly by writ. The certiorari is not taken away from the crown, and therefore might have been brought before me, and I might have looked at it."

Defendant discharged.

In a note to the case of *Hammond*, 9 *Ad. & E.*, 99, *N. S.*, it is said:

"The reporters are informed by Mr. Robinson, the Master of the Crown Office, that the understood practice is, that if the warrant of commitment be bad, and the justices or informer prefer to rely on a good conviction, it is for them to bring up such conviction by certiorari, and that it is not the duty of the defendant to remove a conviction of which he is not supposed to know anything, and which may not exist. If the conviction be not brought before the court, the court will not presume that there is a good one, or any, but will decide on the document actually before them."

In the United States courts the English practice of issuing the writ of certiorari with that of the habeas corpus in cases proper for it, has been followed. *Ex parte Bollman & Swartwout*, 4 *Cranch*, 75.

The power to grant the writ of certiorari is not coextensive with the power to grant the writ of habeas corpus. Yet a court or officer on the hearing of a habeas corpus may admit the record of conviction, although it has no power to compel its production by certiorari.

In England the Court of Exchequer has power to issue a habeas corpus, but none to issue a certiorari. *In re Allison*, 29 *Eng. Law and Eq.*, 406, there was a rule to show cause why a habeas corpus should not issue on the ground of a defect in the commitment. In answer to the rule, cause was shown, and the conviction produced, verified by affidavit.

The reading of the conviction was objected to on the ground that it had not been removed into court by writ of certiorari, and the case of *Regina* v. *Chancy*, 6 *Dowl. Pr. C.*, 281, was cited in support of the objection.

ALDERSON, B. "If the court cannot look at a conviction unless it is regularly brought before it by a writ of certiorari, a prisoner, who was improperly convicted, could never obtain relief by habeas corpus in this court. And, moreover, in a case like the present, the consequence would be, that though, on an application to the Court of Queen's Bench, the rule was discharged, yet the party might obtain a different decision in this court, because it has no power to bring the conviction before it by certiorari."

PARKE, B. "Since there is no other mode of bringing the conviction before the court, it is sufficient to produce it verified by affidavit."

The conviction was read and appeared unobjectionable. The commitment also on further examination was found to be in the form prescribed by the statute and the rule was discharged.

But although the court may admit the record where it has no power to issue a certiorari, it does not follow that it has the same power over it which a court authorized to grant the writ possesses. It may examine it to see whether it be void, and if so may discharge the prisoner although the commitment be regular. But it cannot act upon errors or defects which only render it voidable. And herein lies an important difference between the powers of courts having jurisdiction over both writs and those having power only over the habeas corpus. The former, where both writs have been issued, may for errors which render the conviction only voidable, reverse or quash the conviction and discharge or remand the prisoner. The latter can only remand him and leave him to his remedy by writ of error or certiorari. *Stewart's case*, 1 *Abbott's Pr. Cas.*, 210; *Baker's case*, 11 *How. Pr. R.*, 418.

In a late case, *In re Freestone*, 36 *Eng. Law and Eq.*, 532, the Court of Exchequer discharged a prisoner for a defect which was properly cognizable only on certiorari. By the act 5 *Geo.* IV., *c.* 83, *sec.* 4, it is enacted that "every person playing or betting in any street, road, highway or other open and public place, at or with any table or instrument of gaming, at any game or pretended game of chance," shall be deemed a rogue, &c. The defendant was brought up on habeas corpus and the commitment showed that he was duly convicted, for that, &c., he "did unlawfully play in a certain open and public place, to wit, in a third-class carriage used on the London, Brighton and South-Coast railway," &c.

POLLOCK, C. B. "We are all of opinion that the place of gaming here designated does not come within the statute. For anything that appears to the contrary, the gaming, such as it was, may have taken place in a third-class carriage, used indeed on the line of railway, but at the time of the gaming, shunted away into some yard or warehouse."

Prisoner discharged.

CHAPTER VII.

VALIDITY OF LEGAL PROCESS.

SECTION I.

JURISDICTION OF THE SUBJECT MATTER.

The various subjects of judicial cognizance being apportioned by statute, or usage having the force of law, to the several courts it is not generally difficult to determine whether in a given case a court had jurisdiction of the subject upon which it assumes to adjudicate. It is oftentimes a question of statutory construction, but in all cases the subject matter, whether relating to prosecutions in criminal or remedies in civil cases, must be such as affords a lawful predicate for the imprisonment. If the liability of officers, for acts done under void process, were the subject of inquiry it would be necessary to note the distinction which obtains between magistrates, who issue it, and the executive officers whose duty it is to execute it. It would be seen on such an investigation that the latter are protected in some cases where the former are not. As, where the process is regular upon its face and the subject matter within the jurisdiction of the magistrate, though the officer executing it will be protected by it even if informed that some condition essential to the exercise of such jurisdiction in the particular case has been omitted, yet the magistrate may not. *Welch* v. *Scott*, 5 *Iredell*, 72.

But the test of the officer's liability to the injured party, in an action of trespass or false imprisonment, is not the criterion by which to determine the prisoner's claim to discharge under the writ of habeas corpus. If the process be void the prisoner cannot be held by it, whatever may be the legal character of his claim upon the officers for the injury.

SECTION II.

JURISDICTION OF THE PERSON.

The person must not only be subject, but subjected to the jurisdiction of the court. Even the example of the Creator and judge of men has been quoted in support of this principle of the law. In *Rex* v. *The Chancellor, &c.*, 1 *Str.*, 557, "The laws of God and man," says Fortescue, J., "both give the party an opportunity to make his defence, if he has any. I remember to have heard it observed by a very learned man, upon such an occasion, that even God himself did not pass sentence upon Adam before he was called upon to make his defence."

The accused must "have his day in court." No conviction for crime or misdemeanor can be had without personal notice and for the most part actual appearance, but judgments in civil actions where the service of process is not actually made upon the person may, other statutory conditions being strictly complied with, authorize an execution for the body of the debtor.

The notice to be effectual must be served by some one duly authorized. *Reynolds* v. *Orvis*, 7 *Cow.*, 269.

In the case of *Meade* v. *Deputy Marshal of Virginia*, 2 *Wheeler Cr. Cas.*, 569, it appeared on habeas corpus that the petitioner was detained in custody on account of non-payment of a fine of $48, assessed by a court-martial, and that the court proceeded without notice. "For this reason," said Ch. J. Marshall, "I consider its sentence as entirely nugatory and do therefore direct the petitioner to be discharged from the custody of the marshal."

SECTION III.

JURISDICTION OF THE PROCESS.

Where the statute prescribes the mode of acquiring jurisdiction, it must be strictly followed. *Collins* v. *Batterson*, 3 *Mill Lou. Rep.*, 242, 245.

A warrant was held void where it issued against a man of a family, without the proof required by statute. *Curry* v. *Pringle*, 11 *Johns.*, 444; *Gold* v. *Bissell*, 1 *Wend.*, 210.

So if a justice of the peace issue a search warrant without oath that the goods are stolen, or suspicion that they are concealed in the particular place to be searched. *Grummon* v. *Raymond*, 1 *Conn.*, 40.

A justice's execution was made returnable in sixty days, when by statute it should have been ninety, and it was held void. *Toof* v. *Bentley*, 5 *Wend.*, 276; 9 *Wend.*, 338.

In Massachusetts, an execution misreciting the recognizance as to date and amount, was held void. *Albee* v. *Ward*, 8 *Mass.*, 79.

A justice having power by statute to issue an attachment against a person absconding from his own state, issued one against the resident of a foreign state, and the judgment was held void. *Lessee of Hodges* v. *Deaderick's Heirs*, 1 *Yerg.*, 125.

A justice's warrant of arrest for traveling on Sunday is void, if it issue against one not inhabiting the county, such residence being required by statute. *Pearce* v. *Atwood*, 13 *Mass.*, 324, 342.

A citizen of the United States, not in the military service, being arrested though on a military process valid on its face, even the ministerial officer who detained him was held liable in an action for false imprisonment. *Smith* v. *Shaw*, 12 *Johns.*, 257.

SECTION IV.

JURISDICTION MUST BE EXERCISED IN THE MANNER PRESCRIBED BY LAW.

The jurisdiction may be shown to be defective in some other particulars, as that it is exercised at an improper time or place.

A justice of one county cannot render a judgment in another. *Hamilton* v. *Wright*, 4 *Hawks.*, 283.

A justice convicted a man for a contempt committed in his presence, and issued a warrant of commitment, which was executed, but the conviction was void because it did not take place while the justice was acting officially. *Fitter* v. *Probasco*, 2 *Browne*, 137, 142; *The State* v. *Applegate*, 2 *McCord*, 110.

Time, however, is not always material, the provisions in respect to it sometimes being held to be only directory and not imperative; and this, in regard to proceedings in inferior courts. *Smith's Com. St. Cons, and cases cited*, 783.

The jurisdiction may also be shown to be defective in the organization of the court; as where in Massachusetts, in an action brought for a military fine, the proceedings of the court were adjudged void, because they proceeded without a judge advocate legally appointed. *Brooks* v. *Adams*, 11 *Pick.*, 441.

And it may be defective in respect to the qualification of the officer; as where a magistrate had received a deed of trust from an insolvent debtor, which was fraudulent in law as to creditors, he was held incompetent to sit as a magistrate in the discharge of the debtor under the insolvent laws of Virginia. *Slacum* v. *Simms & Wise*, 5 *Cranch*, 363.

So when the justice was related to one of the parties, and therefore disqualified by statute. *Hill* v. *Wait*, 5 *Verm.*, 124; *Bates* v. *Thompson*, 2 *Chip.*, 96.

SECTION V.

PRESUMPTIONS RELATING TO JURISDICTION.

As the want of jurisdiction renders legal process void and entitles the prisoner imprisoned under it to be set free, the existence of it becomes in all cases a question of leading importance. The power of one court to declare the judgment of another a nullity, where that judgment is only brought collaterally in question, is one which requires in its exercise cautious circumspection, even where the question arises before the highest judicial tribunal; and it becomes one of exceeding delicacy where it arises before a coördinate, or, as it frequently happens in habeas corpus, before an inferior tribunal. The question of want of jurisdiction is, not unfrequently, one of difficulty, and to aid in the solution of it certain rules have been suggested, some of which are well settled.

It is a well established and leading rule, that, "Nothing shall be intended to be out of the jurisdiction of a superior court except that which specially appears to be so; on the contrary, nothing shall be intended to be within the jurisdiction of an inferior court, unless it be so expressly alleged." *Peacocke* v. *Bell and Kendall*, 1 *Saund.*, 74.

This rule is not always of easy application and deserves therefore to be further considered.

1. *Of the distinction between superior and inferior courts.* There is no certain test by which to determine in all cases to which class any given court belongs;

but courts invested with a general common law jurisdiction in law or equity are, when exercising their general jurisdiction, superior courts within the meaning of the rule.

In *Kemple's Lessee* v. *Kennedy*, 5 *Cr.*, 185:

CH. J. MARSHALL, defines inferior courts to be "courts of special and limited jurisdiction, which are erected on such principles that their judgments, taken alone, are entirely disregarded and the proceedings must show jurisdiction."

In *Grignon's Lessee* v. *Astor*, 2 *How. U. S.*, 319, Mr. Justice Baldwin said: "The true line of distinction between courts whose decisions are conclusive if not removed to an appellate court, and those whose proceedings are nullities if their jurisdiction does not appear on their face, is this: a court which is competent by its constitution to decide on its own jurisdiction, and to exercise it to a final judgment, without setting forth in their proceedings the facts and evidence on which it is rendered, whose record is absolute verity, not to be impugned by averment or proof to the contrary, is of the first description; there can be no judicial inspection behind the judgment, save by appellate power. A court which is so constituted that its judgment can be looked through the facts and evidence which are necessary to sustain it; whose decision is not evidence of itself to show jurisdiction, and its lawful exercise, is of the latter description; every requisite for either must appear on the face of their proceedings, or they are nullities."

A court may be limited and subordinate in its jurisdiction and yet not be an "inferior court, in the sense that it ought to certify every thing precisely." *Peacocke* v. *Bell and Kendal*, 1 *Saund.*, 74.

In the application of these principles it has been held that the Circuit, District and Territorial Courts of the United States though of limited jurisdiction are not "inferior" courts under the rule. *Kemple's Lessee* v. *Kennedy*, 5 *Cr.*, 185; 1 *Smith Lead. Cas.*, 5 *ed.*, 846.

In the several states there has been some diversity in the application of the rule to particular courts. In New York the "Surrogate Court" is held to be "inferior;" but in Pennsylvania, Maryland and Alabama the "Orphan's Court," and in Arkansas the "Probate Court" are held to be "superior."

In New York the general sessions of the peace in the several counties are held to be "inferior," while in Pennsylvania, Vermont and Connecticut, a Justice's court is, under the rule, held to be "superior." *Dening* v. *Corwin*, 11 *Wend.*, 647; *Smith* v. *Fowle*, 12 *Ib.*, 911; *South Car. Law Jour.*, 195; 1 *Eng.*, 41, 182, 371; *Fridge* v. *The State*, 3 *Gill & Johns.*, 103, 113; *Wilson's heirs* v. *Wilson's admr.*, 18 *Ala.*, 179; *McPherson* v. *Cunliff*, 11 *S. & R.*, 422; *Herr* v. *Herr*, 5 *Barr.*, 428; 1 *Smith Lead. Cas.*, 5 *ed.*, 847; *Clark* v. *McComman*, 7 *W. & S.*, 469; *Holcomb* v. *Cornish*, 8 *Conn.*, 345; *Wright* v. *Hazen*, 24 *Vt.*, 143.

In the last case the court say:

"We are aware that the decisions in New York, and probably in some other states, have required the justice to know the facts limiting the extent of his jurisdiction at his peril. But no such rule has ever been applied to courts of general jurisdiction either in Westminster Hall or in this country; *and the jurisdiction of justices of the peace has become so important and extensive that we incline to believe sound policy requires us to extend the same rule of construction in favor of their jurisdiction, which is done in favor of courts of general jurisdiction.*"

2. *Of presumptions relating to superior courts.* The following propositions are founded in reason, and appear to be warranted by the authorities. The cases are fully collected and commented on in the American note in 1 *Smith Lead. Cas.*, 5 *ed.*, 816; see also, 2 *Cowen & Hill's Notes, n.* 87, *p.* 779:

1st. If it appears by the record expressly, or by necessary implication that the cause of action was beyond the jurisdiction of the court, or that the court proceeded without notice to the parties, no presumptions in favor of jurisdiction arise, and the judgment will be void.

2d. If the court is not in the exercise of its general jurisdiction, but of some special statutory jurisdiction, it is as to such proceeding an inferior court and not aided by presumptions in favor of jurisdiction.

3d. If the record contains a recital of the facts requisite to confer jurisdiction it is conclusive and cannot be contradicted by extrinsic evidence.

4th. If the record is silent as to the jurisdictional facts, they will be presumed to have been duly established; but such presumption may be rebutted by extrinsic evidence.

3. *Of presumptions relating to inferior courts.* In respect to inferior courts the following propositions appear to be warranted by the authorities:

1st. If the record does not show upon its face the facts necessary to give the court jurisdiction, they will be presumed not to have existed; but this presumption may be rebutted and the jurisdictional facts established by extrinsic evidence.

2d. If the record recites the facts which are preliminary, or conditions precedent to the right to hear and determine the merits of the cause, it is *prima facie* evidence only of their existence, and may be disproved by extrinsic evidence.

3d. If the record recites facts essential to jurisdiction, which must necessarily be considered and decided in determining the merits of the cause, it is as to them conclusive, and cannot be contradicted collaterally.

4th. When the facts required to confer jurisdiction are sufficiently established, the records of inferior courts have the same conclusiveness as those of superior courts, and are aided by the same presumptions.

SECTION VI.

GENERAL WARRANTS.

General warrants, either to arrest persons suspected of crime or to search suspected places for stolen or contraband goods, without describing the particular person to be arrested or the place to be searched, were undoubtedly contrary to the spirit of English liberty and the principles of the common law. 2 *Hale*, 150; 2 *Hawk.*, 132. But they were not unfrequently granted. 4 *Burns' J.*, 130.

It was not, however, until 1763 that their legality was brought in question in the higher courts. In that year, in the case of *Wilkes* v. *Wood*, *Loft.*, 18, Lord Camden appears to have avowed *his* opinion of their illegality. In 1765 in the case of *Money* v.

Leach, 3 *Burr.*, 1743, Lord Mansfield and the whole court declared that general warrants to seize the person, unless in cases specially authorized by acts of parliament, were illegal and void; and yet the point really decided in that case was that the warrant had not been well executed. "On the 22d of April, 1766, the House of Commons passed a resolution condemning general warrants, in the case of libels; and lest this limitation should impliedly authorize the use of them upon other occasions the House, three days afterwards, passed another vote, by which they were declared to be *universally* illegal." 2 *Hawk.*, 131, *n.*

But before these resolutions in the House of Commons, and before the decision of these cases, in the British courts, the oppression of general warrants was felt in America and was resisted with that jealous and dauntless spirit which the ardent and enlightened love of liberty of the colonists could not fail to inspire.

To enforce the Acts of Trade "writs of assistance" had been granted to the officers of the customs, who in some instances exercised their power under them wantonly and with the most exasperating insolence.

These writs possessed the odious features of general warrants—indefinite, transferable, discretionary and irreturnable—detested engines of oppression.

The people grew uneasy; the legality of the warrants was denied. Upon application made to the Court at Boston in February 1761 by one of the custom-house officers for such a writ, an exception was taken to the application.

A day was assigned for the discussion of the question, when OTIS, the champion of the people, before the court and a crowded auditory, with a "tongue of flame and the inspiration of a seer," reasoned of justice, popular rights and liberty to come.

His argument convinced and restrained the court for a season, but its real triumph was in the sacred fire which it kindled in the hearts of the people, for although uttered more than fifteen years before the Declaration of Independence, it was nevertheless a most thrilling strain in the noble prelude of the great drama of the revolution. *Hutch. Hist. Mass. Bay.*, 92; 4 *Bancroft*, 414; 2 *John Adams Works, App. A.*, 521.

It mattered not that the court, disregarding the law, subsequently granted the writs. The people were convinced of their illegality, and the use of them served to show a purpose to oppress and to prepare the minds of the colonists to resist it.

On the formation of the Constitution of the United States it was thought expedient to subject a power so liable to abuse to constitutional restraint. It was accordingly provided by the fourth article of the Amendments to the Constitution that:

"The right of the people to be secure in their persons, houses, papers and effects against unreasonable searches and seizures shall not be violated; and no warrants shall issue but upon probable cause, supported by oath or affirmation and particularly describing the place to be searched and the person or things to be seized."

SECTION VII.

REQUISITES OF SPECIAL WARRANTS.

1. *The direction.*
2. *The name of the accused.*
3. *The offence, how described and supported.*
4. *The conclusion.*
5. *The signature and seal.*

1. *The direction.* The warrant should be directed to some person or officer legally authorized to execute it. The executive officer of the court or magistrate from which the process issues is the most proper party to execute it. 1 *Salk.*, 381; 1 *Chit. Cr. L.*, 38; 2 *Ld. Raym.*, 1192; 4 *Bl. Com.*, 291.

It may be directed to any one of a class of officers without naming him, if the court or magistrate can lawfully command a member of such class, *e. g.*, a justice's warrant may be directed "to any constable of," &c. 1 *East P. C.*, 320; 1 *Chit. Cr. L.*, 49; 6 *Binn.*, 123.

A warrant to arrest, if there be no statutory limitation, may be directed to some indifferent person by name, who is no officer, but who thereby becomes authorized though not compelled to execute it. 2 *Hawk. P. C.*, *ch.* 13, *sec.* 27; 1 *Ch. Cr. L.*, 38; 1 *Hale P. C.*, 581; 2 *Hale P. C.*, 110; 1 *Salk.*, 347; 3 *Wend.*, 350.

If it be directed to no one, but be generally to take the defendant to jail, it will be void and the prisoner will be discharged on habeas corpus. *Rex* v. *Smith*, 2 *Str.*, 934; *Russell* v. *Hubbard*, 6 *Barb. Sup. Ct.*, 654.

2. *The name of the accused.* The warrant must not be general, to apprehend all persons suspected; but must be specific to apprehend some particular individual, otherwise it will be void; and the reason is it is the duty of the court or magistrate and not of the executive officer to judge of the ground of suspicion. 4 *Bl. Com.*, 291; 1 *Hale P. C.*, 580; 1 *Chit. Cr. L.*, 41; 2 *Burr.*, 1766; 1 *Bl. Rep.*, 555; 2 *Wils.*, 151.

If the name of the person to be apprehended be unknown, there must be employed in the place of it some personal description by which he may be identified. 1 *Ch. Cr. L.*, 39, 40; 1 *Hale P. C.*, 577; *The State* v. *Munson*, *Hall's Jour. Juris.*, 257; 1 *Russ. Cr. L.*, 619.

If the name inserted be not the right one, or be fictitious merely, the arrest cannot be justified, even though the person arrested be the one intended; unless indeed, he is known as well by the name in the warrant as by his true name. *Shadgett* v. *Clipson*, 8 *East*, 328; 6 *Cow.*, 456; 7 *id.*, 332; 3 *Wend.*, 350; 4 *id.*, 555; 9 *id.*, 320; 2 *Taunt.*, 400; 1 *Arch.*, 33, *note* 1; *Hoye* v. *Bush*, 1 *M. & Gr.*, 775.

If blanks are left to be filled with the names after the warrant is delivered to the officer, the warrant will be void. 1 *Ch. Cr. L.*, 39; 2 *Hale P. C.*, 114; *Fost.*, 312.

Names may, however, be inserted at any time before the warrant is delivered. 2 *Leach*, 929; *The King* v. *Winwick*, 8 *T. R.*, 454; 1 *East P. C.*, 324.

It seems that the omission of the christian name will render the warrant void, though the accused was described "——— Hood, of the parish of F., son of

Samuel Hood." *Rex* v. *Hood*, 1 *Moody C. C.*, 281; *see also Wells* v. *Jackson*, 3 *Mumford*, 458.

3. *Statement of the offence and how supported.* It is a general rule that the offence must be stated with reasonable certainty and be supported by oath or affirmation.

In considering this rule, it is to be observed that the distinction, already noticed, between superior and inferior courts in respect to their judgments, applies also to their process; and that the process of the former is favored by certain legal presumptions of regularity which are not accorded to that of the latter.

I. *Of the statement in process emanating from inferior courts, or from officers exercising a special statutory jurisdiction.*

1. The offence must be stated with reasonable certainty. *Bac. Abr., tit. Commitment, E.; Hale P. C.*, 94; 2 *Inst.*, 52; 2 *Hawk. P. C., ch.* 16, *sec.* 16.

In 1627 the judges of England, in answer to a question from the King, declared that: "Upon a habeas corpus, brought by one committed by the King, if the cause be not specially or generally returned, so as the court may take knowledge thereof, the party ought by the general rule to be discharged."

The court is to determine whether the cause of commitment and detainer be sufficient in law or not; and such certainty should therefore appear in the commitment as will enable the court to determine this question. For if the commitment be against law as being made by one who had no jurisdiction of the cause, or for a matter for which by law no man ought to be punished, the court are to discharge him, and therefore the certainty of the commitment ought to appear; and the commitment is liable to the same objections where the cause is so loosely set forth, that the court cannot adjudge whether it were a reasonable ground of imprisonment or not. *Impey's Shff.*, 522; *Hale P. C.*, 584; *Skin.*, 676, *pl.*, 2; 12 *Co.*, 130.

A warrant by a justice of the peace to apprehend a person "to answer such matters as shall be objected against him," without expressing the certainty of the crime, is contrary to law and void. 2 *Inst.*, 591; *Hale P. C.*, 577.

A commitment by the mayor of London, "for divers causes well known to the mayor," was held not good, for the commitment ought to show the cause of the imprisonment, so that the court might adjudge whether it was lawful or not. *Boucher's case, Cro. Jac.*, 81.

In a commitment for felony it was necessary that the commitment should specify the species of felony, "as for felony for the death of J. S., or for burglary in breaking the house of J. S." *The King* v. *Wilkes*, 2 *Wils.*, 158; 1 *Ch. Cr. L.*, 111; *Hale P. C.*, 122.

It was not necessary to allege in the mittimus that the offence was "feloniously" committed. 1 *Ch. Cr. L.*, 113.

In *Rex* v. *Croker*, 2 *Chit.*, 138, the defendant was committed for embezzling bank notes. The warrant did not state that the act was done feloniously, and it was therefore claimed that the defendant was entitled to his discharge. But the court said: A commitment need not have the precision of an indictment. The commitment states general evidence, and though not formally sufficient to find him guilty, yet it is sufficient if the corpus delicti be shown to us to warrant the commitment.

In the Constitution of the United States, and most of the several states, it is provided, as has been already stated, that "no warrants shall issue but on probable cause," &c. Probable cause has been defined to be, "A reasonable ground of suspicion, supported by circumstances sufficiently strong in themselves to warrant a cautious man in the belief, that the person accused is guilty of the offence with which he is charged." *Muns* v. *Dupont*, 3 *Wash. C. C.*, 31.

This must be made out by proof before the magistrate, before he can issue his warrant; but it need not be fully set forth in the warrant, for that would be to require him to state all the evidence submitted to him. It should, however, show a reasonable ground for believing that probable cause was shown to the committing magistrate.

"It must state some good cause certain." *Ex parte Burford*, 3 *Cr.*, 448.

It must be a *good cause.* It must show substantially a criminal matter, over which the committing magistrate has jurisdiction and for which the prisoner may legally be committed.

It must be stated *with certainty.* That is, the offence ought to be stated with sufficient particularity to distinguish it from other offences.

Whether it is stating the offence with sufficient certainty, simply to designate it by the name of the class of crimes to which the magistrate may find it to belong; or whether the warrant should not state the material facts proven before the magistrate, which, in his judgment, constitute the offence, or whether at least there should not be added such circumstances of identity, as to distinguish the alleged offence from all others of the same class, may be said to be questions not entirely settled.

To illustrate the point. Suppose a commitment for larceny. Is it enough to state that the accused was charged on oath, &c., "with having committed larceny," and that on examination, &c., "there is probable cause for believing that the accused did commit larceny?" Or should not the warrant state so much of the facts proved and found to constitute the larceny, as may be necessary to mark the legal character of the act, as that the accused was charged, &c., "with having stolen and carried away one gold watch, the property of A," &c., and that, "on examination, &c., there is probable cause for believing that the accused did commit the said larceny?"

Or at least should not the warrant state the name of the person against whom the offence was committed?

One would suppose that at this day such questions could be very readily answered; and yet courts of the highest respectability have differed in regard to them.

In commitments at common law for treason, it was at one time held that some particular species of treason must be expressed in the warrant. 3 *Viner Abr.*, 512; 2 *Hawk. P. C.*, *ch.* 16, *sec.* 16. But afterwards, the commitment was held sufficient where it was simply "for treason." *Rex* v. *Wyndham*, 1 *Str.*, 3; 3 *Viner Abr.*, 515; *The King* v. *Despard*, 7 *T. R.*, 736.

In the last case, the court relied very much upon the practice in commitments for that crime — treason. No cases of commitments for other crimes in such general terms were cited, and it is believed that none can be found. It is indeed intimated by Coke, 2 *Inst.*, 52, that a commitment "for felony," in general, would be good; and it has been said, 2 *Hawk. P. C.*, *ch.* 16, *sec.* 16, that there were precedents of commitments for felony in general, in good authors. Yet Coke, in the same book, at page 591, also intimates that a commitment for felony in general without showing the species of the offence is not good; and such is undoubtedly the received opinion. *Hale P. C.*, 122. It will be observed, that this author did not deem it sufficient to state the offence in the name of the class or species merely, as "burglary" only, but "for burglary in breaking the house of J. S."

The reason given for requiring certainty in the commitment, deserves attention. It is said to be, to enable the Court of King's Bench, when the commitment is returned on a habeas corpus, which is also said to be in the nature of a writ of error, to determine whether the imprisonment be erroneous or not. *Hale P. C.*, 584. This property of the writ of habeas corpus, we have already said was more appropriately ascribed by the same learned jurist, when upon the bench, to the concurrent writs of habeas corpus and certiorari. *Hammon* v. *Howell*, 1 *Mod.*, 119.

The use of the certiorari as ancillary to the writ of habeas corpus, has been explained. And its agency should be borne in mind in considering this question; for the court under that writ, in the exercise of its strictly appellate jurisdiction in criminal matters, on reviewing the grounds of commitment frequently refused to discharge, where it was conceded, if the case had stood on the commitment alone, the prisoner would have been entitled to his discharge.

It has before been stated, that the writ of certiorari usually accompanied the writ of habeas corpus, and that it was through that, that the court not only exercised its corrective jurisdiction, but acquired possession of the examination and depositions upon which the commitment was founded. So that when a question was made on the sufficiency of the commitment, the court had before them, and took into consideration the proofs, and in effect allowed them to help out a defective commitment, or in other words, refused to discharge the prisoner however irregular the commitment, if they discovered in the depositions sufficient evidence of any offence to justify a detainer of the prisoner, and put him upon his trial.

Thus in the case of *The King* v. *Judd*, 2 *T. R.*, 255, it was not alleged in the commitment that the criminal act was done feloniously, nor could the court collect from the facts stated, that the act was felonious; yet, because they were satisfied from the depositions that some offence had been committed by the prisoner, they refused to discharge him. And in *Rex* v. *Marks*, 3 *East*, 166, the practice of remanding on defective commitments where the depositions disclosed any offence is stated to have been settled; though in that case a change was introduced of discharging from the defective commitment, and of committing *de novo*.

In many of the states the testimony of witnesses in criminal examinations is not reduced to writing, and the prisoner must be remanded or discharged according as the court shall determine the sufficiency of the commitment on its face. In such cases, however, if the commitment be found fatally defective there may be a power or a duty enjoined by statute, to proceed and hear the case *de novo*, as will be hereafter shown.

Where there are no depositions to show upon what evidence the commitment was founded, there would seem to be a peculiar reason why the commitment should be required to show the facts claimed to constitute the offence, otherwise the power of the superior courts to determine whether the imprisonment be illegal or not may be seriously abridged.

On the whole it is believed that a commitment, in the absence of any statutory provisions prescribing its form and contents, does not sufficiently state the offence by simply designating it by the species or class of crimes to which the committing magistrate may consider it to belong; but that it ought to state the facts charged or found to constitute the offence, with sufficient particularity to enable the court, on a return to a habeas corpus, to determine what particular crime is charged against the prisoner.

And if the commitment fails to do this, the prisoner ought to be discharged from that commitment whatever else the court may afterwards do with him in the exercise of its appellate jurisdiction in criminal matters, if it have any.

2d. The probable cause must be supported by oath or affirmation, and that ought to appear on the face of the warrant.

It must be supported by oath or affirmation.

It has been said that at common law an oath was not indispensable to justify the magistrate in issuing his warrant. 4 *Bl. Com.*, 290; 2 *Hawk. P. C.*, *ch.* 16, *sec.* 17; 2 *Hale P. C.*, 110; *Rex* v. *Wilkes*, 2 *Wils.*, 158; *Wyndham's case*, *Str.*, 3. Such, undoubtedly, was the law where the offence was committed in the presence of the magistrate; but it is not so clear that a magistrate possessed such power where he was not present at the commission of the offence. It must certainly have been an unsafe course and could perhaps only be justified, if at all, by proving the commission of the offence, for Holt, Ch. J., in *Rex* v. *Pain*, *Comb.*, 359, said, that if a magistrate commit without oath made before him he must make out the cause at his peril. But in a late case the Court of King's Bench have held that at common law a magistrate has no power to issue a warrant to arrest without oath. In the case of *Caudle* v. *Seymour*, 1 *Gal. & Da.*, 454; 41 *Eng. C. L.*, 825, it appearing that the justice's clerk went up stairs, took the informations and swore the informant, the justice remaining below, not seeing or hearing the proceeding above, the justice was held liable to an action of trespass for issuing his warrant.

But whatever may have been the common law on this point, we have seen that in the United States the matter has been made the subject of express provision in the federal and most of the state constitutions.

In *Ex parte Burford*, 3 *Cr.*, 448, the Supreme Court of the United States held the provision in the federal constitution on the subject of warrants included commitments.

And such appears to have been the opinion of the Supreme Courts of Massachusetts, *Sanford* v. *Nichols*, 13 *Mass.*, 236, and of Vermont, *The State* v. *J. H.*, 1 *Tyler*, 444.

In South Carolina, in the case of *The State* v. *Killett*, 2 *Bailey*, 289, it was strongly intimated, but not expressly determined that it was not indispensable that the information for a warrant should be on oath.

In *Conner* v. *Commonwealth*, 3 *Binn.*, 38, a warrant of arrest was held to be illegal, which issued without any previous oath or affirmation; but recited that it appeared to the judge who issued it, from "common rumor and report," that there was strong reason to suspect A. of issuing forged notes, though it stated there was danger of his departing from the county before witnesses could be summoned to enable the judge to issue it upon oath.

And it may be fairly inferred from the cases of *The Commonwealth* v. *Murray*, 2 *Va. Cas.*, 504, and *Welch* v. *Scott*, 5 *Iredell*, 72, that the Supreme Court, of Virginia and North Carolina would have held the process void on a habeas corpus if the charge was not in fact supported by oath or affirmation.

The warrant ought to show on its face that the charge is supported by oath or affirmation.

To this effect was the decision of the Supreme Court in *Ex parte Burford*, 3 *Cr.*, 448, and such is the fair import of the decision in *Conner* v. *Commonwealth*, 3 *Binn.*, 38; *The State* v. *J. H.*, 1 *Tyler*, 444; *Sanford* v. *Nichols*, 13 *Mass.*, 236; and *Caudle* v. *Seymour*, 41 *Eng. C. L.*, 825.

The Supreme Court of Virginia, however, in the case of *The Commonwealth* v. *Murray*, 2 *Va. Cas.*, 504, held that a warrant of commitment was distinguishable from a warrant of arrest in this respect, and that under the Constitution of that state the former was not invalid for omitting to state that the charge was supported by oath or affirmation.

In respect to this decision it may be remarked:

1st. There does not appear sufficient ground for the distinction taken between warrants to arrest and warrants to commit, unless the latter, of which there are several—such as commitments for safe custody, for further examination, for punishment as for contempt—by its recitals refer to some proceeding which would show that the commitment was founded upon oath or affirmation.

In the latter case, if the omission of an express averment, that the charge was supported by oath would not vitiate the commitment, it would not be on the ground that an oath or affirmation was not necessary; but on the ground, that it sufficiently appeared by the references, that the charge was so supported. The distinction is not found in the most approved forms. The necessity of stating the charge to be on oath, is recognized as applying to warrants to commit, as well as warrants to arrest, in 2 *Nun & Walsh Jus. Peace*, 186, 405.

2d. The provision in the Constitution of Virginia, on the subject of warrants, is unlike that in the federal Constitution, or those in the constitutions of most of the other states. The prohibition in that is, perhaps, not quite so comprehensive and emphatic.

Wyndham Case, 1 *Str.*, 3, is relied on by the court in the case of *Commonwealth* v. *Murray*, 2 *Va.*, 504, to support the position, that at common law it was not necessary to set forth in the warrant that the charge was supported by oath.

But as the case is reported in 3 *Viner Abr.*, 515, the reason assigned is not entirely satisfactory.

One objection taken to the commitment was, that it did not appear to be on oath. *Parker*, *Ch. J.*, said: "It was a hard way of arguing, that because no oath was expressed in the warrant, therefore he was committed without oath;" and he answered the argument by saying: "Where a magistrate executed a matter within his jurisdiction, it should never be presumed that he abused that discretion."

In the United States as we have seen, for the most part, the charge is required, either by constitution or statute, to be supported by an oath or affirmation before a warrant can issue. The oath or affirmation becomes, then, essential to the jurisdiction of the magistrate, and it is a general rule that all facts essential to jurisdiction should *expressly* appear in the proceedings of courts of inferior jurisdiction. 2 *Cowen & Hill Notes, Phil. Ev., note*, 87, *p.* 179; 1

Smith Lead. Cas., 5 *ed.*, 816 ; *The State* v. *Staples*, 37 *Maine Rep.*, 228 ; *Gurney* v. *Tufts*, *id.*, 133.

The following cases are cited to illustrate the application of some of the principles which have been discussed in this section.

It will be seen that the courts of Georgia and South Carolina differ on the question, as to the certainty required in stating the offence.

In South Carolina, in the case of *The State* v. *Everett*, 1 *Dud. Law Rep.*, 295, the Court of Appeals held the warrant of commitment sufficiently certain which stated that the prisoner was "charged before A. H. Brown, on the oath of A. Gibson, from circumstances, with larceny of bank bills of the Union Bank of Florida, valued at about seventy dollars, there being other bills, and one $50 and one $20 bill being found on the person of said Jas. E. Everett." And in the case of *The State* v. *Potter*, decided by the same court at the same time, the offence was stated in the warrant of commitment in the following words, "charged before me, upon the oath of Capt. Ross, with having committed larceny."

Exceptions were taken to these warrants that the charges were uncertain and insufficent. But the court held them sufficient. Earle, J., in delivering the opinion of the court, said:

"At this day one would hardly suppose that a question could arise on the subject of proceedings under the habeas corpus act; and yet there seems to be a popular misapprehension in relation to them, indicating a belief that the habeas corpus act is a sort of universal relief-law, a summary general jail delivery.

"In the case of Potter the charge is, that the prisoner had committed larceny without any facts or circumstances to show whether it was grand or petit larceny. In such a case, in favor of liberty, without more appearing from the depositions or examination, I should regard it as a charge of petit larceny and admit to bail. Potter should therefore have been bailed, but not released. The warrant of commitment is sufficiently certain. It is a great mistake to suppose that a warrant for apprehension or a warrant of commitment need contain any statement at all of the evidence on which it is founded or need enumerate any of the facts and circumstances accompanying the offence.

"There are several high authorities that it need not even contain a specification of the particular offence. But the better opinion as well as the general and approved practice, is that it should state the offence with convenient certainty; that it should not be for felony generally, but should contain the special nature of the felony."

In the case of *The State* v. *Killett*, 2 *Bailey*, 289, it appeared that the defendant was in custody under a warrant of commitment for "passing a counterfeit note knowing it to be such." It was objected that the offence was not sufficiently set forth in the warrant.

EARLE, J. "The insufficiency of the form of the warrant in charging the offence cannot avail. It cannot be expected nor is it necessary that a magistrate in framing a warrant should state the offence with the same technical accuracy that is required in an indictment. It is sufficient if it appear on its face that an authority is given to arrest on some charge or on some statement of facts which in the judgment of the magistrate amounts to a charge of a criminal nature. The charge here is that the prisoner 'passed a counterfeit note knowing it to be such,' which is considered quite enough."

In the case of *The State* v. *Munson, Hall's Jour. Juris.*, 257, the warrant was as follows:

"*Kent County* ss: The State of Delaware to the sheriff or any constable of said county, greeting:

"Whereas James Kirbin, of the county of Kent, this day appeared before Mr. James Schee, one of the justices of the peace of the state of Delaware, in and for said county, on his oath did declare that on the 17 day of January, 1817, received two dollar bank note from young man on the Bank of Hagerstown, No. 7263, and dated Hagerstown, 27 April, 1814, having good cause to believe and doth believe that young man did feloniously pass the same to me so counterfeit and forged on the Bank of Hagerstown, and the said young man has this day been brought before me the said justice and have refused to find surety for his appearance at the next court of general quarter sessions of the peace and jail delivery, to be held at Dover for said county, to answer unto the above charge; these are therefore to command you," &c.

It was moved on habeas corpus to discharge the prisoner for the following reasons:

1st. He is not named in the commitment. 2d. He is not described so as to be identified. 3d. He is not charged with any crime or probable crime on oath. 4th. The commitment does not allege the crime was committed in this state.

The Chancellor, was of opinion that the 4th objection had no weight in it. The 3d he thought deserved consideration; but did not afford any ground for the discharge of the prisoner.

"It was urged," he said, "that the prisoner was not charged with any crime. The offence is awkwardly enough stated in the commitment; but it is clearly to be collected that he is charged with passing a counterfeit note; and although the charge is informal, and he is not said to have passed the note knowing it to be counterfeit, yet that is the import of the charge. The justice used the word 'feloniously' improperly; but he has said that the young man did feloniously pass the note, so counterfeit and forged on the Bank of Hagerstown; and the whole shows that he is informally charged with passing a forged bank note, knowing it to be forged.

"A mistaken notion seems to prevail that any error or informality in a warrant of commitment makes it void, and entitles the party to a discharge without bail. The law is not so; neither is it reasonable or just that it should be so.

"It is not necessary that the offence should be described with the nicety and technical precision of an indictment, but that the prisoner should be *charged with some offence*, for it is enough if the commitment shows that an offence has been committed, not to discharge without bail.

"If all the certainty of an indictment were requisite in a commitment, scarcely any crime would be punished, for it would only be necessary for the party to refuse to give bail that he might be committed, and then on a writ of habeas corpus be discharged without bail. *The King* v. *Judd*, 2 *T. R.*, 225; *The King* v. *Despard*, 7 *T. R.*, 736; *The King* v. *Marks*, 3 *East*, 157.

"In this case the defendant is not charged with any felony, for it is not a felony to pass a counterfeit bank note; neither is he charged with any crime according to the act against forgery; but it appearing from the warrant of commitment that he is charged with an offence which is punishable by the laws of the land, he may be bailed, but for this reason he is not to be discharged. His crime, if he has committed any, is that of cheating, and like the case of Ford, he may be indicted for it at common law."

The first and second objections were then considered and sustained and the prisoner discharged.

In Georgia, in the case of *The State* v. *Bundy*, 2 *Geo. Decis.*, 40, under the statute of December 22, 1808, which required the crime to be plainly and clearly set forth, together with the time and place when and where committed, a warrant of commitment before indictment was held defective, where the only description of the offence was "charged with having committed the offence of larceny." The court discharged the prisoner, the judge saying:

"I am of opinion the prisoner is entitled to her discharge upon the illegality apparent on the face of the warrant of commitment. It neither states the time nor place when or where the said offence was committed, nor the property of any person upon which said offence has been committed by the prisoner. These facts, I apprehend, must be stated on the face of the commitment in order to make it a legal one; and such would seem to be the clear spirit and intention of the act of the legislature passed 22d December, 1808."

The court in this case evidently considered the statement of the offence for "larceny" simply, as a fatal defect at common law. After indictment the warrant to arrest or commit the defendant may refer to the indictment and describe the offence for which he is indicted in general terms, as for arson, burglary or the like.

In the case of *Brady* v. *Davis*, 9 *Geo. Rep.*, 73, it was held that a bench warrant to arrest and a warrant of commitment after indictment, are sufficient if they recite the fact of indictment and describe the offence generally. As when the warrant and mittimus stated the offence simply as *a misdemeanor*, founded on the special presentment of the grand jury of Troup county. Neither stated the particular misdemeanor or the time and place when and where committed. These particulars, said the court, will be found in the presentment, and the object of the warrant is to bring in the accused to answer that.

The court might have added that the warrant in such a case was the procees of a superior court, and that it would be presumed that what the law required had been done.

II. *Of process from a superior court of general jurisdiction.*

The favorable presumptions extended to process issuing from courts of general jurisdictions, are very clearly and concisely stated in the case of *Gosset* v. *Howard*, 10 *Q. B.*, 359, 452, *cited in* 1 *Smith Lead. Cas.*, 5 *ed.*, 821.

"The question arose on a warrant of the speaker of the House of Commons, which did not specify the cause for which it issued, and it was held by the Exchequer Chamber, reversing the judgment of the Court of King's Bench, that although the failure to set forth the cause of arrest would have been fatal, had the warrant been issued by an inferior court, yet that as it was the mandate of the Commons, it should be construed with the liberality shown to the proceedings of all superior courts and must consequently be regarded as valid, unless manifestly without jurisdiction. 'The validity of the warrant,' said Parke, in delivering the opinion of the court, 'depends mainly upon a preliminary point: on what principle is the instrument to be construed? Is it to be examined with the strictness with which we look at the warrants of magistrates or others acting by special statutory authority, and out of the course of the common law, or is it to be regarded as the mandate or writ of a superior court acting according to the course of the common law?

"'The judges who composed the majority of the Court of Queen's Bench, seem all to have thought that the speaker's warrant was to be strictly construed; and Lord Denman and my brother Coleridge appear to have assimilated it to the warrant or commitment of a justice of the peace, and applied the same rules of construction to which such an instrument is always subjected.'

"All these three judges held it to be void, because it did not show a sufficient authority on the face of it to justify the defendant in all he admitted to have done, though they did not agree in the nature of the defect. If this had been the case of a magistrate acting under some statute, which gave him a special authority to take a man into custody under the same circumstances as are stated in the three first pleas, we should no doubt have agreed with those learned judges that a warrant in a similar form would have been void, those circumstances not appearing upon the face of it; for, in the case of special authorities given by statute to justices or others acting out of the ordinary course of the common law, the instruments by which they act, whether warrants to arrest, commitments, or orders, or convictions, or inquisitions, ought, according to the course of the decisions, to show their authority on the face of them by direct averment or reasonable intendment. Not so the process of superior courts acting by the authority of the common law. In the argument of the case of *Peacock* v. *Bell*, 1 *Saund.*, 74, the rule as to pleading is well expressed thus: 'The rule for jurisdiction is that nothing shall be intended to be out of the jurisdiction of a superior court, but that which specially appears to be so;' 'nothing shall be intended to be within the jurisdiction of an inferior court but that which is so expressly alleged;' and therefore the majority of the court held that the courts of counties Palatine being superior courts, the record in those courts need not state the cause to have arisen within the jurisdiction. In like manner it is presumed, with respect to such writs as are actually issued by superior courts, that they are duly issued and in a case in which they have jurisdiction, unless the contrary appears on the face of them, as it would for instance, if a writ of capias for a criminal matter issued from the Common Pleas, or a writ in a real action (before the abolition of such remedies) from the King's Bench or a real action, not in the Crown's case, in the Exchequer; in all which cases the want of jurisdiction would appear.

"But writs issued by a superior court, not appearing to be out of the scope of their jurisdiction, are valid, and of themselves, without any further allegation, a protection to all officers and others in their aid acting under them; and that, although they be on the face of them, as a *capias* against a peeress (*Countess of Rutland's case*, 6 *Rep.*, 54, *a.*), or void in form, as a *capias ad respondendum*, not returnable the next term, *Parsons* v. *Lloyd*, 3 *Wils.*, 341; for the officers ought not to examine the judicial act of the court whose servants they are, nor exercise their judgment touching the validity of the process in point of law, but are bound to execute it, and are therefore protected by it. *Turner* v. *Felgate*, 1 *Lev.*, 95; *Cotes* v. *Michill*, 3 *Lev.*, 20.

"Many of the writs issued by superior courts do, upon the face of them, recite the cause of their issuing, and show their legality; writs of execution, for instance; others however, do not, and, though unquestionably valid, are framed in a form which, if they proceeded from magistrates or persons having a special jurisdiction unknown to the common law, would have been clearly insufficient, and rendered them altogether void. A *capias ad respondendum*, for example, issued before the recent statute, 1 and 2 *Vict.*, *c.* 110, states no original writ, no affidavit of debt, nor any plea commenced before the *capias* issued; and it is still unquestionably valid; yet if, instead of being issued by a superior court, it had proceeded from an individual who had a special limited power by statute, after an original writ from Chancery, directed to him, or after a suit instituted and affidavit of debt, to command another to be arrested, a warrant in this form would have been as clearly bad. So the forms of writs of attachment from the superior courts do not state the previous steps of a charge of contempt, the rule of court that it should issue, or the nature of the contempt. That issued from the Common Pleas (not against officers of the court merely, but against individuals,) is simply to order the sheriff to bring the party into court on a certain day, to answer to her Majesty of and concerning *those things* which on her behalf shall then and there be objected against him. There is no recital of any previous proceeding, no statement of the nature of the charge, none of the adjudication of the court that it ought to be answered; yet this writ is as unquestionably good as it would have been unquestionably bad had it been issued by a magistrate or other individual who had a special jurisdiction to punish for such offences as would constitute a contempt of court, or any other particular offence. It appears, indeed, that if a writ of a superior court expressed no cause at all it would be legal, and the dèfendant not liable, according to what Lord Coke says in *The Brewer's case*, 1 *Roll. Rep.*, 134.

"It was a mistake to assert, as was done at the bar, that an adjudication of a contempt was a necessary part of every committal for a contempt, and that an attachment would be invalid without it. It is not so in the superior courts of common law, as has been before stated, nor in the Court of Chancery, as Lord Lyndhurst has lately decided, *Ex parte Van Sandan*, 1 *Phillip*, 445, 605."

In the case of *The People* v. *Tompkins*, 1 *Parker Cr. Rep.*, 224, already cited, Mr. Justice Edmonds, suggests a distinction between "judgments, decrees and convictions" on the one hand, and "writs, warrants and other process before the final judgment" on the other, intimating that the latter might be collaterally impeached, though the former could not. In that case the distinction between superior and inferior courts was not adverted to, and the particular process then under review issued from an inferior court.

The presumption of jurisdiction and regularity which arises in favor of the process issuing from superior courts, and which does not recite the facts necessary to give jurisdiction to grant it, may, as has been shown, be rebutted by proof showing the non-existence of such facts and so the process be invalidated. And in this view the action of the court in the case of *Wade* v. *Judge*, 5 *Ala.*, 130, is consistent with the doctrine maintained in *Gosset* v. *Howard*. In that case the warrant to arrest a debtor was held to be unauthorized where the affidavit upon which it was grounded was in the alternative, as "that the defendant has fraudulently conveyed or is about fraudulently to convey," &c.

So upon this principle — that the presumption may be rebutted — the *action* of the court in *Nelson & Graydon* v. *Cutler & Tyrrell*, 3 *McLean*, 326, is not inconsistent with the doctrine of *Gosset* v. *Howard*, although one observation of the court may appear to conflict with it.

In that case, the court on habeas corpus looked into the affidavit, upon which the capias ad respondendum was issued, and because it was defective in not swearing positively to the amount due under the non-imprisonment act of Ohio, the defendants were discharged.

On objection that the court could not look beyond the capias, the court said: "The writ on which the arrest was made, is produced by the gaoler; but that writ, unsupported by an affidavit, did not authorize the arrest. Indeed, it cannot legally be issued without an affidavit. The affidavit, therefore, is so connected with the writ, as to constitute an essential part of it. Separate it from the writ, and the defendants must be discharged. The personal liberty of the defendants is concerned, and in such a case a presumption does not arise against liberty."

In this case, a sufficient affidavit was a condition without which the court had no jurisdiction to grant the writ; and although in the absence of proof, a sufficient affidavit would be presumed, the prisoner might rebut the presumption by proof showing there was no affidavit, or that it was insufficient. The remark of the learned judge, that "where personal liberty is concerned, presumptions do not arise against liberty" is not sustained by the authorities; for the presumptions in favor of the proceedings of superior tribunals apply as well to criminal as civil cases. *The People ex rel. Johnson*, v. *Nevins*, 1 *Hill*, 154; 1 *Smith Lead. Cas.*, 5 *ed.*, 816.

4. *The conclusion.* The conclusion should be according to the purpose of the commitment. At common law the conclusion usually was, "there to remain until he shall be discharged by due course of law." 2 *Hawk.*, 186.

But if the conclusion be irregular, the warrant will not for that reason be void; but the law will reject that which is surplusage and the rest shall stand. 2 *Hale P. C.*, 584.

5. *The signature and seal.* The warrant should be signed and sealed.

1st. *The signature.*

The warrant should be signed in the official character of the officer issuing it. Though the omission of the designation of his official character, has been held not to vitiate the warrant, if the party issuing it was in fact authorized to issue it. In *Rex* v. *Goodall*, *Sayer*, 129; *S. C.*, 1 *Kenyon*, 122; on motion to discharge the defendant who had been committed for having riotously assembled with divers others, it was contended that it did not appear in the warrant, that the person committing was a justice of the peace; or that he had authority to commit the defendant. But the court was of opinion that it was not necessary that an authority to commit, should appear in a warrant of commitment.

In *Elderton's case*, *Ld. Raym.*, 978; *S. C.*, 6 *Mod.*, 73; it was held that the justice need not mention his office in the warrant of commitment; but that his official character must appear on the return to the writ of habeas corpus.

In *Jones* v. *Timberlake*, 6 *Rand.*, 678, on a motion to discharge on habeas corpus, on the ground of a similar omission in the warrant, the court held that the official character of the person issuing the warrant might be proved *aliunde*.

2d. *The seal.*

At common law, a special warrant for the arrest or imprisonment of a person was required to be under seal; 2 *Inst.*, 52; 1 *Hale*, 577; 2 *Hawk.*, *ch.* 13, *sec.* 21; 4 *Burns' J.*, 393; 4 *Black.*, 290; though a contrary opinion is supposed to have been once held. *Willes Rep.*, 411; 1 *Ch. Cr. L.*, 38.

In the absence of any statutory provision, the omission of a seal will render the warrant void, and entitle the prisoner to be released from the custody claimed under it. *Ex parte Bennett*, 2 *Cranch C. C.*, 612; *Somerville* v. *Hunt*, 4 *Harr. & McHenry*, 113; *The State* v. *Caswell*, *Charlt.*, 280; *The State* v. *Buzine*, 4 *Harr.*, 575; *The State* v. *Munson*, *Hall Jour. Juris.*, 257; *Lough* v. *Millard*, 2 *R. I. Rep.*, 436; *State* v. *Drake*, 36 *Maine*, 366; *Tackett* v. *The State*, 3 *Yerger*, 392. *But see Ex parte Smith*, 5 *Cow.*, 273; *State* v. *Vaughn*, *Harper*, 313.

In Missouri, where the act of the General Assembly, required the governor's warrant for the surrender of a fugitive from justice, to be under the great seal of the state, it was held that where the impression of the seal was wholly unintelligible, the warrant was void. *Vallad* v. *Sheriff*, *&c.*, 2 *Mis.*, 26.

The word warrant, when applied to a written process, authorizing the arrest or imprisonment of a person, imports an instrument under seal. *State* v. *Drake*, 36 *Maine*, 366; *Beekman* v. *Traver*, 20 *Wend.*, 67; *Smith* v. *Randall*, 3 *Hill*, 497.

SECTION VIII.

ORDERS OF COURT.

A court of record may commit without a formal warrant. *Taylor et Beale*, 2 *Roll. Abr.*, 559, *tit. Imprisonment justifiable by officers, D.*, *pl.* 3. Lord Hale says: "The power of a justice of the peace, differs from the power of a court; for the Court of King's Bench may commit by order, and so may the court of sessions of the peace, because there is, or ought to be, a record of the commitment."

And in 2 *Burns' Jus.*, 604, it is said that in a commitment by the sessions or other court of record, the record itself or the memorial thereof, which may at any time be entered of record, is sufficient without any warrant under seal.

Where a commitment is in court to a proper officer there present, there is no warrant of commitment; and, therefore, to a habeas corpus he cannot return a warrant in hæc verba, but must return the truth of the whole matter. *Bac. Abr.*, *Hab. Corp.*, *B.* 9; *Salk.*, 349, *pl.* 5. And the sheriff "without more ado is obliged to take notice of all commitments in court." *Souther's case*, 6 *Mod.*, 133.

This principle was approved and applied in *The People ex rel. Johnson*, v. *Nevins*, 1 *Hill*, 154; and *The State* v. *Heathman*, *Wright*, 691. In the last case, *Wright, J.*, says: "The record of the Common Pleas shows the *order to commit* made in open court. In such case a mittimus is not necessary; the order in court to the sheriff, is his authority, and the evidence of it being preserved of record, no writ or copy of the order was necessary."

SECTION IX.

AUTHORITY OF LAW.

"Process of law is twofold, viz.: by the king's writ, or by due proceeding and warrant, either in deed *or in law without writ.*" 2 *Inst.*, 51. "If treason or felony be done, and one hath just cause of suspicion, this is a good cause and *warrant in law* to arrest any man." A watchman may arrest a night walker by *warrant in law.* A commitment by lawful warrant, either in deed or in law, is accounted in law due *process* or proceeding in law, and by the law of the land, as well as by process by force of the king's writ." 2 *Inst.*, 52.

It has, however, sometimes been claimed that an arrest of this character without a warrant in fact, was a violation of the great fundamental principles of our national and state constitutions, forbidding unreasonable searches and arrests, except by warrant founded upon a complaint made under oath. This objection was met as early as 1814, in the case of *Wakely* v. *Hart*, 6 *Binn.*, 216, and answered by Tilghman, Ch. J., after citing the constitutional provision of Pennsylvania, in the following terms:

"The provisions of this section, so far as concern warrants, only guard against their abuse by issuing them without good cause, or in so general and vague a form as may put it in the power of the officers who execute them, to harass innocent persons under pretence of suspicion; for if general warrants are allowed, it must be left to the discretion of the officer on what person or things they are to be executed.

"But it is nowhere said that there shall be no arrest without warrant.

"To have said so would have endangered the peace of society. The felon who is seen to commit murder or robbery, must be arrested on the spot or suffered to escape; so although not seen, yet if known to have committed a felony and pursued with or without a warrant, he may be arrested by any person. And even when there is only probable cause of suspicion, a private person may, without warrant, *at his peril* make an arrest. I say at his peril, for nothing short of proving the felony will justify the arrest.

"These are the principles of the common law, essential to the welfare of society, and not intended to be altered or impaired by the Constitution. The whole section indeed was nothing more than an affirmance of the common law, for general warrants have been decided to be illegal; but the practice of issuing them had been ancient, the abuses great and the decisions against them only of modern date; the agitation occasioned by the discussion of this important question had scarcely subsided, and it was thought prudent to enter a solemn veto against this powerful engine of despotism."

The same rule of construction has been adopted in New York, Massachusetts, New Hampshire, and doubtless in other states, as no cases are found holding a contrary doctrine. *The People, ex rel. Johnson,* v. *Nevins,* 1 *Hill,* 154; *Rohan* v. *Swain,* 5 *Cush.,* 281; *Mayo* v. *Wilson,* 1 *New Hampshire,* 53.

This authority of law to arrest felons, although vested more fully in peace officers, is not limited to them. It may be exercised by private persons in certain cases.

The true distinction between the powers of peace officers and private persons to arrest offenders, is thus stated by Savage Ch. J. in *Holley* v. *Mix & Clute*, 3 *Wend.*, 350:

"If an innocent person is arrested upon suspicion by a private individual, such individual is excused, *if a felony was in fact committed and there was reasonable ground to suspect the person arrested.* But if no felony was committed by any one, and a private individual arrest without warrant, such arrest is illegal, though *an officer would be justified if he acted upon information from another which he had reason to rely on.*" *Samuel* v. *Payne and others, Doug.*, 359; 1 *Chit. Cr. Law.*, 15; 1 *Arch. Cr. Pl., & Ev., Waterman's Notes*, 212.

For the grounds of suspicion which will justify an arrest of an innocent person, see 2 *Hawk. P. C., book* 1, *ch.* 12, *sec.* 8.

In *Eanes* v. *The State*, 6 *Humph.*, 53, it was held that "the official proclamation by the governor, of the commission of a felony, published as the law directs, is sufficient evidence of the commission of it to justify an arrest of the supposed felon by a peace officer without warrant."

If a writ of habeas corpus be obtained where the arrest is upon suspicion, and without a special warrant, proof must be given to show the suspicion to be well founded. 2 *Inst.*, 52.

SECTION X.

COMMITMENTS IN EXECUTION.

1. *Commitments on summary convictions.*
2. *Commitments for contempt.*

Final criminal jurisdiction over some minor offences, has been in England since 1544, and now is in many of the United States conferred upon justices of the peace acting without a jury. In such cases, "the party accused is acquitted or condemned by the suffrage of such person only as the statute has appointed for his judge." The proceeding being summary in its nature the conviction is called a "summary conviction."

Where a person is committed in execution under such a conviction, he cannot claim under the act 31 *Car.* 2, nor under the acts of several of the states as we have seen, to be discharged under a writ of habeas corpus. Courts however, possessing a common law jurisdiction over the writ, or judges, or other officers, upon whom jurisdiction is conferred without such limit, may in exercise of such common law or unrestricted jurisdiction, discharge the prisoner from such commitment if it be fatally and incurably defective. But as we have also seen, courts are reluctant to interfere then under the writ of habeas corpus without having the conviction before them; and they never do for mere error or irregularity, unless they have the record before them in such form as to enable them to act expressly and conclusively upon such error or irregularity.

Hence, the importance of the writ of certiorari, and hence also, the necessity of applying for relief from imprisonment in such cases, to a court which by its constitution and relation possesses a corrective or revisory jurisdiction over the conviction, so that if it be erroneous it may be reversed, and then the prisoner be discharged.

"Though all the King's courts at Westminster have power to issue the writ of habeas corpus, it is seldom sued out of any other than the Court of King's Bench, by persons committed upon convictions by justices; because the other courts can only remove the body and the warrant of commitment, but cannot send for and examine and set aside the conviction itself; which is the prerogative of the King's Bench." *Paley on Convictions*, 272.

When a record of a summary conviction is properly presented for revision, it is subjected to strict rules of construction.

The power to convict without a jury being in derogation of the common law, has always been watched with great care by the courts; and it has long been settled, that the record of conviction must clearly show the guilt of the prisoner or he will be discharged. *Nash's case*, 4 *B. & A.*, 295; *Rudyard's case*, 1 *Skin.*, 678; *Bac. Abr.*, *Hab. Corp.*, *B.* 10; *The King* v. *Gibson*, *Fort.*, 272; *Rex* v. *Symonds*, 1 *Ld. Raym.*, 699; *Rex* v. *Harper*, *D. & R.*, 222; *Thomlinson's case*, 12 *Co.*, 104.

Indeed this jurisdiction has been regarded with such disfavor by the courts that a body of rules has gradually been established for the construction of the conviction, so searching and rigorous that in England and New York the legislature has deemed it expedient to prescribe forms of convictions. 1 *Smith Lead. Cas.*, 5 *ed.*, 810: 1 *Parker Cr. Rep.*, 96, *n.*

The general nature and requisites of summary convictions are thus stated by Burns:

"The power of a justice of the peace is in restraint of the common law, and in abundance of instances is a tacit repeal of that famous clause in the great charter, that a man should be tried by his equals, which also was the common law of the land long before the great charter, even from time immemorial, beyond the date of histories and records.

"Therefore, generally, nothing shall be presumed in favor of the office of a justice of the peace, but the intendment will be against it. Therefore, where a special power is given to a justice of the peace by act of parliament to convict an offender in a summary manner, without a trial by jury, it must appear that he hath strictly pursued that power, otherwise the common law will break in upon him and level all his proceedings. Therefore, where a trial by jury is dispensed withal, yet he must proceed, nevertheless, according to the course of the common law in trials by juries, and consider himself only as constituted in the place both of judge and jury. Therefore there must be an information or charge against a person, then he must be summoned or have notice of such charge, and have an opportunity to make his defence, and the evidence against him must be such as the common law approves of, unless the statute specially directeth otherwise; then if the person is found guilty, there must be a conviction, judgment and execution, all according to the course of common law, directed and influenced by the special authority given by statute; and in the conclusion there must be a *record* of the whole proceedings, wherein the justice must set forth the particular manner and circumstances, so as if he shall be called to account for the same by a superior court it may appear that he hath conformed to the law, and not exceeded the bounds prescribed to his jurisdiction." 1 *Burns' Jus.*, 409.

It will not be practicable here to consider at length all the objections which may be taken to these convictions when under revision for error or irregularity. They have been made the subject of able and elaborate treatises and occupy no inconsiderable space in the reports, as the following collection by Mr. Justice Edmonds, in the case of *The People* v. *Phillips*, 1 *Parker Cr. Rep.*, 95, will show. The following propositions will also be found fully discussed in the treatises of Paley and Hulton on convictions, and of Nun and Walsh on the powers and duties of justices of the peace.

A conviction must contain the following particulars:

An information or charge against the defendant — a summons or notice of the information, in order that he may appear and make his defence — his appearance or non-appearance — his confession or defence — the evidence, if he does not confess — and the judgment or adjudication. All these matters must be particularly set out on the conviction. 2 *Robinson's Justice*, 542; *Brackett* v. *State*, 2 *Tyler*, 167; *People* v. *Miller*, 14 *Johns. R.*, 371; 4 *Johns. R.*, 292.

"The information should state correctly the time when taken, the place, the jurisdiction before which taken, and the charge preferred. *Ld. Raym.*, 509; 2 *Bl. Com.*, 141; *Lacon* v. *Hooper*, 6 *T. R.*, 224. So that it may appear that it had been given within the time limited by the statute; that the power was exercised at a place commensurate with the jurisdiction before a magistrate having jurisdiction at that place, 2 *Salk.*, 473; that the offence was directly charged, and not by implication, and contained in express terms every ingredient necessary to constitute the crime described by the statute. *Rex* v. *Bradley*, 10 *Mod.*, 155; *R.* v. *Trelawney*, 1 *T. R.*, 122; 2 *Lord Raym.*, 791; 2 *T. R.*, 34.

"In describing the offence, a mere compliance with the terms of the statute will not suffice, for if a magistrate merely states the facts of the offence in the words of the act, when the evidence does not warrant the conclusions, he subjects himself to a criminal information. *R.* v. *Thompson*, 2 *T. R.*, 18; *R.* v. *Pearce*, 9 *East*, 358; *R.* v. *Davis*, 6 *T. R.*, 171; *Ardry* v. *Hoole*, *Cowp.*, 825.

"The particular circumstances which conduce the opinion of the magistrate must be set forth, and not the mere result or conclusion from them. 2 *Rob. Jus.*, 546.

"It must appear that the accused was summoned or appeared before the magistrate, *Rex* v. *Allason*, 2 *Str.*, 678; *R.* v. *Venables*, *ib.*, 630, and if he neglects to appear after proof of being duly summoned, the justice may proceed to judgment, but he must state all these facts in their proper order in the conviction. *R.* v. *Simpson*, 1 *Str.*, 44; *State* v. *Stokes*, 1 *Coxe*, 392; *Bigelow* v. *Stearns*, 19. *J. R.*, 41; *Son* v. *People*, 12 *Wend.*, 348; *Chare* v. *Hathaway*, 14 *Mass. R.*, 224.

"The plea of the defendant must be set forth, whether of denial or confession. *Paley on Conv.*, *Deacon's ed.*, 139, § 5.

"If he denies the charge it must be supported by evidence, and the names of the witnesses must be set out, that the court may judge whether they are competent. *Rex* v. *Tilly*, 1 *Str.*, 16; *Rex* v. *Blaney*, *Andr.*, 240.

"The evidence should be stated to have been given in the presence of the accused, that it may appear he had an opportunity of cross-examination. *Rex* v. *Vipont*, 2 *Burr.*, 1163; *Rex* v. *Crowther*, 1 *T. R.*, 125; *Rex* v. *Swallow*, 8 *T. R.*, 284; *Rex* v. *Selway*, 2 *Chit.*, 522.

"The whole evidence which applies to the charge must be particularly set out in the conviction, that the court may judge whether sufficient proof appears on the face of it to sustain every material allegation and to justify the adjudication. *Rex* v. *Killer*, 4 *Burr. Rep.*, 2063; *Rex* v.

Vipont, 2 *Burr. R.*, 1165 ; 2 *Rob. Jus.*, 550, *per Lord Mansfield ; Rex* v. *Lloyd*, 2 *Stor.*, 999, *per Lord Hardwicke ; Rex* v. *Theed*, 2 *Str.*, 919, *per Lord Raymond ; vide also* 2 *Doug.*, 486 ; *Rex* v. *Smith*, 8 *T. R.*, 588, *per Lord Kenyon ; Rex* v. *Taylor*, 2 *Chit. R.*, 578 ; *Commonwealth* v. *Hardy*, 1 *Ashmead R.*, 411.

"It will not be sufficient to state 'that the said offence was duly and fully proved,' for that is to state the result of the evidence and not the evidence itself. *Rex* v. *Reed*, *Doug.*, 490 ; *Rex* v. *Lovet*, 7 *T. R.*, 122.

"And the evidence for the defendant, as well as that for the prosecution must be set out. 2 *Rob. Jus.*, 561 , *Rex* v. *Clarke*, 8 *T. R.*, 220.

"The record must contain an adjudication of the magistrate upon the evidence, as to the guilt or innocence of the prisoner. *Rex* v. *Harris*, 7 *T. R.*, 238 ; *Mayor* v. *Mason*, 4 *Dall.*, 266.

"And the adjudication, on every point to which it refers, must be precise and exact, a judgment for too little being as bad as a judgment for too much. *Rex* v. *Clark*, *Cowp.*, 610 ; *Morgan* v. *Brown*, 6 *N. & M.*, 59 ; 4 *Ad. & E.*, 515 ; *Rex* v. *Patchett*, 5 *East*, 339 ; *Rex* v. *Hazell*, 13 *East*, 139 ; *Cumming's case*, 3 *Greenl. R.*, 51 ; *Power* v. *People*, 4 *Johns. R.*, 292.

"That the design of the conviction is not merely to record the fact of the judgment, but to show that the proceedings required by justice had been regularly observed and the sentence legally supported by evidence, is everywhere evinced by the language and sentiments of the ablest judges from the time of Lord Holt, who himself, on all occasions, regarded the obligation of recording the whole proceeding as a necessary counterpoise against the liability to error or misapplication to which a private and discretionary tribunal is naturally exposed. *Intro. to Paley on Con.*, xxxiii.

"Everything requisite to support a conviction should appear on the conviction itself. 6 *T. R.*, 538. And its validity must be determined by what appears on the face, not by reference to matters dehors. 3 *T. R.*, 338.

A distinction has been taken between the record of conviction and the warrant of commitment, and it has been held that the latter should be viewed with less strictness.

In the case of *The King* v. *Rogers*, 1 *Dowl. and Ryl.*, 156, Abbott, Ch. J., stated this distinction as follows:

"The difficulty I have in this case is in subjecting this warrant of commitment to the same rules of construction which are applicable to convictions.

"We are bound to presume, until the contrary is shown, that there has been a good conviction, and that the magistrate has done everything required of him by law. This is a commitment in execution, and recites that the party has been convicted, and there is no distinction in the cases cited which authorizes us to look at the warrant of commitment with the same strictness of a conviction. The commitment is for two months unless the money shall be sooner paid. I think it is not necessary that the commitment should state to whom it should be paid. If the defendant pays the money to the gaoler, he will be discharged forthwith.

"It is not suggested that the magistrate did not direct to whom the money was to be paid before the conviction took place" (and if the suggestion had been made it could not have been listened to unless the records were brought up on certiorari, *Regina* v. *Chancy*, 6 *Dowl. Pr. Cas.*, 281,) "and as we are bound to presume that there was a good conviction before commitment, I think we ought not to discharge the defendant."

If the commitment misrecite the name of the person through the medium of whom the conviction took place, it will be rejected as surplusage. *Mossey* v. *Johnson*, 12 *East*, 67.

But if it fails to show before whom the conviction took place, it will be void. *Rex* v. *York*, 5 *Burr.*, 2684.

And if it show a conviction with conditions annexed, not authorized by law, and indivisible, it cannot be sustained. *Rex* v. *Barnes*, 2 *Str.*, 917. But if the sentence be divisible, a part authorized by law and a part not, the commitment will stand good for that which is authorized, and the prisoner will be discharged as to that part which is not. *Phinney's case*, 32 *Maine*, 440; *Rex* v. *St. Nicholas*, 3 *Ad. & Ell.*, 79.

Commitments in execution in civil cases. The same strictness has not been applied to commitments grounded upon *civil* proceedings.

In *Ex parte Pardy*, 1 *Lowndes, Maxwell & Pollock*, the court refused a habeas corpus, holding that the warrant of commitment, being partly in the nature of a civil proceeding, was not bad for not stating that the examination was "upon oath," or for showing two offences; or for uncertainty in the description of the offence; or for requiring the defendant to be kept in a prison for forty days, or until he should be discharged by due course of law.

EARLE, J., said: "If the warrant of commitment, now under consideration, were in the nature of a conviction, it might be bad; but it is in the nature of a civil execution, for the defendant may at any time pay the debt and cost, and release himself from the consequences of his refusal or neglect to pay."

2. *Commitments for contempt.* The right of punishing for contempts by summary conviction is inherent in all courts of justice, and essential to their protection and existence. A commitment under such conviction is a commitment in execution, and the judgment of conviction is not subject to review in any other court unless specially authorized by statute. It cannot be attacked under the writ of habeas corpus except for such gross defects as render the proceeding void.

Brass Crosby's case, 3 *Wils.*, 183; *Kearney's case*, 7 *Wheat.*, 38; *Yates' case*, 4 *Johns.*, 318; *McLaughlin's case*, 5 *Watts & Serg.*, 275; *Johnson* v. *Commonwealth*, 1 *Bibb*, 602; *Ex parte Alexander*, 2 *Am. Law Reg.*, 44; *Ex parte Nugent*, 7 *Penn. Law Jour.*, 107; *State* v. *White*, *T. U. P. Charlt.*, 123; *Ex parte Hickey*, 4 *S. & M.*, 749; *State* v. *Tipton*, 1 *Blackf.*, 166; *Clark* v. *The People*, 1 *Breese*, 266; *Bickley* v. *Commonwealth*, 1 *J. J. Marsh*, 575; *Gist and others* v. *Bowman and others*, 2 *Bay*, 182; *Matter of Smithurst*, 2 *Sandf. Sup. Ct.*, 724; *Lockwood* v. *The State*, 1 *Carter*, 161; *Ex parte Adams*, 25 *Miss.*, 883; *The State* v. *Woodfin*, 5 *Iredell*, 199; *Ex parte Williamson*, 4 *Am. Law Reg.*, 27; *Ex parte Nugent*, 1 *Am. Law Jour. (N. S.)*, 111.

It is necessary in this as in all other judicial proceedings affecting persons, that the court should have jurisdiction of the offence and of the person. The proceeding for contempt is regarded as a distinct and independent matter, so far at least as to require notice to the party affected, and the omission to serve him with notice renders the proceeding void. *Ex parte Langdon*, 25 *Verm.*, 680.

"The right to interfere on habeas corpus with commitments for contempt by a *superior* court, came under consideration in *The People* v. *Nevins*, 1 *Hill*, 154. There it was held that a rule of court without a precept is valid as process to the sheriff, even though the prior proceedings be not specified in the rule; that it is enough if the rule show briefly a commitment for contempt, with the sum of money ordered to be paid either directly or by reference to some other rule or proceeding. It was also held that the rule being defective in form, is not sufficient objection; and though irregular, the commissioner ought not for that reason to interfere by habeas corpus. It was also held that jurisdiction must be intended.

"The Supreme Court of the United States in *Ex parte Kearney*, 7 *Wheat.*, 38, where another court had committed for a contempt, held the conviction equivalent to a judgment and execution, and it appearing that the court rendering the judgment had competent jurisdiction, they refused to interfere on habeas corpus." 3 *Hill*, 665, *note* 38.

The controversy growing out of the commitment of John V. N. Yates for contempt by the Chancellor of New York, John Lansing, Jr, in 1808, is remarkable for the great ability and learning displayed in the arguments of counsel and the opinions of the judges and senators. As a judicial proceeding, however, it is more valuable for what was *said* than for what was *done*.

Yates was committed for contempt and mal-practice, on 18th August, 1808. On the 19th August he was discharged on a writ of habeas corpus by Mr.

Justice Spencer of the Supreme Court. The Chancellor on the 5th September ordered him to be recommitted, and he was again arrested on the 12th September and on the same day discharged by the same judge on another habeas corpus. The Chancellor again, on the 5th December, ordered him to be recommitted which was done on the 7th February, 1809, when the prisoner applied to the Supreme Court for a habeas corpus. On final hearing the prisoner was remanded to the custody of the sheriff. 4 *Johns.*, 315. The judges stood three to two. A writ of error was brought upon this judgment and it was reversed. 6 *Johns.*, 337.

In the mean time Yates brought an action against the Chancellor to recover the penalty provided in the habeas corpus act for recommitting after discharge on habeas corpus. The Supreme Court held the law to be with the Chancellor. 5 *Johns.*, 282. The judges were divided as in the case of habeas corpus. A writ of error was brought on this judgment and it was affirmed. 9 *Johns.*, 394.

The result appears to be that Yates escaped the prison and the Chancellor, the penalty. The cases are not much cited as authority. The following instances, however, may serve to show the estimate in which they are held.

Ch. J. Gibson, of Pennsylvania, in the case of the *Commonwealth* v. *Leckey*, 1 *Watts*, 66, refers to the case in 4 *Johns.*, 318, with approbation, although it was reversed in 6 *Johns.*, 337; while Chancellor Pirtle, of Kentucky, in *Ex parte Alexander*, 2 *Am. Law Reg.*, 44, relies on the case in 6 *Johns.*, 337, which was in effect overruled in 9 *Johns.*, 394.

Where a person committed for contempt was brought before a judge on a writ of habeas corpus, and it did not appear from the return that there had been a conviction or judgment that he had been guilty of a contempt, it was held that his commitment was unlawful. *Ex parte Adams*, 25 *Miss.*, 883.

In commitments for contempt, where the imprisonment is intended as a punishment for the offence, it should specify some definite time. But where it is designed to compel obedience to an order of the court, it should be for so long only as the contumacy should continue. *Goff's case*, 3 *M. & S.*, 203; 1 *Burns' Jus.*, 382.

In *Rex* v. *James*, 5 *B. & A.*, 894; *S. C.*, 1 *D. & R.*, 559, the defendant was committed by two justices for a contempt towards them in their office, until discharged by due course of law. Being brought up under the habeas corpus act he was discharged, the court being clearly of the opinion that the commitment was bad, as it ought to have been for a time certain; and as there was no course of law by which the defendant could be discharged, such a commitment, if valid, amounted to perpetual imprisonment. See also *Rex* v. *Hall*, 3 *Burr.*, 1636; *Baldwin et ux.* v. *Blackmore*, 1 *Burr.*, 602; *Bracy's case*, 1 *Ld. Raym.*, 100.

A commitment which states that the party committed was adjudged guilty of a contempt in refusing to answer questions while giving his deposition as a witness, "*specially and plainly*" charges a contempt under the act of Missouri concerning habeas corpus, although it does not in terms state that the questions were relevant or were decided to be relevant. *Ex parte McKee*, 18 *Miss.*, 599.

In the case of *The State* v. *White*, *T. U. P. Charlt.*, 123, it was said: "In proceedings for contempt, if the return shows a good cause for commitment, it will be valid, though it may want form."

In *Ex parte Nugent*, 7 *Penn. Law Jour.*, 107, *Cranch, J.*, held that "the warrant of commitment need not set forth the particular facts which constitute the alleged contempt."

In *Ex parte Summers*, 5 *Iredell*, 149, it was held that where a court imposes a fine or imprisonment for a contempt, and the court does not state the facts constituting the contempt, and the court is not bound to set them out; no other tribunal can reverse their decision. But if the court does state the facts upon which it proceeds, a *revising* tribunal may, on a habeas corpus, discharge the party if it appear that the facts do not amount to a contempt.

SECTION XI.

WARRANT DEFECTIVE, PRISONER NOT ALWAYS DISCHARGED.

Ordinarily if the warrant be found invalid for the want of the essential requisites or conditions which have been considered, the prisoner will be entitled to be discharged. But this is not an invariable rule even where there is no statute to direct the action of the court or judge under the writ.

Where the proofs upon which the committing magistrate acted have been certified up or otherwise properly presented to the court or officer hearing the habeas corpus, or the further proofs, which may be adduced at the hearing where such further proofs are permitted, create a reasonable ground of suspicion of the prisoner's guilt of the crime specified, or any other, it has been held to be the duty of such court or officer, if invested with the power of a committing magistrate, not to discharge the prisoner absolutely, however defective the warrant may be, but to remand him or commit him *de novo*.

In England the *Stat.* 31 *Car.* 2 conferred no power to discharge the prisoner absolutely except where he had not been indicted and tried the second term after his commitment or had been tried and acquitted. In all other cases he was required to be remanded or let to bail. At common law, however, the Court of King's Bench had unlimited power to bail, and general, original and appellate jurisdiction in all criminal matters. It had power also, quite independent of the statute of 31 *Car.* 2, to issue the writ of habeas corpus in all cases, and not only to admit to bail under it in all cases, but to discharge absolutely. Under the statute they could not let to bail when the commitment was for felony or treason plainly expressed in the warrant; but at common law they could not only let to bail in such cases but might examine the grounds of commitment, and if on the facts it was plain that no crime had been committed, discharge the prisoner altogether; or if the facts disclosed a crime, but different from that for which the prisoner had been committed, they might simply remand him or commit afresh. The Court of King's Bench therefore exercised under its common law jurisdiction, as the court of supreme criminal judicature, higher powers under the writ of habeas corpus than were conferred by the act of 31 *Car.* 2 on the officers named in it.

Prior to 1802 it was the practice in that court, where the commitment was found defective, and yet the depositions showed some crime to have been committed by the prisoner, simply to remand him by a rule in general terms. But as this left the prisoner free to sue out another writ of habeas corpus upon the same defective original commitment, the practice was changed in that year.

In the case of *The King* v. *Marks*, 3 *East*, 157, *Grose*, *J.*, said:

"There is no doubt of the power of this court" (Kings Bench) "to bail, if they see occasion, in all cases of felony, even in case of murder, though there should be no doubt of the validity of the warrant of commitment. On the other hand, there is as little doubt as to their power of remanding, notwithstanding the warrant of commitment be defective; and it is the constant practice of this court to remand prisoners in such cases if it appear on reading the depositions that there is a fair ground to authorize them."

Le Blanc, J., said: "This court have clearly a right to bail the parties accused in all cases of felony, if they see occasion, whenever there is any doubt either on the law or the fact of the case. And it is equally clear that though the warrant of commitment be informal, yet if upon the depositions returned the court see that a felony has been committed, and that there is reasonable ground of charge against the prisoners, they will not bail but remand them. The same rule applies with respect both to the law and the fact; unless we see reason to doubt the truth of the fact charged, prisoners must be remanded; and the same consequence follows, unless we see reason to doubt whether the fact charged constitute any offence within the law."

The reporter adds: "In cases of defective commitments the practice has heretofore been merely to draw up a rule remanding the prisoners in general terms to the same custody as before, and this was at first designed to be done in the usual form in the present instance; but it occurred to the officers of the crown office to suggest an alteration of the practice in this respect, founded upon the consideration that prisoners thus remanded might renew the same application to another court or judge; and therefore the rule was ultimately drawn up in this form:

"'Friday next, after 15 days of St. Martin, in the forty-third year of King George the Third.

England, Wiltshire, } George Marks being brought here in custody of the keeper of his Majesty's gaol at Devizes, in and for the county of Wilts, by virtue of a writ of habeas corpus, it is ordered that the said writ, and the return made thereto, be filed. And upon reading the several informations upon oath of, &c., returned in obedience to a writ of certiorari directed to R. L. and T. H. P., two of his Majesty's justices of the peace in and for the county of Wilts, and upon hearing counsel upon both sides, it is ordered that he, the said George Marks, be now discharged from his imprisonment by virtue of the warrant in the said return mentioned; and that he the said George Marks be recommitted to the custody of the said keeper, for unlawfully and feloniously being aiding and assisting at, and present at and consenting to the administering and taking of an oath or engagement, purporting, &c., &c., to be by him kept in safe custody until he shall be from thence discharged by due course of law.' "

This course has been pursued in some of the courts of the United States. In the case of the *Commonwealth* v. *Hickey*, 2 *Pars. Select Cas.*, 317, the defendant was bound over by an alderman to answer to a charge of obtaining goods under false pretences. He was surrendered by his bail and sued out a writ of habeas corpus. The court on examining the evidence was of opinion that the charge of obtaining goods under false pretences was not sustained, yet another offence appearing the defendant was held to answer. *Parsons, J.*, said:

"But I am asked to hold the prisoner to bail, under the 20th section of that law (1842), upon the charge of having assigned his property with a design to defraud his creditors; and it is objected by the defendant's counsel, that inasmuch as he was only charged before the committing magistrate with an offence for which the judge who hears this cause will not hold him to bail, no other or different offence should be a ground for detaining him when brought up on this writ. In my opinion, this position cannot be maintained. The value of the writ of habeas corpus to the citizen, and the importance to the people of this city and county of judges carrying into full effect the act of the Assembly authorizing this writ, is, to my mind, daily becoming more apparent; and while a judge feels himself bound to investigate fully the facts in each case brought before him, and see if any offence against the law has been committed, and if convinced that there has been no infraction of it, to discharge at once the accused from arrest; so if on the hearing he believes that an offence has been perpetrated by the party charged, which is the subject of indictment, a faithful discharge of duty demands that he should hold him to bail—although no oath was made before the magistrate accusing the defendant with such a crime. All the judges of this court are, *ex officio*, magistrates, fully authorized to hold to bail or commit any one charged with a crime. A complaint is made on oath by the testimony of witnesses. Why should he not then hold the accused to bail? In my opinion, his oath of office requires it, and such is the practice of this court."

And in the case of *The Commonwealth* v. *Crans*, 3 *Penn. Law Jour.*, 459. *King, P. J.*, said:

"It is a settled doctrine of the criminal jurisprudence of Pennsylvania, that on the hearing of a relator under a writ of habeas corpus, the court are not confined to the sufficiency of the cause of detainer, as set forth in the commitment, but may look into the facts adduced by the Commonwealth in support of such commitment. If the result of such examination establishes that any breach of the criminal law has been sufficiently proven against the relator, he will be held to answer for such offence, although the proof submitted may not amount to the crime originally charged, or although the crime intended to be charged is defective in technical accuracy."

The same rule prevails in *Delaware*. In the case of *The State* v. *Buzine*, 4 *Harr.*, 575, where the warrant of the mayor was defective—having no seal—the judge says:

"But, in my opinion, the petitioner is not entitled to his discharge on account of the insufficiency of the warrant, provided the fact disclosed by the evidence affords a reasonable presumption that he is guilty of the offence imputed to him, or such probability as would be sufficient to put him upon his trial. If such were the case, although I should discharge him from imprisonment under the warrant of the mayor I should consider it my duty to order him to be immediately committed," &c.

The same rule was recognized in the case of *Ex parte Bennett*, 2 *Cranch C. C. Rep.*, 612, where a majority of the court say: "If the commitment be so bad on its face that the court must discharge the prisoner from that commitment, the court will, if they have sufficient evidence before them, commit the prisoner *de novo*, and order the witnesses to recognize," &c. And in New York, *Ex parte Taylor*, 5 *Cow.*, 12.

When the court examines the proofs, it will only inquire whether there is *probable cause to believe* that the person charged has committed the offence, &c. *The United States* v. *Johns*, 4 *Dallas*, 413.

"Unless it clearly appears that a prisoner, brought up on habeas corpus, is entirely innocent, the judge is bound to bail or remand. But difficulty or hesitation as to the law, arising from facts indisputably established, is not that kind of doubt of guilt which justifies in refusing to discharge, where the mind inclines, after full consideration, to pronounce in favor of innocence." *Gibson, J.*, *Com.* v. *Carlisle*, *Brightly Rep*, 36.

Previous to the trial of Burr, a motion was made to the Circuit Court to commit him, pending the investigation before the grand jury. A doubt was stated whether the court, sitting as a court, possessed the power to commit one charged with an offence, &c., though it was expressly given to the judges severally.

Ch. J. MARSHALL said: "It is believed to be a correct position that the power to commit for offences of which it has cognizance, is exercised by every court of criminal jurisdiction, and that courts, as well as individual magistrates, are conservators of the peace.

"Were it otherwise, the consequence would only be that it would become the duty of the judge to descend from the bench, and in his character as an individual magistrate to do that which the court is asked to do." 1 *Burr's Trial*, 79.

A dangerous lunatic is not to be discharged as a matter of course, because the order of confinement does not fulfill the requisites of the statute under which the custody is claimed. In the matter of *Shuttleworth*, 9 *Ad. & E.*, 651, it was contended that if the orders were deficient, the court would be under the necessity, however inconvenient, of allowing the lunatic his common law liberty. But Lord *Denman* answered:

"If the court thought that a party, unlawfully received or detained, was a lunatic, we should be betraying the common duties of members of society if we directed a discharge. But we have no power to set aside the order, only to discharge. And should we, as judges or individuals, be justified in setting such a party at large? It is answered that there may be a fresh custody. But why so? Is it not better, if she be dangerous, that she should remain in custody till the Great Seal or the Commissioners act? Therefore being satisfied, in my own mind, that there would be danger in setting her at large, I am bound by the most general principles to abstain from so doing; and I should be abusing the name of liberty if I were to take off a restraint for which those who are most interested in the party ought to be most thankful."

The English Court of Exchequer *In the matter of Parker and others*, 5 *M. & W.*, 31, did not follow the practice adopted in the case of *Rex* v. *Marks*, 3 *East*, 157. They declined to decide the questions involving the validity of the express commitment which it was claimed, justified the detention of the prisoners and refused to discharge them because the return disclosed a crime confessed by them, for which they ought to be tried if they were not already legally convicted and in the proper custody under the sentence.

The prisoners had been indicted in Lower Canada for treason, and under a statute of that province had applied for and received pardon upon the condition of transportation to Van Dieman's Land for fourteen years. In the execution of this condition, they were taken to Liverpool, and whilst means were preparing there to transport them to Van Dieman's Land they were delivered to the jailor of the city for safe-keeping.

The court having stated the substance of the return, proceeded:

"This is the substance of the return, against which many ingenious objections have been urged; the principal of which seem to be, that the legislature of Upper Canada had no authority to make any such law; that if they had, it could be binding only within the precincts of that province; that it could communicate no authority to any person out of that province, and therefore could give none to the jailor of Liverpool; that even if it could have that effect, the pardon granted under that law being conditional, it was not competent to the prisoner to accept a pardon, whereby he submitted himself to imprisonment or transportation; or that if it were competent to him to accept a pardon with such a condition, he has still a right to retract his consent, and to be set free from the obligation imposed upon him by the condition.

"All these topics have been elaborately argued on both sides, and have received due attention from the court; but in the view which we take of the case, we do not think it necessary to pronounce any opinion upon them. If the condition upon which alone the pardon was granted be void, the pardon must also be void. If the condition were lawful, but the prisoner did not assent to it, nor submit to be transported, he cannot have the benefit of the pardon; or, if having assented to it, his assent be revocable, we must consider him to have retracted it by this application to be set at liberty, in which case he is equally unable to avail himself of the pardon. Looking then at the return, the position of the prisoner appears to be this: that he has been indicted for high treason committed in Canada against her Majesty; that he has confessed himself guilty of that treason; that he is liable to be tried for it in England; that he cannot plead the pardon which he has renounced; and that he is now in the custody of the jailor of Liverpool, under such circumstances as would justify any subject of the Crown of England in taking and detaining him in custody, until he be dealt with according to law. Any subject who held him in custody with a knowledge of the circumstances, would be guilty of a crime in aiding and assisting his escape, if he be permitted to go at large without lawful authority. How then can we order the jailor of Liverpool, or any other person who has him in custody, with knowledge of these circumstances, to let him go at large?

"If the prisoner cannot be lawfully transported under his present circumstances, it is to be presumed that the government, upon being so certified, will take proper measures for prosecuting him for the crime of treason in England. For these reasons we are of opinion that the prisoner must be remanded."

In pondering these reasons the prisoner may be supposed to have asked two questions, which he could not very readily answer.

1st. How was the government to be certified that he could not "lawfully be transported under his present circumstances," when the court expressly refused to decide that question.

2d. How long was he to be detained in prison under the presumption that the government would one day take *proper measures* for prosecuting him?

The Court of Queen's Bench had just had the same questions under consideration and evaded none of them. They also remanded the prisoners because they held them to be legally detained under the commitment, &c., as set forth in the return. *Leonard Watson's case*, 6 *Ad. & Ellis*, 731; 36 *Eng C. L.*, 384.

But if the court granting the habeas corpus, does not possess the jurisdiction of a committing magistrate over the alleged offence, it must discharge the prisoner if the commitment be illegal. As where the power to arrest and deliver up fugitives from justice from France was by the Convention *Act of* 6 *and* 7 *Vic.*, *c.* 75, vested in certain officers, the Court of Queen's Bench in Besset's case, after holding the commitment insufficient, refused to act upon the proofs and remand the prisoner on their own authority, on the ground that they had "no authority of the kind in such a case." *Ex parte Besset*, 51 *Eng. C. L.*, 480.

In INDIANA it is provided in the habeas corpus act, *sec.* 21, *Rev. Stat.*, 931, that "if any person be committed to prison, or be in custody of any officer, on any criminal charge, by virtue of any warrant or commitment of a justice of the peace, such person shall not be discharged from such imprisonment or custody, by reason of any defect or informality of such warrant or commitment, if such warrant or commitment substantially allege against such person a criminal offence, of which such justice had jurisdiction.

And if the charge be "defectively or unsubstantially set forth," the court or judge granting the writ may subpœna witnesses, and hear the proofs at large and discharge, let to bail or recommit the prisoner as may be just and legal.

So in KENTUCKY, *Rev. Stat.*, 1852, *p.* 379, *sec.* 16; and in ALABAMA, *Clay Dig.*, 469, § 40; and in ARKANSAS, *English's Dig.*, 577, *sec.* 13.

In DELAWARE, *Rev. St.*, 1852, *p.* 412, *sec.* 14, it is provided: "But no person shall be discharged for a mere defect in the commitment, if the evidence before the court or judge is sufficient to require that he should be committed or bound for his appearance. In such case the committing magistrate shall be summoned, proper witnesses examined, and the accused committed properly."

And for this trouble of doing the work over, it is provided in the 15 *sec.* that the magistrate shall have "no compensation."

SECTION XII.

WARRANT PERFECT, PRISONER NOT ALWAYS REMANDED.

If the warrant be legally sufficient in all respects, the prisoner should ordinarily be remanded or in a proper case let to bail. Yet this is not an invariable rule.

In England it is said that "even though the commitment be regular the court will examine the proceedings, and if the evidence appear altogether insufficient will admit the prisoner to bail; for the court will rather look to the depositions which contain the evidence than to the commitment, in which the justice may have come to a false conclusion." 1 *Chitty Cr. Law*, 129.

In the United States the inquiry has not been always limited to the commitment. In *Ex parte Bollman*, 4 *Cranch*, 75, it was moved to discharge the prisoners on the ground of illegality in the commitment. But Chief Justice Marshall "stated the clear opinion of the court to be, that it was unimportant whether the commitment was regular or irregular in point of form. The court having gone into an examination of the evidence on which the commitment was grounded, they will proceed to do that which the court below ought to have done."

At common law, however, the court would look only to the depositions, taken before the committing magistrate, for their direction, and where a felony was positively charged refused to bail, though an alibi was offered to be proved by the "affidavits of eight credible persons." *Rex* v. *Greenwood*, 2 *Str.*, 1138. Nor would the court at all admit of extrinsic evidence, so that they refused to examine whether a man brought up before them had been previously acquitted of a charge precisely similar. 1 *Ch. Cr. L.*, 130. So where the defendant was charged with receiving stolen goods, knowing that they were stolen, his affidavit that he did not know they were stolen was rejected. *Rex* v. *Parnam*, *Cunningham Rep.*, 96. This practice, in the absence of any statutory regulation, has been sometimes followed in the United States.

In the case of *The State* v. *Asselin*, *T. U. P. Charl.*, 184, the defendant had been committed under a warrant for "feloniously carrying off certain negroes," and being brought up on habeas corpus his counsel moved for his discharge (upon exhibition of evidence written and parol), on the ground that no felony had been committed. The judge admitted the evidence with reluctance, and afterwards held that it was inadmissible for the prisoner, on return to the habeas corpus, to go into a full defence of his case.

"I am tied down," said the judge, "by precedents when they do not militate with the Constitution or the law. It is the glory of our people that their rights are dependent upon fixed principles, and those fixed principles are contained in the fundamental provisions of the Constitution, in the adjudications of our courts, in the precedents established by our ancestors. The imperial legibus solutus is established so soon as a judge sets up his opinion against an uniform current of authorities which have been stamped with the seal of wisdom and acquiesced in by the people." Referring to the cases of *King* v. *Horner*, *Leach Cr. L.*, 226, and *Rex* v. *Greenwood*, 2 *Str.*, 1138, he concludes "that no evidence, extraneous to the depositions and informations taken by the magistrate, ought to be admitted to controvert the facts contained in those depositions or the charge exhibited in the warrant of commitment." He adds also, "These cases are fortified, too, by another principle of law, that no one can, in any case, controvert the truth of the return to a habeas corpus or plead or suggest any matter repugnant to it."

CHAPTER VIII.

RIGHT TO BAIL.

The case being fully submitted, the court is to consider whether they will discharge, bail or remand the prisoner.

If the prisoner is entitled to an unqualified discharge he is set free at once; if not, he must be bailed or remanded.

If the offence be bailable and he offers sufficient surety he must be let to bail; and "excessive bail shall not be required."

SECTION I.

BAILABLE OFFENCES.

By the ancient common law all felonies were bailable; and though the power of inferior courts has been somewhat limited by statute in England, the Court of King's Bench or any judge thereof in vacation may, in the plenitude of that power which they enjoy at common law, in their discretion admit persons to bail in all cases whatsoever, though committed by justices of the peace or others, for crimes in which inferior jurisdictions would not venture to interfere. They may bail for high treason, murder, manslaughter, forgery, rapes, libels and for all felonies and offences whatever. The only exception to their discretionary authority is where the commitment is for a contempt or in execution, for then such imprisonment without bail is part of the sentence and punishment. 1 *Chitty Cr. Law, pp.* 93, 98. But this power is to be exercised in the discretion of the court, and none can claim its benefits, *de jure.* 2 *Hale,* 129. Accordingly, unless it were doubtful whether the prisoner was guilty or not, they refused to bail except in very special cases. "Bail is only proper where it stands indifferent whether the party be guilty or innocent of the accusation against him, as it often does before his trial; but where that indifferency is removed, it would, generally speaking, be absurd to bail him." *Hawkins, B.* 2, *ch.* 15, *sec.* 40.

In the United States the right of bail has been thought worthy of constitutional protection. In the federal Constitution and in the constitutions of nearly all the states it is provided that "excessive bail shall not be required," and in all the states but nine, the power of discretionary denial is strictly limited. The provisions relating to bailable offences are not precisely alike in the several states.

MAINE. "All persons, before conviction, shall be bailable, except for capital offences, where the proof is evident or the presumption great."

RHODE ISLAND. "All persons imprisoned ought to be bailed by sufficient surety, unless for offences punishable by death or imprisonment for life, when the proof of guilt is evident or the presumption great."

CONNECTICUT. "All prisoners shall, before conviction, be bailable by sufficient sureties, except for capital offences, where the proof is evident or the presumption great."

NEW JERSEY. "All persons shall, before conviction, be bailable by sufficient sureties, except for capital offences, when the proof is evident or presumption great."

PENNSYLVANIA. "All persons shall be bailable by sufficient sureties, unless for capital offences, when the proof is evident or presumption great."

DELAWARE. "All prisoners shall be bailable by sufficient sureties, unless for capital offences, when the proof is positive or the presumption great."

FLORIDA. "All persons shall be bailable by sufficient securities, unless in capital cases, where the proof is evident or the presumption strong."

ALABAMA. "All persons shall, before conviction, be bailable by sufficient securities, except for capital offences, when the proof is evident or the presumption great."

MISSISSIPPI. "All prisoners shall, before conviction, be bailable by sufficient securities, except for capital offences, where the proof is evident or the presumption great."

NORTH CAROLINA. "All prisoners shall be bailable by sufficient sureties, unless for capital offences, where the proof is evident or presumption great."

LOUISIANA. "All prisoners shall be bailable by sufficient sureties, unless for capital offences, where the proof is evident or presumption great."

TENNESSEE. "All prisoners shall be bailable by sufficient sureties, unless for capital offences, when the proof is evident or the presumption great."

VERMONT. "All prisoners, unless in execution or committed for capital offences, when the proof is evident or presumption great, shall be bailable by sufficient sureties."

KENTUCKY. "All prisoners shall be bailable by sufficient securities, unless for capital offences, when the proof is evident or presumption great."

INDIANA. "Offences, other than murder and treason, shall be bailable by sufficient sureties. Murder or treason shall not be bailable when the proof is evident or the presumption strong."

ILLINOIS. "All persons shall be bailable by sufficient sureties, unless for capital offences, where the proof is evident or the presumption great."

MICHIGAN. "All persons shall, before conviction, be bailable by sufficient sureties, except for murder and treason, when the proof is evident or the presumption great."

MISSOURI. "All persons shall be bailable by sufficient sureties, except for capital offences, when the proof is evident or the presumption great."

ARKANSAS. "All prisoners shall be bailable by sufficient securities, unless in capital offences, where the proof is evident or the presumption great."

TEXAS. "All prisoners shall be bailable by sufficient sureties, unless for capital offences, when the proof is evident or the presumption great; but this provision shall not be so construed as to prohibit bail after indictment found upon an examination of the evidence by a judge of the Supreme or District Court, upon the return of the writ of habeas corpus, returnable in the county where the offence is committed."

IOWA. "All persons shall, before conviction, be bailable by sufficient sureties, except for capital offences, where the proof is evident or the presumption great."

WISCONSIN. "All persons shall, before conviction, be bailable by sufficient sureties, except for capital offences, when the proof is evident or the presumption great."

CALIFORNIA. "All persons shall be bailable by sufficient sureties, unless for capital offences, when the proof is evident or the presumption great."

OHIO. "All persons shall be bailable by sufficient sureties, except for capital offences, where the proof is evident or the presumption great."

In Ohio, California, Texas, Arkansas, Illinois, Indiana, Kentucky, Tennessee, Louisiana, North Carolina, Florida, Delaware, Pennsylvania and Rhode Island the right to bail in the unexcepted cases is unlimited; in all the rest it is limited by the "conviction."

In Indiana the right to bail in the excepted cases, is expressly prohibited; in all the rest if prohibited, it is by implication only.

In Alabama it has been denied that there is an implied prohibition. In *Ex parte Croom and May*, 19 *Ala.*, 561, the court in speaking of this section in their Bill of Rights say:

"It is believed that the history of the legislation of the state, both before and since the adoption of the Constitution, and the numerous decisions of this court upon similar statutes as well as the spirit of other portions of the constitution, very satisfactorily show that the above clause in the Bill of Rights, was not designed to deny to the legislature the power to pass laws providing for bail in capital cases, when the proof was evident or the presumption great.

"At common law, all cases were bailable; but it was competent for the legislature in the absence of a constitutional inhibition, to deprive the citizen of this right, or so to modify it as to render it valueless. The clause was designed not to place a perpetual restriction upon the common law right of the citizen, in the matter of bail, but on the contrary to secure by the fundamental law of the state, and to place this right in the given cases, beyond the power of either legislative or judicial interposition, creating however, no restriction upon the legislature as to the excepted cases, when the 'proof is evident or the presumption great."'

In Pennsylvania however, it was said in *Commonwealth* v. *Keeper of Prison*, 2 *Ash.*, 227, that "where a crime is charged which is short of a capital felony, the judges are bound to admit the prisoner to bail; but where a capital felony is charged and the proof of it is evident, or the presumption great, *no power exists anywhere to admit to bail.*"

In those states where the right has not been secured by constitutional provisions, it is protected by the court in as ample a manner as by the Court of King's Bench in England. *Ex parte Tayloe*, 5 *Cow.*, 39; *Jones* v. *Kelley*, 17 *Mass.*, 116; *Evans* v. *Foster*, 1 *N. Hamp.*, 374; *The State* v. *Everett*, *Dudley Law Rep.*, *S. Car.*, 295, *cited* 1 *Hill*, *Rep.*, 398, *note.*

It may be doubted whether the right to the writ of habeas corpus, as it is regulated by the habeas corpus acts in several of the states, is co-extensive with the constitutional or common law right to be let to bail. There are cases excepted in those acts, from the benefit of that writ in which the prisoner may clearly be entitled to be bailed. If in those cases where the imprisonment is not, and is not alleged to be, illegal, the writ of habeas corpus may be granted for the sole purpose of admitting the prisoner to bail, as has sometimes been done, it must be by virtue of some special statute or of that "sovereign jurisdiction in criminal matters," which belongs only to the highest courts. The writ of habeas corpus was a common law remedy, where bail was improperly refused. 4 *Inst.*, 290; *Hand's Pr.*, 522.

And has been granted where excessive bail was exacted. *Jones* v. *Kelley*, 17 *Mass.*, 116.

The practice in Alabama where bail was alleged to have been unlawfully denied, was much considered in *Ex parte Croom*, 19 *Ala.*,*561. In that case it was held that a prisoner charged with a capital offence, after having been refused bail by a circuit judge, on application by habeas corpus, may petition the supreme court for a revision of the decision of the circuit judge. That the proper practice in such case, is, for the prisoner to petition the supreme court for the writ of habeas corpus, and such other remedial process as may be necessary to render its control effectual, setting forth under oath such a state of the case as will show that the circuit judge erred to his prejudice, and that he was entitled by the case then made to the relief which he seeks; and if the supreme court deems the showing *prima facie* sufficient to entitle the prisoner to bail, the writs of habeas corpus and certiorari will be awarded to bring before the supreme court the body of the prisoner and the proceeding had before the circuit judge, that if upon a full hearing on the return of the writs, the prisoner should be adjudged entitled to bail, he may be allowed to give bail in such sum as may be prescribed.

In the United States then the excepted cases are "capital offences, when the proof is evident or the presumption great." In these cases the common law right to bail has been extended; for the King's Bench may refuse to bail on a slight preponderance of proof against the prisoner. 2 *Hawk. P. C., ch.* 15. Here the proof must be evident or the presumption great. The court must find there is proof evident or a strong presumption of the prisoner's guilt, or allow him to give bail.

2. *Inquiry before indictment.* We have seen that it is not competent in this summary proceeding to try the question of the guilt or innocence of the prisoner with a view to his absolute discharge. It has also been held in some cases in England, that extrinsic evidence would not be heard even with a view to bail: as where a felony was positively charged the court refused to bail though an alibi was supported by numerous affidavits. 2 *Str.*, 1138. So they refused to examine whether a man brought up before them had been previously acquitted of a charge precisely similar. 2 *Str.*, 751. So they refused to bail a person for receiving stolen goods, the defendant's affidavit admitting the receipt of the goods but denying that he knew them to be stolen. *Rex* v. *Parnham, Cunningham Rep.*, 96. Nor would they allow, at the request of the party accused, an inspection of a person whom he had stabbed, in order to ascertain that he is out of danger, that the prisoner may be admitted to bail. 1 *Str.*, 546.

These decisions, however, cannot be reconciled with those cited in 2 *Hawk., ch.* 15, *sec.* 79, where a more liberal and humane rule was acted upon.

In the United States, where in all such cases it is the prisoner's *right* to be bailed, such evidence is admissible to guide the court in determining the amount of the bond.

In the case before cited of *The State* v. *Asselyn, T. U. P. Charlton*, 184, where affidavits and oral evidence, not produced before the committing magistrate, were offered to show that no felony had been committed, although the judge felt constrained to reject it on the motion to discharge, he did receive and consider it on the motion to bail, saying: "Though I cannot receive this evidence on a motion to discharge the prisoner, yet I am not precluded by any principle of law from permitting it to regulate the bail which I conceive it proper to require."

Similar proofs were held admissible in Texas. *Yarborough* v. *The State*, 2 *Texas*, 519.

What state of facts is necessary to bring the case within the constitutional prohibition cannot be easily defined.

It is said to be "a safe rule, where a malicious homicide is charged, to refuse bail in all cases where a judge would sustain a capital conviction if pronounced by a jury on such evidence of guilt as was exhibited to him on the hearing of the application to admit to bail, and in instances where the evidence of the commonwealth is of less efficacy to admit to bail." *Commonwealth* v. *Keeper of Prison*, 2 *Ashm.*, 227.

3. *Inquiry after indictment.* The grand jury acts upon evidence taken usually viva voce, always in secret and never preserved; the evidence, therefore, does not admit of that summary revision which is applied to coroners' inquests and the proceedings of

committing magistrates, where the evidence is for the most part reduced to writing. 1 *Chit. Cr. Law*, 129; *The People* v. *McLeod*, 1 *Hill*, 377. At common law, however, the court sometimes admitted the prisoner to bail after indictment, and it is said, "The court will sometimes examine by affidavit the circumstances of a fact on which a prisoner brought before them by an habeas corpus hath been indicted, in order to inform themselves, on examination of the whole matter, whether it be reasonable to bail him or not. And agreeably hereto, where one Jackson, who had been indicted of piracy before the sessions of admiralty on a malicious prosecution, brought his habeas corpus in said court in order to be bailed, the court examined the whole circumstances of the fact by affidavits, upon which it appeared that the prosecutor himself, if any one, was guilty, and carried on the present prosecution to screen himself; and thereupon the court, in consideration of the unreasonableness of the prosecution and the uncertainty of the time when another session of admiralty might be holden, admitted the said Jackson to bail, and committed the prosecutor till he should find bail to answer the facts contained in the affidavits." 2 *Hawk. P. C., ch.* 15, *sec.* 79.

In some of the United States the indictment has been held to preclude all inquiry as to the guilt or innocence of the accused, whether with a view to discharge or bail.

In Louisiana, in the case of *The Territory* v. *Benoit*, 1 *Martin Rep.*, 142, the grand jury had found an indictment against the defendant for an assault with intent to murder, then a capital offence. A motion having been made to bail him, the court said:

"It cannot be done. Bail is never allowed in offences punishable by death, when the proof is evident or the presumption great. On a coroner's inquest finding a person guilty of a capital crime, the judges have often looked into the testimony which the coroner is bound to record, and when they have been of opinion that the jurors had drawn an illogical conclusion, admitted the party to bail. But as the evidence before the grand jury is not written, and cannot be disclosed, the same discretion and control cannot be exercised, *and the judges cannot help considering the finding of a grand jury as too great a presumption of the defendant's guilt to bail him.*"

In NORTH CAROLINA, in the case of *The State* v. *Mills*, 2 *Dev. Rep.*, 421, RUFFIN, J., said: "After bill found, a defendant is presumed to be guilty to most, if not to all purposes, except that of a fair and impartial trial before a petit jury. This presumption is so strong that in the case of a capital felony, the party *cannot be let to bail.*"

In IOWA, in the case of *Hight* v. *U. S.*, *Morris Rep.*, 407, the court say: "A prisoner under an indictment for murder cannot, as a matter of right, claim to be admitted to bail on habeas corpus. An indictment furnishes no presumption of guilt against a prisoner when he is upon his trial, but, so far as it regards all intermediate proceedings between the indictment and trial, it furnishes the very strongest possible presumption of guilt. The provisions of our habeas corpus act, so far as they require the hearing of original testimony, contemplate cases where no indictment has been found.

"The finding of the grand jury is conclusive, so far as to control proceedings up to the time of trial before the petit jury."

On the other hand, in *South Carolina*, affidavits were received on the question of guilt, and bail allowed. *State*

v. *Hill*, 1 *Const. Rep.*, 242. *Smith, J.*, dissented: He, however, admitted the *power* of the court, but denied the propriety of its exercise.

And in the case of *The State* v. *Hill*, 3 *Brevard*, 89, it was held that, after a bill of indictment found for a capital felony, the defendant may be admitted to bail at the discretion of the Court of General Sessions, and that court may hear and consider affidavits tending to show that the prosecution was instituted from malice or mistake.

In TEXAS, prior to her annexation to the United States, it was decided in the case of *The Republic* v. *Wingate, Dec. Term*, 1845, that after an indictment for murder the prisoner was entitled to an examination of the witnesses as to his guilt or innocence, upon an application for bail. The 9th section of the Texas Bill of Rights, before cited, seems to have been intended as an affirmance of the principle of this decision. *Yarborough* v. *The State*, 2 *Texas*, 519.

In INDIANA, it is said that the indictment should not be taken as conclusive of the grade of the offence, in determining the question of bail, *because upon an indictment for murder in the first degree, the accused may be convicted of murder in the first or second degree, or of manslaughter*—the last two offences not being "capital." *Lum* v. *The State*, 3 *Porter*, 393. Under the provisions of the statute in that state, it is held that after indictment on habeas corpus, where the prisoner admits the legality of the arrest and detention, but claims the right to give bail for his appearance, witnesses may be summoned and the court proceed fully to investigate the case on this point. *Ib.*

In VIRGINIA, if a prisoner, remanded for trial by the examining court to the superior court on a charge of felony, apply to the latter court to be let to bail, on the ground that there is only a slight suspicion of his guilt, an *indictment found against him and the judgment of the examining court are not conclusive against the application. Commonwealth* v. *Rutherford*, 5 *Rand.*, 646.

In NEW YORK, where there is no constitutional provision on the subject, the English practice has been pursued, of denying bail after indictment found, though the *power* of the court to admit to bail in such a case is not understood to be denied. *The People* v. *McLeod*, 1 *Hill*, 377; *The People* v. *Martin*, 1 *Parker Cr. Rep.*, 191.

And in the case of *The People* v. *Hyler and others*, 2 *Parker Cr. Rep.*, 570, it was held that on a motion to admit to bail, on an indictment for murder, the court would consider the testimony taken before the coroner and grand jury, but would not hear further proof either by affidavits or oral testimony tending to establish the innocence of the defendants as affecting the question of bail.

And the same practice appears to have been adopted in the courts of the United States. On Burr's trial, after indictment, the defendant, on the question of his right to be admitted to bail, proposed to show that the indictment against him had been obtained by perjury; but Ch. J. Marshall thought it inadmissible after indictment found, and refused to let him to bail. 1 *Burr's Trial*, 310.

So in the case of *The United States* v. *Ruse*, 3 *Wash. C. C. Rep.*, 224, the defendant being indicted for piracy, his counsel proposed to go into evidence against him, to show that he ought to be bailed; but, per *Washington, J.*, "The bill of indictment being found, we do not feel ourselves at liberty to inquire into the evidence against him."

There is certainly great force in the suggestion of the court in Indiana, 3 *Porter*, 393, that the indictment should not be taken as conclusive of the grade of the offence. The indictment may be for murder in the first degree, an offence not bailable; the true offence and the conviction under the indictment may be for manslaughter, an offence which is bailable. The distinction between the two offences depends upon questions of law upon which the grand jury may be wholly uninstructed. To refuse then to look beyond the indictment on the question of bail is greatly to embarrass the prisoner's constitutional right, and in some cases must operate as a practical denial of it.

In the late case of *The People* v. *Hyler and others*, 2 *Parker*, 570, above cited, the court did not hold that the mere finding of the indictment precluded inquiry; and they did examine the testimony taken before the coroner, and that taken before the grand jury upon which the indictment was found.

Upon what principle can the rejection of the additional testimony, offered on the single question of bail, be justified in such a case? If any evidence should be considered, why not all that may tend to inform the judgment of the court? Must the preliminary examination before the coroner, taken suddenly with a view to commitment only, and the evidence taken before the grand jury, ex parte and in secret, be conclusive upon the prisoner on his motion, to be allowed his constitutional or common law right of bail?

The court advance as a reason for rejecting the testimony offered by the prisoner that "to open the whole question of guilt or innocence to proof, on a motion to admit to bail, would be attended with most serious public inconvenience."

Is "*public inconvenience*" a sufficient ground for withholding a *private right*, especially in those states which have deemed it worthy of a constitutional guaranty?

In some states the examinations before the committing magistrate or grand jury are not required to be reduced to writing. To refuse, in such, to hear testimony, on the motion to bail, would be in the case of a commitment by a magistrate, to commit to him almost an exclusive jurisdiction on that important question; and in the case of the institution of the prosecution by indictment to deny it in capital cases, if not in others.

Circumstances not connected with the merits of the prosecution. It is said by Mr. Hill, in his note to 3 *Hill*, 671, that "independently of and collateral to the merits on which the prosecution is founded, there are several circumstances, whether arising before or after indictment, which may entitle to bail. One is a clear want of jurisdiction over the subject matter. *The People* v. *McLeod*, 1 *Hill*, 406; 25 *Wend.*, 573.

"So if the facts returned be falsified; as if the officer return an order of commitment or process for a crime not bailable, when in fact it is for some other crime which is bailable. So if a prisoner be not indicted within the time required by statute, or if indicted be not tried as speedily as he is by statute entitled, in which instances he may be discharged or bailed, as the case may require. *State* v. *Stalmaker*, 2 *Brev. Rep.*, 44.

"It is said if the prisoner be so sick as to be in danger of his life, he may be bailed, even after indictment for murder; though bail was denied, the sickness not endangering life. *Kirk's case*, 5 *Mod.*, 454. Bail was allowed on this ground in a case of piracy, after indictment, though the sickness was not immediately dangerous. *United States* v. *Jones*, 3 *Wash. C. C. Rep.*, 224. In cases of crime not capital, bail is sometimes allowed at any time before trial, with consent of the attorney-general or district attorney. 1 *Chitty Cr. Law*, 129; *Selfridge Tr. Pamphlet.* If a jury have disagreed in such a case, and been discharged, and the case appear to be one on which they might fairly so disagree without perverseness, that may also form a ground for bail. *Goodwin's case*, 5 *City Hall Rec.*, 11, 49, 52; 1 *Wheel. Cr. Cas.*, 443. So where an indictment is plainly frivolous, as if it be for a crime not known to the law, the prisoner may, perhaps, be let to bail" [and, *perhaps*, instantly and absolutely discharged].

In order to warrant a discharge because of delay in bringing on the trial, the *state* must be in fault. *Bird* v. *The State*, 1 *How. Miss. Rep.*, 163; *State* v. *Marco*, *Charlt. Rep.*, 24;" [see also *The State* v. *Rogers*, 7 *Louis. Rep.*, 382; *Ex parte Simonton*, 9 *Port.*, 390; *State* v. *Buych*, 2 *Bay*, 563.]

The prisoner may be bailed where the prosecution is unreasonably delayed, or where he may be in danger of losing his life, either by famine or dangerous distemper, &c., unless he be bailed. *Bac. Abr.*, *Bail*, *Cr. Cas.*, *D*.

The indisposition upon which the court will bail, must be a present indisposition, arising from the *con-*

finement and not from any constitutional or family distemper, or from the act of the prisoner. *Rex* v. *Wyndham*, 1 *S. P.*, 4; *Cowp.*, 333; 11 *Leigh*, 665, *Archer's case*, 6 *Gratt.*, 705.

Where several indictments were founded on one criminal transaction, and might have been all included in one indictment, though prosecuted as several offences and the prisoner was acquitted in one case, it was held that it afforded such a presumption of his innocence in the others as entitled him to be bailed. *Green's case*, 2 *Leigh*, 677; *State* v. *Simmons*, 19 *Ohio Rep.*, 139.

But mere disagreement of the jury does not entitle the prisoner to be let to bail in Ohio, 19 *Ohio Rep.*, 139.

4. *Inquiry, after conviction.* At common law the prisoner might be let to bail after conviction if that appeared to be erroneous. 2 *Hawk. P. C.*, 175; 1 *Bac. Abr.*, 353.

In Mississippi, a prisoner after conviction in a case not capital, may be discharged from imprisonment on bail to appear and abide the sentence of the court. *Davis* v. *The State*, 6 *How. Miss.*, 399.

The right of a prisoner to bail, after conviction, is governed by the rules and practice of the common law; and the power of the court ought to be exercised with great caution. *Ex parte Dyson*, 25 *Miss.*, 356.

The prisoner's constitutional right after conviction in non-excepted cases. It has been made a question in those states where there is no express limitation as to time, whether the prisoner could claim to be let to bail as a matter of constitutional right, and it has been variously decided.

The provision in the Constitution of North Carolina is as follows: "All persons shall be bailable by sufficient sureties, unless for capital offences where the proof is evident or presumption great."

In that state in the case of *The State* v. *Ward*, 2 *Hawks.*, 443, it was held, on appeal to the Supreme Court, to be discretionary with the court to bail the prisoner after conviction for an offence not capital; and that bail should be refused unless the case be very doubtful on the merits.

In Louisiana the constitutional provision on the subject, (108*th Art.*) is identical with that in North Carolina. The same question decided in 2 *Hawks.*, 443, arose in the case of "*Longworth, praying for a writ of Habeas Corpus*," 7 *La. Rep.*, 24, in 1852. In that case it appears the prisoner was prosecuted for larceny, convicted and sentenced. He then took an appeal, in the nature of a writ of error to the Supreme Court. The general assembly had passed a law in effect denying the right to bail after conviction, notwithstanding an appeal pending.

The question was as to the prisoner's constitutional right to bail, during the pendency of the appeal. The court say: "The convention in providing by the 108th *Art.*, for the liberty of the citizen, though accused of crime, must have referred to the principles of bail in criminal cases as they existed at the time of the adoption of the Constitution. It becomes necessary therefore, by a thorough search to ascertain what those principles were."

They find that the courts and judges at common law exercised an unbounded discretion to bail or refuse to bail, "without certain rules to guide it, which has ever been regarded with jealousy by a people tenacious of liberty," and proceed: "The people of Louisiana have therefore by their constitution restrained the discretion, and enlarged the liberty of the citizen by declaring that 'all persons shall be bailable by sufficient sureties unless for capital offences, where the proof is evident or presumption great; and the privilege of the writ of habeas corpus shall not be suspended unless when in cases of rebellion or invasion the public safety may require it.'

"A judge or court authorized to issue a writ of habeas corpus, cannot therefore refuse bail by sufficient sureties except for capital offences, where the proof is evident or presumption great.

"It is the constitutional right of the prisoner to demand it, and it is not in the discretion of the judge to deny it.

"Does the conviction of the prisoner deprive him of this constitutional right? A conviction did not deprive the judges of the power to bail according to their discretion at common law. *Str.*, 9, 531, 794; 2 *Shower*, 96; *Salk.*, 60.

"In many of the states an appeal or writ of error is allowed by law, to obtain relief from an improper conviction. Where that means of relief is accorded until the appeal or writ of error can be tried, the party prosecuting it has often been bailed, notwithstanding his conviction. 1 *Caine's R.*, 148, 72; 1 *Wheeler Cr. Cas.*, 431. In some states express provision is made by law enabling convicts to give bail until their appeal or writ of error is tried. *Miss.*

Rev. St., 138, *Mass. Rev. St.*, 763. And it is probable that in most of the states where appeals or writs of error are allowed in criminal cases, similar relief is extended to prisoners either by statute or by the practice of their courts, by suspending the execution of the sentence and all the effects of the conviction during the pendency of the appeal or writ of error; otherwise the hope of relief would be attended with certain evil, rendering its advantage doubtful. The case of *The State* v. *Ward.* 2 *Hawks.*, 443, is a decision directly in point against the application in the present case. We cannot so interpret the clause in our Constitution, the words of which are plain, unambiguous and imperative 'that all persons shall be bailable by sufficient sureties unless,' &c. They are entitled to be bailed as a matter of right, and the judge has no discretion except in fixing the amount of the security.

"The prisoner is not undergoing the sentence of the law for his crime, but is a prisoner awaiting the final determination of his case by the Supreme Court, to which the 63d *Art.* of the Constitution allows him to appeal."

Let to bail, $5,000.

One judge, the court consisting of four, dissented.

CHAPTER IX.

CLAIMS FOR PRIVATE CUSTODY FOUNDED ON THE DOMESTIC RELATIONS.

SECTION I.

GENERAL OBSERVATIONS.

It has been seen that at common law, the writ of habeas corpus might be granted on the application of the husband, parent, guardian and master for the purpose of inquiring into any alleged illegal restraint, respectively, of the wife, child, ward or apprentice.

The object, it will be observed, in such cases is not to enforce a right of custody; but to remove unlawful restraint. The party thus interested in the custody will be presumed to represent the wishes of the person restrained, so far as to enable him to set the remedial power of the court in motion. But the right properly speaking, extends no farther than that.

In the case of adults, other than idiots and lunatics, where the writ issues at the instance of one claiming the custody, the court makes no order in relation to the custody, but leaves the person brought up free to go where he or she pleases. If the writ issues at the instance of the person restrained to be set free from a legal custody, the court may discharge or remand according as it finds the custody to be legal or illegal, and if legal whether grossly abused or not.

SECTION II.

HUSBAND FOR HIS WIFE.

In the case of *Rex* v. *Clarkson*, 1 *Str.*, 447, Dibley pretending to have married Mrs. Turberville, a lady of fortune, took out a habeas corpus directed to her guardians, commanding them to bring her into court. When she was brought into court, and the return had been read, the chief justice asked her if she desired to be taken out of the hands of the person she lived with and go with Dibley? She denied him to be her husband, and desired she might continue with her guardians.

THE COURT. "We have nothing to do to order her to go with Dibley, but only to see that she is under no illegal restraint; all we can do is to declare that she is at her liberty to go where she pleases; but lest this writ be made use of by Dibley as a means to get her abroad and seize her, we will order our tipstaff to wait upon her home to her guardians; and so it was done in Lady Harriet Berkley's case." *3d vol. St. Tr.*, 78.

In the case of *Rex* v. *Mead*, 1 *Burr.*, 542, the writ issued at the instance of the husband for his wife directed to her mother. On the return it appeared there had been articles of separation executed in which the husband had covenanted "never to disturb her or any person with whom she should live." It was suggested that the writ had been obtained by the husband with a view of seizing her by force or for some other bad purpose.

The court held the argreement to be a formal renunciation by the husband of his marital right to seize her, or force her back to live with him. And they said that any attempt of the husband to seize her would be a breach of the peace, and that any attempt by the husband to molest her in her present return from Westminister Hall would be a contempt of the court.

They told the lady she was at full liberty to go where and to whom she pleased.

In such a case a court of Chancery will interfere by injunction to restrain the husband from infringing his covenant. *Sanders* v. *Rodway*, 13 *Eng. Law and Eq.*, 463.

But even without articles of separation, if the wife voluntarily leaves her husband and remains absent without any restraint, the husband is not entitled to the writ of habeas corpus.

This point was determined in a late case, *Ex parte Sandilands*, 12 *Eng. Law and Eq.*, 463. In that case a rule *nisi* had been obtained on the application of Mr. Sandilands, for a writ of habeas corpus to bring up the body of his wife. It appeared by the affidavits, upon which the rule was founded, that Mrs. Sandilands was staying with her son, against whom the application was made, by her own consent, and that no coercion or imprisonment had been used towards her, except that it was suggested that she was incapable of exercising a sound discretion and that her son used undue influence over her. The court hesitated, being of opinion that this was, in effect, an indirect mode of suing for a restitution of conjugal rights; but the case of *The King* v. *Mead*, 1 *Burr.*, 542, being cited, they reluctantly granted a rule to show cause.

Lord CAMPBELL, Ch. J.: "The court granted this rule with very great reluctance, and against the impression of every member of it; but we were told that there was an authority which supported the application, and as we always feel a great tenderness in dealing with writs of habeas corpus, we acceded to the application for a rule *nisi*.

"That rule has now been discussed, and, after hearing the argument, I think it should never have been granted. This invaluable writ could always be obtained where a person had been improperly deprived of liberty. From the earliest times, before the habeas corpus act, a writ issued in such cases, calling upon the party detaining to show cause if any just cause existed for the detention; but this was always on the supposition that liberty was interfered with. Here this lady is living with her son by her own free consent, and is under no restraint whatever. Whether her husband can or cannot compel her return is a question *alieno foro*. We have no jurisdiction on that subject. If this writ were to go and the lady were to be produced before us in court, she would be at perfect liberty to return to her son as at present, if she so pleased, and we could make no order for her to live with her husband. If she has no good cause for living absent from him, he may have a decree in the Ecclesiastical Court for her to return and live with him.

"The case of an infant, to which allusion has been made, is quite different, because there the parent has the right to the custody of the child, and if the infant is of tender years, the court will order it to be delivered to its father. But a husband has no such right at common law to the custody of his wife."

SECTION III.

PARENT FOR HIS CHILD.

1. *Degree of restraint necessary to authorize the writ.* The use of the writ of habeas corpus in this class of cases, infers some modification of the general idea of imprisonment, and an extension of the original design of the writ.

The term *imprisonment* usually imports a restraint contrary to the wishes of the prisoner; and the writ of habeas corpus was designed as a remedy for *him*, to be invoked at *his* instance, to set him at liberty, not to change his keeper.

But in the case of infants an unauthorized absence from the legal custody has been treated, at least for the purpose of allowing the writ to issue, as equivalent to imprisonment; and the duty of returning to such custody, as equivalent to a wish to be free.

It has been held that the writ may not only issue without privity of the child, *The People* v. *Mercein*,

3 *Hill*, 399; but against its express wishes. *Commonwealth* v. *Hamilton*, 6 *Mass.*, 273.

"To confine the writ of habeas corpus at common law," said the judge, *In the matter of Mitchell, R. M. Charl.*, 489, "exclusively to cases of illegal confinement would be destructive of the ends of justice. I apprehend it is not going too far to say, that the interests and welfare of society require, that, under peculiar circumstances, the fact that the child of tender years is *detained* improperly from the person entitled to its possession is sufficient ground to maintain the writ of habeas corpus."

To the same effect, were the observations of *Patteson, J.*, in *Ex parte McClellan*, 1 *Dowl. P. C.*, 81: "With respect to the argument, that some force or improper restraint must be used in order to authorize the court to remove an infant from the custody of any one, the authorities referred to show that it is not necessary that any force or restraint should exist on the part of the person having the custody of the infant towards it."

In the case of *Mercein* v. *The People*, 25 *Wend.*, 64, *Bronson, J.*, said: "For all legal purposes the child is in the custody of those with whom it lives."

2. *Nature and extent of the jurisdiction.* "The father may obtain the custody of his children by the writ of habeas corpus, when they are improperly detained from him; but the courts, both of law and equity, will investigate the circumstances and according to sound discretion, and will not always and of course interfere upon habeas corpus, and take a child, though under fourteen years of age, from the posses-

sion of a third person and deliver it over to the father against the will of the child. They will consult the inclination of an infant, if it be of sufficiently mature age to judge for itself, and even control the right of the father to the possession and education of his child, when the nature of the case appears to warrant it." 2 *Kent*, 194.

The nature and extent of the jurisdiction under the writ of habeas corpus in this class of cases have sometimes been spoken of in terms of great indefiniteness; and sometimes a plenitude of power has been exercised which it might be difficult completely to defend.

The court or judge, in these cases, exercises a degree of equity jurisdiction; but it is far short of the power exercised by a court of equity sitting as the representative of the sovereign in the character of *parens patriæ*.

Before proceeding to notice the difference between the jurisdiction under the writ of habeas corpus and that under a bill in equity in reference to the custody of infants, it may be observed,

1st. The power of a judge or other officer in vacation, in respect to the custody of infants, when the jurisdiction under the writ is conferred in general terms and without particular qualifications, is the same as that of a court of general jurisdiction in term when acting under the writ alone.

2d. The powers of a judge or court of law are the same as those of a chancellor or court of equity under the writ. It has sometimes been supposed that a chancellor or a court of equity possessed ampler powers under the writ of habeas corpus, than a judge or court of law could exercise.

But this is a mistake. The jurisdiction in such cases and the powers under the writ are "exactly the same." *Crowley's case*, 2 *Swanst. Rep.*, 79; *Lyons* v. *Blenheim*, *Jac.*, 245, *n.*; *Matter of Wollstonecraft*, 4 *John. C. R.*, 80. In the case of *The People* v. *Mercein*, 8 *Paige*, 47, the Chancellor, observed: "The right to the guardianship of an infant cannot be tried upon a habeas corpus. The Court of Chancery upon such a writ will exercise, in disposing of the custody of the infant, its discretion, *upon the same principles* which regulate the exercise of a similar discretion by other officers and courts, who are authorized to allow the writ in similar cases."

The grounds upon which courts of equity proceed, in questions of parental custody are more numerous, and sometimes of a different character from those upon which orders in habeas corpus are founded.

"Although in general parents are intrusted with the custody of the persons and the education of their children, yet this is done upon the natural presumption that the children will be properly taken care of, and will be brought up with a due education in literature and morals, and religion; and that they will be treated with kindness and affection; but whenever this presumption is removed, whenever (for example) it is found that a father is guilty of gross illtreatment or cruelty towards his infant children; or that he is in constant habits of drunkenness and blasphemy, or low and gross debauchery; or that he professes atheistical or irreligious principles; or that his domestic associations are such as tend to the corruption and contamination of his children; or that he otherwise acts in a manner injurious to the morals or interests of his children; in every such case the Court of Chancery will interfere and deprive him of the custody of his children, and appoint a suitable person to act as guardian and take care of them, and to superintend their education. *Story Eq. Juris.*, § 1341.

"'The Court of Chancery' says Lord Hardwicke in *Butler* v. *Freeman*, *Ambler*, 302, 'has a general right delegated by the crown, as parens patriæ to interfere in particular cases for the benefit of such as are incapable to protect themselves.'

"'But there *must be a suit depending* relative to the infant or his estate, to entitle the court to this jurisdiction.' *Ib.*

"In the case of *Wellesley* v. *The Duke of Beaufort*, 3 *Eng. Con. Ch. Rep.*, 10, which was a proceeding in chancery, Lord Eldon in discussing the subject of the jurisdiction of a court of chancery in these cases, says: 'So much has passed with reference to this subject as to make it not altogether inexpedient to say something on the nature of the law, as between parent and child, which is administered in this court. I do apprehend that notwithstanding all the doubts that may exist as to the origin of this jurisdiction, it will be found to be absolutely necessary that such a jurisdiction should exist. With respect to the doctrine that this authority belongs to the king as parens patriæ, exercising a jurisdiction by this court, it has been observed at the bar, that the court has not exercised that jurisdiction, unless where there was property belonging to the infant to be taken care of in this court. Now whether that be an accurate view of the law or not; whether it be founded on what Lord Hardwicke says in the case of *Butler* v. *Freeman*, *Ambler*, 303, 'that there must be a suit depending relative to the infant or his estate,' (applying, however, the latter words rather to what the court is to do with respect to the maintenance of infants;) or whether it arises out of a necessity of another kind, namely, that the court must have property in order to exercise this jurisdiction; that is a question to which perhaps sufficient consideration has not been given. If any one will turn his mind attentively to the subject he must see that this court has not the means of acting, except where it has property to act upon. It is not, however, from any want of jurisdiction that it does not act, but from a want of means to exercise its jurisdiction; because the court cannot take on itself the maintenance of all the children in the kingdom. It can exercise this jurisdiction usefully and practically only where it has the means of doing so; that is to say, by its having the means of applying property for the use and maintenance of the infants.

"If this court has not the power to interpose what is the provision of the law that is made for the children? You may go to the Court of King's Bench for a habeas corpus to restore the child to the father; but when you have restored the child to the father, can you go to the Court of King's Bench to compel that father to subscribe even to the amount of five shillings a year for the maintenance of that child? A magistrate may compel a trifling allowance, but I do not believe that there was ever a mandamus from the Court of King's Bench upon such a subject. It is an eligible thing that children of all ranks should be placed in this situation, that they shall be in the custody of the father; although, looking at the quantum of allowance which the law can compel the father to provide for them, they may be regarded as in a state little better than that of starvation.

"The courts of law can enforce the rights of the father, but they are not equal to the office of enforcing the duties of the father. Those duties have been acknowledged in this his Majesty's court for centuries past."

No judge or court in a simple habeas corpus proceeding assumes any such amplitude of jurisdiction. They do, however, act upon some of the grounds upon which the Court of Chancery proceeds. But it is not to be forgotten that their proceeding is emphatically a summary one, and that its chief end and aim is to relieve from illegal restraint. It acts upon the present actual condition of the parties and for the present. It does not undertake to prescribe what their *future* relations shall be. It takes care that the infant shall not leave the court under injurious custody, and *expects* that the custody to which it is committed will continue while the circumstances shown in evidence remain unaltered, but it does not *command* that it shall thus continue. Orders have sometimes been made, it is true, of a somewhat more mandatory and prospective character, but they do not appear to rest upon very satisfactory ground

The true idea was very nearly expressed by the court *In the matter of Kottman*, 2 *Hill C. R.*, 363:

"Perhaps it might be more correctly said that the office of the court," on habeas corpus, "is to discharge the infant from illegal restraint, *and the discretion is to protect the infant in returning*."

The distinction between the powers of a court of common law and a court of equity is stated by Lord Redesdale, in *Wellesley* v. *Wellesley*, 2 *Bligh, N. S.*, 126, thus:

"The care of the person to protect from violence belongs to the Court of King's Bench, but the care of the person with respect to education, does not belong to the Court of King's Bench, and the Court of King's Bench disclaims any such right; therefore as to the care and protection for the purpose of education, it belongs to this court (of Chancery) which has exercised the jurisdiction. The same view of the matter was taken in *Ex parte Skinner*, 9 *Moore*, 278, in the Common Pleas by Best, Ch. J., who said: 'In cases of similar applications to the Court of King's Bench they generally refer the parties to a master in chancery who may ascertain whether there is sufficient property to provide for the support of the child, or whether it might be made a ward of that court or he might appoint a guardian to take care of it; and that, therefore, appears to me to be the wisest course, at all events our authority can only be coequal with that of the Court of King's Bench. But the Court of Chancery has a jurisdiction as representing the King *parens patriæ*, and that court may accordingly, under circumstances, control the right of the father to the possession of his child and appoint a proper person to watch over its morals and see that it receives a proper education; and if a sum equivalent to its maintenance can be obtained the Lord Chancellor will order it to be done without inquiring where the funds are to come from.'

"Lord ELDON also said, *Jac.*, 254, that where the infant was a ward of the court there were many circumstances to which he could give attention, which could not weigh with him on a habeas corpus alone, without any cause in court. He said also that he apprehended that the jurisdiction which he had upon a habeas corpus was *exactly the same* as if it was before a judge, and that a judge attended to nothing but cruelty or personal ill-usage to the child as a ground for taking it from its father. *But where there was a cause in court* there were many other considerations to be attended to, as in the case then under discussion, where an aunt of the children made an appointment in their favor, which she would not continue if they resided with their father. The Lord Chancellor proceeded to say that he could not attend to that circumstance on a writ of habeas corpus, but in a *cause* it might have some weight.

"Lord ELDON here states that a judge at common law in considering the question, whether an infant shall be taken from the custody of its father or not, does not attend to anything as a ground for such removal except cruelty or personal ill-usage to the child. But we shall find that this is too limited a rule unless we give the words 'cruelty or personal ill-usage' a wider sense than that which they usually bear, and make them embrace cases of moral contamination; for a well founded apprehension that a female infant, for instance, will by residence with its father be exposed to moral pollution, is sufficient to deprive him, at common law, of the right to the custody of the child." *Forsyth on Custody of Infants*, 56.

SECTION IV.

GENERAL RULES AS TO CUSTODY OF LEGITIMATE CHILDREN.

In exercising the jurisdiction in habeas corpus the following principles deduced from the cases are of general application:

1st. The court is in no case bound to deliver the child into the custody of any claimant, or of any other person; but may leave it in such custody as the welfare of the child at the time, appears to require.

2d. In controversies between parents for the custody of their legitimate children, the right of the father is held to be paramount to that of the mother; but the welfare of the child and not the technical legal right is the criterion by which to determine to whom the custody of the child shall be awarded.

3d. In controversies between parents for the custody of their illegitimate children, the right of the mother is paramount: but, as in the last case, the welfare of the child and not the technical legal right determines the custody.

4th. In all cases, if the child has arrived at the age of discretion it will be permitted to elect in whose custody it will remain, provided its choice, under the circumstances, does not, in the opinion of the court, lead to an improper custody.

In some of the states the order in these cases, as will be seen hereafter, has been held by the courts or declared by statute, to have the force of *res adjudicata*. In others, where a repetition of the application may be permitted, the decision is entitled to weight on the question of allowing a second hearing, according to the fullness, fairness, patience and judgment with which the proceeding shall appear to have been heard and considered.

It is not the object of the proceeding to establish a permanent custody, nor has the order anywhere been adjudged to be *res adjudicata*, except for so long as the material circumstances existing at the time of the order remain unchanged. Yet the order in its effects may reach far into the future, and the court therefore, proceeds with that circumspection which it would exercise if its continued obligation were to be a term or a probable consequence of the mandate.

The question of custody between the conflicting claims of parents, being one of discretion rather than strict law, the duty of determining it is not only important in all cases, but in some exceedingly delicate and embarrassing. The welfare of the child is the object to be secured, and that requires attention to many circumstances; such as its sex, age, health and social position as affected by that of its parents; its just expectations of property from them or either of them or from others; and the state of its morals and education, and the surest means, under the circumstances, of securing for it that discipline and instruction necessary to qualify it for that station in life which the parents, had no controversy arisen, it may reasonably be supposed, would have desired and been able by their fortune or industry to prepare it to occupy.

The comparative qualifications also of the parents to provide for these various wants require consideration, such as their temper, morals, habits, judgment.

It cannot be otherwise than that there should be some diversity of opinion upon questions addressed so much as these are, to the discretion of the court, to that rule of judgment which is graduated by the individual experience and observation of the judge.

It will be no disqualification to the judge, if from that experience he can testify upon the one hand, how precious is the devoted mother's love, how vigilant and how self-sacrificing her care; and upon the other, how salutary is the loving father's correcting hand, how disinterested and wise his ever ready counsel and how instructive his own consistent life.

The following cases drawn from the English and American reports will exhibit the spirit of the law upon this subject more satisfactorily than any condensed statement of the points decided could possibly do.

SECTION V.

SPIRIT OF THE ENGLISH CASES ON CONFLICTING CLAIMS OF PARENTS FOR THE CUSTODY OF THEIR CHILDREN.

The leading case upon this subject, and which has been generally approved and followed in the American courts, is that of *Rex* v. *Delaval and others*, 3 *Burr.*, 1434; 1 *W. Bl.*, 409, *S. C.*, determined in 1763. It was in that case that the rule was distinctly declared under the writ of habeas corpus, to be "The court is bound *ex debito justitiæ* to set the infants free from an improper restraint: but they are not bound to deliver them over to anybody nor to give them any privilege. This must be left to their discretion, according to the circumstances that shall appear before them."

"In this case it appeared that ANNE CATLEY, about 18 years of age, who was produced in court by Sir Francis Delaval, in obedience to a writ of habeas corpus directed to him, had been bound when about 15, by her father apprentice to Bates a *music master*. During her apprenticeship being then about 17, she was debauched by Sir Francis, and was at the time of applying for the writ by her father, notoriously *kept* by Sir Francis, actually resided in his house and publicly rode out on his horses attended by his servants. On the hearing she declared her attachment to Sir Francis, and her unwillingness to go home with her father, who thereupon attempted to seize her in court, but was not permitted, and was reprimanded for the contempt.

Lord Mansfield referring to the cases of *Rex* v. *Clarkson and others*, *Str.*, 444; *Rex* v. *Johnson*, *Str.*, 579, and *Rex* v. *Smith*, *Str.*, 982, said that "he thought what was *done* by the court in every one of them was right, though he did not agree with the sayings that were reported in the books, to have been made use of in determining them.

"In the first case the infant was a marriageable young lady who lived with her guardian. A man claimed her as his wife; she denied the marriage. The court could not try the marriage by affidavit, and they could not deliver her to the man *as her husband* without allowing the marriage. She chose to remain with her guardian: and the court upon being informed 'that the man had a design to seize her,' sent a tipstaff home with her, to protect her.

"In the second, *Rex* v. *Johnson*, the child was too young to judge for itself; she was not more than 9 or 10 or as some accounts say, six years old; but certainly not old enough to exercise any judgment of her own. And there was a legal guardian appointed by her father; and therefore it was right to let the legal guardian take her, as she was too young to judge for herself. The guardian appointed in that case by the spiritual court, was nothing at all: for they appoint any body guardian in that court, for the mere purpose of appearing.

"In the third case, *Rex* v. *Smith*, the child wanted but six weeks of 14. And that case was determined right (barring the dictums that were used in it); for the court were certainly right in refusing to deliver the infant to the father, of whose design in applying for the custody of his child, they had a bad opinion.

"The true rule is, 'That the court are to judge upon the circumstances of the particular case, and to give their directions accordingly.'

"Let the girl therefore be discharged from all restraint, and be at liberty to go where she will. And whoever shall offer to meddle with her, *redeundo*, let them take notice that they do it at their peril. But I see no reason in *this* case to send an officer with her to protect her, upon a mere apprehension or supposition that anybody will behave improperly upon the occasion."

The English cases might be left here, for the equitable doctrine maintained in this case, has been commonly practiced in this country and may now be considered as thoroughly incorporated in the American common law.

The English courts however it is said, have repudiated this doctrine, and some recent cases are frequently cited as proof of it, which do not however fully sustain the assertion. Before adverting to those cases, mention should be made of *Blisset's case Lofft.*, 748, occurring a few years after that of *Rex* v. *Delaval.* That was a habeas corpus issued at the suit of the father of the child. The return showed that the child who was six years old, was by choice with her mother who lived separate from her husband. At Chambers before Mr. Justice Aston, the father threatened to take the child by force if it was not delivered to him, and the justice threatened to commit him. It appeared the father was bankrupt, and the mother was forced to live separate from him on account of ill-treatment; also, that the child was likely to receive an improper education with the father, and was not well used.

Lord MANSFIELD said: "The court, if the parties are agreed, will make no determination. If the parties are disagreed, the court will do what shall appear best for the child; fix on a boarding school and the court will have no objection. Let the child in the mean time stay, so that the rule may be made with the concurrence of the family. The natural right is with the father; but if the father is a bankrupt, if he contributed nothing for the child or family and if he be improper, for such conduct as was suggested at the judge's chambers, the court will not think it right that the child should be with him."

The cases usually referred to as showing that the courts of common law in England have renounced the exercise of the discretion which was claimed by Lord Mansfield are *Rex* v. *De Mandeville*, 5 *East*, 220; *Ex parte Skinner*, 9 *J. B. Moore*, 278; *The King* v. *Greenhill*, 4 *Adol. & Ell.*, 642.

In the case of *Rex* v. *De Mandeville*, 5 *East*, 220, the defendant, the father of the child, had forcibly taken the child, then eight months old, from its mother who had separated herself from him on account of ill-treatment, and kept the child, whom she was nursing, with her. In delivering the judgment, *Lord Ellenborough, Ch. J.*, said:

"We draw no inferences to the disadvantage of the father. But he is the person entitled by law to the custody of his child. If he abuse that right to the detriment of the child, the court will protect the child; but there is no pretence that the child has been injured for want of nurture or in any other respect. Then he having a legal right to the custody of the child, and not having abused that right, is entitled to have it restored to him."

In *Ex parte McClellan*, 1 *Dowl. P. C.*, 85, Patteson, J., said: "The case of *Blissett*, *Loft.*, 748, was doubted a great deal by the court of Common Pleas in the case of *Ex parte Skinner*, an infant, in which the court doubted its authority so to interfere," and in the case of *The People* v. *Porter*, 1 *Duer*, 718, the court say that Blissett's case was "in effect overruled" in *Ex parte Skinner*.

But Mr. *Forsyth*, in his work on the *Custody of Infants*, 65, very justly remarks, that:

"The report of *Ex parte Skinner* does not state any expression of doubt on the part of the court as to the authority of Blissett's case. The exact words there used by Best, Ch. J., were the following, and they contain the only allusion that was made to the decision of Lord Mansfield: 'I was referred to Blissett's case, and it certainly is extremely strong to show that the power of assigning the custody of a child brought before the Court of King's Bench was discretionary, if the father appeared to be an improper person to take it; and I therefore thought that the most prudent course would be to assign it over to the care of a third person, which was acceded to by both its parents. But it now appears that the father has removed the child and has the custody of it himself; and no authority has been cited to show that the court has jurisdiction to take it out of such custody for the purpose of delivering it to its mother.'

"The distinction, therefore, that seems to be here taken is this, that so long as the infant is not in the custody of the father, the court will, under certain circumstances, prevent him from obtaining possession of it; but if he has already got possession of the child, the court will not interfere to take it from him, at least unless there be apprehension of ill treatment or moral contamination by him."

In *Ex parte McClellan*, *Patteson*, *J.*, did not dissent from the doctrine laid down in Blisset's case. He said, "It is not necessary to say to what extent that case is an authority. I do not mean to say that this court has not authority so to do"— *i. e.*, to change the custody of the child and to take it from the father.

In *Rex* v. *Greenhill*, 4 *Ad. and El.*, 624, the mother had separated herself from her husband, on account of the open and avowed adultery of the latter, and she had taken away with her her three children, females, aged respectively five years and a half, four and a half, and two and a half, to the house of their maternal grandmother, where they were residing at the time when Mr. Greenhill obtained a writ of habeas corpus, commanding his wife to produce the bodies of his three children before Patteson, J., at his house. It was stated on affidavits, and not denied by Mr. Greenhill, that when he obtained the writ he was living under a feigned name, with a woman who passed as his wife at a lodging in London, and that he acknowledged that the adultery was still continuing. It was also stated, that he could at any time have, and had in fact had, access to his children, where they then were. The grandmother deposed, that if the children were placed with their father there was great probability that they would be brought into contact with a female of an abandoned and profligate character. Mr. Justice Patteson, after taking time for consideration, ordered that the children should be delivered up to the father.

"The order was made a rule of court, but Mrs. Greenhill refused to give up the children, and a rule nisi was obtained for an attachment against her for contempt. She, however, in the same term obtained a rule nisi, calling upon Mr. Greenhill to show cause why the order of Patteson, J., should not be set aside and the rule making it a rule of court discharged.

"The matter thus came before the court. Mrs. Greenhill had already instituted proceedings (which were then pending), in the Ecclesiastical Court for a divorce and alimony.

"Affidavits were put in on behalf of Mr. Greenhill, in which he stated that he had offered, if his wife would forgive him, to live with her whenever she wished, and to give up his adulterous connection, but without success; that the children, if taken out of his custody would lose materially by family arrangements, which, to his knowledge and belief, would essentially affect their future interests; that his wife had no means of supporting them; that the children, if separated from him, would, as he believed, be brought up in detestation of him, and that his mother was a very proper person to be intrusted with them; that he never contemplated for a moment depriving his wife of the privilege she had as a mother of seeing her children and had repeatedly expressed himself to her to that effect; that he had never taken either of his children near to his mistress's residence, or his mistress to his own house, or any other place where his wife or children were, nor had he entertained the thought of bringing his wife and children in contact with her. It was afterwards sworn by Mr. Greenhill, that he believed that Mrs. Greenhill had taken the children with her out of the kingdom.

"On the part of the mother it was said, that she was willing to abide by any direction of the court, which might leave her access to her children. Upon this, Lord Denman, Ch. J., remarked: 'The children are not in court; nor have we any certainty that the order we might make would be complied with.'

"The court ultimately discharged the rule obtained by Mrs. Greenhill, and thus decided that the father was entitled to the custody of the children. LORD DENMAN said: 'There is in the first place no doubt that where a father has the custody of his children he is not to be deprived of it except under particular circumstances; and those do not occur in this case, for, although misconduct is imputed to Mr. Greenhill, there is nothing proved against him which has ever been held sufficient ground for removing children from their father; here it is impossible to say that such danger exists. Although there is an illicit connection between Mr. Greenhill and Mrs. Graham, *it is not pretended that she is keeping the house to which the children are brought*, or that there is anything in the conduct of the parties so offensive to decency, as to render it improper that the children should be left under the control of their father. And he promises the same conduct with respect to them for the future.' "

Mr. JUSTICE COLERIDGE said: "A habeas corpus proceeds on the fact of an illegal restraint. Where the writ is obeyed and the party brought up is capable of using a discretion, the rule is simple and disposes of many cases, namely, that the individual who has been under restraint is declared to be at liberty, and the court will even direct that the party shall be attended home by an officer, to make the order effectual. But when the person is too young to have a choice, we must refer to legal principles to see who is entitled to the custody, because the law presumes that where the legal custody is, no restraint exists."

The law as declared in this case was so shocking to the moral sense of the British public "that *Sergeant Talfourd*, to his everlasting honor, although he had been the counsel for the husband, immediately brought a bill into parliament to change the law and to restore the mother to her natural right to be put upon an equality with her husband in relation to the care and custody of her children within the age of nurture, and finally succeeded in carrying his bill through both houses of parliament by a large majority, though it was once defeated in the house of lords." *Per Walworth, Chancellor*, *Mercein* v. *The People*, 25 *Wend.*, 64.

This law, which was passed in 1839, authorizes the Lord Chancellor, and also the master of the rolls, to make an order for the access of the mother to her infant children, and if the infant be within the age of *seven years*, to make an order that it be delivered to and ramain in the custody of the mother until attaining such age.

A similar statute was soon after passed in New York, in reference to which *Bronson, J.*, in the case of *The People* v. *Chegaray*, 18 *Wend.*, 542, said: "it conferred a power upon the Supreme Court which it did not before possess; and that it was not the object of the common law writ of habeas corpus to try the rights of parents or guardians to the custody of infants, but merely to deliver them from unjust imprisonment, and all illegal or improper restraint."

The provisions of the statute in New York on this point are as follows:

Sec. 1. "When any husband and wife shall live in a state of separation without being divorced, and shall have any minor child of the marriage, the wife, if she be an inhabitant of this state, may apply to the Supreme Court for a habeas corpus, to have such minor child brought before it.

Sec. 2. "On the return of such writ the court, on due consideration, may award the charge and custody of the child, so brought before it, to the mother, for such time, under such regulations and restrictions, and with such provisions and directions as the case may require.

Sec. 3. "At any time after the making of such order the Supreme Court may annul, vary or modify the same." 2 *R. S.*, 1852, *p.* 332.

Mr. FORSYTH observes that: "During the debate in the House of Lords (July 18, 1839,) on the Custody of Infants bill, Lord DENMAM, Ch. J., said: 'In the case of *The King* v. *Greenhill*, which had been decided in 1836, before himself and the rest of the judges of the Court of King's Bench, he believed that there was not one judge who had not felt ashamed of the state of the law, and that it was such as to render it odious in the eyes of the country. The effect in that case was to enable the father to take his children from his young and blameless wife and place them in charge of a woman with whom he cohabited.' *See Hansard's Parl. Deb., Vol.* 49, (3*d series*,) *p.* 493. But according to the report of the case, the court thought that there was no evidence that the children were likely to be brought into contact with the father's mistress. If the fact had been so the decision would probably have been different.'" *Forsyth Custody of Infants*, 69, *note*.

SECTION VI.

SPIRIT OF THE AMERICAN CASES ON CONFLICTING CLAIMS OF PARENTS FOR THE CUSTODY OF THEIR CHILDREN.

It is gratifying that the American reports furnish no such case as that of *Rex* v. *Greenhill*, to make the judges "ashamed of the law."

Chancellor Walworth in the case of *Mercien* v. *The People*, 25 *Wend.*, 64, alluding to the cases in the English courts since the days of Lord Mansfield, says:

"The American cases show it to be the established law of this country that the court or officer are authorized to exercise a discretion; and that the father was not entitled to demand a delivery of the child to him, upon habeas corpus, as an absolute right. This was also the law of England at the time of the separation from the mother country; though the decisions of the English courts since that period appear to have gone back to the principles of a semi-barbarous age, when the wife was the slave of the husband because he had the physical power to control her, and when the will of the strongest party constituted the rule of right."

In *Ex parte Schumpert*, 6 *Rich.*, 344, the English cases are commented on and the American vindicated.

"This was an application by the writ of habeas corpus ad sub. by the father, Peter M. Schumpert, for an order for the delivery to him of his infant daughter, Frances, aged between four and five years, who, it is alleged, was unlawfully detained by the grandfather, Honorius Shepperd, with whom the mother, Mary Schumpert, wife of the petitioner and daughter of Honorius Shepperd, resided. Two similar applications had been made before his Honor Judge O. Neall. On the first application, made March 19, 1850, the following order was made: 'The sheriff having returned the writ of habeas corpus, and the parties appearing before me, and the child being of very tender years, a little more than a year old; it is ordered that for nurture and care the child remain for the present in the possession of the mother; the father to be at liberty to apply hereafter for the custody of the child if he should think proper so to do.'"

The second application, January 14, 1851, the order was, for the present the child remain in the custody of the mother.

On the third application it was ordered that the mother, Mary Schumpert, be permitted to retain the possession of the child, Frances, and that she be responsible for its maintenance, and that Honorius Shepperd, her father, do give to the petitioner, P. M. Schumpert, bond with sufficient surety to indemnify said P. M. Schumpert for all liability for the support and maintenance of the child. Bond, penalty $5,000.

Motion to reverse this order of the circuit judge heard before the court. The opinion was delivered by *Whitner, J.*:

"The legal power of the father over his infant child, irrespective of age and the claims of the mother, has been strongly pressed by the counsel for the petitioner. Many cases have been adjudged, principally in England, going far to deny to the common law judge any discretion on the subject; whilst others, in conceding a discretion, have so limited and restrained it as almost to amount to a denial.

"Lord Mansfield in 1763, in *Delaval's case*, 3 *Burr.*, 1434, laid down a safe rule which has been recognized by our own case of *Kottman*, 2 *Hill's C. R.*, 363: 'That in cases of writs of habeas corpus directed to bring up infants the court is bound *ex debito justiciæ* to set the infant free from an improper restraint, but they are not bound to deliver them over to anybody, nor to give them any privilege. This must be left to their discretion, according to the circumstances that shall appear before them.' And again, some ten years after, in *Blissett's case*, *Loft.*, 748, he held 'that if the parties disagreed, the court will do what shall appear best for the child.' Yet, as above stated, the principle and practice became more stringent. Those who choose to consult the authorities will find, in order of succession, the courts proceed from *DeMandeville's case*, 5 *East*, 221, where the paramount title of the father became the favorite doctrine, although the welfare of the child might require the mother's custody, decided, I think, in 1804, down to the celebrated case of *Greenhill*, 4 *Ad. & El.*, 624, which so shocked public sentiment, that, under the lead of distinguished jurists of that day, an act of Parliament was adopted more in consonance with the dictates of humanity and sound reason, whereby the rights and feelings of the injured mother were taken into the account.

"It is a matter of congratulation that but little additional weight has been given to this class of cases by American judges. In this state we are committed to no such extreme doctrine, and the day of danger I trust has passed. Pursuing the rule of Lord Mansfield, we have heretofore sought to free the infant from improper restraint; hence at the age of choice the infant is instructed and advised, and if need be protected, in his choice. *Judge Strony* says, in 3 *Mason*, 382: 'It is an entire mistake to suppose that the court is bound to deliver over the infant to its father, or that the latter has an absolute vested right in the custody.'

"The wise principles of the earlier English cases have been liberally incorporated into our American cases in the several states, that 'it is the benefit and welfare of the infant to which the attention of the court ought principally to be directed.' 13 *Johns.*, 418.

"In these delicate and difficult questions, what safer principle can be adopted? What parent can object that the welfare of the child shall be deemed paramount to the claims of either? This is the proposition made by each parent, and neither should condemn the practical operation of the rule. *D'Hauteville* v. *Sears.* Motion to reverse order of circuit judge dismissed."

The order actually made in the foregoing case appears more prospective and absolute than is usual in such cases, and approaches so nearly an order in chancery, that it is not so easy to approve of all that was done as of all that was said.

Pennsylvania. The case of the *Commonwealth* v. *Nutt*, 1 *P. A. Browne*, 143, was decided in the Court of Common Pleas, Philadelphia county, in 1810:

"This case arose upon a habeas corpus taken out by Levi Nutt, the father, and directed to Rhoda Nutt, the mother, commanding her to bring Acha B. Nutt, his daughter, before the court, together with the cause of detention. Rhoda Nutt returned, &c., 'that Levi Nutt, the father, was an immoral man, and neglected to maintain his family.'

"*Per Curiam.* 'The general opinion is correct, that the father has a right to the custody of his children. But exceptions have been very properly admitted. In the case now before us the court have been furnished with the most disgusting evidence of the immoral character and conduct of both parties. They have quarreled, broken up housekeeping and separated. The children have been separated and dispersed into different places. The mother at this time keeps house for Amos Howell, a tavern keeper and married man, who has also parted from his wife. There is too much reason to believe they live in constant habits of adultery, and that acts of the grossest indecency have been exhibited in the presence and view of the daughter. Fiddling, dancing and frolicking are frequent at the house. This certainly is not a scene in which virtue and innocence can be trusted with safety.

"'With respect to the father, his general neglect to provide for his children is but too apparent and he is at this time destitute of a settled habitation; his profligate language, in the presence of his wife and daughter, is too indelicate to be repeated.

"'As the court cannot deliver Acha B. Nutt either to the father or the mother, they are precisely in the situation of the court in the case of *Ann Cutley*, 3 *Burr.*, 1436. But here the analogy between the two cases must stop. It is not our intention to turn Acha B. Nutt adrift upon the wide world, and to tell her, as the court told Ann Cutley, "you are at liberty to go where you please;" but we mean to put her under the custody of a relative, where we think she will be best taken care of, and her mind and morals in the least danger of being corrupted. In the case of Ann Cutley, Lord Mansfield stated the law to be that the court is *bound* to set infants free from any improper restraint, but they are *not bound* to deliver them over to anybody or to give them any privilege. They must be left to their discretion according to the circumstances that shall appear before them. The court has received satisfactory information that Ann Nutt, sister to Acha B. Nutt, is a person to whose custody Acha may be with safety confided. They therefore direct that Acha shall remain in the custody of her sister Ann, who has consented to take her; and they do further direct that the said Ann shall permit the father and mother of Acha to see her at all reasonable times, and that she shall also permit them to offer such aid towards her support and education as they may be able or willing to contribute.

"'We desire the father and mother to take notice that it will be at their peril if they or either of them shall take away or withdraw Acha B. Nutt from the custody of her sister Ann, where she is now placed by the order and authority of this court, and that any infraction of this sentence will be punished according to law.'

"The age of the infant is not stated."

The case of *The Commonwealth* v. *Addicks and Wife*, 5 *Binn.*, 520, occurred in 1813, in the Supreme Court.

"The court upon the application of Joseph Lee, the father, granted a habeas corpus to the defendants to bring up two female children, his daughters, in their custody, and they were accordingly brought into court, under the care of their mother, Barbara Addicks, with whom, as was stated in the return, they had lived ever since their birth. The petitioner had been divorced from the defendant, Barbara, for adultery. She afterwards married Addicks. It was claimed in extenuation of her conduct that Lee had made no provision for his wife and family for four years, that she had been compelled to keep a boarding house, &c., and that she had educated the children well."

TILGHMAN, Ch. J. "We have considered the law and are of opinion that although we are bound to free the person from all illegal restraint we are not bound to decide who is entitled to the guardianship, or to deliver infants to the custody of any particular person. But we may in our discretion do so, if we think that under the circumstances of the case it ought to be done. For this we refer to the cases of *The King* v. *Smith*, 2 *Stra.*, 982; *and The King* v. *Delaval*, 3 *Burr.*, 1436.

"The present case is attended with peculiar and unfortunate circumstances. We cannot avoid expressing our disapprobation of the mother's conduct, although so far as regards her treatment of the children, she is in no fault. They appear to have been well taken care of in all respects. It is to *them* that our anxiety is principally directed; and it appears to us, that considering their tender age, they stand in need of that kind of assistance which can be afforded by none so well as a mother. It is on their account, therefore, that exercising the discretion with which the law has invested us, we think it best at present not to take them from her. At the same time, we desire it to be distinctly understood that the father is not to be prevented from seeing them. If he does not choose to go to the house of their mother, she ought to send them to him, when he desires it, taking it for granted that he will not wish to carry them abroad, so much as to interfere with their education."

These parties were before the same court three years after to have the same question redetermined, 2 *Serg. & Rawle*, 174, when the custody of the children, then respectively 10 and 13 years of age, was transferred to the father, "the children not standing before the court in the same situation as formerly," because they had arrived at an age when their morals were in danger of contamination by the mother's evil example. *Per Barton, D'Hauteville's case*, 292.

The *D'Hauteville case*, decided by the Court of General Sessions for the city and county of Philadelphia, in 1840, was a habeas corpus proceeding. The writ was obtained July 3, 1840, by the father to recover possession of his infant son not then two years old, and was directed to his wife and to her father and mother.

This case attracted much attention at the time but is chiefly remarkable for the personal history it contains of a young American lady of some fortune, venturing, on very short acquaintance, less than six months, upon matrimony in Europe, with "the son of a private Swiss gentleman, a lieutenant in the militia," supposed to possess an adequate estate. It is also somewhat remarkable for the intolerable length of the pleadings or "suggestions," as they are called under the statute of 1785. The marriage proved an unhappy one. The wife with her husband's consent returned to America on a visit, and was delivered of the son for which the writ was issued. On refusing to return to her husband, he came seeking her and the child. She resided at that time with her father in Massachusetts. Thinking the law of Pennsylvania "more favorable to the preservation of the child in this country than the practice in Massachusetts," she repaired with her child to Philadelphia, thereby giving a practical illustration of the difference between the case of *The Commonwealth* v. *Briggs*, 16 *Pick.*, 203, and that of *The Commonwealth* v. *Addicks and wife*, 5 *Binn.*, 520.

The court was invoked to disregard the Addicks case as a judicial anomaly, "to ride over it and ride it down;" but it was deaf to the entreaty. So far from overriding that case it gave full play to all its dreaded principles.

"The reputation of a father" said the court, "may be stainless as crystal; he may not be afflicted with the slightest mental, moral or physical disqualification from superintending the general welfare of the infant; the mother may have separated from him without the shadow of a pretence of justification; and yet the interests of the child may imperatively demand the denial of the father's right, and its continuance with the mother. In this case 'the tender age and precarious state of the infant's health' make the vigilance of the mother indispensable to its proper care; for not doubting that paternal anxiety would seek for and obtain the best *substitute* which could be procured, every instinct of humanity unerringly proclaims that *no* substitute can supply the place of HER, whose watchfulness over the sleeping cradle or waking moments of her offspring is prompted by deeper and holier feelings than the most liberal allowance of a nurse's wages could possibly stimulate. Not yet two years of age when the writ of habeas corpus was issued, this child has already been the subject of several distressing maladies, and has been apparently threatened with others of not inferior aggravation."

Indorsed on the writ of habeas corpus.

"DECREE."

"And now, 14 November, 1840, this cause having been heard upon the returns and amended return, suggestions and further suggestions, filed by the respective parties, and remaining of record, and upon the evidence written and oral, adduced before the court, it is considered that the within named infant, Frederick Sears Grand d'Hauteville, is not unlawfully restrained of his liberty, or detained by the parties to whom the writ is directed, or any or either of them, and, that the said infant be remanded and restored to his mother, Ellen Sears Grand d'Hauteville, in the said writ named."

Massachusetts. One of the most interesting cases in this state is that of *The Commonwealth* v. *Briggs*, 16 *Pick.*, 203.

SHAW, Ch. J. "This writ was sued out upon the petition of Samuel Thacher, and directed to Mehitable Thacher his wife, and Wales Briggs her father, requiring them to bring in the body of Samuel W. Thacher, a child of the petitioner and Mehitable, between three and four years of age.

"Upon the return of the writ it appears that Briggs admits that his daughter with her child are residing at his house, but he claims no custody of the child. It further appears that the wife is living separate and apart from her husband without any divorce or separation by mutual agreement; and she claims the custody of the child on the ground that the father is intemperate, and, in other respects, an unfit person to take care of the child. Upon the first application for this writ, a doubt was entertained whether the writ could be properly issued against the wife on the application of the husband. This doubt originated in the well known rule, that there can be no adverse interest between husband and wife, but that in contemplation of law, the custody of both wife and child belongs to the husband and father, and is actually in him. But, on consideration, the writ being in the name of the Commonwealth, the technical objection of a suit between husband and wife is avoided; and inasmuch as the writ is designed to secure and promote personal liberty, slight objections ought not to be entertained. The process may be often useful and highly beneficial as the only efficient and peaceful remedy for a husband to obtain the custody of his child, when he is entitled to it. The court, therefore, are of the opinion that a writ of habeas corpus might issue to a wife at the instance of her husband.

"On hearing the evidence the court were satisfied that the charge of intemperance on the part of the husband was not established. They were of opinion that unless there is some justifiable cause of separation, the court ought not to sanction the unauthorized separation of husband and wife by ordering the child into the custody of the mother, thus separated and out of the custody of the father. If there be any good cause of divorce, either *a vinculo* or *a mensa* and proceedings are instituted, the court will then take such order as to the custody both of the wife and children as the circumstances of the case may require. *As a general rule, the writ of habeas corpus and all action upon it are governed by the judicial discretion of the court, in directing which all the circumstances are to be taken into consideration. In the case of a child of tender years, the good of the child is to be regarded as the prominent consideration.* There may be cases in which the court would not interfere in favor of a father to take the child from any safe custody to deliver it to him; as when he is a vagabond and apparently wholly unable to provide for the safety and wants of the child. But, in general, as the father is by law clearly entitled to the custody of his child, the court will so far interfere as to issue the writ and inquire into the circumstances of the case, in order to prevent a party entitled to the custody of a child, from seeking it by force or stratagem.

"And the court will feel bound to restore the custody where the law has placed it, with the father, unless in a clear and strong case of unfitness on his part to have such custody. The unauthorized separation of the wife from her husband, without any apparent justifiable cause, is a strong reason why the child should not be restored to her. On all the circumstances of the case, the court are of opinion that no sufficient cause has been shown for taking the custody of this child from the father, and, therefore, that the child be restored to him."

New Hampshire. In the case of *The State* v. *Smith*, 6 *Greenl.*, 462, a husband and wife having separated pursuant to articles previously entered into, in which he had stipulated, "if in consequence of any ill-treatment by him his wife should be rendered unhappy and unwilling to cohabit with him, and should make affidavit that she is so treated by him as that she cannot live happily with him, then she may live separately from him at her own pleasure and shall be at liberty to take the children under her own control and custody and keep them so long as they, the petitioner and wife, should live apart." The court on habeas corpus sued out at his request, ordered the children into the custody of the mother, pursuant to the articles of separation; she living with her father and they being of an age to require her care. The eldest child was between ten and eleven, and the youngest between four and five years old.

Parris, J., in deciding the case, said:

"The children being now in the custody of the mother and in court by her permission and consent, the petitioner seeks to reclaim them through the interposition of the law, alleging his paramount right to their custody, and that the court is not at liberty, in the exercise of any discretionary power, to deny his petition.

"That the father is generally entitled to the custody of his infant children is a principle resulting from his obligation to maintain, protect and educate them. These are duties thrown upon him by the law of nature as well as of society, which he is not permitted to disregard and which he could not conveniently discharge if the object of those duties were withdrawn from his control.

"The right, however, is neither unlimited nor unalienable. It continues no longer than it is properly exercised; and whenever abused or whenever the parent has become unfit by immoral or profligate habits to have the management and instruction of children, courts of appropriate jurisdiction have not hesitated to interfere to restrain the abuse or remove the subject of it from the custody of the offending parent." The judge then reviews the authorities and proceeds: "From an examination of these authorities I consider the law well settled that it is in the sound discretion of the court to alter the custody of these minor children or not, and that the father cannot claim them as a matter of right. In the exercise of that discretion, under which I am presumed to act in this case, I cannot forget that the eldest of these children is a daughter requiring peculiarly the superintendence of a mother; that the others, although males, being of tender years may probably be as well governed and instructed by her as by the father, especially as it is in evidence from the petitioner's witnesses that she is a 'smart, industrious woman, and a kind, good mother;' that the parental feelings of the mother toward her children are naturally as strong and generally stronger than those of the father; that the separation of the heads of this family has been caused by the imprudent conduct" (he was charged with being the father of a bastard child and gave his notes with sureties to settle it; 'imprudent conduct!') "and that by his voluntary act he consented, in case of such separation, to relinquish to the mother the right of custody and control of her children, and conveyed a moiety of his real estate in trust for her support, and that the residue of his property is mortgaged and conveyed to indemnify his sureties and for the payment of his debts. All these considerations seem to require that this application should not be granted; and in this opinion my brethren unanimously concur."

Tennessee. In the case of *The State, ex rel. Paine,* v. *Paine,* 4 *Humph.,* 523, it appeared that on the 1st of March, 1841, William L. Paine presented a petition to William C. Dunlap, one of the judges of the Circuit Court of Tennessee, in which he stated that his wife, Eliza Paine, had abandoned him and taken with her his three children, Henry, Sarah and John, minors, and that she detained them from the custody and possession of the petitioner and prayed the issuance of the states' writ of habeas corpus, commanding the said Eliza to bring the said children before him at a day and place, &c. She filed her answer alleging ill-usage, &c.; claimed the petioner was incompetent; the children of tender years, Henry seven, Sarah five, and John three years old. The relator replied denying ill-usage, &c. The proof showed relator, widower, having competent estate real and personal, and three children by former wife; married Eliza Paine who had some property. They had three children and were both members of the Methodist church at the time she abandoned him. Some witnesses proved him to be a man of good moral character in his public deportment. The preponderance of testimony was that he was hypochondriacal, peevish and capricious, and instances of coldness and neglect toward his wife were shown. Both were shown to be competent and fit to have the custody and control of the children in most respects. The judge decided that the children were not unlawfully restrained and directed that they be restored to their mother, and that the petition be dismissed and relator pay the cost. From this judgment he prayed and obtained an appeal.

TURLEY, J. "Among the multiplied duties of a court there are none the discharge of which is attended with more pain and regret than those which interfere with the domestic relations of husband and wife, parent and child. This difficulty is increased by the difference of the sources from whence our law is derived.

"On the one hand the common law with its stern and iron-bound principles, based upon the manners and customs and thoughts of our ancestors, a rude and undigested people of rough energy and indomitable pride, addicted to arms, and considering battle and conquest as the only great and glorious duties of life, making all their institutions, civil and domestic subservient to these ends, giving a paramount right to the superior over the services, liberty and even life of the inferior, embracing in this view the relations of landlord and tenant, husband and wife, parent and child, guardian and ward; and fixing their duties and rights without regard to justice or humanity, upon the principles of concentrated power upon which the feudal system rested.

"On the other hand the jurisprudence of a refined race, one that had emerged from its barbarism, and after having subdued the world, had been for centuries polished by philosophy, poetry, eloquence and art even to enervation.

"In the case before the court we are only called upon to expound what is the common law relation between the father, the wife and the child, and to enforce the rights as thus recognized. That the father is entitled upon the principles of the common law to the exclusive custody of his children, is not and cannot be controverted; and that if he have it, a court of common law will not deprive him of it, but for an abuse of his trust, affecting their persons either by improper violence or improper restraint, and which would justify the issuance of a writ of habeas corpus for their protection. *Shelford on Marriage and Divorce*, 409, *and cases.*

"But in this case he has lost their possession, and the question is presented under a different phasis. The probability is that the rigid principles of the common law would have restored the possession of a minor child to the father, under all the circumstances; for, as has been observed, this would have been in conformity with the social principles. But if it ever were so, it is so no longer, and perhaps the mitigation, so far as it has extended, is adopted from the civilians. The mitigation of the principle is 'that the court is not bound in a proceeding upon habeas corpus to deliver the child to the father, but may act upon its discretion according to the circumstances of the particular case.' The first, and so far as we know, the earliest case referred to in support of this position, is the case of *The King* v. *Delaval, decided by Lord Mansfield*, 3 *Burr.*, 1434. The predilections of that jurist for the civil code, and his strong disposition to engraft its principles upon the rude stem of the common law are well known. However the principle thus laid down has been so repeatedly recognized both in England and the United States, that it is now at all events a part of the common law.

"The principle being thus established, that the court is not bound by a fixed principle of right to restore a child to its father, but may, at its discretion, withhold it, the question occurs, under what circumstances may that discretion be exercised? This must, of necessity in many instances, be a thing difficult for judicial determination, and no fixed and determined principles can be established upon the subject, every case resting upon its own peculiar circumstances. It is to be observed that in all cases the interest and welfare of the child is the great leading object to be attained, and therefore, if it be of an age sufficiently matured to judge for itself, the court will free itself from the responsibility of determining the controversy, by leaving it at liberty to go where it pleases. *Rex* v. *Smith*, 2 *Stra.*, 982; 8 *John.*, 328.

"But if it be not of such an age, the court will judge for it. There are certain principles upon the subject recognized by all the authorities, and controverted by none; such as if the father be unworthy, or incapable morally or physically to take care of the child, if there be apprehensions of improper restraint, the court will not restore the possession to him. In the case of *D'Hauteville*, it was held that if the health and age of the child were such as to make the vigilance and attention of the mother necessary for its care, it would not be taken from her and giv en to the father We deem it useless to enter into an investigation of the particular circumstances upon which the different cases rest with a view to reconcile them.

"They completely establish the principle that the court has a discretion upon the subject, and a conflict of judgment is, under such circumstances to be expected. But the principle that it is the interest of the child which is to be looked to, without regard to the right of others being established, relieves us, to a great extent, from the difficulty resulting from a want of certainty in the exercise of the right of discretion. We will not, as we ought not, attempt to establish any general rule on the subject, but confine ourselves to the inquiry as to the rights of those interested in the case under consideration. The wife, by common law, has no right to the children against the husband.

"Therefore she cannot be looked to in this case except so far as she may be considered by the court the most suitable person, under the circumstances, to have their control for their benefit. The father is not shown to be disqualified, either morally or physically, for their care and culture; and the only question left for consideration is, in whose possession will the interest of the children be best provided for, the father's or the mother's. There are three, the oldest a boy aged near eight years, the second a girl aged near six years, the third a boy aged near four years.

"We think exercising our discretion from the best light that our knowledge of society gives us, that the oldest boy can be better raised by the father than the mother, under the existing circumstances; but that the other two are of too tender an age to be removed at present from the protecting care of the mother, who is proved to be worthy and well qualified for their protection. We therefore direct that the oldest son be restored to the father, and that the daughter and youngest son remain with the mother until upon a change of circumstances it may be otherwise directed. We do this the more readily because the subject is now before the Chancellor, who has more power over it than we have by this proceeding."

It appears that a divorce was afterwards granted for abuse &c., on petition of the wife, April 9, 1844, 41 *Humph.*, 500. The case of *Ward* v. *Roper*, 7 *Humph.*, 111, although in chancery was evidently controlled by the same principles which governed the case of *State* v. *Payne.* In that case *Reese J.*, delivered the opinion of the court.

"The complainant by the last will and testament of his son, was appointed testamentary guardian of two children, a son and daughter, the latter now 11 years old, and the former about 9.

"This bill is brought against the maternal grandfather to obtain the custody of the ward. The parents of the children are both dead, the mother died first. But long before the death of either, they surrendered the daughter to the maternal grandfather, in her earliest infancy for nurture, and under an agreement that she was to be brought up by him. The daughter was of very delicate health, and the grandmother has much skill as well as great tenderness, in the treatment of children, and has always had this child in her possession. The uniform wish of both parents was that the daughter should remain with the grandmother, and this wish was distinctly repeated by the father, even after he had appointed the complainant testamentary guardian.

"The complainant has lost his wife, and is now a widower. The testamentary guardian has a legal right to the custody and possession of his wards. But the case of *Payne* v. *Payne and others*, settles as a principle, that this legal right will not be impaired, but will be controlled in a case where the interest of the child obviously requires that it should be done. Such we regard as being the case in the present instance as relates to the daughter. Those strong ties arising from nature and nurture between her and her grandmother, must not be broken. With respect to the son, his home at the death of his father was with the complainant, and he was taken to the defendants under promise to be returned. The legal right is with the complainant, and we are not satisfied that such circumstances exist as to control that legal right. It would be wished, indeed, that the children should be much together; and we hope that when the feelings, unfortunately engendered by this contest shall somewhat abate, that the complainant will permit his male ward to pass much of his time with his sister.

"Our decree is, that the daughter remain with her maternal grandfather; and that the son be restored to the custody of his guardian, the complainant."

Mississippi. In the following case, the petitioner was a testamentary guardian and the powers of the court appear to be made very ample by statute, yet as the questions under notice now were discussed, the case is given as one of interest.

Foster and wife, appellants, v. *Alston*, 6 *How. Miss.*, 406. This was a proceeding by habeas corpus by a testamentary guardian to recover possession of his infant wards. A. J. Alston died in the State of

Tennessee in 1834, having by will appointed his brother, Jas. J. Alston, guardian of his children. The guardian qualified, and the children with their mother resided with him until the winter of 1840, when their mother, who had in the mean time married Foster, the plaintiff in error, and removed to Holly Springs, in the State of Mississippi, went with an armed force and forcibly took possession of the children and brought them to the residence of the mother, in this state, where Foster and wife obtained letters of guardianship.

MR. JUSTICE TURNER. "In cases of this kind we are bound to consider the interests of the child as paramount to all other considerations. Are these children restrained of their liberty? Are they under the care and control of improper persons? Are they so situated as to prejudice their health or to expose them to improper or immoral influences? All these questions must be answered in the negative. They are with their mother, the proper place for all female children, and decidedly to be preferred to any other, whether nursery or boarding-school, unless there be something in the conduct or character of the mother to operate against the *interest* of the child. The law has given to our courts the most unbounded jurisdiction over minors. Fathers may be preferred to mothers, mothers to fathers, relatives to parents, or strangers to either, for the custody and care of infants where the interests of the child require its exercise. *Rev. Code, p.* 64, *sec.* 401.

"In cases like the present proceeding under the writ of habeas corpus, the technical legal rights of the parties do not govern. A guardian, whether appointed by the parent or the court, has his ordinary civil remedy if any of his legal rights are violated. The courts and juries of the country will respect those rights and grant redress according to the circumstances of each particular case and the rules of law. But in this summary proceeding these rights cannot be redressed; no damages can be assessed, no restoration of property can be decreed, except in cases of slaves under our statutes." After reviewing the evidence the judge proceeds: "What is this court under these circumstances called on to do? It is in proof that these children are fond of their mother; and after trying both situations, first with their uncle, grandmother and aunt, and then with their mother and stepfather, decidedly prefer remaining with their mother, expressing at the same time an affectionate regard for their grandmother. Does this show illegal restraint, the very thing necessary to give this court the right to change their custody? I think not.

"But what are we called on to do with these children by the petitioner, the testamentary guardian? To tear these tender female children aged nine and ten years from the care and custody of a fond, devoted and capable *mother* and place them under the care of a *bachelor uncle*, residing some seventy-five miles from their mother. To state the proposition would seem to decide it. Let every mother, let every father answer this question!" Judge TROTTER concurred.

Chief Justice Sharkey, dissented, however, and, in this general survey of the grounds of judicial discretion, his observations are worthy of notice.

"The first question," said he, "is as to the right or power of the father over his children, as contrasted with that of the mother. Amongst the various authorities introduced, none have gone so far as to deny the superior claims of the father to the control of his children. We are informed by the first elementary books we read, that the authority of the father is superior to that of the mother. It is the doctrine of all civilized nations. It is according to the revealed law and the law of nature, and it prevails even with the wandering savage who has received none of the lights of civilization. The father is considered the head and governor of the family. He controls even the mother, and must, of necessity, control the children. Some writers, I am aware, have contended for the equal authority of the mother on the ground of her superior affection for her offspring. Their efforts to prove that the law should be so, are of themselves evidence that it is otherwise, and the warmer attachment of the mother, instead of proving the error of the law may serve to prove its policy. We are all aware that children must be brought up under a proper state of discipline, faults must be corrected and errors avoided.

"A system of training must be adopted which is often repugnant to the wishes of the child. Which is best calculated to do these things, the doting, partial mother with whom every fault is virtue, every wish a command, or the less partial father who looks to future welfare rather than the gratification of childish folly? I am sensible that there are kind offices which none can so well discharge as the mother, but these are not inconsistent with the father's superior authority; and that his authority is superior in controlling the destiny and custody of his children, is manifest from the statute which authorizes him to appoint a guardian by will or deed. The true rule is laid down in *Nickeson's case*, 19 *Wend.*, 16."

Georgia. In Ex parte Rosetta Ralston, R. M. Charl., 119, *Charlton, J., said:*

"This is an application (Hab. Corp.) by the guardian of the infant, for the possession of her person, for the purpose of better care and education than she can now receive from her grandmother, Mrs. Drake, to whom the writ was directed. The infant is only *seven* years old, and cannot make a free and unbiassed election between her guardian and grandmother. Upon different circumstances, this court upon the authorities adduced, would permit the infant to go where she pleased.

"The grandmother is to have access to the infant on her own request, and at convenient periods.

"It is ordered that the infant Rosetta Ralston, be delivered to the custody of her guardian, John Shellman."

The State v. *Nathan S. King*, 1 *Geo. Decis*, 93.

"In this case the writ of habeas corpus was obtained by Anna King, the wife of the defendant, to produce the body of their infant child about 2½ years old, called Emily. In the petition she complains that her husband has taken possession of said infant and detains it, when the tender years of said infant require the constant care of its mother. Upon this application the court granted the writ, and the same being served on the defendant, he produced the child and made his return, in which he admits he went to another state and took the child with him, and claims the custody of it by virtue of his parental rights, that the mother is not a fit person to take care of the child, that she neglected it, and is not qualified to attend to its morals and personal comfort, and that he and his wife have separated, and that he has brought a libel for a divorce in this country, and that the mother still retains her youngest child, a boy, and that he has a sister with him who will take charge of the child. And thus stands the case by the pleadings between the parties.

"When the cause came to a hearing a mass of evidence was produced relating to the various causes which produced their separation; and evidence was also adduced, in relation to their capability as parents to discharge their duties to their children. * *

"In the first place, the conduct and character of the father is that of a good moral man, and no objection can be raised against him as a father.

"On the part of the mother, there has been a mass of evidence showing some improper conduct about their money matters, and some imprudent expressions at times when laboring under feelings of despondence, and from which, and the appearance of the wife, the court believes that she is at times subject to feelings of great despondence, and was induced to make imprudent expressions, which she never executed, and never intended to execute, and which she has not attempted to fulfill; and so far as relates to her fondness, for her children and her anxious care about them, and her industry to maintain them, the evidence is ample in her favor, as well as for chastity; and that by her labor she can support them; and that both father and mother have to live by their labor; and it further appears that the father assisted the mother to depart for Charleston with both their children, and that one a boy, is now about 9 or 12 months old, and the child Emily is about two years and four months old, and that the father went to Charleston, took the child Emily from the mother whilst absent from her home, and brought it to Augusta, and now has it in his possession, and the before stated writ is brought to have it restored to the mother.

"The first objection which is urged by the defendant, is that the writ being entitled at common law, the court is bound by the law to return the child to the father; but the jurisdiction which is exercised by the Chancellor, is the same as at common law. *Law Lib.*, 685, *No.* 99. Where the Chancellor grants the writ, he as *parens patriæ*, possesses power over the legal rights of the father, which a common law judge does not. In this case the judges of the Superior Courts being clothed with both law and equity powers, will look to the prayer of the writ and see in which capacity the court is called on to act, and proceed to make its decision accordingly. This court, therefore sees nothing in the address of the writ, which will not allow it to exercise its equity powers; as the case made by the petition shows that those powers are involved in this case.

"Where this writ is granted, and the facts show that the court is called on as *parens patriæ*, to exercise its equitable powers, its great and paramount duty is to look to the interest and safety of the child, as well as its morals, its education, and even its pecuniary interest. And the legal rights of the father to the custody of his child, will not be enforced if those rights in any manner conflict with these interests or the welfare of the child. All the authorities agree as to this rule. It is the application of it to each particular case, that has created some difference of opinion between judges, and as the judges shall under the facts of each case, believe it to be either for the safety and welfare of the child or its pecuniary interests, so will they exercise or refuse to exercise this jurisdiction. The question now presented by the facts before the court is, will it be for the welfare of this child to leave it in the possession of the father or return it to its mother?

"Upon this point we have the testimony of Doctors Eve and Garvin, as well as the opinion of several other witnesses, that this child will be better attended to and more closely watched in its present state and very tender years by the mother, than it can be attended to by the father, or any other person, as a nurse for it; and particularly as the child is a female. And the court being of the same opinion with the doctors and other witnesses on the subject: It is therefore ordered by the court, that the defendant, Nathan S. King, deliver the infant child Emily back to his wife Anna, to be by her nurtured and taken care of as the exigencies of said child may require; but upon this express condition, and it is hereby ordered that said Anna King suffer and permit the said Nathan S. King to have reasonable access to the said child, through the agency of their friends or otherwise.

"But as this court is not allowed by law to make an order which will deprive itself of jurisdiction over the person of this child, and as the father has the same right to apply to this court when he thinks the welfare of his child may require it as the mother; and as it appears by the evidence that Mrs. King is now residing in Charleston and without the jurisdiction of this court, it is further ordered that the said Anna King by her friends appear before the clerk of this court, and enter into bond by such friend or friends, payable to the state of Georgia in the penal sum of $500, conditioned that the child Emily King be not removed without the jurisdiction of this state. And it is further ordered, that if the said Anna King is unable to procure her friends to give such bond, then the said child Emily is to remain under the care of her father, the said Nathan S. King, and he permitting the said Anna King to have reasonable access to the said child Emily, through her friends or otherwise, from time to time as may be reasonable. And it is further ordered, that said Nathan S. King pay the cost of this proceeding."

It has been shown that the court in this case was mistaken in supposing it had any greater authority under the habeas corpus, because the equity powers of the court were invoked in the petition for the writ, than they would have possessed had the writ issued on the law side of the court. And it is obvious the court did not stand much upon the distinction, for, *it would seem*, they would consider the application addressed to the equity side of the court whenever the nature of the case required the exercise of that discretionary power which they supposed appertained to them only in their character as a court of Chancery.

The legislature of the state, however, seem to have determined that the judges should not have any occasion to avow themselves ashamed of the law; for four years after the decision of the last case, they passed "An Act to give mothers certain rights in relation to the guardianship and custody of their minor children." *Cobb's Dig., A. D.* 1851, *p.* 335, the second section of which provides that:

"In all cases where a controversy may arise on the return to a habeas corpus, in relation to the custody of the persons of minor children, the common law rule vesting said custody always in the father shall be abolished; and it shall be within the discretion of the judge of the superior courts or justice of the inferior courts, or a majority of them, in the absence of the judge of the superior court, to award the custody of said minor or minors either in the father or mother, as may appear most beneficial to the interest of said children."

A reviewing court will not interfere with the exercise of the discretion of the court to which the writ of habeas corpus is returnable, unless there is some flagrant abuse of it. *Lindsey* v. *Lindsey*, 14 *Geo.*, 657.

New York. In this state the earliest case reported is that of the *McDowles*, in 1811. 8 *Johns.*, 328.

"Writs of habeas corpus were awarded by the recorder of Albany to Nathan Spicer to bring up the body of Hugh McDowle, and to Nathan Slosson to bring up the body of John McDowle. The recorder certified the writs and returns into this court and recognized the parties to appear at this term and produce the infants. They now appeared and the infants were produced in court. The return of Spicer stated that on 3d May, 1808, Matthew McDowle, father of the infant, sealed and delivered to him an indenture which was set forth by which he bound his son Hugh, then six years of age, to Nathan Spicer (a member of the society of Shakers) to be by him, or under his care, fed, clothed, taught to read and write and instructed in the carpenter and joiner's trade, provided circumstances would admit it and the boy inclined, and instructed in other matters according to his faith and the faith and practice of the church and society to which he belonged until the age of 21. If the boy inclined to depart before, the father agreed to take him away on being duly notified. The indentures were excuted by Spicer and the father of the infant. The return further stated that the infant had never manifested any desire to depart but an inclination to stay, &c.

"The return to the other writ was similar. John was bound by his father 23d April, 1808, being then eight years old, to be taught the trade of blacksmith, &c.

"*Per Curiam.* Two objections are taken to the validity of the indentures stated in the return:

"1st. That it is not executed by the infant. 2d. That the word apprentice is not inserted in the deed.

"The first objection is founded on statute (2 *R. S.*, 154, § 1,) which evidently requires the deed to be executed by the infant as well as his parent or guardian. At common law a parent may bind his infant an apprentice; but the statute must be considered as controlling the common law in this respect, and as requiring the infant to be a party to the deed. The infant in the present case is not therefore bound, and the question is as to the relief which ought to be granted on the present writ.

"The father who on his part executed the indenture with the master sues out the writ. There is nothing before the court to show any improper treatment of the infant, nor that the party to whom the father intended to bind him has not hitherto faithfully performed the stipulations in the indenture.

"This is not a case then in which the father has any equity or any right to complain. He may be bound still by the covenants in the indenture, though the infant is not. It is for the infant alone to take advantage of the defect; and if he does not choose to do it, he may waive the defect and avail himself of the benefit of the apprenticeship. All that the court are required to do under the present writ is to see that the infant is not restrained against his will.

"In the present case, then, the court can only declare that the infants are at liberty to go where they please. They may go and put themselves under the protection and care of their father, or they may return to the service of their masters.

"N. B. The chief justice then asked the infants where they chose to go; and they answered that they wished to return to the masters. The counsel for the masters suggesting that violence might be used on the part of the father to gain possession of the boys, the court directed a constable to attend them.

"Afterwards the counsel for the father suggested to the court that improper means and constraint had been used by the masters and others belonging to the society of Shakers to induce the children to declare their election to return and that the answers were not fairly given by them to the court. The parties then agreed that the boys should be privately examined by three gentlemen of the bar as to their election; and the court appointed three counsellors to examine the boys in order to discover their true wishes. The counsellors after making the inquiry reported to the court that the boys, after being carefully informed of the purpose of the inquiry, expressed a decided and unequivocal desire to return to their masters and a strong and unaccountable repugnance to go back to their father. The court thereupon ordered the boys to be delivered to their masters and directed an officer to attend and protect them in their return according to their choice. It was mentioned that the mother of the children, now deceased, had been a member of the society now called Shakers."

The next case occurred in 1816, in the same court. *In the matter of Waldron*, 13 *Johns.*, 418.

"A habeas corpus was issued in this case in May term last to Andrew McGowan, to bring up the body of Margaret Eliza Waldron, an infant alleged to be detained in his custody. It appeared from the affidavits which were read to the court, that John P. Waldron had married the daughter of Andrew McGowan, and that having become embarrassed and insolvent, McGowan in Feb. 1813, took his daughter to his house, without her or her husband's consent, as was alleged on the part of Waldron; but positively denied by the affidavits on the other side. Mrs. Waldron lived with her father until her death, and during her residence with her father Margaret Eliza Waldron was born, who has always been supported by her grandfather. Waldron used to visit his wife shortly after her removal to her father's, but had discontinued his visits for a long time previous to her death; and had not visited his child, being deterred as he alleged, but which was denied by the other side, by the unkind and repulsive treatment which he met with from McGowan and his family.

"McGowan is a man in very affluent circumstances, and abundantly able to educate and maintain his granddaughter; and it appeared that Waldron was insolvent and unable to pay certain trifling debts which he had contracted, although it was alleged that his mother, with whom he lived, was competent and willing to support him and his daughter. It appeared also that the infant's mother was the only daughter of McGowan, and the infant the only remaining grandchild in the family, and would most probably receive the greater part of the property of her grandparents on their death.

THOMPSON, Ch. J. "The general principle applicable to cases of this kind is laid down by Lord Mansfield in *Rex* v. *Delaval*, 3 *Burr.*, 1436, 'That in cases of writs of habeas corpus directed to private persons to bring up infants, the court is bound ex debito justitiæ, to set the infant free from an improper restraint. But they are not bound to deliver the infant over to any particular person. This must be left to their discretion, according to the circumstances that shall appear before them.'

"In the present case, the child cannot be considered under any improper restraint. She was born at the house of her grandparents, and has always lived with and been brought up by them. The case of the *Commonwealth* v. *Addicks*, 5 *Binn.*, 520, is very much in point and a strong corroboration of the principle that it is a matter resting in the sound discretion of the court, and not a matter of right which the father can claim at the hands of the court. It is the benefit and welfare of the infant to which the attention of the court ought principally to be directed.

"We think, therefore, that it will be a due exercise of the discretion with which the law has invested us, to deny the present application, leaving the father to pursue his remedy, if any he has, in the Court of Chancery, where questions of this kind more properly belong; there being no actual improper restraint of the infant. We think proper, however, to suggest that the father ought on all suitable occasions to be permitted to see the child, taking it for granted that he will not attempt to take her away from the care and custody of her grandparents, except by the aid of some judicial proceeding."

The next case reported occurred in 1819, before the Chancellor. *Matter of Wollstonecraft*, 4 *Johns. C. R.*, 80.

"From the affidavit upon which the writ was granted and the return of Joseph T. Jackson, it appeared that the infant Jane N. Wollstonecraft was born in Louisiana, that her father procured a divorce from her mother on the ground of her adultery; he kept the child and married again; he died leaving his second wife testamentary guardian, who declined and Alfred Hennen was appointed guardian in Louisiana, who sent the child by her step-mother to New Hampshire for education, and placed her under the care of Richard Hall, from whose custody she was forcibly taken away to Putnam county, New York, by her own mother, who there procured the appointment of guardian of the person of the infant, by the surrogate of that county, and placed her in the family of Joseph T. Jackson, who married the aunt of the infant. The writ was granted on the application of said Hall.

"The CHANCELLOR examined the infant touching her situation and wishes; and thereupon observed, that the object of the court was to release the infant from all improper restraint, and not to try, in this summary way, the question of guardianship or to deliver the infant over to the custody of another. That the course and practice of the courts in these cases was only to deliver the party from illegal restraint; and if competent to form and declare an election, then to allow the infant to go where she pleased, and if the infant be too young to form a judgment then the court is to exercise its judgment for the infant. That in the case of *Rex* v. *Johnson*, 1 *Str.*, 579, 2 *Ld. Raym.*, 1333, *S. C.*, *and* 3 *Burr.*, 1436, *S. C.*, the infant was so young (nine years old), as to have no judgment of her own, and the court delivered the child over to the party suing out the writ; but that case was afterwards overruled in *Rex* v. *Smith*, 2 *Str.*, 982, 3 *P. Wm.*, 155, *note*. The practice sufficiently appeared from the cases of *Rex* v. *Clarkson*, 1 *Str.*, 444; *Ex parte Hopkins*, 3 *P. Wms.*, 151; *Rex* v. *Delaval*, 3 *Burr.*, 1434, 2 *Cox*, 242; *Matter of McDowles*, 8 *Johns.*, 328; and *Matter of Waldron*, 13 *Johns.*, 418."

The following order was thereupon entered:

"The above named Jane N. Wollstonecraft being brought up before the Chancellor, by Joseph T. Jackson, upon a writ of habeas corpus, heretofore awarded in this case, and being examined, and appearing to be of the age of thirteen years or thereabouts, and declaring herself to be of that age, and that she was unwilling to be delivered up to Richard Hall, on whose behalf the writ of habeas corpus was awarded, and that she wished to remain under the care, and in the custody of her mother and Joseph T. Jackson, who married her aunt, and under whom she was placed by her mother, and she appearing to be of competent judgment to make a choice: Ordered that she be restored to the custody of Joseph T. Jackson and of her mother."

The next case was in 1836, *The People, ex rel. E. Ordronaux,* v. *Chegaray and Condert,* 18 *Wend.,* 637.

This was an application for a habeas corpus by the wife, under the statute, 2 *R. S.*, 148, *sec.* 1, which provided that "Where any husband and wife shall live in a state of separation without being divorced, and shall have any minor child of the marriage, the wife, if she be an inhabitant of this state, may apply to the Supreme Court for a writ of habeas corpus, to have such minor child brought before it; on the return of such writ, the court, on due consideration, may award the charge and custody of the child so brought before it, to the mother, for such time, under such regulations and restrictions, and with such provisions and directions as the case may require. At any time after making such order the Supreme Court may annul, vary or modify the same."

On the 8th of August, 1836, Elizabeth Ordronaux, the wife of John Ordronaux of the city of New York, presented a petition to the court, verified by her oath, stating that she was an inhabitant of this state, and that she and her husband were living in a state of separation, without being divorced; that there were three minor children of the marriage, to wit, Clara, aged 15 years, Florine, aged 13 years, and John, aged 9 years, that her husband, in April, 1855, placed the two daughters in the boarding school of Madame Chegaray, the wife of the defendant Chegaray, in the city of New York, where they still remain; and that the son was placed in a boarding school kept by the defendant Condert, who is the principal of the New York Lyceum, where he still remains.

"On the hearing, counsel for the relator offered to read the affidavit of Mrs. Ordronaux, who was in court. It was objected: 1st. That the return could not be contradicted; 2d. That she could not be a witness against her husband, it was against the policy of the law.

By the court, BRONSON, J.: "The practice of the courts has not been entirely uniform on this subject; but independent of any statutory provision, I think it the better opinion that the return to a writ of habeas corpus could not be controverted. But this rule is changed by statute. The proper course has thus far been pursued on the part of the applicant. A copy of her petition was served with the writs, and the father and the persons having the immediate charge of the children under his authority, have had an opportunity to answer. It is true that they may now be surprised by the introduction of new matter; but this would not be a greater evil than that which might possibly result from holding returns conclusive.

"In a summary proceeding either party may suffer injury from not being able to anticipate all the allegations which may be made on the part of his adversary. But the court as far as practicable, will take care that no improper advantage shall be obtained by either party. The proofs offered by the mother will be received, and the father will also be at liberty to give further evidence on his part. The affidavit of Mrs. Ordronaux will be received, subject to all legal exceptions."

The admissibility of the affidavit of the wife was finally left undetermined, the court remarking on the next morning that "if the facts stated by Mrs. Ordonaux were important to the conclusion at which I have arrived on the main question, I should not receive her affidavit without taking time for consideration.

"In relation to the general question it can hardly be doubted that the father is entitled to the custody of his infant children; and where, as in the present case, differences unfortunately exist between the parents, the right of the father is preferred to that of the mother. I shall not stop to inquire into the fitness of the rule. It is enough that it is settled by authority. The statute under which these writs were sued out, proceeds upon the assumption that the father has the better right. It authorizes the court to interfere on the application of the wife only; and evidently supposes that she alone needed any extraordinary remedy. It is true that the courts on the common law writ of habeas corpus have not always committed the children to the custody of the father.

"It is not the object of that writ to try the right of parents or guardians to the custody of infants; but to deliver from unjust imprisonment and all illegal and improper restraint. When therefore infants have been brought into court, who were of the age of discretion, they have frequently been consulted in relation to their wishes; and have been informed they were at liberty to go where they pleased. Cases of this kind prove nothing in favor of the mother, and many of them admit the superior right of the father.

"The father, however, has not an absolute, unalienable right to the custody of his infant children. This like other rights may be forfeited by misconduct. And although courts of law have not interfered by habeas corpus, in such cases the father has been controlled in the exercise of his parental power by the Court of Chancery in England."* *

"I have entertained some doubt whether this was a proper case for consulting the children in relation to their wishes. This is not a proceeding for the purpose of relieving them from any improper restraint; but it is a contest between parents in relation to the future charge and custody of their children. But as the legislature has not declared on what grounds the court shall proceed, but has confided the whole matter to our discretion, I have concluded that it was not improper to consult the children, and have conversed with them severally in relation to their present condition and their wishes for the future.

"It only remains that I examine the evidence which has been adduced for and against the granting of this application." * *

"This is not a case where the court is to interfere as a matter of course, but only upon sufficient grounds. The children are in good health. They are in schools of the best repute, where their morals and comfort as well as their education, receive all proper attention. Their mother is permitted to visit them at pleasure, and they occasionally visit her. Their father is a man of good character, and it is abundantly proved that he is a fit and proper person to have the charge and custody of the children. On the evidence before me I am unable to make the same remark in relation to the mother.

"On the whole, there does not appear to be any sufficient ground for the interference of the court, and the application of Mrs. Ordronaux must be denied."

The next case occurred the year following, 1837, and is that of *The People, ex. rel., I. Nickeson* v. ——, 19 *Wend.*, 16.

This was a habeas corpus for a minor child and the question was one of custody between the parents. The mother had withdrawn herself from the protection of her husband and resided with her father. She took with her an infant child, to obtain the custody of which the father sued out the writ of habeas corpus. On the return of the writ numerous affidavits were produced on both sides and after hearing counsel the following opinion was pronounced.

By the court, NELSON, Ch. J.: "The father is the natural guardian of his infant children and in the absence of good and sufficient reasons shown to the court, such as ill-usage, grossly immoral principles or habits, want of abilty, &c., is entitled to their custody care and education. All the authorities concur on this point. * * * *

"I have diligently and carefully examined the facts disclosed in the affidavits and feel myself bound to say that upon the whole nothing appears that can justify the conclusion that the father is not a fit and proper person to have the care and education of his child or that it would be for the interest of the child pecuniarily or otherwise to commit its custody to the mother according to the principles of the common law and the numerous adjudged cases aleady referred to. Mrs. Nickeson is now living in a state unauthorized by law. The statute, 2 *R. S.*, 145, 6, 7, *arts.* 3, 4, enumerates the cases in which a separation may be legalized either by a dissolution of the marriage contract or by a divorce from bed and board. The course of the decisions of the Court of Chancery clearly shows that no divorce or separation could be decreed upon the facts before me. It is no doubt possible that the home of the wife may be made intolerable without any actual violence committed on her person; harsh and cruel usage that would justify a separation may be practiced towards her short of this by an unkind husband, and this is what seems to be *intimated* in the affidavits opposing this motion. Upon questions, however, involving such solemn considerations and so deeply affecting the future condition and character of the parties we cannot act upon *insinuations*." We regard only the facts. Proof in opposition insufficient. "*Order* that the child be delivered to the father."

The controversy between John A. Barry and his wife, for the custody of their daughter, was made a subject of repeated examination in the courts of New York and of the United States. The respective rights of father, mother and child were more fully discussed than in any other case which has occurred, and the case may be referred to as supporting the rules before given relating to the custody of children. It also establishes some important principles relating to the practice under the writ. The following are the leading facts:

John A. Barry, from Nova Scotia, a British subject and widower, having four children, in 1835 married, in the city of New York, Eliza Anna Mercein, daughter of Thomas R. Mercein a citizen of the United States. They had two children, a son and a daughter. Difficulties arose between them. He desired to take his wife and their children to Nova Scotia. She complained of cruel usage at his hands and refused to go with him. A temporary separation was agreed upon, she to go to her father's with her daughter and he to retain the custody of the son. Subsequently he endeavored to induce her to accompany him to his home in in Nova Scotia which she declined to do, but continued to reside with her father retaining the daughter.

On the 18th of May, 1839, the daughter then being about fifteen months old, Barry obtained a writ of habeas corpus from the recorder of the city of New York, directed to Thomas R. Mercein, commanding him to produce the bodies, &c., of Mrs. Eliza Anna Barry and Mary M. Barry, her daughter. The return disclaimed all right of custody but stated the differences between the husband and wife, and was accompanied with the wife's affidavit justifying herself for refusing to live with her husband, and praying to be left in custody of the child which was represented to be in a delicate state of health. After hearing the parties the recorder, on the 1st of July, 1839, ordered that the child remain in custody of the mother 'until the said John A. Barry and Eliza Ann Barry shall make some arrangement or compromise, or until the custody of the said child shall be changed by a judicial decision.'

"On the 13th of July, 1839, Barry obtained another habeas corpus issued by the Chancellor, directed to Thomas R. Mercein, commanding him to produce the same persons named in the first writ. A similar return was made to this writ. Indeed copies of the former return and of Mrs. Barry's affidavit were set out and made a part of the return. After hearing the parties the Chancellor, on the 10th of August, 1839, made the following order:

"It appearing that so far as relates to the said Ann Eliza Barry, she is under no restraint whatever, but on the contrary that she is now and at all times has been at perfect liberty to go wheresoever she pleased; and there appearing to exist no sufficient reason for depriving the said Eliza Ann Barry of the care and nurture of her said infant child Mary Mercein Barry: It is therefore adjudged and declared that the said infant daughter is not improperly restrained of her liberty by the said Thomas R. Mercein, and that no good reason now exists for taking the said infant child from the care or protection of the said Thomas R. Mercein with whom the said Eliza Ann Barry now voluntarily resides; and this court therefore will not make an order to take the said infant child from the custody and nurture of its mother and the care and protection of the defendant, Thomas R. Mercein, for the purpose of delivering it up to the relator, John A. Barry."

On the 29th October, 1839, he obtained a third habeas corpus from Hon. Wm. Inglis, associate judge common pleas, city and county of New York, directed to the defendant to bring up the child before him. To this writ defendant returned, stating the issuing of the first writ of habeas corpus by the recorder and the proceedings had thereon; also the issuing of second writ of habeas corpus by the Chancellor and the proceedings had thereon; and insisted that such proceedings were a bar to any further proceeding on the habeas corpus then pending, and that the matter should be adjudged *res adjudicata* and the habeas corpus dismissed. If, however, the matter should be otherwise adjudged he then returned the facts and circumstances under which the child was in his house and prayed that the return made by him to the habeas corpus issued by the Chancellor and the affidavit accompanying the same made by his daughter, might be deemed part of his return and he accordingly annexed a copy of such return. He also verified the facts set forth in his return to the habeas corpus issued by the recorder. He stated also his belief of the relator's purpose to vex and harass his wife and him, and to carry off the child to foreign lands. He also stated that the relator had greatly frightened the child by the abduction of it, deranged its nervous system, &c., and concluded by saying the child was there with her mother, Mrs. Barry, in his custody; but that Mrs. Barry was and at all times had been at liberty to go whithersoever she pleased and take the child with her.

On the coming in of this return the relator did not *demur* to it as *informal* in referring to other papers but merely objected to it as being *evasive* and that the doctrine of *res adjudicata* was not applicable to the writ of habeas corpus.

The judge decided that an adjudication of the same subject matter between the same parties was not a bar to the issuing of a new writ of habeas corpus, and to the investigation of *new matters arising subsequently to the prior adjudication*, and that the return should set forth that no new state of facts between the parties, in relation to the child, had arisen subsequently to the prior adjudication. The return was amended accordingly, by stating therein the *continuance of the same facts* upon which the decisions of the recorder and Chancellor were founded at the time of the return to the associate judge, who thereupon, after argument decided; "that the proceedings before the Chancellor and the order of the 26th day of August, made by him were well pleaded in bar to any investigation of any matters in relation to the detention or imprisonment of the child; and that the matters in difference between the parties up to the time of the making of that order must be considered *res adjudicata*."

Subsequent to this decision the relator produced in evidence a letter in defendant's hand writing, dated after the Chancellor's decision, to wit, August 28, 1839, also one from his wife dated August 29, 1839, on the subject of allowing relator to visit the child. Other evidence was also offered by defendant as to Mrs. Barry's good character and defendant's good family; also at a subsequent hearing the defendant produced the agreement of June 7, 1838, which was objected to by the relator as inadmissible under the decision, that evidence of facts transpiring previous to the order of the Chancellor, 26th August, 1839, could not be read, but the judge overruled the objection and received the paper and a declaration of the relator that he intended to take the child out of the state was proved on the part of the defendant.

On the 30th April, 1840, Judge Inglis made his final decision, whereby he held there was no imprisonment or restraint or unlawful withholding of the infant child, Mary Mercein Barry, and accordingly *dismissed* the habeas corpus.

The relator sued out a certiorari removing the proceedings before Judge Inglis into the Supreme Court. To which writ the judge returned, stating the proceedings before him in which he certified, that the *original order* of the recorder directing the child to remain in the custody of her mother, and an *exemplification* of the order of the Chancellor of the 26th August, 1839, were produced in evidence before him, and that at the several hearings before him the relator offered no testimony except in relation to matters that had taken place previously to the said two orders, and offered none except in relation to the character and circumstances of the *defendant*, which he subsequently did not follow up with proof.

"The Supreme Court reversed the decision of Judge Inglis, whereupon the respondent sued out a writ of error removing the record into the Court of Errors. In this court by a vote of 19 to 3, the judgment of the Supreme Court was reversed, and a resolution adopted declaring that the decision of Judge Inglis upon the question of *res adjudicata*, was correct and in conformity to law."

In October, 1840, Barry obtained another writ of habeas corpus issued by Justice Oakley of the Superior Court of New York; but the judge not finding the circumstances of the case materially different from what they were at the time of the decision by Judge Inglis, decided against the relator in March, 1841. In the summer of 1842, he obtained another writ issued by the Supreme Court, consisting of the same judges who composed the court when the decision of Judge Inglis was reversed, viz.: Nelson Ch. J., Bronson and Cowen, JJ., a majority of the court being of opinion that the circumstances of the case were materially changed from the time of the hearing before Justice Oakley, by reason of the increased age, (about 18 months) of the child, made an order for the delivery of the child to the father. Nelson, Ch. J., dissented.

"This decision was reversed in the Court of Errors on substantially the same grounds, upon which the former judgment of the Supreme Court had been reversed.

"The relator afterwards in January, 1844, applied to the Supreme Court of the United States for a writ of habeas corpus, which was refused on the ground that the Supreme Court had no original jurisdiction in such cases. He then in April, 1844, applied for the writ to the Circuit Court of the United States for the Southern District of New York, which was refused for the following reasons, by Judge Betts:

"1st. If granted and a return was made admitting the facts stated in the petition, I should discharge the infant on the ground that this court cannot exercise the common law functions of *parens patriæ*, and has no common law jurisdiction over the matter.

"2d. Because the court has not judicial cognizance of the matter by virtue of any statute of the United States.

"3d. If such jurisdiction is to be implied, that then the decision of the Court of Errors of New York supplies the rule of law, or furnishes the highest evidence of the common law rule, which is to be the rule of decision in this case.

"4th. Because by that rule the father is not entitled on the case made by this petition, to take this child out of the custody of its mother.

"Upon this refusal to grant the writ, Barry sued out a writ of error from the Supreme Court of the United States, which in 1847, was dismissed for want of jurisdiction."

The foregoing facts and decisions will be found stated in the cases, *The People, ex rel Barry*, v. *Mercein*, 3 *Hill Rep.*, 399; *Barry* v. *Mercein*, 5 *How.*, 108; *Mercein* v. *The People*, 25 *Wend.*, 64, *and*, *The People, ex rel Barry*, v. *Mercein*, 8 *Paige*, 47.

The last decision, however, of the Court of Errors, reversing the order of the Supreme Court, has never been reported.

This litigation was no less remarkable for the great research and ability displayed in the discussion of the questions involved, than for the exceeding pertinacity with which it was pursued by the relator.

The only important question of law, however, which it may be said to have settled, at least for the

State of New York, is that an order in habeas corpus determining the question of custody of a child, between contending parents is conclusive, while the material facts relating to the circumstances of the parties remain unchanged, and may be relied on as a bar to a subsequent writ of habeas corpus.

The following case occurred in 1847, and may be considered as stating fairly the law in New York upon this interesting question as derived from the cases adjudged in their highest courts.

In the matter of Gregg, 6 *Penn. Law Jour.*, 528. In the Superior Court of the city of New York before the *Hon. T. J. Oakley*, assistant J., June 1, 1847:

OAKLEY, J. "The writ of habeas corpus in this case was sued out by Dr. Wm. Gregg, of the city of Philadelphia, to bring up the body of his infant son" (about 6 years old) "detained illegally, as was alleged, in the custody of his wife in the city of New York.

"*Return.* Cruel treatment, &c.

"*Answer.* Denies the allegations in the return.

"*Proofs.* Oral and documentary.

"It appears that both father and mother are persons of good moral character, and both of sufficient pecuniary means to enable them properly to take charge of the child, and that the child, though never having been subject to any complaints other than those which are ordinarily incident to childhood, is of delicate health, and, in the judgment of the only physician who has been examined in relation to it, still requires the care of a mother. The general doctrine, that the father has an absolute right to the custody of his child if personally unobjectionable, does not seem to be sustained by the law in this state as expounded by its highest tribunals. It is a matter of frequent occurrence that this supposed absolute right is made to yield to the mere will of the child. In cases where the child is of sufficient discretion, though still an infant in the eye of the law, to make a choice for itself as to the disposition of its own person, all the court does under the writ of habeas corpus is to see that all restraint is removed and that such choice may be freely made; and this choice may not only be in favor of either parent against the other, but is not unfrequently opposed to the wishes and claims of both, the child preferring to place himself in the care and custody of strangers. The question there as to the alleged superior right of the father can only arise where the child cannot, as in the present case, choose for itself, and here the real point at issue between the parties presents itself; the relator contending that in such case the law determines that the safest place for the child is under the care and custody of the father; and the respondent insisting that the question is left at large to be determined by the court exercising a sound legal discretion and acting solely in reference to the interests of the child under the circumstances of the case.

"It would seem, then, that the real question in these cases is not what are the rights of the father or mother to the custody of the child, or whether the right of one be superior to that of the other, but what are the rights of the child; and I cannot but think that much of the apparent conflict in the various decisions of the courts in these cases and in the reasoning which has been resorted to to sustain them has arisen from loose and undefined notions as to the nature of the questions involved. They have not unfrequently been treated as if they were cases involving the rights of property rather than mere personal rights, and as if the parents were setting up conflicting claims of property in the child.

"The true view is that the rights of the child are alone to be considered, and those rights clearly are to be protected in the enjoyment of its personal liberty, according to its own choice if arrived at the age of discretion, and if not to have its personal safety and interests guarded and secured by the law acting through the agency of those who are called upon to administer it.

"In all the cases, even in those in which the superior right of the father seems to have been most strongly maintained, the principle is clearly recognized that there may be circumstances irrespective of any personal disqualification of the father which may defeat his claim. The discretion which is thus to guide in the decision of cases, like the present, is not an unregulated or arbitrary discretion of the judge, for that has justly been styled 'the law of tyrants,' but a discretion governed as far as the case will admit by fixed rules and principles. It is certainly somewhat difficult to define these rules and principles with precision, but keeping in mind that the present interests of the child are alone to be consulted, I think they may safely be sought for in considerations connected with its age and health.

"When a child is found in the custody of its mother, of tender years or of feeble and delicate health and when the necessity of maternal care is evident, the law will not interfere to remove it from such custody and could not do it without shocking the common sense and feelings of mankind. But where the child has arrived at an age at which t becomes important to determine upon its course of education and mental training, in reference to future business and establishment in life, it may reasonably be supposed that the superintendence and judgment of the father will better subserve its true interests than those of the mother. While the physical safety of the child and the incipient stages of its education are the chief objects to be regarded, it is quite clear from observation and experience that these may be safely entrusted to the mother, and that in general, under such circumstances, maternal is more safe and effectual than paternal care and superintendence."

Let the child remain with its mother.

New Jersey. *In the State* v. *Stigall & Turney*, 2 *Zabr.*, 286, RANDOLPH, J., said:

"But where the child is of tender years and the father and mother have separated, or the wife has left the abode of her husband, it often becomes necessary for the court or judge, on return of the habeas corpus, to determine as to the custody of the child, without waiting for the slower action of the Chancellor, or referring the matter to him as the parens patriæ in the place of the sovereign.

"Under the general rule of the common law, courts have not felt authorized to take the child from the father and give it to the mother, although some very strong cases have arisen which seemed to demand the interference of the court. 5 *East*, 00; 9 *J. B. Moore*, 279; *Ball* v. *Ball*, 2 *Sim.*, 35; *Wellesley* v. *Duke of Beaufort*, 2 *Russ.*, 9.

"But where the father had asked a court of law or a judge to grant an order to reinvest him with the actual custody of his child, the court before making the order would look into the case and notwithstanding the presumed right of the father, would exercise a discretion in the matter. Such ever was and still is the law, with much less change in the rule than in the mode of exercising the discretion or the extent of its exercise.

"The principle of the action of the court or refusal to act is this: The power and right of the father is allowed for the benefit of the child, and not to enable him to govern with arbitrary caprice or tyrannical control, so as to subvert the very object of the law in giving him the authority. Thus where the children would be exposed to cruelty or gross corruption, immoral principles or habits, or the father is not of ability to provide for the support, education and future prospects of the child, and the mother or person with whom the child resides is able, the court will make no order granting the custody of the child to the father. And, too, if the child is of tender years and especially if a female or of sickly constitution, in the custody of the mother, against whom there is no charge but inability to live with her husband, the court would make no order of removal.

"*The discretion is pretty broad, and perhaps extending with the improvements and refinements of the age, yet it is not arbitrary, but based on sound principles; and yet like all other discretionary proceedings will take its hue from the officer exercisiny it.*

"In this case there were three children, Charles, aged 5 years and 3 months; Robert, 3 years and 5 months, and Elizabeth, 13 months.

"The two younger children are too young to be removed for any practical or useful purpose to themselves at least; and as nothing is found against the mother, but her inability to live with her husband, they should, for the present, remain with her; but an order may be entered to deliver the eldest to the father."

SECTION VII.

CUSTODY OF ILLEGITIMATE CHILDREN.

The English cases show a want of unanimity of opinion upon this question also. *See Forsyth's Custody of Infants*, 77.

In *Rex* v. *Soper*, 5 *T. R.*, 278, Lord KENYON, Ch. J., said that the putative father of a bastard child had no right to the custody of it. And when this case was cited in *R.*

v. *Mosely*, 5 *East*, 224; and see *R.* v. *Hopkins*, 7 *East*, 579, *and* 1 *Madd. Ch. Pr.*, 432, *n. z.*, where a writ of habeas corpus was moved for to bring up the body of a bastard infant, of which the defendant was the father, the same learned judge said: "Where the father has the custody of the child fairly, I do not know that this court would take it away from him, though I do not mean to impeach the propriety of the case cited. But where he has got possession of the child by force or fraud, as is here sugested, we will interfere to put matters in the same situation as before."

Yet the learned judge does not appear to have been consistent in that opinion; for in an anonymous case, cited by Sheppard, Serg't, *arguendo*, in the case of *Strangeways* v. *Robinson*, 4 *Taunt.*, 506, where a writ of habeas corpus was sued out on behalf of the mother to prevent a legitimate child, little more than seven years old, from being carried to the West Indies by his father, though the father had obtained the possession of the child from a school both by fraud and force, he held that as he found it in the possession of the father he must leave it there, though he said he would have preferred to have left the child in the custody of the mother.

In a late case, *Ex parte Knee*, 1 *Bos. & Pul. N. R.*, 148, the Court of Common Pleas did take away an infant illegitimate child from the custody in which it had been placed by the father, although there was no imputation against him, and ordered it to be delivered to the mother, who was willing and anxious to receive it.

Sir J. MANSFIELD, said: "It is not unlikely, indeed, that by granting this application we may be doing a great prejudice to the child, but still the mother is entitled to the child if she insists upon it."

It is, however, by no means clear that such a right on the part of the mother would now be recognized. In *Rex* v. *Hopkins*, 7 *East*, 579, Lord Ellenborough expressed a doubt whether the court could interfere by a writ of habeas corpus on behalf of the mother of an illegitimate child, who had no legal right to the person of the child, the question of guardianship belonging to another forum, and the child not being of an age to complain for itself of any illegal restraint on its person. As, however, the infant had been taken away from the mother by force, the court ordered it to be restored to her."

The last case in which the point was much considered, *In re Lloyd*, 3 *Man. & Gr.*, 547, does not clear away all the difficulty.

"An illegitimate child, between eleven and twelve years of age, was produced under the care of a female attendant, by the father with whom it resided, in the court of Common Pleas, in obedience to a writ of habeas corpus, and as he made no claim to the custody, the court allowed the infant to choose for herself the party with whom she wished to remain. In delivering the judgment, TINDAL, Ch. J., said: 'This is a case of some difficulty, and we cannot help feeling distressed at being obliged to come to a decision upon it. The writ of habeas corpus has been obtained by the mother of an illegitimate child, for the purpose of bringing her up from the custody of a party with whom she had been placed by her putative father. The child is now in court in obedience to the writ, and appears as she has been sworn to be, between eleven and twelve years old. *Had she been under seven years of age, the court would have said that she could exercise no discretion;* but she is old enough to choose for herself, and, therefore, we do not feel called upon to exercise a discretion for her.

If she is willing to go with her mother, she may, but if she does so it must be her own free will, for no force shall be used.'

"His lordship then asked the child if she would go with her mother, but she expressed a strong disinclination to do so. He then told her she was at liberty to go where she would; whereupon she left the court with a female who had accompanied her there. Upon quitting the court the mother attempted to take forcible possession of the child; but upon this being made known to the Chief Justice, one of the officers of the court was sent with her for her protection."

The same difficulty has not embarrassed the American courts. They hold the putative father to have no right to the custody of his illegitimate child as against its mother. *Wright* v. *Wright*, 12 *Mass.*, 109; *Robalina* v. *Armstrong*, 15 *Barb.*, 247.

The bastard, however, is entitled when brought before the court upon a habeas corpus, to the same liberty of election when of proper age, and to the exercise on the part of the court of the same considerate discretion when too young to choose, as is accorded to the child of lawful wedlock.

The People, ex rel. Davenport, v. *Kling*, 6 *Barb. Sup. Ct.*, 366: On certiorari. The relator was the mother of a bastard child, named Martin Kling, born in November, 1844. The defendant was the putative father of the child. In October, 1847, relator presented a petition to the Hon. Demosthenes Lawyer, County Judge of Schoharie, stating that on the 2d day of that month, the defendant had illegally and forcibly taken the child from her custody and carried it away, and that he still illegally detained the child. A writ of habeas corpus was thereupon allowed, commanding the defendant to bring the child before the judge, &c.

The defendant, among other things, returned to the writ that the relator was in very indigent circumstances; that she was of weak and imbecile mind, and was not a proper or fit person to have the care and custody of the child; that while with her, the child had suffered greatly for the want of sufficient and proper food and clothing; that at the time mentioned in the petition for the writ, he had applied to the relator for leave to take and bring up the child; that no objection or opposition having been made by her, he took the child and delivered him to his father, Henry Kling, who took the child into his family and adopted him as his own child.

Witnesses were examined, and after hearing the parties the judge dismissed the habeas corpus. Relator obtained a certiorari removing the proceedings to the Supreme Court.

HARRIS, J: "Were this a controversy between the mother of the child and the putative father, as to which had the better right to the custody and guardianship of the child, as the relator's counsel seemed to suppose it to be, there could be no doubt that the decision of the county judge was erroneous.

"As against the mother of a bastard child, the putative father has no legal right to the custody. The mother as its natural guardian is bound to maintain it, and is entitled to the control of it. But the difficulty with the relator's case is, that this is not a question to be determined upon habeas corpus.

"This writ is, by eminence *the writ of liberty*. Its office is, to inquire into the ground upon which any person is restrained of his liberty and, when it is found that the restraint is illegal, to deliver him from such illegal restraint. Ordinarily this end is attained by allowing the person improperly detained the free exercise of his volition. But in the case of a child too young to be capable of determining for itself, the court or officer assumes to determine for it. In making such election for the child, its welfare is chiefly if not exclusively to be had in view. * *

"I admit that this discretion is not to be arbitarily exercised. Nor are the rights of the parent to be wholly disregarded. In this case although a matter addressed to the discretion of the court, if it had appeared that the relator had possessed the capacity and the means of maintaining and educating the child as well as the grandfather, who had received it into his family, I think a judicious exercise of his power would have required the judge to deliver the child into the custody of the mother. But such a state of facts was not presented. * * I am entirely satisfied with the determination of the county judge to leave the child with its grandfather."

In the case of *The People* v. *Landt*, 2 *John.*, 375, a writ of habeas corpus was sued out by the putative father of a bastard child, directed to the defendant who had married the mother. It was claimed by the relator that the child had been illtreated by the defendant, and several affidavits read on both sides.

Per Curiam. "The only question before the court is, who has the legal right to the custody of the child. In the case of illegitimate children, and especially as to females, the mother appears to us to be the best entitled to the custody of them; but this right is not of such a nature as to prevent the court from interfering to take the infant from the custody of its mother, under special circumstances of illtreatment. In the present case, the evidence of illtreatment has been so far obviated by the affidavits which have been read on the part of the defendant, that we do not think it necessary to interfere at this time, to take the child from the custody of the defendant and his wife. But we think proper to admonish the defendant that he be careful to restrain his passions in future; and that, if hereafter, it should be made to appear that the child is illtreated, the court will interfere for her protection, and remove her from his custody."

In the matter of Doyle, Clark Ch. Rep., 154, The *Vice Chancellor* held that the father of an illegitimate child had no right to its care and custody, as against the rights of the mother. He said:

"The paternal and filial relation, in all its endearing and legal consequences, does not exist between such a father and such a child. The law looks coldly upon this relation, and takes no further care of it than to see that the community is not put to expense. In such a case there seems to be more than a legal doubt who is actually the father, the sworn father being termed merely the *putative* father, while there can be no doubt who is the mother. As the mother is the only parent such a child can have with legal certainty, she is the parent to whom the custody of such a child seems properly to belong."

SECTION VIII.

INFANT'S LIBERTY OF CHOICE.

In cases of any doubt or difficulty, a practice prevails, both in England and the United States, of consulting the wishes of the infant, when of sufficient age and discretion, as to its custody. And so common is the practice, that it has come to be supposed, by some, that the infant possesses a controlling right of choice. But this an error. An infant has no controlling legal right of election as to its custody. It was never designed to subject the legal right of custody to the caprice of infant children, nor to emancipate them from the rightful custody.

It was said by *Starkey, Ch. J.*, in his dissenting opinion in the case of *Foster & wife* v. *Alston*, 6 *How*

Miss., 472, that: "An infant is not entitled to his freedom, an adult is. When a habeas corpus is granted to an adult the object is to inquire whether he is legally restrained of his liberty, because if he is not he must be set free for the plain reason that by law he is entitled to his freedom. But if the court is also to set the infant free they give him a right to which he is not entitled; and deprive the parent or guardian of a right to which he is entitled, to wit; the custody of the infant. The law, it seems to me, does not clothe the infant with power to say whether he will be set free or not; it does not give the infant a discretion on the subject. If it did the habeas corpus would cease to be a remedy for the father."

The true view of the matter appears to be this. The jurisdiction of the question of custody under the writ of habeas corpus, is of an equitable nature. The welfare of the infant is the polar star by which the discretion of the court is to be guided. But the legal rights of the parent or guardian are to be respected. They are founded in nature and wisdom and are essential to the peace, order, virtue and happiness of society. But they may have been abandoned, transferred or abused.

The parent may have parted with the custody under circumstances which would render it injurious to the child and unjust to others to permit him to reclaim it. He may have grossly abused his right and thus have forfeited it and rendered the interference of the court necessary for the protection of the child. In the former case he may not be permitted to recover the child because of an equitable estoppel arising from his own conduct. In the latter he shall not be permitted to exercise a right which he has grossly abused. The original legal right being surrendered it shall not be reasserted to the manifest injury of the child, or, being grossly abused, the strict legal custody ceases to be a rightful custody and should therefore be changed. In neither case can the court be properly said to emancipate the child from the strict legal right of custody; it only protects it against a wrongful and injurious assertion or a gross abuse of the right.

The welfare of the child, then, being the object to be attained, no consideration, calculated to influence the decision of the question, should be overlooked. Hence the wishes of the child are consulted, not because it has a legal right to demand it, but because it is material for the court to understand them, that it may be the better prepared to exercise its discretion wisely. It is not the whim or caprice of the child which the court respects, but its feelings, its attachments, its reasonable preference and its probable contentment.

Consulting the wishes of the infant, we may conclude, is a mere rule of procedure founded upon the duty of the court to exerise a wise circumspection, and not upon any legal right of the infant to decide for himself and the court the question of custody.

Such being the nature and ground of this practice, it is impossible to prescribe the precise weight which should be given to these wishes when ascertained. It may, however, be safely said that where the parent has voluntarily parted with the custody and seeks to recover it, if his right to recover it be doubtful or the assertion of the claim would be inequitable to others or injurious to the child, or if no legal right to the custody be preferred by any one, the reasonable wishes of the child should be allowed a controlling influence. And a similar effect should be given to similar wishes where the parent has grossly abused the right of custody and the safety, the health or morals of the child are in imminent danger under the parent's custody; and this, whether the inquiry arises under a proceeding instituted by the parent to recover the custody not voluntarily surrendered, or by the child to be freed from the custody of the parent in consequence of the abuse and apprehended danger.

In the absence of any transfer of the custody of the child, or of any abuse or real danger of abuse of it by the parent, it is competent for the court, and in many cases, perhaps, its duty, to order the infant into the legal custody, notwithstanding the child may have wishes to the contrary. But it is not clear that the court is bound to proceed to that extent. In *Rex* v. *Delaval*, 3 *Burr.*, 1436, Lord Mansfield said: "The court is bound *ex debito justitiæ*, to set the infants free from an improper restraint; *but they are not bound to deliver them over to any body*, nor to give them any privilege." In the case of *Rex* v. *Isley*, 5 *Ad. & Ell.*, 441, the Court of King's Bench thought they were bound to deliver them into the legal custody, no circumstances of injury or the apprehension of it appearing.

In this country the doctrine of Lord Mansfield generally prevails. The court does not feel bound in all cases to deliver the child into the legal custody where it has not been abused or transferred. On the contrary, where the parent seeks by the writ to recover the custody and it stands indifferent as to the welfare of the child whether he shall be restored to the legal custody, and especially where the welfare of the child will probably be promoted by not restoring him to the legal custody, as, where parental government is relaxed, inefficient, not salutary, leading to idleness and the unnumbered evils always in her train, and the child manifests an appreciation of the disadvantages of such custody and affords reasonable ground to believe that it will be better for him not to be restored to the legal custody, the court may and often does refuse to make any order in regard to his custody, and will suffer him to go at large.

And such action or refusal to act, affords no just ground of reproach to the habeas corpus proceeding. It has been said, indeed, that in such cases the habeas corpus "ceases to be a remedy for the father." It does not *cease* to be a remedy, it never was a remedy to that extent.

It may appear like inefficiency to say, as was said in the *Matter of Kottman*, 2 *Hill C. R.*, 363, to the infant: "You are at liberty to go where you please," and to the father: "You have the legal right to take him wherever you find him, after he gets home from court; but it must be at your risk if you commit a breach of the peace in so doing."

But it is to be remembered that the primary and great use of the writ is to set at liberty any person illegally restrained or imprisoned, and that at least no right of liberty is violated, when the child is permitted to go free. The parent is not without other remedies.

SECTION XI.

INFANT'S AGE OF DISCRETION.

It has been said the child must have *discretion* to entitle its wishes to be consulted. The law, in this country at least, prescribes no age at which the child shall be presumed to have discretion adequate for this purpose. The court prefers to exercise its own judgment in each case upon the competency of the child. It looks to the capacity, information, intelligence and judgment of the child. It removes, as far as possible, all improper influences by which parties interested in its custody may seek to bias its choice. And if it finds the child able to reason sensibly, though as a child, in regard to its condition and its preferences and prospects, it will take its wishes into consideration.

It is notorious that children attain this capacity at different ages; some, indeed, hardly ever. A procustean rule, then, that a child's fitness to choose should be determined by his age and not his mental capacity might save the court some trouble, but would not be likely to subserve the best interests of the child.

In England, after what appeared to be at least strong intimations to the contrary, it has been decided that during the age of nurture, which continues until the child arrives at the age of fourteen, no child's wishes shall be consulted against the claim of the guardian by nurture.

In the United States this species of guardianship has no existence, the guardianship by nature, which continues until majority, leaving no room for it. *Reeves Dom. Rel.*, 315; 2 *Kent's Com.*, 221. It would be necessary, therefore, if years are to be the measure of capacity, to adopt some other rule than that adopted in England, or the liberty of choice would be quite gone.

But for reasons already suggested, mental capacity and not any certain number of years is regarded with us as the true criterion of the child's qualification to choose where choice is permitted.

The following cases from the English and American authorities will serve to illustrate the application of these general rules.

In *R.* v. *Greenhill*, 4 *Ad. & El.*, 624, Lord DENMAN, Ch. J., said: "When an infant is brought before the court by habeas corpus, if he be of an *age to exercise a choice*, the court leaves him to elect where he will go. If he be not of that age, and a want of direction would only expose him to dangers or seductions, the court must make an order for his being placed in the proper custody."

In re Preston, 5 *Dowl. & L.*, 247, Patteson, J., refused an application for a writ of habeas corpus, made on behalf of an infant's mother, then in India (the father being dead), in order to remove her son from the guardianship of the persons who had for some time had the custody of him, saying:

"In deciding this question it seems to me it is altogether useless to question the child, as to with whom he might wish to be. *It is difficult to say at what age a child is capable of exercising a sound discretion, and judging for itself in matters of this kind;* but it seems to me that it is but a mockery to ask a child of nine years of age whether he would sooner remain with the person who has brought him up, or go with a stranger."

In the case, *Rex* v. *Johnson*, 1 *Stra.*, 579, the infant was nine years old, the court said: "*this being the case of a young child, who had no judgment of her own,* they ought to deliver her to her guardian," and he took possession of her in court.

"Very recently," says *Forsyth, Custody of Infants*, 106, "an illegitimate child seven years old, about whose custody there was a dispute in the Bail Court, was called up to the bench by Mr. Justice Wightman, and after having been privately questioned by him, found to be very intelligent, she was allowed to choose the person, although neither her father nor mother, with whom she was to reside. It was, however, agreed that the mother should have access to her at all reasonable times." *In re White, Jan'y* 25, 1848.

In re Lloyd, 3 *Man. & Gr.*, 547, the child was between eleven and twelve years of age, and was allowed to choose. And the court *intimated* that she would have been allowed the privilege had she been only seven years old, for Tindal, Ch. J., said: "*Had she been under seven years of age, the court would have said that she could exercise no discretion.*"

In Regina v. *Clarke*, 21 *Jurist*, 335; *S. C.*, 5 *Am. Law Reg.*, 537, an infant of the age of ten years was brought up on habeas corpus upon the application of the mother, who was surviving parent, the father, who was a marine, having died without appointing a guardian. The father was a protestant, and the child had been baptised under his directions by a clergyman of the Church of England; but he had permitted the mother, who was a Roman Catholic, to give the child such religious instruction as was in accordance with her religious profession. The child, after the death of the father, had been placed by the mother at the Sailor's Orphan Girl's School, where she would be educated, &c., in the Protestant faith. The object of the mother, in suing out the habeas corpus, was to remove the child to a Roman Catholic school. The Court of Queen's Bench held that the mother, as guardian for nurture, was entitled to the custody of the person of the child; that the court could not examine the infant as to her wishes or religious belief; that the mother was not bound to educate her in the protestant faith, nor had she lost her right over her by sending her to the Sailor's Orphan Girl's School; and therefore the court was bound to order her to be delivered to her mother.

In the United States the courts have generally inquired as to the capacity and intelligence of the child. In the *Commonwealth* v. *Taylor*, 3 *Met.*, 72, *Shaw*, *Ch. J.*, said:

"In point of law, a child of such tender years, seven or eight, has no will, no power of judging or electing; and therefore his will and choice are to be wholly disregarded. The natural and strong feelings of a child, which induce him to cling instinctively to those whom he has been accustomed to regard as his natural protectors, cannot be regarded as the exercise of a legal will or an intelligent choice.

"*In Commonwealth* v. *Hammond*, 10 *Pick.*, 274, the child was between *eleven and twelve*, and its wishes were consulted.

"In the case of *The People, ex rel. Ordronaux* v. *Chegaray*, 18 *Wend.*, 637, there were three children, aged respectively 15, 13 *and* 9 *years*. They were all consulted respecting their wishes.

"In the case of *McDowles*, 8 *John*, 328, the youngest child was not more than *nine* years old, and was consulted in respect to his wishes, not only by the Chief Justice, but afterwards on a suggestion that improper means had been used by the master, by three gentlemen of the bar appointed by the court, and his wishes were respected.

"*In the matter of Doyle*, *Clark's Chy. Rep.*, 154, the putative father petitioned for the custody of his bastard child, then only six years old, alleging in his petition that the mother was of dissolute habits and unfit to have the custody &c. The case was heard upon affidavits. *The Vice Chancellor* held that the mother was entitled to the custody, as against the putative father, yet deemed it proper to examine, and accordingly did examine the child privately in respect to its wishes, and says: 'I find she is very well educated; that due care has been paid to her morals, her manners and her education; that she loves her mother and prefers to live with her; that she is daily sent to school; and that few girls of her age are better taught, either in mind or heart.'"

In the case of the *State* v. *Scott & wife*, 10 *Foster*, 274, the child was eleven years old. The court appointed a committee of three members of the bar to interrogate the child, who reported that she was of sufficient understanding to choose, and the court suffered her to make her election.

In the case of *The People* v. *Pillow*, 1 *Sandf. Sup. Ct. Rep.*, 672, the writ issued at the instance of the master against the father for three children, aged respectively 14, 11 and 9, and they were all privately consulted by the court as to their wishes.

"The eldest elected to go to the master, and the others to remain with their father, and ordered accordingly."

SECTION X.

VOLUNTARY TRANSFER OF CUSTODY.

It has been seen that a parent may emancipate his minor child by voluntarily relinquishing his claim to the services of the child, or by permitting the child to contract marriage or other relations inconsistent with filial subjection, and may also forfeit his right of custody by cruelty or gross neglect of duty.

Why, then, may he not transfer to another this right of custody which he may thus abandon or forfeit, especially where the interests of the child are not prejudiced by the assignment? And how can the court pronounce that custody, which is held under a fair agreement with the parent and not injurious to the welfare of the child, to be an *illegal restraint?*

It is true of this as of many other questions, in habeas corpus proceedings, that the authorities do not all speak one opinion.

In *Regina* v. *Edward Smith; In re Boreham*, 16 *Eng. Law and Eq.*, 221, on a writ of habeas corpus the return showed *Emma Susan Boreham* born 1847, daughter of Nathaniel Boreham and Susan his wife, sister of defendant, Edward Smith. In May, 1852, an agreement was entered into between N. Boreham and E. Smith, which recited that the wife, being dangerously ill, with the consent of her husband, requested Smith, her brother, in the event of her death to take charge of and educate and bring up her infant daughter, and by which Smith agreed to take such charge on condition that the daughter was permitted to remain with him until she was grown up and able to provide for herself. N. Boreham agreed to the condition, that he would in no manner interfere, and that he would pay Smith fourteen shillings per month for the child's support and education. Proviso, that he might visit his daughter at reasonable times. The mother died July, 1852. Smith, by virtue of the agreement, took possession of the daughter and took charge of and maintained her.

ERLE, J. "I have looked into the cases and it seems to me the arrangement between the father and the uncle is in the nature of a consent given by the father that the uncle should have the custody of the child, and a contract by the father to pay the uncle for its support. I am of opinion that the father is at liberty to revoke the consent, and I am bound to say that he is entitled, legally, to the custody of his child."

The report is too short to inform us what the court thought was the nature of the undertaking on the part of the uncle to maintain the child. The cases cited by counsel for the father were, as might be supposed, *The King* v. *Mandeville*, 5 *East*, 221; *The King* v. *Greenhill*, 4 *Ad. & El.*, 624; *and Ex parte Skinner*, 9 *J. B. Moore*, 278, very strong and very hard cases. The American reports furnish two cases of a similar tenor.

In *The State* v. *Clover*, 1 *Harr.*, 419, a child twelve years old, brought up on habeas corpus, was ordered to be delivered to the mother where the return of the defendants stated that the child was placed with them, with the mother's consent, to live and remain with them until of full age, and that she wished to remain.

And in *Mayne* v. *Bredwin*, 1 *Halsted Ch. R.*, 454, the Supreme Court of New Jersey held that a father might recover possession of his infant child, although he had committed her to the care and custody of another until the child should attain the age of twenty-one years, and in pursuance thereof the child had been adopted by such third person.

In the matter of Mitchell, R. M. Charl., 489, the court do not deny the power of the father to assign the custody of his child, but on the contrary intimate an opinion that he could lawfully do so upon a legal consideration. In that case the father sued out the writ of habeas corpus for his child, then three months old. The respondents were the grand-parents, at whose house the wife died in child-bed. It appeared that the applicant *promised his wife*, on her death bed, that the child should remain with her parents.

"This," said the court, "was without any legal consideration; and I cannot hold it to be an entire surrender of his legal or parental right. It might with great propriety be called *nudum pactum*."

On the other hand, in the case of *The State* v. *Smith*, 6 *Greenl.*, 462, the court, in refusing to deliver the children into the custody of the father, laid stress upon the fact that he had agreed in a certain event, which had come to pass, that his wife should have the custody and control of their children.

The opinion of the Supreme Court of Massachusetts, in the case of *Pool* v. *Gott and wife*, 14 *Law Rep.*, 269, breathes the true spirit, and is in unison with the general tone of our American authorities on the subject of parental custody where the controversy is between the parents.

The petitioner, Ebenezer Pool, was a merchant of Bangor, Maine, and sued out the writ of habeas corpus for the purpose of getting possession of his daughter, Lydia Gott Pool, aged thirteen years, in the custody of her grand-parents, the respondents. The other facts appear sufficiently in the opinion of the Chief Justice.

Chief Justice SHAW, in pronouncing judgment, remarked substantially as follows: "This case presents circumstances of interest and delicacy, involving both legal rights and the dearest feelings of parties. On the one hand is the legal right of the only parent, and on the other, the feelings of the child, and the feelings and rights, such as these rights may be, of the grand-parents. In either event the decision must cause pain and disappointment. I have carefully examined the pleadings and testimony, and find the facts to be but little controverted and to be substantially these: In 1837, Mr. Pool married the only daughter of Mr. and Mrs. Gott, who died the next year, upon the birth of this her only child. Under such circumstances the attachment of the grand-parents to the child was naturally strong, and as Mr. Pool had no home or wife, and was at that time in an embarrassed pecuniary condition, they took the child to their own home, with the father's consent. There is no evidence as to the nature of the agreement made, if indeed there was any agreement at that time; but the child has remained under the sole care of the grand-parents, to the present time, educated at their expense, the father neither offering nor being called upon for any contribution to its support. About ten years ago, Mr. Pool removed to Bangor, married again, has retrieved his affairs, has now a comfortable home, and a wife, and a family of three children, the fruit of this last marriage, of the ages of eight years and under. There was a period of three years when there was no intercourse between Mr. Pool and the grand-parents, but it appears that during the last five or six years he has visited the child about once a year, more or less. He has however never made any demand, or given the child or its grand-parents any reason to suppose that he ever would demand the restoration of the child to his own care. On the contrary, I have no doubt that it was understood on all sides that the child was to remain under the respondents' charge and that they were to stand in *loco parentis*. The present demand grows out of a refusal by the child to make a vist of four weeks or so to the father, at his request, and a refusal of the grand-parents to part with her for that purpose.

"It is to be regretted that the law leaves cases of this description with so few rules for the government of the courts. This is perhaps unavoidable, on account of the illimitable variety of circumstances by which they are attended—circumstances that cannot be anticipated or provided for. There is no doubt that the father is *prima facie* entitled to the custody of his child. But this is not an absolute right. It may be controlled by other considerations. If unable or unfit to take charge of the child and educate it in a suitable manner, the court will not interfere to take the child from the care of persons who are fit and able to maintain and educate it properly. This is an exception, however, which need not be considered in this case; for the evidence shows that the father is in a good situation, pecuniary, domestic and social, and of a character and reputation against which no objection can be made. On the other hand, the respondents are persons of entire respectability, in independent pecuniary circumstances, and have so far educated, and will undoubtedly hereafter educate the child in a proper manner, and make her a suitable provision in case of their death.

"I have taken an opportunity to examine the child in private. I find her devotedly attached to her grand-parents, and am satisfied that a termination of this relation would be, for a long time at least, the cause of great suffering to her and them. It cannot be supposed that, under the circumstances of the last six or eight years, and in the father's present situation, a failure to secure the custody of the child would be of as much consequence to him. It is suggested that the child has been prejudiced against the father, by the respondents, for the purpose of retaining her to themselves.

"I think there is a feeling on the part of the respondents, towards the father, which is unreasonable, though natural, and it has doubtless been communicated, to some extent, to the child, but I see no reason for supposing that the respondents have intentionally or culpably instilled prejudices into her mind for any sinister purpose. Making due allowance for this consideration, I am yet of opinion that it is clearly for the interest and happiness of the child to remain where she now is.

"It is a leading principle that when the right of the parent is not clear, the interest of the child will govern the decision of the court. Is then the right of the father clear in this case? Although there is no agreement proved, yet the conduct of the father, during nearly the whole life of the child, furnishes reason for supposing that he surrendered his rights over the child by a tacit understanding, if not by an express agreement. He has, for eight years or more, been able to retake the child, and has made no offer to do so. No demand or offer has been made on either side, that he should contribute to her support. His present assertion of his right is in consequence of what he deems an unreasonable refusal of a different request. By his own acquiescence, he has allowed the affections on both sides to become engaged in a manner he could not but have anticipated, and permitted a state of things to arise, which cannot be altered without risking the happiness and interest of his child. He has allowed the parties to go on for years in the belief that his legal rights were waived, and this relation of adoption sanctioned and approved by him. Under such circumstances I do not think that the petitioner is in a position to require the interference of the court, in favor of a controlling legal right on his part, against the rights, such as they are, the feelings and the interests of the other parties.

"This is eminently a case for amicable arrangement between the parties. Some agreement might be made by which the child should spend part of her time with her father, to allow opportunities for mutual affections and interests to grow up between herself and her paternal relations.

"But it is not in the power of the court, in this proceeding, to decree any arrangement, or to modify at all the relations of the parties. The judgment must be simply for the custody of the child. The decree, therefore, is that the child be restored to the custody of the respondents."

In *McDowle's case*, 8 *John.*, 328, where the father applied for the writs to obtain possession of his sons, whom he had undertaken to apprentice to the defendants, the indentures were held inoperative as to the infants because they did not conform to the requisitions of the statute, yet the court intimated that the father might still be bound by the covenants, and said he "had no equity and no right to complain."

The following case was decided in Pennsylvania, in 1851, by the District Court of Alleghany county, and the decision was afterwards brought up before the Supreme Court in banc and the same order made.

The Commonwealth at the instance of Mary Gilkeson v. *James Gilkeson*, *Wallace Phila. Rep.*, 194.

This was a habeas corpus by a daughter to be discharged from the custody of her father. It appeared that about six years before the granting of the writ the father and mother of the petitioner by contract under seal transferred the custody of her to her uncle and aunt, who by the same writing agreed to adopt her as their child. The contract, though of such a character as could not be enforced against the child, was performed by the uncle and aunt and sanctioned by the father until the child had grown from 9 to 15 years of age. Her mother and uncle having died the father obtained possession of her and insisted on retaining the custody though she preferred remaining with her aunt.

LOWRIE, J., said: "We have never in this state held that the courts are bound to a strict adherence to the old common law rules as to the right to the custody of children; and this writ being used as a remedy for the improper interference with that right we must treat it as a Pennsylvania remedy, governed by the principles of the common law of Pennsylvania, of which equitable principles constitute an illustrious part. * * * *

"In this case the parental authority has been solemnly renounced for six years, and the child has grown to the age of fifteen years. She has been estranged from the customs and government of her father's house. She has formed new habits and views, and become accustomed to different associations and modes of living. And now the father disregarding his own contract and the wishes and comfort of his child, seeks to re-establish the parental authority. We should be glad he could effect it by the influence of parental kindness, and consistently with honesty. We dislike to see the parental and filial relation severed, and should love to see the broken bond re-united. But it cannot well be done by the enforcement of it as a legal right.

"The father himself broke the bond, and the law will not help him now to mend it. He emancipated his daughter by his own solemn act, and all restraint upon her by him is now improper.

"We must, therefore, discharge her from restraint, and leave her to elect with whom she will remain."

SECTION XI.

MASTER FOR HIS APPRENTICE.

It is sometimes said that a master is entitled to the writ of habeas corpus to enable him to obtain the custody of his apprentice; and some cases have gone upon this ground; thereby converting the proceeding into a species of personal replevin.

But the true principle seems rather to be that the writ may issue on behalf of the apprentice at the suggestion of the master.

It has indeed been held that it could not issue at the instance of the master. In *The King* v. *Reynolds*, 6 *T. R.*, 497, a writ had been granted at the instance of the master to recover his impressed apprentice. On motion to quash the writ, *Lord Kenyon*, Ch. J., said:

"I think the writ of habeas corpus was improperly issued. The writ ought not to be issued at the instance of the master: but the apprentice, who is of sufficient age to judge for himself, should have applied for it if he had wished it. * * Suppose this apprentice had been taken into the service of any other master, we should not have granted a habeas corpus at the instance of his first master, but should have left him to his action for seducing his apprentice."

The same doctrine was held in the case of *The King* v. *Edwards*, 7 *T. R.*, 741, where the master moved for a habeas corpus to bring up his apprentice, who had entered into the sea service, in order that he might be restored to him.

The court, referring to the case of *The King* v. *Reynolds*, above cited, said: "The distinction was properly taken in the case cited; that though the apprentice might obtain the writ the master could not, for that its object was the protection of the liberty of the party. That the master was not without his remedy, for that he might have his action against those who detained the apprentice."

In Pennsylvania at an early day the writ was granted on the application of the master, and the apprentice delivered to him, 1 *Bro. Rep.*, 277, and in cases of doubt an issue was sometimes directed to a jury, *Graham* v. *Graham*, 1 *Serg. & Rawle.*, 331.

But in the case of *Commonwealth* v. *Robinson*, 1 *Serg. & R.*, 352, where the writ had been issued on the application of the master to recover his enlisted apprentice, who was upwards of 18 years of age, and on examination expressed his wishes to remain in the army, the Supreme Court said: "A habeas corpus may be issued at common law, under which courts have gone so far as to deliver the body of an infant to his parent, and sometimes an apprentice to his master. It is discretionary however, whether to proceed to that length or not. In a case like the present there is no occasion for a summary proceeding, because the master has his remedy by action against the person who takes away his apprentice."

The court also said: "the object of the act of Assembly (1785,) was to secure personal liberty, not to decide disputes about property."

In a late case *Commonwealth* v. *Harris*, before Rogers, one of the justices of the Supreme Court, March 7, 1848, *cited* 1 *McKinney's Justice*, 344, it was held: "If an apprentice enlist in the army, the court will not, upon a habeas corpus, issued at the relation of the master, remand the prisoner to the custody of the master, if the minor is unwilling to return, but will leave the master to his suit against the officer who enlisted the minor for damages suffered by loss of the services of the apprentice."

In New Jersey the master petitioned for the writ to obtain his enlisted apprentice, but it appearing on the hearing that he had assented to the enlistment, the writ was dismissed. *The State* v. *Brearly and others*, 2 *South*, 555.

In Massachusetts in the case of *Commonwealth* v. *Harrison*, 11 *Mass. Rep.*, 63, the writ was granted at he instance of the master; but it does not appear from the report that the apprentice was ordered into his custody. He was released from the custody of the defendant and "set at large."

From the reasoning of the court it may be inferred that they considered they had authority, if the circumstances of the case required it, to commit the apprentice to the custody of the master.

The action and observations of the court in the following case in New York, appear to indicate a safe middle course by which a master can always get the writ, but very rarely his apprentice. They concede as much as the spirit of the writ would seem to justify.

In the case of *The People* v. *Pillow*, 1 *Sandf. Sup. Ct.*, 672, it was held that the writ of habeas corpus might issue at the instance of the master directed to the father of the children, who had been replevied from the master by the father, and that the proceeding under the writ de homine replegiando, was no bar to the proceeding in habeas corpus. The three children were aged 14, 11 and 9, and being privately consulted by the court as to their wishes the oldest elected to return to his master, and the two youngest elected to remain with their father and ordered accordingly. The court said:

"In these cases, the court acts for and in behalf of the children, to see that they are under no improper restraint. The master may set its powers in motion, and the court will interfere so far as to permit the children to go where they please, when they are old enough to understand their own wishes, and those wishes lead to no improper custody."

SECTION XII.

GUARDIAN FOR HIS WARD.

The guardian may have the writ to bring up his ward as has been seen; but it is in the discretion of the court whether the ward shall be restored to his custody.

In the case of the *Commonwealth* v. *Hammond*, 10 *Pick.*, 274, the court refused to deliver the ward to the guardian, saying "We do not think proper to decide upon the relative rights of the mother and the guardian in respect to the custody of the child, as they are only incidentally drawn in question. The application is to the discretion of the court, and the court will not interfere where the liberty of the party is not injuriously or unwarrantably infringed. In that case the child had been placed by her mother with the defendant on a verbal contract for her support and education, until she should arrive at the age of 21 years, for which she was to render the defendant reasonable services. She had not been illtreated, was 11½ years old, and desired to remain with the defendant.

In the case of *The State* v. *Cheeseman*, 2 *South*, 445, it appeared from the return to the habeas corpus that the boy, then 13½ years old, and for whom the relators had been appointed guardians, was living in the family of his step-father, the defendant and his mother; and had been, since his father's death and mother's marriage to the defendant, and desired to remain with her, and that the defendant had never detained him contrary to his will. It also appeared that two years before the taking out of the writ, the guardians demanded the boy of the defendant, who replied: "Take him, but I'll make you bring him back faster than you take him away."

SOUTHARD, J., said: "The first inquiry is the right of these guardians to the person of the child. This I consider complete and perfect. The nature of the guardianship created by our statute, nay the very relation of guardian and ward gives the right. The principles applicable to this subject before the enactment of our statute and the words of the statute, place the guardian *in loco parentis;* and as the father is entitled to the possession of the person of his child so is the guardian of that of his ward. It is not then, either from the right of a guardian to the person of his ward, or from any doubt that these applicants really are the guardians and are so to be considered that any difficulty results in the present case. But it is from doubt whether the writ of habeas corpus be the proper mode of contesting the rights of those parties under facts like these. What is the writ of habeas corpus? The writ used in this case is the great and efficacious writ, *ad subjiciendum*, which is directed to a person detaining another and commanding him to produce the *prisoner* with the day, &c. 3 *Bl.*, 131; 8 *St. Tr.*, 142. It is called a high prerogative writ, and issuing by common law and running throughout the kingdom, because the King is entitled at all times to have an account why the *liberty* of his subject is restrained. *Cro. Jac.*, 543.

It is for the relief of the *prisoner* and the *prisoner* only. It is to inquire why the liberty of the citizen is restrained.

"This, then, is its legitimate and only object; to relieve from restraint and imprisonment. Whenever there is no imprisonment there is no ground for the writ of habeas corpus. And I apprehend no case can be cited where this writ is either used to determine a question of property, or the conflicting rights to the possession of the person; it looks to another object altogether. If one of two parties unlawfully restrain and imprison the person about whom the contest arises, the writ steps in and relieves from the restraint but leaves the contest, as to possession, to be decided in another mode. *Rex* v. *Smith*, 2 *Str.*, 982; *King* v. *Reynolds*, 6 *T. R.*, 497; *Rex* v. *Edwards*, 7 *T. R.*, 745.

"When we look into this case I am free to say that I think the guardians entitled to the infant. They have a right to take possession of it, and the step-father has no right to resist. But when we inquire *why this court on this writ*, should interfere I do not find any imprisonment or restraint, which alone authorizes us to interfere, and therefore I am of opinion that no order for delivery of the infant to the guardian should be made; but let the child go where he will; and let the guardian, if he pleases, either take possession of him or by course of law enforce his right to the custody of his person."

The practice of granting the writ at the instance of one claiming the custody of another has in some instances been extended beyond the relations already considered; and the writ has sometimes been granted in a free state to a master for his escaped slave. *United States, ex rel. Wheeler,* v. *Williamson,* 3 *Am. Law Reg.*, 729.

And in *Ex parte Williamson,* 3 *Am. Law Reg.*, 741, Lewis, Chief Justice of Pennsylvania, said: "It is true that the habeas corpus act was not intended to decide rights of property, but the writ at common law may be issued to deliver an infant to a parent, or an apprentice to a master. *Commonwealth* v. *Robinson,* 1 *S. & R.*, 353. On the same principle, I see no reason why the writ at common law may not be used to deliver a slave from illegal restraint, and restore him to the custody of his master."

It has been shown in the preceding pages that the writ of habeas corpus is not, properly speaking, issued to deliver an infant to a parent, though the court sometimes in the exercise of its sound discretion orders the infant to be thus delivered. It has also been shown that in the case of the master and apprentice, although it may issue at the instance of the master, the courts very rarely make any order in favor of the master for the custody of the apprentice.

But if the practice in those cases were clearly settled, as assumed by the learned judge, then all the beneficent principles of practice applicable in those cases, should be extended to the case where the writ was granted to the master for his slave.

The writ should be granted at the instance of the master, on some sufficient showing of illegal restraint;

and if mere absence from his custody is to be held equivalent to such illegal restraint, then on the simple application of the master; but in either case where the slave is brought before the court under the writ, he, as well as the apprentice or infant, must, if of sufficient capacity, be allowed his liberty of choice, and if of tender years or insufficient capacity he must be disposed of under the writ, as the sound discretion of the court shall dictate.

CHAPTER X.

STATUTORY PROVISIONS RELATING TO PRISONER'S DISCHARGE.

Section I. DISCHARGE FOR WANT OF PROSECUTION.
II. RECOMMITMENT AFTER DISCHARGE.

SECTION I.

DISCHARGE FOR WANT OF PROSECUTION.

By the 7th section of the act 31 *Car.* 2 it was provided that:

"If any person or persons, committed as aforesaid, upon his prayer or petition in open court, the first week of the term on the first day of the sessions of oyer and terminer and general gaol delivery, to be brought to his trial, shall not be indicted and tried the second term sessions of oyer and terminer or general gaol delivery after his commitment, or upon his trial shall be acquitted, he shall be discharged from his imprisonment."

In Georgia, where the act 31 *Car.* 2 was adopted, it was held in the case of *The State* v. *Monguo et Segar*, *Charl.*, 24, that where the prisoners had been confined two terms, were ready for their trial at each term, and at the second term did, by their counsel, petition to be brought to trial, they were entitled to be discharged on a writ of habeas corpus.

In South Carolina, where the act of 31 *Car.* 2 was also adopted, it was held in the case of *Logan* v.

The State, Const. Rep., 493, that a prisoner who had been let out on bail was not entitled to his discharge though he had demanded his trial. Nor can he claim his discharge under the act, where there has been a mistrial under the indictment, though the state is not ready for trial at the next term. *State* v. *Sprague*, 1 *McCord*, 563.

Nor can the accused be discharged from his recognizance under the act, for the provisions of the 7th section apply only to actual prisoners. *The State* v. *Buyck*, 1 *Brevard*, 460.

The provision in the statute of Pennsylvania, is as follows:

"If any person shall be committed for treason or felony, and shall not be indicted and tried some time in the next term, session of oyer and terminer, general gaol delivery, or other court, where the offence is properly cognizable, after such commitment, it shall and may be lawful for the judges or justices thereof, and they are hereby required upon the last day of the term, sessions, or court, to set at liberty the said prisoner upon bail, unless it shall appear to them, upon oath or affirmation, that the witnesses for the Commonwealth, mentioning their names could not then be produced; and if such prisoner shall not be indicted and tried the second term, sessions, or court, after his or her commitment, unless the delay happen on the application or with the assent of the defendant, or upon trial shall be acquitted, he or she shall be discharged from commitment." *Dunlop's St.*, 143, *sec.* 3.

It has been held by the Supreme Court of Pennsylvania, that by the fair construction of their habeas corpus act, (although no provision was referred to except the preamble, which "confines itself to *all wrongful* restraints of personal liberty,") a prisoner who had not been tried at the second term was not in all cases entitled to be discharged, although the delay did not happen on his application nor with his assent.

In the case of *The Commonwealth* v. *The Sheriff and Gaoler of Alleghany County*, 16 *Serg. & Rawle*, 304, in 1827 the prisoner had been indicted as an accessory. Two terms of the court had passed, but the principal had not been convicted, nor had the process of outlawry been completed against him, nor could it be for another term, the statute requiring at least three terms to complete it. So that the proof which the rules of law made indispensable to the conviction of the prisoner could not be given within the time mentioned in the habeas corpus act. He sued out the writ of habeas corpus to be discharged.

The court, however, held that the section above quoted was intended to provide against the abuse of a protracted trial, to provide not only against the malice of a prosecutor, but against his negligence, against all *his* delays whether with cause or without cause, against every possible act or want of action of the prosecutor; but not to shield a prisoner in any case from the consequences of any delay made necessary by the law itself.

The court also intimated that a prisoner would not be entitled to his discharge if the second term should pass without his trial in consequence of his sickness, insanity, or the limited term of the court (that being prescribed by law) not admitting of the trial.

Chief Justice Gibson dissented. But eleven years after, in the case of the *Commonwealth* v. *The Jailer of Alleghany County*, 7 *Watts*, 366, in a somewhat weaker case he appears to have concurred with the other members of the court in refusing a discharge. That was a case of habeas corpus. The prisoner had not been tried at the second term: he had been sick of the small pox and though convalescing, his aspect was so loathesome, as to spread a general panic; and on the testimony of the physician of the prison that he might still communicate infection, he was remanded, though insisting on being tried,

The court remanded him, saying: "There is no doubt that necessity, moral or physical, may raise an available exception to the letter of the habeas corpus act. A court is not bound to peril life in an attempt to perform what was not intended to be required of it. The legislature intended to prevent willful and oppressive delay; and it is sufficient that there is no color for an imputation of it."

In *Ex parte Walton*, 2 *Whart.*, 501, the court refused to discharge the prisoner on habeas corpus, who had moved to quash the indictment at the second term, which motion, the court being unable to determine, was continued under advisement, the court holding that such postponement should be construed to be with the assent of the prisoner.

The court also held that the power of discharging a prisoner when he had not been tried at the second term, was confined to the court in which he was indicted, and that although they were bound to allow the writ of habeas corpus, they should not for the future, if the commitment was unexceptionable in the frame of it, consider themselves bound to look farther. This construction of the act was approved in the case of *Commonwealth* v. *The Sheriff*, 7 *Watts & Serg.*, 108.

In Mississippi when their code contained a provision similar to that in Pennsylvania, it was held in the case of *Byrd* v. *The State*, 1 *How. Miss.*, 163, that a prisoner charged as accessory to a murder is not entitled to a discharge because he has not been indicted, although the *stated times* of holding two terms of court have elapsed. To bring the prisoner within that statute it must appear that the state has been in default, that two terms have actually been holden without being indicted; for if no terms are holden the state cannot be in default.

SECTION II.

RECOMMITMENT AFTER DISCHARGE.

By the sixth section of the *Act* 31 *Car.* 2, it was provided: "And for the prevention of unjust vexation by reiterated commitments for the same offence; Be it enacted, by the authority aforesaid, That no person or persons which shall be delivered or set at large upon any habeas corpus, shall at any time hereafter be again imprisoned or committed for the same offence, by any person or persons whatsoever, other than by the legal order and process of such court wherein he or they shall be bound by recognizance to appear, or other court having jurisdiction of the cause; and if any other person or persons shall knowingly, contrary to this act, recommit or imprison, or knowingly procure or cause to be recommitted or imprisoned, for the same offence or pretended offence, any person or persons delivered or set at large as aforesaid, or be knowingly aiding or assisting therein, then he or they shall forfeit to the prisoner or party grieved the sum of £500; any colorable pretence or variation in the warrant or warrants of commitment, notwithstanding, to be recovered as aforesaid."

The provisions of this section have been in substance incorporated in the statutes of the several states.

In New York, under a similar section, in the case of *Yates* v. *Lansing*, 5 *John.*, 282; *S. C.* 9 *ib.*, 395, where the chancellor had committed one of the officers of chancery for malpractice and contempt, and a judge of the Supreme Court, on a habeas corpus, discharged the officer; and he was afterwards recommitted by the chancellor for the same offence, it "was held that the chancellor was not liable to an action by the officer for the penalty; that the penalty given by the statute is imposed on individuals acting ministerially out of court, and does not apply to the acts of a court done of record."

In Ex parte Milburn, 9 *Peters*, 704, it appeared that the petitioner for the writ after having been discharged on habeas corpus from an arrest under a capias, on the ground that it had been irregularly issued, was again arrested on another capias upon the same indictment; and this being urged as a ground of illegal imprisonment, &c., the court said:

"A discharge of a party under a writ of habeas corpus from the process under which he is imprisoned discharges him from any further confinement under the process; but not under any other process which may be issued against him under the same indictment."

It was very confidently maintained by Chief Justice Kent in the case of *Yates* v. *Lansing*, 5 *John.*, 282, that "if a person convicted at court of oyer and terminer or sessions of the peace of a felony, and imprisoned in a state prison, be discharged by a judge on habeas corpus, on the ground that the court had no authority to commit, or that the order of commitment was invalid, the court might cause the convict to be further reimprisoned either upon the same warrant, if it judged it sufficient, or by awarding a new and better one. And this upon the ground that the statute never intended such a destruction of principle as to entrust to a judge in vacation the power to control the judgment or check the jurisdiction of a court of record."

This view, however, was combatted with great earnestness by Senator Clinton in the same case on error, 9 *Johns.*, 440, who maintained that the commitment on conviction determined the jurisdiction of the court, in which the conviction was had, over the *cause*. He argued that it was one thing to have jurisdiction over the subject matter, and another to have it over the cause. That *the subject matter is the crime in the abstract. The cause is the case of the individual.* That to give jurisdiction of the *cause* there must therefore be jurisdiction of the person, which being lost by the process of final commitment, the court was without jurisdiction over the *cause*, and could not recommit under the exception in the statute.

The argument of the Senator did not prevail. The judgment of the Supreme Court was affirmed.

The provisions of the Statute of New York, on this subject, are as follows:

"§ 75. No person who has been discharged by the order of any court or officer, upon a habeas corpus or certiorari, issued pursuant to the provisions of this article, shall be again imprisoned, restrained or kept in custody, for the same cause; but it shall not be deemed the same cause,

"1. If he shall have been discharged from a commitment on a criminal charge, and be afterwards committed for the same offence, by the legal order or process of the court wherein he shall be bound to appear, or in which he shall be indicted or convicted for the same offence: or

"2. If after a discharge for defect of proof, or any material defect in the commitment, in a criminal case, the prisoner be again arrested on sufficient proof, and committed by legal process for the same offence: or

"3. If in a civil suit, the party has been discharged for any illegality in the judgment or process, hereinbefore specified, and is afterwards imprisoned by legal process for the same cause of action: or

"4. If, in any civil suit, he shall have been discharged from commitment on mesne process, and shall afterwards be committed on execution, in the same cause, or on mesne process in any other cause, after such first suit shall have been discontinued." 2 *Rev. St.*, 1852, *p.* 804.

In Pennsylvania, in the case of *Hecker* v. *Jarrett*, 1 *Binn.*, 374, it was held that under the habeas corpus act of that state, the penalty for recommitting a person who has once been delivered for the same cause on a habeas corpus, is limited to recommitments for the same *criminal offence*, and is not incurred by taking the party a second time in custody upon civil process; and the reason for the distinction in the law was suggested to be "that the object of the habeas corpus act was to protect the liberty of individual citizens; and the danger of oppression is not so great in civil matters, as in case of crimes or supposed crimes. Governments often magnify real crimes, and sometimes impute offences falsely to innocent persons, for the purpose of oppression. From this quarter has generally arisen the danger to liberty; and this might have induced the legislature of Pennsylvania to omit the penalty in civil cases."

In Mississippi it was said in the case of *Byrd* v. *The State*, 1 *How. Miss.*, 163, that a discharge under the provision authorizing the discharge of the accused if not tried at the second term, &c., was no bar to another prosecution for the same offence.

CHAPTER XI.

SECTION I.

WRIT OF ERROR.

It has never been decided in England that a writ of error will lie to a final order made on a habeas corpus. But it has repeatedly been said that it would not.

" *The City of London's case*, 8 *Co.*, 121, *b*, was a case of a habeas corpus, issuing out of the court of Common Pleas to the mayor, aldermen and sheriffs of London, to bring up the body of one Wagoner, who was in their custody upon civil process for breach of a by-law. A return was made to the writ, and upon an objection to its sufficiency, the court resolved it sufficient upon this ground, that, upon the return, no issue could be taken or demurrer juined; that the return was only to inform the court of the truth of the matter, and that a writ of error would not lie upon the award of the court, to be made upon the return."

The doctrine of this case was recognized in the case of *The King* v. *The Dean and Chapter of Trinity Chapel, in Dublin*, 8 *Mod.*, 27. That was a case of a writ of error from the King's Bench in Ireland to the King's Bench in England, brought upon the award of a peremptory *mandamus*. The principal point in the case was whether a writ of error would lie upon such an award. The K. B. unanimously resolved that the writ would not lie, and it was quashed. They said that it was against the nature of a writ of error to lie on any judgment, but in causes where issue might be joined and tried, or where judgment might be had upon demurrer, and therefore that it would not lie on the return of a habeas corpus.

Upon this decision a writ of error was brought into the House of Lords; and all the judges of England being of opinion that the decision was correct, the judgment of the King's Bench was affirmed. 2 *Bro. P. C.*, 554.

To the objection that these were but opinions of the courts, not adjudications upon the point, *Ch. J. Kent.*, in *Yates* v. *The People*, 6 *Johns.*, 429, answered:

> "The doctrine was laid down in Lord Coke's day, as of course, as being then the known and established law. The principle is of immemorial standing. It has become the uncontroverted maxim of ages. A great part of the magnificent structure of our jurisprudence is not built upon a sounder basis. * * It has now stood the test of two centuries as an uncontrovertible principle, without a precedent or *dictum* to oppose it. To overthrow it would be tearing up the common law by the roots."

The case of *The Queen* v. *Paty and others*, 2 *Salk.*, 503; 2 *Ld. Raym.*, 1105, being one of the cases growing out of the *Aylesbury* election in 1703, is sometimes cited as supporting a contrary opinion. The history of the Aylesbury cases is stated more at large in 8 *How. St. Tr.*, 142.

"It appears that Matthew Ashby, a burgess of the town of Aylesbury, brought an action upon the case at common law against the constables of the town of Aylesbury, (being the proper officers to return members to serve in parliament for that place), for having by contrivance fraudulently and maliciously hindered him, to give his vote at the election. In this action a verdict was found for him; but judgment was given against him in the court of Queen's Bench, which was reversed in the House of Lords on error, when he obtained judgment for his damages, and had execution.

"Five others, burgesses, who complained of like wrong, brought their several actions. For this they were sent to the bar of the House of Commons, and committed prisoners to Newgate, during the pleasure of the House, as having acted contrary to the declaration, in contempt of the jurisdiction, and in breach of the privileges of that House.

"They sued out writs of habeas corpus to the Court of Queen's Bench, but were remanded to Newgate by three of the judges. *Contra*, Lord Ch. J. Holt.

"The House of Lords then petitioned the Queen to grant a writ of Error to the order of the Queen's Bench, remanding the prisoners, reserving themselves upon the question whether a writ would lie in such a case until the question should come regularly before them, and claiming that they being the court to which the writ was returnable, and of the last resort, were the only proper court to decide the question.

"The House of Commons resolved that, 'there is no judgment pronounced in the case of a habeas corpus, or in anything relating thereto.' 'That it had been the uniform opinion of former times, that a writ of error did not lie in any proceeding on a habeas corpus;' and they prayed the Queen not to grant the writ.'

"The Queen referred it to all the judges to advise whether the Queen ought to grant the writ of error, of right, or *ex debito vel merito justitiæ*, or *ex gratia*.

"Ten of the twelve advised that the writ ought to be granted of right, and not of grace. They added however,

'But we give no opinion whether a writ of error does lie in this case, because it is proper to be determined in parliament, where the writ of error and record are returned and certified." *Burdett* v. *Abbott*, 14 *East*, 91 *n*.

The Queen at last replied to the prayer of the House of Lords: "I should have granted the writ of error desired in this address; but finding an absolute necessity of putting an immediate end to this session, I am sensible there could have been no further proceeding upon that matter."

Ch. J. Kent, in *Yates* v. *The People*, 6 *Johns.*, 429, after reviewing the foregoing cases concludes that by the English law a writ of error would not lie to a decision on a habeas corpus, and says: "We have the unanimous opinion of the court of C. B. in the time of Lord Coke. We have the resolutions of the House of Commons in the reign of Queen Anne. We have the unanimous opinion of the court, of K. B. in the time of Geo. I., and lastly we have the sanction of Lord Ch. Baron Comyns; and all this without a single case or decision, or precedent, or opinion to oppose such a stream of authority."

To this may be added the testimony of the practice in England of renewing the application for the writ as often as the party desires, which is inconsistent with the supposition that a decision upon it is understood to be of that conclusive character which is necessary to support a writ of error.

The right to make repeated applications was recognized and strongly stated in *Ex parte Partington*, 13 *M. & W.*, 678, which was an application for the writ of habeas corpus on affidavit.

PARKE, B., said: "This case has already been before the Queen's Bench on the return of a habeas corpus; and before my Lord Ch. Baron, at chambers, on a subsequent application for a similar writ. In both instances the discharge was refused. *The defendant, however, has a right to the opinion of every court as to the propriety of his imprisonment*, and therefore we have thought it proper to examine," &c.

In the United States there has been exhibited in the opinions of the courts and acts of legislation, a tendency to attach to a decision in habeas corpus, the legal incidents belonging to *res adjudicata.*

In the case of *Yates* v. *The People*, 6 *Johns.*, 337, it was decided by the Court of Errors of New York, contrary to the opinion of the Chancellor and a majority of the judges of the Supreme Court, including Ch. J. Kent, that a writ of error did lie upon the award remanding the prisoner on a habeas corpus.

Since that decision the principle has been embodied in the legislation of the state.

In the Supreme Court of the United States the question was discussed in the case of *Holmes* v. *Jennison*, 14 *Peters*, 540. In this case a writ of error was brought on the order of the Supreme Court of Vermont remanding on habeas corpus the plaintiff who had been committed on the governor's warrant to be surrendered to the Canadian authorities as a fugitive from justice. The Supreme Court of the United States were divided on the question of jurisdiction, so that no decision was pronounced in the case.

Several judges expressed their opinions upon the questions in the case including the question whether, a writ of error would lie on a decision on habeas corpus.

From these it may be collected that five of the judges, viz.: Taney Ch. J., Story, McLean, Wayne and Catron, concurred in the opinion that the writ would lie in such a case. Justices Barbour and Thompson expressed no opinion on this point. Mr. Justice Baldwin alone held that the writ would not lie to a decision on habeas corpus.

Mr. Justice McLean afterwards in *Ex parte Robinson*, 6 *McLean*, 360, said: "It must be admitted that the authorities are not uniform on the point, whether the decision on a habeas corpus is final. This may be said of the authorities in this country and in England. I have been myself inclined to think such a decision should be considered final, where there was clearly jurisdiction and a full and fair hearing; but that it might not be so considered when any of these requisites were wanting, or when new and important evidence could be obtained."

The current of authority in the state courts is that a review of a decision on habeas corpus, independently of statutory provisions, cannot be had by writ of error, or appeal, and that on the ground that the decision is not a final judgment. *Bell* v. *The State*, 4 *Gill.*, 304; *Russell* v. *The Commonwealth*, 1 *Penrose & Watts*, 82; *Wade* v. *Judge*, 5 *Ala.*, 18; *Howe* v. *The State*, 9 *Miss.*, 690; *Matter of Perkins*, 2 *Cal.*, 424; *Ex parte Mitchell*, 1 *La Ann. R.*, 413. But an appeal was allowed in Louisiana, in the case of *Ex parte Lafonta*, 2 *Rob.*, 495; *Weddington* v. *Sloan*, 15 *B. Monroe*, 147; *Commonwealth* v. *Biddle*, 6 *Penna. Law Jour.*, 287.

It has been held that a decision on a habeas corpus in one state will not be considered as *res adjudicata* in another. *The State* v. *Brearly*, 2 *South.*, 555; *Maria* v. *Kirby*, 12 *B. Monroe*, 550.

But although not strictly a final judgment, and therefore not subject to review on a writ of error, the decision is held to be entitled to some consideration on a second application; and may warrant the refusal of the second.

In *Ex parte Lawrence*, 5 *Binn.*, 304, the Supreme Court of Pennsylvania said they did not think it expedient to grant the writ, in that case, because it had been already heard upon the same evidence.

In *Ex parte Campbell*, 20 *Ala.*, 89, the Supreme Court of Alabama held that notwithstanding a judgment refusing a discharge upon an application for bail, does not conclude the party from applying again, yet it is within the sound discretion of the court, after having fully examined the facts and circumstances on the previous application, whether it will retry them upon a renewed application or repose upon its former judgment.

Provision is made by statute for reviewing the decision on habeas corpus by writ of error or appeal in New York, Virginia, Florida, South Carolina, Mississippi, Texas and Ohio.

In some the review may be had at the instance of the state when the prisoner is discharged, as well as at the instance of the prisoner where he is remanded. In the cases of *The State* v. *Everett and The State* v. *Potter, Dudley Law Rep. S. Car.*, 295, which were appealed by the attorney-general, the end to be attained by an appeal on the part of the state, was thus stated by the court: "No decision that can be made by this court will recapture the defendants and bring them to justice. But it has been urged upon us, by the attorney-general, to express an opinion which may prevent their former discharge from being urged in their behalf, in case they should be retaken, and may serve to guide magistrates in like cases." But where the appeal suspends the order of discharge the prisoner will be remanded if the order be reversed. *The People* v. *Cavanagh*, 2 *Parker Cr. Rep.*, 650.

Giving to the order on habeas corpus the effect of a final judgment may lead in a degree to the gradual introduction into the practice under the writ of the stricter rules of proof and the more circumspect delays of regular actions; and must deprive the prisoner of the right of repeated application for the benefit of the writ, not only to the court of last resort, but to the several judges of it in vacation.

On the other hand questions of the most serious moment are often raised in this proceeding; questions relating to the constitutionality of an act of the state legislature or of Congress, and to the jurisdiction of courts, the highest, it may be, in the land, and to the validity of process emanating from them. These questions, when they arise, it is supposed to be the duty of the judge hearing the habeas corpus to determine.

Such questions claim the most deliberate consideration of the wisest who are charged with the administration of justice; and it is neither safe nor consistent with the general spirit of American law, to entrust their final decision, in a summary proceeding, to a single judge sitting apart at chambers without a record, shorn of the majesty of a court.

BOOK III.

THE

LAW OF EXTRADITION OF FUGITIVES.

THE

LAW OF EXTRADITION OF FUGITIVES.

CHAPTER I.

EXTRADITION OF FUGITIVES FROM JUSTICE, FROM FOREIGN STATES.

SECTION I.

NATURE OF THE OBLIGATION.

The duty of extradition of fugitives from justice from foreign states, as understood in America, supposes a reciprocity of obligation founded upon an express agreement between sovereign powers.

"In the year 1791, the governor of South Carolina made a request that the President of the United States should demand of the governor of Florida certain persons who had committed crimes in South Carolina, and fled to Florida. Mr. Jefferson, the Secretary of State, in his report to President Washington, says: 'England has no convention with any nation for the surrender of fugitives from justice, and their laws have given no power to their executive to surrender fugitives of any description, they are accordingly constantly refused; and hence England has been the asylum of the Paolis, the La Mottes, the Calonnis; in short, of the most atrocious offenders, as well as the most innocent victims, who have been able to get there. The laws of the United States, like those of England, receive every fugitive; and no authority has been given to our executives to deliver them up. If, then, the United States could not deliver up to General Quesnada (Governor of Florida), a fugitive from the laws of his country, we cannot claim as a right the delivery of fugitives from us.'"

In the year 1793, Mr. Jefferson answered an application of Mr. Genet, the French minister, in the following terms:

"The laws of this country take no notice of crimes committed out of their jurisdiction. The most atrocious offender coming within their pale, is received by them as an innocent man; and they have authorized no one to seize and deliver him. The evil of protecting malefactors of every dye is sensibly felt here, as in other countries, but until a reformation of the criminal codes of most nations, to deliver fugitives from them, would be to become their accomplices. The former is viewed, therefore, as the lesser evil."

Mr. Monroe, as Secretary of State under President Madison, in his instructions to our Commissioners at Ghent, said: "Offenders, even conspirators, cannot be pursued by one power into the territory of another, nor are they delivered up by the latter, except in compliance with treaties, or by favour."

The treaty of 1794, between the United States and Great Britain having expired, the former maintained the same views which had been advanced before the treaty was made.

"In March, 1825, the Governor of Vermont forwarded to Mr. Clay, the Secretary of State of the United States, a communication addressed to him by 'the acting Governor of Canada,' stating that two soldiers of a British regiment, who had committed a robbery on two officers of the regiment, were then in confinement in jail in Burlington, Vermont, and asked that the offenders should be delivered up to a person to be authorized to receive them, to be brought to justice in the province of Canada. The Governor of Vermont, in the letter to the Secretary of State, expresses his readiness to attend to any directions the Secretary of State of the United States might please to give on the subject.

"The reply of Mr. Clay, which was transmitted by Governor Van Ness to the acting governor of Canada, states: 'I am instructed by the President to express his regret to your excellency, that the request of the acting Governor of Canada, cannot be complied with under any authority now vested in the executive government of the United States; the stipulation between this and the British government, for the mutual delivery of fugitives from justice, being no longer in force; and the renewal of it by treaty being, at this time, a subject of negotiation between the two governments."'

Other instances have occurred in which the government has maintained the same views. *Story Confl. Laws*, § 628, *note.*

The subject has in a few cases been brought under consideration in the courts. In 1819 Chancellor Kent in a learned and elaborate opinion in the *Matter of Washburn*, 4 *John. C. R.*, 108, maintained that independent of any treaty stipulations, "it is the law and usage of nations, resting on the plainest principles of justice and public utility, to deliver up offenders charged with felony and other high crimes, and fleeing from the country in which the crime was committed into a foreign and friendly jurisdiction."

But this opinion has been followed in no other state. On the contrary it has been rejected in several. In 1823 the question was considered by the Supreme Court of Pennsylvania, in the case of *The Commonwealth* v. *Deacon*, 10, *S. & R.*, 125, and an opinion pronounced by *Ch. J. Tilghman*, distinguished for research and ability, in which he upholds the doctrine advanced by the American government, and concludes: "that no state has an *absolute and perfect right* to *demand* of another the delivery of a fugitive criminal, though it has what is called an *imperfect right*, that is a right to ask it as a matter of courtesy, good-will and mutual convenience. In 1822, *Ch. J. Parker* of Massachusetts, in the case of *The Commonwealth* v. *Green*, 17 *Mass.*, 547, recognises the same doctrine, observing that in respect to the several states of the Union: "The constitution has made that obligatory between the states, which between nations entirely foreign to each other was done from comity." In 1837, in the case of *U. S.* v. *Davis*, 2 *Sumner*, 482, on the acquittal of the defendant, on the ground that jurisdiction over the offence belonged to a foreign government, it was suggested by the district judge, that the court should remand the prisoner to the foreign government for trial. But *Mr. Justice Story* said:

"He had never known any such authority exercised by our courts, except where the case was provided for by the stipulations of some treaty. He had great doubts whether upon principles of international law, and independent of any statutable provisions or treaty stipulation, any court of justice was either bound in duty or authorized in its discretion to send back any offender to a foreign government whose laws he was supposed to have violated."

The prisoner was thereupon discharged.

See also the case of *Jose Ferreira de Santos*, 2 *Brock R.*, 493, *Commonwealth* v. *De Longchamps*, 1 *Dall.*, 111.

SECTION II.

BY WHOM THE SURRENDER IS TO BE MADE.

The duty of surrendering the fugitive arising only from treaty stipulations, its performance is supposed to appertain to the executive department of our government which, "by and with the advice and consent of the Senate," constitutes the treaty making power. *Sergt. Const. Law*, 408 ; 1 *Curtis' Comm.*, 96.

It has been thought that the several states were not exempt from this duty, and some of them have at different times made provisions by statute for discharging it. It was the subject of statutory regulation in Virginia, as early as 1784. 11 *Hen. Stat. p.*, 471, *ch.* 24, cited in 1 *Rob. Pr.*, 7. In New York also, the governor was authorized by statute, in his discretion to surrender fugitives from foreign countries, but the governor in 1839, refused to act under it, upon the ground that the national government had exclusive jurisdiction over the subject; and such appears to have been the opinion of the Supreme

Court of the United States the next year, 1840, as expressed in the case of *Holmes* v. *Jennison and others*, 14 *Peters*, 540. For although no judgment was given in the case, a majority of the court concurred in the opinion that the governor of Vermont had not the power to deliver up to a foreign government a person charged with having committed a crime in the territory of that government.

The Supreme Court of Vermont having before remanded the prisoner to be surrendered, subsequently acquiesced in this view and finally discharged him on habeas corpus, 14 *Peters*, 598, *note*.

SECTION III.

BY WHAT AGENCY THE SURRENDER IS TO BE MADE.

Whether in the execution of a treaty stipulation there being no legislation by Congress on the subject, it is competent for the executive, by his warrant to cause the fugitive to be arrested and surrendered; or whether it is necessary to appeal to the judiciary to determine whether the case of the alleged fugitive is embraced by the treaty, or whether the aid of the judiciary can be invoked at all, and if it can, at whose instance, that of the executive or the representative of the foreign government, are questions which have not escaped discussion.

In 1797, Thomas Nash, better known by the name of *Jonathan Robbins*, which he assumed in the jail at Charleston, was committed to jail in Charleston South Carolina, at the instance of the British consul on suspicion, grounded on two affidavits, of having been concerned in a mutiny on board the British frigate Hermoine, in the year 1791, which ended in the murder of the principal officers, and carrying the frigate into a Spanish port.

The District Judge, Bee, having declined to deliver him up to the British authorities because no requisition had been made upon the President; a requisition was subsequently, on the 23d of May, 1799, addressed by the British Minister at Washington to the President under the 27th article of "Jay's Treaty," who thereupon, on the 3d of June, 1799, caused a communication to be made to the judge by the Secretary of State, conveying his (the President's,) "advice and request," that on production of such evidence as was contemplated by the treaty, Robbins should be delivered up.

The prisoner being afterwards, on the 1st of July, 1799, brought before the judge on a writ of habeas corpus, the following order was made:

"*United States* v. *Nash*, alias *Robbins*.

"The prisoner is brought before me by writ of habeas corpus from which and from two affidavits, filed with the clerk of this court, it appears that the prisoner is charged with having committed murder on board of a ship of war belonging to his Britannic Majesty, on the high seas. Requisition has been made by the British Minister that he be delivered up by virtue of the 27th article of the treaty of amity between the United States and Great Britain, and as there is sufficient evidence of criminality to justify his apprehension and commitment for trial and justice may be more fully done, if the prisoner be tried where the witnesses reside, or their evidence may be better procured, I do (in consideration of the circumstances and at the particular request of the President of the United States, Mr. John Adams,) order that the prisoner, Thomas Nash *alias* Jonathan Robbins, be delivered over by the Marshal of this court to Benjamin Moodie, Consul of his Britannic Majesty, agreeably to the 27th section of the treaty aforesaid." *Bee's Admiralty Rep.*, 266.

The judgment being pronounced, the court was immediately adjourned; the irons were replaced on the prisoner and he was delivered over by the constables to a detachment of federal troops, who had before been placed under arms opposite the courthouse and had continued there during the sitting of the court. The troops immediately delivered up the prisoner to Lieut. Jump, of his Britannic Majesty's sloop, Sprightly, then lying in the harbor, and which sailed on Saturday morning for Jamacia. He was afterwards tried by a court martial of the British navy, convicted, hung and gibbetted. 1 *Hall's Jour. of Jur.*, 18; *Wharton, St. Tr.*, 392.

The surrender of Robbins and the participation of the executive therein became immediately the subject of thorough discussion, enlisting some of the ablest pens in the country, Pinckney of South Carolina and Madison and Marshall of Virginia. Great principles were involved and there were not wanting great men to comprehend and discuss them. Pinckney, on the 3d August, 1799, under the signature of "A South Carolina Planter," published a letter, in which the power of the court to act under the Treaty, in the absence of any legislation on the subject by Congress, was denied, and the letter of the Secretary of State to the judge, "advising and requesting," the delivery of the fugitive was characterized as an act of "extreme impropriety," and a dangerous interference on the part of the executive power with the judicial.

Marshall, afterwards Chief Justice of the United States, in a letter published in the Virginia "Federalist," argued with his accustomed clearness:

"It is a certain fact that Great Britain, by the express words of the Treaty had a right to demand Robbins in the present case, who was accused of murder, one of the enumerated offences for which fugitives were to be delivered up.

"There must, therefore, have been some mode of carrying the provision of the Treaty, in this respect, into execution, or else the articles would be nugatory; and it would be absurd to suppose the parties meant to stipulate for a thing which could not be performed.

"The question then is, what mode should be pursued when a requisition of this kind is made, and what proceedings should take place in order to comply with it.

"The Treaty has not pointed out any mode, and therefore we must recur to principles and the nature of things in order to discover it.

"As nations do not communicate with each other but through the channel of their government, the natural, the obvious and the proper mode, is an application on the part of the goverment (requiring the fugitive) to the executive of the nation to which he has fled, to secure and cause him to be delivered up.

"1. Because the government being the only channel of communication between the nations, the British government, in cases of this kind, has nothing to do with the detail and internal regulation of ours, nor we with theirs. For, as the governments have respectively undertaken to do the thing which is required, the injured nation is not concerned any further with the business than merely to exhibit the proofs and call on the other for the performance of the Treaty; and the nation called on must attend to the details and internal regulations themselves.

"2. Because the government to which the fugitive has fled ought to be informed why an inhabitant is forced away from its territories; and, therefore, a removal of any person therefrom, without an application to the Chief Magistrate, would not only be dangerous to the personal safety of individuals, but would be an indignity and an affront which ought not to be offered.

"3. Because without such application, the injured nation could not complain of an infraction of the Treaty on the part of the other government in not delivering up the fugitive. For it would be an irresistible argument to such a complaint, that no application was ever made to the government itself. Nor would it strengthen the complaint, that an application was made to some inferior authority; because an application to subordinate officers who do not represent the general national concerns, would not only be improper on account of the inconvenient practices it might introduce (for by that means a man might be carried off without government having an opportunity of protecting him), but in case the requisition were not complied with, could not be a just ground of reproach to the government itself, which was never informed of the application.

"4. Because it is manifest from what has been said, as well as from the very nature of things, that government must have a right to decide whether a fugitive should be delivered up or not. For it is a mere question of state, and all questions relative to the affairs of the nation emphatically belong to the government to decide upon. Therefore in case of a requisition for a fugitive by the United States from Great Britain, the application would be to the Executive, and not to the judiciary or any other inferior department of government.

"It follows, therefore, that an application to the government itself is essential; and, accordingly, in the case under consideration, such an application was actually made. But surely the business was not to rest there; some further steps were necessary, or else the application would have been to no purpose.

"The government, as we have already seen, was bound by engagement to cause delivery to be made; and, therefore, the President was under the necessity of taking some order in the business which might produce the object of the application. For, having been informed that the man was under confinement, upon the charge on which the application was made, until the determination of government upon the subject could be known, he was bound to give some directions in the business, so that the prisoner might either be liberated or delivered up, and those directions could only be given in writing."

In the next Congress, 1800, the matter was made the subject of investigation in the House of Representatives, and resolutions of censure introduced by Livingston of New York, supported by Gallatin of Pennsylvania, and others. The administration was defended by Bayard of Delaware, Chief Justice Marshall of Virginia, and others. The argument of Chief Justice Marshall was written out by himself, and is said by Justice Story to be "among the very ablest arguments on record." In that he maintained the same views he had previously advanced in his published letter.

"1st. That the case of Robbins as stated to the President, was completely within the 27th article of the Treaty.

"2d. That the question of surrender of a fugitive was one of 'political law,' the power to decide which rests alone with the executive department.

"3d. That in deciding it the President was not chargeable with an interference with judicial decisions."

The opposition was silenced for the time, and the course of the administration approved by a large majority of the house, the vote standing 62 to 35.

Mr. Pinckney, in his letter, had questioned the proceeding on the ground, amongst others, that it placed in jeopardy "the invaluable right of habeas corpus."

Chief Justice Marshall, in his speech in Congress, did not deny that the objection had force; and weakened his conclusion that the executive possessed the *exclusive* power of deciding whether the fugitive should be surrendered by conceding that his decision might be made the subject of review before the judiciary, for he says:

"If the President should cause to be arrested, under the treaty, an individual who was so circumstanced as not to be properly the object of such an arrest, he may, perhaps, bring the question of the legality of his arrest before a judge, by a writ of habeas corpus." *Bee's Rep.*, 287.

He admits, also, the power of Congress to legislate upon the subject, contending that in the absence of such legislation it was the duty of the executive to execute the treaty.

"The treaty," he argues, "which is a law, enjoins the performance of a particular object. The person who is to perform this object, is marked out by the Constitution, since the person is named who conducts the foreign intercourse, and is to take care that the laws be faithfully executed. The means by which it is to be performed, the force of the nation, are in the hands of this person. Ought not this person to perform the object although the particular mode of using the means has not been prescribed? Congress, unquestionably, may prescribe the mode; and Congress may devolve on others the whole execution of the contract; but, till this be done, it seems the duty of the executive department to execute the contract by any means it possesses."

Although the very able argument of Ch. Jus. Marshall silenced opposition at the time, it did not, as Justice Story declares, "put the question at rest forever." The discussion has been revived in recent times in the case of *Metzger*, 1 *Parker Cr. Rep.*, 108.

"Nicholas Lucien Metzger was a notary public in one of the departments of France, which he left and came to this country. After he had left his residence, it was charged against him that he was a defaulter to his clients to a large amount, for moneys of theirs which he had embezzled, which embezzlement he had attempted to conceal by means of forgeries.

"Complaint to that effect was made against him before a French committing magistrate, who issued a warrant for his arrest. He was not, however, apprehended on the warrant, but the papers, duly authenticated, were transmitted to this country, and the French minister to this country demanded his surrender under the treaty with France of 1843. That functionary was referred by the Secretary of State to the courts or magistrates of the country, and accordingly made application to one of the police magistrates of New York or a warrant on which Metzger was arrested. An examination was had before that officer, who adjudicated that the prisoner was within the treaty, and issued his warrant committing him to prison until the President of the United States should demand him.

"Before that demand was made, the prisoner was taken before the Circuit Judge, Edmonds, of the first circuit of New York, on habeas corpus. That officer decided that the police magistrate had no jurisdiction in the matter, and the prisoner was discharged.

"The French diplomatic agent then made application to the United States District Judge Betts, who determined the case as the police magistrate did, and issued a like warrant of commitment.

"Judge Betts held that as a treaty is the supreme law of the land, it is entitled, when coming before the courts, to the same effect as an act of Congress, though no act has been passed to define the method of its operation; that under such treaty a fugitive is subject to apprehension and commitment for a crime committed against the laws of the country demanding him as a fugitive, whether such crime be an offence in the country to which he has fled or not; and that whether the *casus fœderis* has arisen, or whether the compact will be executed, is a political question to be decided by the President, the courts having no power to direct or contravene his decisions in the first instance.

"Whether the judiciary has authority in habeas corpus, after the fugitive is under arrest, to prevent his extradition, if the President decides to make it, was not decided. 5 *New York Legal Observer*, 83; *Wharton St. Tr.*, 457.

"After the commitment by Judge Betts, the prisoner applied to the Supreme Court of the United States for a writ of habeas corpus to review the action of the district judge. The application was denied on the ground that that court had no power to review the action of the district judge at chambers. 5 *How.*, 176.

"Thereupon the President issued his mandate to the marshal of New York, commanding him to surrender the prisoner to the diplomatic agents of the French government. Before, however, the surrender was actually made, a writ of habeas corpus issued, directed to the marshal returnable before Edmonds, circuit judge of New York.

"The case was twice argued by counsel for the prisoner, and the French government and the United States District Attorney.

"The judge finally in March, 1847, held that the provisions in the Treaty with France to be executed *in futuro*, were in the nature of a contract, and did not become a rule for the courts until legislative action was had upon the subject. That the stipulation in that treaty providing for the surrender of fugitives from justice, could not be executed by the President of the United States, without an act of Congress, and that no person could be surrendered under *that* treaty, who is merely charged with crime before a committing magistrate."

He ordered the prisoner to be discharged.

The "legislative action" which Ch. Justice Marshall thought would be proper, and which Judge Edmonds held to be indispensable, was afterwards had.

An act was passed by Congress on the 12th August, 1848, intitled "An act for giving effect to certain treaty stipulations between this and foreign governments, for the apprehension and delivering up of certain offenders," 9 *St. at Large*, 302.

By this act it is provided:

"That in all cases in which treaties of extradition may exist between the United States and foreign governments, the justices and judges of the United States and state courts and Commissioner, authorized by the United States Courts, may upon complaint made under oath or affirmation, charging &c., issue warrants for the apprehension of any person charged with having committed certain offences within the limits of such foreign governments. That if on hearing, the evidence be deemed sufficient to sustain the charge, the same shall be certified with a copy of the testimony to the Secretary of State, that a warrant may issue upon requisition from the proper authority for the surrender of such offender. That copies of the depositions upon which an original warrant in such foreign country may have been granted, certified under the hand of the person issuing such warrant, and attested upon the oath of the party producing them, to be true copies of the original depositions, may be received in evidence of the criminality of the person apprehended. That the Secretary of State under his hand and seal of office may order such offenders to be delivered to such person as may be authorized by such foreign government to receive them. That if such offender be not conveyed out of the United States within two months after commitment, over and above the time actually required to convey him from the jail where committed by the readiest way out of the United States, any judge of the United States or state courts may discharge him on proof of reasonable notice to the Secretary of State, unless sufficient cause be shown to the judge why the discharge should not be ordered. That the Courts of the United States may authorize any person to act as commissioner under the act."

Thus, at length, all the powers of the government, legislative, judicial and executive are brought into harmonious coöperation, each performing its appropriate office, and all contributing to the same end, the double duty of preserving public faith and at the same time protecting private liberty.

Since the passage of the act of 1848, a majority of the judges of the Supreme Court of the United States in *The matter of Kaine*, 14 *How.*, 103, expressed the opinion that under that act a commissioner appointed by an order in general terms, may issue a warrant for the arrest of a fugitive from justice. That he may do so on the application of the representative of a foreign government, without special instruction or warrant being first issued to him by the U. S. government, and that proof that the magistrate in Ireland, before whom the prosecution was instituted, publicly discharged the duties of a justice of the peace, was prima facie evidence of his official character.

CHAPTER II.

EXTRADITION OF FUGITIVES FROM JUSTICE, FROM THE SEVERAL STATES OF THE UNION.

SECTION I.

NATURE OF THE OBLIGATION.

The colonies recognized the obligation without formal compact. *Ch. J. Tilghman*, in the case of *The Commonwealth* v. *Deacon*, 10 *S. and R.*, 129, says: "That prior to the American revolution, a criminal who fled from one colony, found no protection in another. He was arrested wherever found, and sent for trial to the place where the offence was committed."

The following extract from the Colonial records of Pennsylvania will show that in 1685, the rights of sovereignty were duly respected and the law of national comity readily conceded.

"The 24th of ye 5th Mo., 1685."

"Wm Haigue request ye secret^{ry} that a hue and cry from East Jersie after a servant of Mr John White, march^{t} at

New York, might have some force and authority to pass this Province & Territoryes; the Secret[ry] indorsed it and sealed it with y[e] seale of y[e] Province." 1 *Penn. Col. Laws, &c.*, 96.

The "articles of confederation," contained the following clause; "If any person guilty of or charged with treason, felony *or other high misdemeanor* in any state, shall flee from justice and be found in any of the United States, he shall, upon the demand of the government or executive power of the state from which he fled be delivered up *and removed* to the state having jurisdiction of the offence."

The provision as it now stands in the Constitution, *Art.* 4, *sec.* 2, is in these words:

> "A person charged in any state with treason felony *or other crime*, who shall flee from justice and be found in another state, shall, on demand of the executive authority of the state from which he fled, be delivered up, *to be removed* to the state having jurisdiction of the crime."

It is stated by Mr. Madison that the word "crime," was substituted for the words "high misdemeanor," in order to comprehend all proper cases, it being doubtful whether "high misdemeanor" had not a technical meaning too limited. 1 *Rob. Pr.* 11; *Madison Papers, vol.* 3, *p.* 1447.

The executive of Virginia having, in 1791, in consequence of the want of direction as to the mode of discharging the duty, shown some hesitation to deliver up a fugitive from justice on the demand of the executive of Pennsylvania, the attention of Congress was called to the subject by President Washington, and on 12th Feb., 1793, was passed the "Act respecting fugitives from justice, and persons escaping from the service of their masters." 1 *U. S. Stat. at Large*, 302. By the 1st and 2d sections of this act it is provideed:

"Sec. 1. That whenever the executive authority of any state in the Union, or of either of the Territories northwest or south of the river Ohio, shall demand any person as a fugitive from justice, of the executive authority of any such state or territory to which such person shall have fled, and shall, moreover, produce a copy of an indictment found or an affidavit made before a magistrate of any state or territory as aforesaid, charging the person so demanded, with having committed treason, felony or other crime, certified as authentic by the governor or chief magistrate of the state or territory from whence the prisoner so charged fled, it shall be the duty of the executive authority of the state or territory to which such person shall have fled, to cause him or her to be arrested and secured, and notice of the arrest to be given to the executive authority making such demand, or to the agent of such authority appointed to receive the fugitive, and to cause the fugitive to be delivered to such agent when he shall appear. But if no such agent shall appear within six months from the time of the arrest, the prisoner may be discharged. And all costs or expenses incurred in the apprehending, securing and transmitting such fugitive to the state or territory making such demand, shall be paid by such state or territory.

"Sec. 2. That any agent, appointed as aforesaid, who shall receive the fugitive into his custody, shall be empowered to transport him or her to the state or territory from which he or she shall have fled. And if any person or persons shall by force set at liberty, or rescue the fugitive from such agent while transporting, as aforesaid, the person or persons so offending, shall, on conviction, be fined not exceeding five hundred dollars and be imprisoned not exceeding one year."

Mr. Justice Story, speaking of these sections in the case of *Prigg* v. *Commonwealth of Pennsylvania*, 16 *Peters*, 620, says: "Not a doubt has been breathed upon the constitutionality of this part of the act; and every executive in the Union has constantly acted upon and admitted its validity."

Although the constitutionality of the law of 1793 has not in respect to the first and second sections been questioned, and the obligation imposed by the Constitution has been uniformly recognized; there nevertheless has occurred an occasional conflict of opinion among the executive magistrates of the states as to their respective right and duties under them. Some of the points thus raised remain undetermined, the contending parties standing respectively upon their convictions and their sovereignty, and calling no umpire; and some have experienced those vicissitudes of fortune to which all legal questions connected with the politics of the day are exposed in a country of free and earnest and incessant discussion. Several particulars contemplated in the statute will be considered in following sections.

SECTION II.

THE CRIME COMMITTED.

The words of the Constitution are, "treason, felony or other crime." No controversy has arisen as to the crimes enumerated, viz.: "treason and felony" ; but the words, "or other crime" have been the subject of frequent discussion.

The opinion has been advanced by some that the provisions referred only to such "crimes" as were offences by the laws of the respective states at the time the Constitution was adopted. Others have maintained that the character of the alleged criminal act is to be determined by the laws of the state to which the fugitive has fled, or, rather, that it cannot be considered a crime under the Constitution which is not regarded as an offence by the laws of that state, of the other states of the Union, or the law of nations.

Others again contend that these provisions embrace only "offences known as crimes at the common law, or recognized as such by the state of which the fugitive is demanded;" and in support of this view it has been argued that:

"In almost every state of the Union, the criminal code embraces offences unknown to the common law, and peculiar to the state. An act not *malum in se*, nor the subject of punishment anywhere else, is often made criminal in the code of a particular state. It can hardly be supposed that the constitutional provision was intended for such offences.

"The crimes enumerated in the Constitution are of the highest class, and the general description which is added, must, in some degree, be qualified by that enumeration, and especially by the character of the remedy itself. The surrender and extradition of our citizens or of persons claiming the protection of our laws is a matter of great consequence. Although as between the states of the Union it does not stand upon the footing of courtesy but of positive obligation, yet it is essentially of an international character and should not be exercised in doubtful cases." *Attorney-General of Ohio, Report, January* 25, 1850.

But the true construction of this section of the Constitution appears to be that it embraces, as a general rule, all such acts as are made criminal by the laws of the state where they are perpetrated.

This construction is warranted by the letter of the article and required by the spirit of the Constitution.

1. *As to the letter of the article.* "Charged with treason, felony or other crime." A "crime" is "an act committed or omitted in violation of public law, either forbidding or commanding it." 4 *Bl. Com.*, 5. "The violation of a right, when considered in reference to the evil tendency of such violation as regards the community at large." 4 *Steph. Com.*, 55; 1 *id.*, 127, 128.

The states are sovereign and independent, having entire control over their municipal legislation, and may declare any act a crime which they may deem detrimental to the public interest, except only in those cases which are excluded from their cognizance by the national Constitution. To charge a person with committing an act declared by the laws of the state where committed to be criminal is certainly to charge him with "crime."

2. *As to the spirit of the constitution.* The motive suggesting this provision was the desire of the several states to vindicate their violated laws—to arm themselves with the power to maintain those laws by making the punishment of their breach inevitable.

This article is not a mere treaty stipulation. The Constitution of the United States is not a mere treaty. It is a plan of government and its provisions are to be construed with reference to the grand objects for which it was established. Listen to its preamble: "We, the people of the United States, in order to form a more perfect union, establish justice, insure domestic tranquillity, provide for the common defence, promote the general welfare and secure the blessings of liberty to ourselves and our posterity, do ordain and establish this Constitution for the United States of America."

The founders of the republic looked to the future. They adopted *principles* of justice and comity which they deemed adequate to regulate the conduct of the states towards each other for all time. The extradition of fugitives from justice is one of them. If designed as a rule of government, a fundamental law it should reach to and control all modifications of the subject matter comprehended in its general terms.

There was a diversity of criminal laws among the states at the time of the adoption of the Constitution. Identity could not have been anticipated. Moreover such laws have always been subject to frequent change. "Ourselves and our posterity" were to be provided for.

Nations remote from each other might concern themselves to treat only for the surrender of the more atrocious offenders. The hope of escape by flight in countries so situated, it could hardly be supposed would abet the incentive to commit the lesser crimes.

But here was territorial contact on almost every side. The means of transit, and consequently the chances of escape from one state to another, were multiplying daily.

Did any state anticipate that any other state would ever become so barbarous as to enact criminal laws so bloody and inhuman as to cause a shudder at the demand to surrender up the guilty fugitive for trial and punishment? Or that any one would become so debased or so deluded or transcendental as to repeal all criminal laws and thus offer a secure retreat to all the criminals in the land?

On the other hand, did they not confide in one another's *sense of justice*, rather than in any particular limitation to the *general* term used? And did they not agree "in order to insure domestic tranquillity, promote the general welfare," &c., not only to tolerate one another's peculiarity in administering punitive justice, but also so far to assist therein as to deny protection to fugitive offenders?

This point has been discussed by the executive authorities of some of the states, and very different views appear to have been entertained by them. In 1839 the governor of Virginia made application to the governor of New York for the surrender of three men charged by affidavit with being fugitives from justice, in feloniously stealing and taking away from one Calley, in Virginia, a negro slave, Isaac, the property of Calley. The governor of New York refused to surrender the supposed fugitives on the ground that slavery and property in slaves did not exist in New York; that the offence was not a crime known to the laws of New York and consequently not a crime within the meaning of the Constitution and statute of the United States. He contended that by the law of nature there could be no property in slaves, that it was not allowed by the municipal laws of most countries, nor recognized by the law of nations. The executive and legislative authorities of Virginia, on the other hand, considered the case to be within the Constitution and law, and that the refusal was a denial of right. Extracts of the material points in the correspondence may be found in 6 *Penna. Law Jour.*, 412.

Chancellor Kent expressed himself upon the question as follows: "In my humble view of the question, I cannot but be of opinion that the claim of the governor of Virginia was well founded, and entitled to be recognized and enforced." 1 *Kent Com.*, 37, *n.*

In another case, the executive of New York refused to comply with a demand made upon him by the governor of Virginia, for the surrender of Peter Johnson, and other persons named, charged with the crime of stealing a slave within the jurisdiction and against the laws of Virginia. But in this he was not sustained by the legislative authority of the state, for on the 11th April, 1842, the legislature of New York passed a resolution expressing the opinion, that the act charged against Johnson and the others, was a crime within the meaning of the Constitution of the United States.

Laws of N. York, 1842, *p.*, 419; 1 *McKinney's Jus.*, 84.

"In Pennsylvania the ordinary practice with the executive is to issue his warrant of surrender, whenever a requisition is supported by an indictment, duly accompanied by *executive averment that the particular offence is a crime in the State where it was committed*, and by an affidavit that the defendant has fled from such state into one where the warrant is demanded." 6 *Penna. Law Jour.*, 412. "Why are the words 'or other crimes' added (asks the Attorney-General in an early opinion,) if felonies alone were contemplated? In the penal code of almost every state, the catalogue of felonies is undergoing a daily diminution. But it is not by the class of its punishment that the malignity of an offence is always to be determined. Crimes going deep into the public peace may bear a milder name and consequence; and yet it would be singular to afford shelter to those who were guilty of them, because they were not so called and punished." *Id.*

The governor upon whom the demand is made, may however consider whether the state making the demand, has the constitutional power to declare the act criminal, of which it accuses the fugitive, and may refuse to surrender him, if the state seeking him has undertaken by indirection to do the work allotted by the Constitution to Congress.

In December, 1834, the legislature of Maryland passed a law, making it felony in a slave "to escape into the District of Columbia, or into any state of the union, against the will and consent of his master and owner, with a view to escape from servitude." In 1847, the governor of Maryland made his requisition upon the governor of Pennsylvania for the surrender of John Mark and others as fugitives from justice; an indictment having been found against them under that statute for escaping into Pennsylvania. Governor Shunk, under the advice of the Attorney-General, refused to comply with the demand, upon the ground that the Constitution and laws of the United States having embraced the case within the provision for the surrender of fugitives from servitude, no state legislation could evade those provisions, or alter the character of the transaction, so as to introduce the case under the provisions for the surrender of fugitives from justice.

The act of Congress of 12th February, 1793, in pursuance of the Constitution of the United States, made ample provision for the surrender of these individuals as fugitives from labor, on the "claim of the party to whom such labor is due." It was, therefore, an infringment of the federal Constitution to pass a law transferring to the governor of Maryland, the right to demand a surrender; thus making the very act of escape which under the constitution and laws, gave the owner a right to demand a surrender of his property into his own custody, a ground for depriving him of that right, and conveying his property to the custody of a state government, which might or might not respect his constitutional rights of property. 7 *Penna. Law Jour.*, 253; *Lewis Cr. Law*, 260.

In Maine it was objected, 1840, that the provision of the constitution includes only crimes of a high and aggravated nature. Governor Fairfield answered, "The phraseology is 'treason, felony or other crime,' not other crimes of a high and aggravated nature; but crimes in their absolute and unqualified sense."

6 *Am. Jurist*, 226. There is not wanting judicial authority on the point.

In the matter of John L. Clark, 9 *Wend.*, 212, on habeas corpus, 1832, it appeared that the prisoner was in custody by virtue of a warrant issued by the Governor of New York, under a requisition by the Governor of Rhode Island, charged with fraudulently abstracting money from the Burrilville Bank in that state, by the laws of which the act was made criminal and punishable by fine only. It was objected that no "crime" had been committed. The answer of the court was: "An offence of a highly immoral character is stated in the warrant, and is certified by the Governor of Rhode Island to have been made criminal by the laws of that state. This is evidence enough in this stage of the proceedings, of the nature of the offence."

It was further objected then that a crime of greater atrocity was intended by the Constitution than was charged in that case. The court answered: "It seems that when proceedings are instituted by the comity of nations, they apply only to crimes of great atrocity, or deeply affecting the public safety. But with the comity of nations we have at present nothing to do, unless, perhaps, to infer from it that the framers of our Constitution and laws intended to provide a more perfect remedy; one which should reach every offence criminally cognizable by the laws of any of the states; the language is, 'treason, felony or other crime;' the word crime is synonymous with misdemeanor, 4 *Black. Com.*, 5, and includes every offence below felony, punished by indictment as an offence against the public."

In the matter of Hayward, 1 *Am. Law Jour. N. S.*, 271, 1848, the Superior Court of the city of New York, said: "It is immaterial to consider what is the nature of the offence charged against the prisoner, for we have only to consider whether it be a crime according to the law of the state from which the party is alleged to have been a fugitive."

And of that opinion was the Supreme Court of Georgia, as expressed in the case of *Johnston* v. *Riley*, 13 *Geo.*, 97.

The Supreme Court of Maine, in 1837, gave to the Governor of that state, their opinion on this and other points, in the following terms:

"In our opinion it is the duty of the executive of this state to cause to be delivered over to the agent of another state, at the request of the executive thereof, a citizen of this state, charged by indictment with the fraud before set forth, *which, being indicted in such state, may be presumed to be there regarded as a crime*, if the executive of this state is satisfied that such citizen has fled from justice from the state making demand, and not otherwise." 6 *Am. Jurist*, 226.

The Supreme Court of New Jersey, *In the matter of Fetter*, 3 *Zab.*, 311, held that it is not necessary, in order to warrant the surrender or detention of the fugitive, that the crime with which he stands charged should constitute an offence at the common law. It was objected in that case that the indictment did not show an offence at common law. It purported to be for grand larceny, but the facts stated, it was claimed, did not constitute the crime. The court said: "Admitting the position taken by counsel, it is nevertheless certified by the Governor of

California, under the laws of that state. It is moreover an offence of a highly immoral character, and as appears by the bill of indictment, *which must be regarded as prima facie evidence of the fact*, is a *crime* by the law of the State of California."

SECTION III.

THE ACCUSATION.

Its form and when to be made. The act of Congress, Feb. 12, 1793, requires that the accusation should be by "indictment found, or an affidavit made before a magistrate of any state or territory." It is not necessary that the accusation should be made *before* the flight of the criminal. *Gov. Fairfield's opinion*, 6 *Am. Jurist*, 226.

Its sufficiency. A copy of the indictment or affidavit, "certified as authentic by the Governor or chief magistrate of the state or territory from whence the person so charged fled." "The object of this provision of the law is to enable the executive upon whom the demand is made, to determine whether there is probable cause for believing that a crime has been committed. The affidavit, therefore, when that form of evidence is adopted, must be at least so explicit and certain that if it were laid before a magistrate it would justify him in committing the accused to answer the charge." *Gov. Seward of New York to Gov. McDonald of Georgia, June* 15, 1841; *Attorney Gen. of Penn. to Gov. Shunk, May* 15, 1847, 6 *Penn. Law Jour.*, 412; *Ex parte Smith*, 3 *McLean*,

121; *Matter of Hayward*, 1 *Sandf. Sup. Ct. R.*, 701; *Matter of Fetter*, 3 *Zab.*, 311.

SECTION IV.

THE FLIGHT OF THE ACCUSED.

There must be an actual fleeing from justice, and of this the governor of the state of whom the demand is made as well as of the state making it should be satisfied. This is commonly shown by affidavit. "In Hall's case in 1845, a long and angry controversy arose between the governors of New York and Pennsylvania. Judge Kane, then Attorney-General of Pennsylvania, advised against surrender of the alleged fugitive, for want of an affidavit of actual fleeing. He based his opinion upon usage more than upon the words of the act of Congress." *Kane's Letter to Gov. Shunk, March* 14, 1845; 6 *Penn. Law Jour.*, 412.

To the same effect was the advice of the Supreme Court of Maine before quoted, given to the governor in 1837.

Governor Fairfield in his opinion, 6 *Am. Jurist*, 226, says: "Each governor has the right of determining the fact whether the person charged be a fugitive from justice or not," and in respect to *small crimes*, at least, he thinks, that the mere production of an indictment should not be regarded as proof of the fact that the person indicted is a fugitive.

"Where a person, who committed a crime in a state where he was temporarily sojourning, departed from it for his ordinary and permanent residence in Pennsylvania; the Attorney-General of the latter state, advised the Governor thereof that the person could not be considered a fugitive from justice under the Constitution and act of Congress." *Lewis's Cr. Law*, 266.

The Governor of Maine, 6 *Am. Jurist*, 226, expresses himself upon this point as follows:

"Now what will constitute a *fleeing* within the meaning of the Constitution? Making the charge in one state and finding the accused in another, will not. I am clearly of the opinion that where one is conscious of having committed 'treason, felony or other crime' in one state and leaves that state, knowing that by remaining he is subject to prosecution, a sufficient time not having elapsed or other circumstances occurred to remove all reasonable apprehension of a prosecution, he may fairly be regarded as a fugitive from justice within the meaning of the 4th art. of the Constitution."

The Superior Court of the city of New York, in 1844, *In the matter of Adams*, 7 *Law Rep.*, 386, said:

"If a man within a state secretly commits a crime and suddenly departs, the crime not being discovered till months after his departure, though he may have left for purposes other than fleeing from the justice of the state against which he offended; yet he surely might be treated and proceeded against as a fugitive from justice. The consciousness of his having committed the crime, of his being amenable to the laws of the state against which he offended, might and would probably be regarded as the motive for going out of its limits, and form a legitimate basis for an executive requisition and surrender."

SECTION V.

THE DEMAND OF THE FUGITIVE.

This consists of a written application by the governor of the state where the crime was committed, addressed to the governor of the state to which the offender has fled, requesting his delivery to some person therein appointed to receive him. It states the crime of which the fugitive is accused, the fact that he has fled from the justice of the state, and must be accompanied by a copy of the indictment found or affidavits showing the charge.

SECTION VI.

THE ARREST AND SURRENDER.

The arrest may be before the requisition. In some states statutes have been passed authorizing magistrates to apprehend fugitives from other states before any warrant issues from the executive. *In Ohio* it may be doubted whether the intervention of either executive is required. Very ample powers are conferred upon the justices of the peace to hear and examine the charge preferred against any person brought before him, and "charged with the commission of any criminal offence against the laws of any other state or the territories of the United States," and upon proof by him adjudged sufficient, to commit, &c., or "cause such person to be delivered to some suitable person to be removed to the proper place of jurisdiction," &c. *Swn. St.*, 541.

In NEW-YORK "To enable a magistrate to arrest and examine an alleged fugitive from justice from another state, it must be shown to him by a complaint, in writing, on oath, that a crime has been committed in the foreign state; that the accused has been charged in such state with the commission of such crime, and that he has fled from such state and is found here. The judge said: 'I think the affidavit on which the warrant was issued is defective in not showing positively that the alleged crime was committed in the State of Pennsylvana, and because it does not state positively that the prisoner had fled from the state. It is true that it may be readily inferred from the affidavit, the residence of the parties and the facts in the case, that the alleged crime was committed within the State of Pennsylvania, and that the prisoner fled from that state to avoid the consequences of the alleged offence. But mere inference is not sufficient to found the exercise of criminal jurisdiction. The facts sufficient to confer that jurisdiction must be alleged positively.'" *Matter of Hayward*, 1 *Sanf. Sup. Ct. R.*, 701.

In PENNSYLVANIA it is said: "The principle appears to be recognized that in order more effectually to accomplish what is intended by the Constitution and laws of the United States, it is the duty of the magistrates, as it has been the practice, to cause to be arrested, offenders who have fled from one of the United States to another, even before a demand has been made for them by the executive of the state from which they fled." *Opinion of Ch. J. Tilghman*, 10 *Sergt. & R.*, 135.

"It is not necessary in order to arrest a fugitive that a requisition should be produced from the governor at the time of the arrest. If the oath on which the warrant issues is sufficient to raise a good reason for believing that a crime has been committed in a sister state, it is the duty of the magistrate to commit the accused till time be given to take the legal steps for demanding a surrender." *Vaux' Cases*, 32; *Lewis' Crim. Law*, 260.

In the case of Goodhue, charged with obtaining money in Kentucky by false pretences, the recorder of the city of New York remanded the prisoner to be detained in custody six weeks in order to give time for the executive of Kentucky to demand him under the Constitution and laws of the United States. 2 *Johns.*, 477. Similar authority was recognized in *Ex parte Smith*, 5 *Cow.*, 273, and in *The People* v. *Lynch*, 11 *Johns. Rep.*, 549. In these cases the relators were accused of offences against the United States, but the principle for the detention is the same. The court in the former case say: "Detaining a prisoner by state authority in order that he may be delivered over for prosecution to the United States is by no means an unusual exercise of power." But unreasonable delay would be ground for discharge.

In GEORGIA "A person charged with committing a felony in one state may be detained in another on the principle of comity, 'under the law of nations and the common law of this land,' to afford the former an opportunity to demand the accused." *R. M. Charlt. Rep.*, 228; *State* v. *Loper*, 2 *Geo. Decis.*, 33.

In *Delaware*, in 1847, in the case of *The State* v. *Buzine*, 4 *Harring.*, 575, the same views are maintained in an elaborate opinion by Ch. J. Booth. That was a proceeding in habeas corpus. The petitioner had been committed by the Mayor of the city of Wilmington on a complaint of having committed a crime in Pennsylvania and fled, &c. No demand had been made for his surrender, and one ground relied on for his discharge was that the Mayor had no authority to arrest and commit a fugitive from justice from another state prior to a demand, &c. But the court everruled the objection, and in observing upon the act of Congress, of 1793, and the constitutional duty of the states, said: "To enable the executive to perform this duty, it is necessary that magistrates should have the power to arrest and commit the fugitive *before as well as after* a demand has been made. The exercise of the power is essential to carry into effect the provision of the constitution; otherwise an immunity may be offered to the most atrocious criminals. If a felon notoriously guilty of murder can, by escaping into another state, set the law at defiance until a demand is regularly made on the executive, and a warrant is issued for his arrest, the object of the Constitution may be defeated and the act of Congress rendered nugatory. By the time a requisition is obtained and a warrant granted in due form, the offender may fly to another state, where he again finds a sanctuary until the same formalities are repeated. He may thus escape from state to state exempted by his own vigilance or that of his friends from arrest and punishment."

The Chief Justice held the warrant of commitment insufficient for the want of a seal, but refused to discharge the prisoner until the proofs were examined to see whether the facts disclosed afforded a reasonable presumption of guilt, or such probability as would be sufficient to put him upon his trial, saying that "if such were the case, although I should discharge him from imprisonment under the warrant of the Mayor, I should consider it my duty to order him to be immediately committed to the public jail of New Castle county, for a reasonable time to give notice and await the demand of the executive authority of Pennsylvania. If no demand should be made in such reasonable time it would become my further duty to make a final order for his discharge."

The judge then examined the proofs and found they did not show the commission of a criminal offence but a breach of trust only, and so ordered the petitioner to be discharged.

In *Ex parte Thornton*, 9 *Texas*, 635, the Supreme Court on discharging a fugitive from justice from Arkansas on the ground of defect in the Governor's warrant, refused to detain him that another warrant might be obtained saying they had no power to detain him.

In New Jersey in the *Matter of Fetter*, 3 *Zab.*, 311, the relator had been arrested on an affidavit made before a justice of the peace. The affidavit was held defective because it did not allege that any crime had been committed in California, from which he was alleged to be a fugitive.

But the court refused to discharge him and received other affidavits and also the requisition of the Governor of California and accompanying bill of indictment, which had been made upon the Governor of *Pennsylvania*, none as yet having been made on the Governor of New Jersey.

The commitment of the justice directed that he should be detained in custody, "to await the requisition of the Governor of California, or otherwise be thence discharged by due course of law."

The prisoner was remanded.

Where no arrest has been made at the time of the requisition, the governor upon whom the demand is made if satisfied that the case is properly made out under the constitution and act of Congress, issues his warrant for the arrest and surrender of the fugitive. This warrant is commonly addressed to the sheriff or other proper officer, and terminates the agency of the governor in the matter of extradition. *Matter of Clark*, 9 *Wend.*, 212.

It is however competent for the governor if satisfactory reasons appear therefor to recall his warrant before execution. *Opinion of Governor Fairfield*, 6 *Am. Jurist*, 226. The governor of Ohio, in 1844, countermanded and revoked an order for the surrender of Richard Seymour. *Matter of Adams*, 7 *Law Rep.*, 386.

In Pennsylvania instead of issuing final process of arrest and surrender, the governor in case of a requisition issues his precept to some judicial officer of the state, requiring and authorizing him to issue his warrant for the arrest of the criminal, to be brought before him in the usual way, and he proceeds to make the necessary examination so far as to ascertain that the act of Congress has been complied with; and then (the identity of the accused being established, and the authority of the agent shown), to make an order for the surrender of the fugitive, in pursuance of the warrant of the governor. *Lewis's Cr. Law*, 261.

This precept or warrant is required to possess the usual requisites of criminal process. In the case of Henry Thomas, alias Thomas Dean, who was arrested in Lancaster county, Pennsylvania, for murder committed in the State of Ohio, the warrant from the governor of Pennsylvania, merely recited that the "governor of Ohio had given *information* that one Thomas Dean had been guilty of murder in that state," and Lewis, president judge of the district, to whom the warrant was directed, decided that such a recital unaccompanied by evidence, was insufficient; and the prisoner was not delivered up until a certified copy of the affidavit was furnished. *Lewis Cr. Law.*, 262. The governor's warrant to arrest and surrender where it recites the facts necessary under the constitution and law, to give him jurisdiction ought to be at least *prima facie* evidence of the existence of these facts. The requisition and accompanying documents which form the basis of his official action, are or should be deposited amongst the public archives of the state, and may there be appealed to if their existence is so denied as to render their production necessary. They cannot reasonably be required to accompany the warrant of arrest and surrender, so as to make their absence a ground of discharge on habeas corpus, where the warrant properly recites them. *Matter of Clark*, 9 *Wend.*, 212.

The opinion has been entertained in Pennsylvania, that the governor's warrant is not obligatory upon a *judicial* officer of the state; the judiciary being a coördinate department of the government, deriving its power equally with the executive, under the constitution. In one case a judge of the Court of Common Pleas refused obedience to the warrant. 2 *Pa. Law Jour.*, 150; *Lewis Cr. Law.*, 262.

It has been held that the Constitution and laws of the United States only refer to fugitives at large, and that if a fugitive be in actual confinement on criminal or civil process, he cannot be surrendered. In such cases the requisition should be lodged with the sheriff, whose duty it would be upon the prisoner's discharge from his previous arrest, to detain him thereon until notice could be given to the party presenting the requisition. *In the matter of Troutman*, 4 *Zabr.*, 634.

SECTION VII.

THE REVISORY POWER OF THE JUDICIARY.

How far the action of the governor commanding the surrender of a fugitive from justice under the act of 1793, is subject to review before the judicial tribunals of the state is not well settled. It has been held in South Carolina (1814) that the demanding, apprehending and conveying away fugitives from justice under these provisions of the constitution and laws are ministerial acts, wholly entrusted to the management and discretion of the executive authority; that the making the demand, the transmission of the documents, the mode of their authentication, their validity and legal operation, are exclusively of executive cognizance, and that the judicial authority of the state from which they are sent has no control or jurisdiction over the subject. Where, therefore, certain persons were brought up before a judge of that state by habeas corpus, who were under arrest by order of the executive of South Carolina for the purpose of being delivered to an agent of the executive of New York, who had demanded them as fugitives from justice in that state, bills of indictment being found against them in New York for bigamy, and their discharge was moved for on various grounds, the judge decided that he had no power or authority to discharge the prisoners, or in any way whatever to interfere with the mandate of the executive; and that it must be considered as a case excepted out of the state habeas corpus act by the operation of the Constitution and laws of the United States. *Sergt. Const. Law*, 395.

In the case of *The State* v. *Schlemn*, 4 *Harr.*, 577, it appears that after the petitioner, Adams, was discharged by the Chief justice; in the case of *The State* v. *Buzine*, a requisition having been obtained from the governor of Pennsylvania and a warrant from the governor of Delaware, he was again arrested; whereupon he sued out another writ of habeas corpus before *Ch. J. Booth*, who was asked to look behind the warrants which were all regular, but he refused.

"Every person," says the Ch. Justice, "in this state who is restrained of his liberty under any color or pretence whatever, either for a civil or a criminal cause and apprehends or is advised that his imprisonment is illegal, is entitled as a matter of right to the writ of habeas corpus; unless his petition clearly and distinctly shows that he is legally detained for treason or felony plainly and fully set forth in the warrant of commitment; or detained under the judgment or the process thereon of a court of competent civil or criminal jurisdiction; or that he is legally imprisoned by the authority of the United States or detained for such other legal and sufficient cause as satisfies the court or judge that no relief could be granted to the petitioner upon the return of the writ. It is in the nature of a writ of error to examine into the legality of the commitment; and for that purpose to bring up the body of the prisoner with the cause of his detention.

"Suggestions or exceptions against the return may be filed for the purpose of ascertaining material facts to enable the court or judge to determine whether the party ought to be bailed, remanded or discharged. In cases of imprisonment under warrants from our magistrates for offences committed within this state; or for offences perpetrated in another state, and the accused is committed to await the demand of the executive authority of such state, an inquiry is made into the circumstances of the case to ascertain the material fact, whether there is such proof or reasonable presumption of guilt as would be sufficient to put the party on trial. But if the return alleges that the prisoner was committed and is detained by virtue of the judgment and process thereon, of a court of competent jurisdiction, the existence of such judgment and process is the material fact to be ascertained. When ascertained it is sufficient legal cause for the prisoner's detention, and precludes all further inquiry. The court or judge awarding the habeas corpus cannot examine into the matters on which the judgment was rendered, and must remand the prisoner. So, in like manner, if the return to the habeas corpus sets forth that the party is a fugitive from justice, that he was demanded as such and was arrested and committed for the purpose of being surrendered; the only inquiry is, whether the provisions of the act of Congress of 1793 have been complied with. If that fact is shown by the return and by the warrant of the executive authority under which the fugitive has been arrested, it constitutes a just and legal cause for his imprisonment and detention. The right and power under the Constitution of the United States and the first section of the act of Congress of 1793 to demand, arrest, commit and surrender fugitives from justice, are exclusively vested in and confided to the executive authority of the state from which the fugitive has escaped and that of the state where he has taken refuge. * * * The warrant of the executive under the great seal of the state reciting the facts necessary under the act of Congress to give him jurisdiction of the case, would, in my opinion, at the hearing of the habeas corpus be conclusive evidence of the existence of those facts, of his judgment in relation to them, and of a compliance with the Constitution of the United States and the act of Congress.

"No investigation, therefore, in such a case, can be made beyond the warrant of the executive, and no examination into the facts and circumstances of the alleged offence with which the party stands charged.

"The case would not be within the operation of the habeas corpus act of this state, even were it not excepted by the 4th section. *Dig.*, 295.

"In the present case the return fully sets forth copies of all the documents transmitted by the governor of Pennsylvania to the executive of this state, with the warrant of the latter and the appointment of Schlemn as the agent of the State of Pennsylvania, to receive the prisoner as a fugitive from justice and carry him to that state. It appears that all the requisites of the act of Congress have been complied with. No suggestions or exceptions have been made to the return. It is therefore admitted to be true.

"And although my belief is that the alleged offence with which the petitioner is charged is the same, which upon the examination of witnessess at the hearing of the former habeas corpus clearly appeared to be a breach of trust and not a larceny, he must be remanded because the return in this case is conclusive."

The prisoner was taken to Pennsylvania and put in prison at Bellefonte. He then obtained a habeas corpus, and after an examination into the facts of the case was discharged on the ground that they did not constitute larceny, but amounted merely to a breach of trust.

In the *Matter of Adams*, 7 *Law Rep.*, 386, the Superior Court of the city of New York, in 1844, expressed great doubt, and declined to decide "whether on habeas corpus they could look behind the acts of the Governors of Ohio and New York, and inquire whether there was sufficient ground to authorize the requisition of the one and the surrender by the other."

An interesting case was determined by the U. S. District Judge for Illinois, in 1842, and reported in 3 *McLean*, 121, *Ex parte Joseph Smith, the Mormon Prophet*.

The case came before the court upon a return to a writ of habeas corpus, which was issued by the Circuit Court, Dec. 31, 1842, upon a petition for a habeas corpus on the relation of Joseph Smith, setting forth that he was arrested and in custody of Wm. F. Elkin, sheriff of Sangamon county, upon a warrant issued by the governor of Illinois upon a requisition of the governor of the State of Missouri, demanding him to be delivered up to the governor of Missouri as a fugitive from justice; that his arrest, as aforesaid, was under color of a law of the United

States, and was without the authority of law in this; that he was not a fugitive from justice, nor had he fled from the State of Missouri. The sheriff returned that he detained the said Joseph Smith in custody by virtue of a warrant issued by the governor of the State of Missouri, made on the affidavit of Lilburn W. Boggs. Copies of the affidavit, requisition and warrant were annexed to the return, and were as follows:

Affidavit.

STATE OF MISSOURI, }
County of Jackson, } ss.

This day personally appeared before me, Samuel Weston, a justice of the peace within and for the county of Jackson, the subscriber Lilburn W. Boggs, who being duly sworn, doth depose and say, that on the night of the 6th day of May, 1842, while sitting in his dwelling in the town of Independence, in the county of Jackson, he was shot with intent to kill and that his life was despaired of for several days; and that he believes, and has good reason to believe, from evidence and information now in his possession, that Joseph Smith, commonly called the Mormon Prophet, was accessory before the fact of the intended murder; and that the said Joseph Smith is a citizen or resident of the State of Illinois and that the said deponent hereby applies to the Governor of the state of Missouri, to make a demand on the Governor of the State of Illinois, to deliver the said Joseph Smith, commonly called the Mormon Prophet, to some person authorized to receive and convey him to the state and county aforesaid, there to be dealt with according to law.

LILBURN W. BOGGS.

Sworn to and subscribed before me, }
this 20th day of July, 1842. }

SAMUEL WESTON, *J. P.*

Requisition.

The Governor of the State of Missouri, to the Governor of the State of Illinois—GREETING:

Whereas, it appears by the annexed document, which is hereby certified to be authentic, that one Joseph Smith is a fugitive from justice, charged with being accessory before the fact, to an assault with intent to kill, made by one O. P. Rockwell, on Lilburn W. Boggs, in this state, and it is represented to the executive department of this state, has fled to the State of Illinois:

Now, therefore, I, Thomas Reynolds, Governor of the said State of Missouri, by virtue of the authority in me vested by the Constitution and laws of the United States, do by these presents demand the surrender and delivery of the said Joseph Smith to Edward R. Ford, who is hereby appointed as the agent to receive the said Joseph Smith, on the part of this state.

In testimony, &c.

Warrant of Arrest and Surrender.

The People of the State of Illinois, to the Sheriff of Sangamon County—GREETING:

Whereas, It has been made known to me by the executive authority of the State of Missouri, that one Joseph Smith stands charged by the affidavit of one Lilburn W. Boggs, made on the 29th day of July, 1842, at the county of Jackson, in the State of Missouri, before Samuel Weston, a justice of the peace within and for the county of Jackson aforesaid, with being accessory before the fact, to an assault with an intent to kill, made by one O. P. Rockwell, on Lilburn W. Boggs, on the night of the 6th day of May, 1842, at the county of Jackson, in said State of Missouri, and that the said Joseph Smith has fled from the justice of said state, and taken refuge in the State of Illinois:

Now, therefore, I, Thomas Ford, Governor of the State of Illinois, pursuant to the Constitution and laws of the

United States and of this state, do hereby command you to arrest and apprehend the said Joseph Smith, if he be found within the limits of the state aforesaid, and cause him to be safely kept and delivered to the custody of Edward R. Ford, who has been duly constituted agent of the said State of Missouri, to receive said fugitive from the justice of said state, he paying all fees and charges for the arrest and apprehension of said said Joseph Smith, and make due return to the executive department of this state, the manner in which this writ may be executed.

In testimony, &c.

The court caused the Governor and Attorney-General of the State of Illinois, to be informed of the issuing of the habeas corpus; and on the day appointed for the hearing, the Attorney-General of the state appeared and moved to dismiss the proceedings, and filed the following objections to the jurisdiction of the court, viz.:

"1st. The arrest and detention of Smith was not under or by color of authority of the United States, or of any officers of the United States, but under and by color of authority of the State of Illinois, by the officers of Illinois.

"2d. When a fugitive from justice is arrested by authority of the governor of any state, upon the requisition of the governor of another state, the courts of justice, neither state nor federal, have any authority or jurisdiction to inquire into any facts behind the writ."

The counsel of Smith then offered to read in evidence affidavits of several persons, showing conclusively that the said Joseph Smith was at Nauvoo, in the county of Hancock, and State of Illinois, on the whole of the 6th and 7th days of May, in the year 1842, and on the evenings of those days, more than three-hundred miles distant from Jackson county, in the State of Missouri, and that he had not been in the State of Missouri at any time between the 10th February, and 1st July, 1842, the said persons having been with him during the whole of that time.

The reading of these affidavits was objected to by the Attorney-General of the state, on the ground that it was not competent for Smith to impeach or contradict the return to the habeas corpus. It was contended by the counsel for Smith: 1st. That he had a right to prove that the return was untrue. 2d. That the affidavits did not contradict the return, &c.

The court heard the affidavits subject to objections.

The court held that the statute of the State of Illinois, making it the duty of the governor to issue his warrant, in case of a requisition did not enlarge or alter the power which was vested in him by the Constitution and laws of the United States, and that the warrant did issue under and by authority of the United States. Upon this point the court say:

> "If the legislature of Illinois, intended to make it the *duty* of the governor to exercise the power granted by Congress, and no more, the executive would be acting by authority of the United States. It may be that the legislature of Illinois, appreciating the importance of the proper execution of those laws, and doubting whether the governor could be punished for refusing to carry them into effect, deemed it prudent to impose it as a duty, the neglect of which would expose him to impeachment.
>
> "If it intended more the law is unconstitutional and void."

The court did not decide upon the admissibility of the affidavits offered by Smith, inasmuch as it held that he was entitled to his discharge for defect in the affidavit.

"The affidavit is insufficient, said the court; 1st, because it is not positive; 2d, because it charges no crime; 3d, it charges no crime committed in the State of Missouri. Therefore he did not flee from the justice of Missouri.

"Boggs swears to his *belief*. Having the 'evidence and information in his possession,' he should have incorporated it in the affidavit, to enable the court to judge of their sufficiency to support his belief. Again he swears to a legal conclusion, when he says that Smith was '*accessory before the fact*.' What constitutes a man accessory is a question of law, and not always of easy solution. He should have given the facts and sworn they were committed in Missouri, to enable the court to test them by the laws of Missouri, to see if they amounted to a crime. The affidavit is fatally defective in this, that Boggs swears to his *belief*. The language of the Constitution is, 'charged with felony or other crime.' Is the Constitution satisfied with a *charge upon suspicion? Suspicion* does not warrant a commitment, and all legal intendments are to avail the prisoner. The return is to be strictly construed in favor of liberty.

"The proceedings in this affair, from the affidavit to the arrest, afford a lesson to governors and judges, whose action may hereafter be invoked in cases of this character. The affidavit simply says that the affiant was shot with intent to kill, and he believes that Smith was accessory before the fact to the intended murder, and is a citizen or resident of the state of Illinois. It is not said who shot him, or that the person is unknown.

"The governor of Missouri, in his demand, calls Smith a fugitive from justice, charged with being accessory before the fact to an assault with intent to kill, made by one O. P. Rockwell on Lilburn W. Boggs in this state, (Missouri). The governor expressly refers to the affidavit as his authority for that statement. Boggs, in his affidavit does not call Smith a *fugitive from justice*, nor does he state a fact from which the governor has a right to infer it. Neither does the name of O. P. Rockwell appear in the affidavit, nor does Boggs say Smith *fled*. Yet the governor says he fled to the State of Illinois. Boggs only says he is a *citizen* or *resident* of Illinois.

"The warrant of the governor of Illinois recites facts which do not appear in the affidavit.

"The court can only regard the *facts* set forth in the affidavit of Boggs as having any legal existence.

"The misrecitals and over statements in the requisition and warrant, are not supported by oath, and cannot be received as evidence to deprive a citizen of his liberty, and transport him to a foreign state for trial. For these reasons Smith must be discharged."

In *Ex parte Thornton*, 9 *Texas*, 635, the relator was in custody under the following warrant:

"*State of Texas:*

"To all and singular, the sheriffs, constables and other civil officers of the said state, GREETING:

Whereas, It has been represented and made known to me by his excellency, Elias N. Conway, Governor of the State of Arkansas, that Abner E. Thornton, late of the county of Pulaski in said State of Arkansas, stands charged therein with the crime of forgery; and that the said Abner E. Thornton has fled from justice in said state and taken refuge in the State of Texas; and whereas the said Elias N. Conway, Governor of said State of Arkansas, has in pursuance of the Constitution and laws of the United States demanded of the executive of this state, the surrender of the said Abner E. Thornton, and that he be delivered to Benjamin F. Danley, who is duly authorized to receive him:

"Now therefore know ye, that I, P. Hansborough Bell, Governor of the State of Texas, do, by virtue of the power and authority in me vested by the Constitution and laws of the United States, issue this my warrant, commanding all sheriffs, constables and other civil officers of said state, to arrest and to aid and assist in arresting the said Abner E. Thornton, and to deliver him, when arrested, to the said Benjamin F. Danley, agent of said State of Arkansas, in order that he may be taken back to said state to be dealt with according to law.

"In testimony, &c.

HEMPHILL, Ch. J. "The relator insists on his discharge on the ground of the insufficiency and illegality of the warrant in this, that it does not show by recital that the representation and demand of the Governor of the State of Arkansas was accompanied with a copy of an indictment found or an affidavit made before some magistrate of the State of Arkansas, certified by the said executive as being duly authenticated and charging the relator with having committed the crime of forgery within said state. And we are of the opinion that on the ground set forth he is entitled to his discharge.

"By the act of Feb. 1793, it is essential that there should be:

"1st. A copy of the indictment found, or affidavit made charging the alleged fugitive with having committed the crime.

"2d. The certificate of the executive of, &c., that such copy was authentic.

"This was the evidence and the only evidence on which the warrant was authorized to issue. But so far from it appearing on the face of the warrant that such copy has been produced to the executive, and that the warrant had issued in consequence thereof, it appears on the contrary that the executive acted on the representations of the executive of the state of Arkansas, to the effect that the relator stood charged with the crime of forgery in that state. These were altogether insufficient to give the governor jurisdiction in the case. The representations of the executive of the demanding state are of no effect unless supported by a duly authenticated copy of the indictment found, or affidavit made. These are prerequisites to the issue of the warrant; and without these it is void and gives no authority to arrest or detain the person alleged to be charged. We are of opinion that the warrant should show on its face that such authentic copy of the indictment or affidavit had been produced to the executive."

Before the prisoner was discharged the court was moved to detain him until another warrant could be procured, which motion was supported by the affidavit of the sheriff from Arkansas, who was appointed in the requisition, agent, &c., that he had seen the indictment, that he knew a copy had been presented to the Governor of Texas with the requisition, &c.

But the court said they had no power to detain him.

In Missouri it has been held that the governor's warrant should be under the seal of the state and a warrant upon which an impression of the seal of the state was not discoverable was held void and the prisoner discharged. *Vallad* v. *Sheriff, &c.*, 2 *Mis.*, 26.

SECTION VIII.

STATE LEGISLATION.

It does not appear that the constitutionality of the act of Congress of 1793, in relation to the apprehension and surrender of fugitives from justice has ever been contested, or that the executives of the several states were not thereby invested with power to discharge the constitutional obligation resting upon them.

At the same time it must be confessed that the circuity and consequent delay of the proceeding prescribed renders it sometimes ineffectual; and has led to occasional trespasses upon territorial sovereignty which, between "states dissevered," could never be tolerated.

The testimony of the late very able and experienced Chief Justice of Pennsylvania would doubtless find some corroboration in every state in the Union. *In Dow's case*, 18 *Penn.*, 37, Ch. Jus. *Gibson* says:

"The constitutional provision was not devised for the benefit of the fugitive. It was intended to obviate the principle that one government may not execute the criminal laws of another. The practice has been to arrest on hot pursuit, a fugitive from justice wherever found; and were not the violation of territory consequent on it, tolerated by common consent, few fugitives from justice would be brought back. In its practical results the constitutional provision is nearly inoperative. The tardy publicity of laying a ground for demand by indictment or affidavit, of transmitting the documents to the proper executive, and of procuring a warrant of arrest from him, necessarily warns the fugitive of his danger, and leads to another flight. It was formerly the practice of the governor of this state to act in the matter by the instrumentality of the judiciary; and though I have issued many warrants, none of them has ever been followed by an arrest. The consequence of the inefficiency of the constitutional provision has been that extra-territorial arrests have been winked at in every state."

This "*constitutional provision*" however, it must be remembered, was devised as a rule of conduct between sovereign and independent states, and contains all they could concede with a just regard to their right of exclusive dominion over their respective territories. The *act of Congress* may be imperfect and imperfectly executed, yet it will not be denied that the sovereign power of the state, in a matter seriously affecting the liberty of its citizens, should act with the greatest circumspection. And the law itself may appear less exceptionable when we remember that if the guilty sometimes escape by the delay which it permits, the innocent are sometimes saved by the deliberation which it requires.

The states have not however been insensible to this obligation, nor have they excused themselves by doing only what the act of Congress required. *That* requires no arrest of the fugitive until *after* demand made upon the executive, &c. But we have seen that in several of the states the judiciary, without special state legislation have found authority in the principles of the common law to arrest the fugitive *before* the executive demand is made, and to detain him in custody until notice could be given to the proper authorities, and his surrender regularly demanded.

In some states laws have been passed conferring this power upon justices of the peace, and other judicial officers; and in some, a summary hearing and surrender appear to have been authorized without requiring the delay incident to executive intervention.

Whether the states have any power to legislate upon this subject, since Congress has legislated upon it, whether the power of Congress over it is exclusive, or if concurrent, being exercised it is exhausted, are questions which have not been determined. The rule of construction applied in other cases may, per haps, be applicable to this.

In the case of *Prigg* v. *The Commonwealth of Pennsylvania*, 16 *Peters*, 608, the Supreme Court say:

"If Congress have a constitutional power to regulate a particular subject, and they do actually regulate it in a given manner, and in a certain form, it cannot be that the state legislatures have a right to interfere; and, as it were, by way of complement to the legislation of Congress, to prescribe additional regulations, and what they may deem auxiliary provisions for the same purpose. In such a case, the legislation of Congress in what it does prescribe, manifestly indicates that it does not intend that there shall be any further legislation to act upon the subject matter. Its silence as to what it does not do, is as expressive of what its intention is as the direct provisions made by it. This doctrine was fully recognized by this court in the case of *Houston* v. *Moore*, 5 *Wheat.*, 1, 21, 22; where it was expressly held that where Congress have exercised a power over a particular subject given them by the Constitution, it is not competent for state legislation to add to the provisions of Congress upon that subject; for that the will of Congress upon the whole subject is as clearly established by what it had not declared, as by what it has expressed."

This rule was recognized and applied by the Supreme Court of New York in the case of *Jack* v. *Martin*, 12 *Wend.*, 311.

It is of course quite obvious that the states cannot add to the conditions specified in the act of Congress, nor release their executives from the duty which it enjoins. They cannot in any manner or to any extent contravene or embarrass the execution of its provisions. But that they may not by statute enforce the performance of the duty which it enjoins upon their executives by subjecting them to a *state* accountability for neglecting it, or otherwise *facilitate* the discharge of the constitutional obligation, are questions which ought not to be considered as altogether foreclosed by the rule applied in cases not identical.

Perhaps such legislation by the states when in no sense opposed to the law of Congress, may be rested upon the general police power of the states which was so ably contended for by Mr. Justice Baldwin in his opinion delivered in the case of *Holmes* v. *Jennison*, 14 *Peters*, 540, where the power of the states to surrender fugitives from justice from *foreign states* was in question, and which was conceded in the case of *Prigg* v. *The Com. Penn.*, to exist in the states, in the following terms: "We entertain no doubt whatsoever that the states, in virtue of their general police power, possess full jurisdiction to arrest and restrain runaway slaves, *and remove them from their borders*, and otherwise to secure themselves against their depredations and evil example, as they certainly may do in cases of idlers, vagabonds and paupers."

In KENTUCKY, *Rev. Stat.* 1852, *p.* 365, it is provided that on a requisition from the executive of another state, the warrant of arrest shall require the alleged fugitive to be apprehended and brought before a circuit judge, who shall upon testimony determine whether the person apprehended be the fugitive demanded, and if satisfied of the identity, order him to be delivered to the agent of the state or territory demanding him, otherwise he shall discharge him. If, however, the charge be for kidnapping a person of color, the judge shall not confine his inquiry to the single question of identity, but also whether he is the owner of the person charged to have been abducted, or whether he acted as the agent or friend of the owner, or had his sanction for what was done.

Any person guilty of felony any where in the United States, may be arrested on a warrant issued on an affidavit of the facts, and on examination be committed to the jail of the county for sixty days, unless sooner demanded.

In FLORIDA it is by statute, *Thompson Dig.*, 527, made the duty of the governor, on requisition being made, to cause the fugitive to be arrested and secured, either by making public proclamation or by issuing an order to that effect, which order shall be issued under his hand and the seal of the state, directed to all and singular the sheriffs of the state, and be executed forthwith by any sheriff receiving the same.

In INDIANA, *Rev. St.*, 1843, *p.* 1030, it is enacted: "That if any person shall commit any crime in any of the United States or the territories thereof, and shall flee into this state, it shall be lawful for any judge of the Supreme or Circuit Court, or any justice of the peace within this state, on the oath or affirmation of any person charging such fugitive with a crime, to issue his warrant and cause such fugitive to be arrested and brought before him, and after hearing the proofs and allegations for and against such fugitive, if, in the opinion of such judge or justice the proof is evident or presumption strong as to the guilt of the person charged, it shall be the duty of the judge or justice to commit such fugitive from justice to the common jail of the county where such arrest may be made, for any length of time not exceeding one month; or, in case any sheriff, coroner or constable shall have pursued such fugitive, it shall be the duty of such judge or justice to give such sheriff, coroner or constable a warrant to remove such fugitive, which shall be a sufficient authority to remove such fugitive from this state to the state or territory from which he fled."

CHAPTER III.

EXTRADITION OF FUGITIVES FROM SERVICE.

SECTION I.

NATURE AND EXTENT OF THE OBLIGATION.

By the 3d clause of the 2d section of the 4th article of the Constitution of the United States, it is provided that:

"No person held to service or labor in one state under the laws thereof, escaping into another, shall, in consequence of any law or regulation therein, be discharged from such service or labor, but shall be delivered up on claim of the party to whom such service or labor may be due."

By the 3d and 4th sections of the act of Congress of February, 1793, 1*st U. S. Stat. at Large*, 302, it is provided:

"Sec. 3d. That when a person held to labor in any of the United States, or in either of the territories on the north-west or south of the river Ohio, under the laws thereof, shall escape into any other of the said states or territory, the person to whom such labor or service may be due, his agent or attorney is hereby empowered to seize or arrest such fugitive from labor, and take him or her before any judge of the circuit or district courts of the United States, residing or being within the state, or before any magistrate of a county, city, or town corporate, wherein such seizure or arrest shall be made, and upon proof to the satisfaction of such judge or magistrate, either by oral testimony or affidavit taken before and certified by a magistrate of any such state or territory, that the person so seized or arrested, doth, under the laws of the state or territory from which he or she fled, owe service or labor to the person claiming him or her, it shall be the duty of such judge or magistrate to give certificate thereof to such claimant, his agent or attorney, which shall be sufficient warrant for removing the said fugitive from labor to the state or territory from which he or she fled.

"Sec. 4. That any person who shall knowingly and willingly obstruct or hinder such claimant, his agent or attorney in so seizing or arresting such fugitive from labor, or shall rescue such fugitive from such claimant, his agent or attorney, when so arrested pursuant to the authority herein given or declared; or shall harbor or conceal such person after notice that he or she was a fugitive from labor, as aforesaid, shall, for either of the said offences, forfeit and pay the sum of five hundred dollars; which penalty may be recovered by and for the benefit of such claimant, by action of debt, in any court proper to try the same; saving moreover to the person claiming such labor or service, his right of action for or on account of the said injuries or either of them."

Speaking of the foregoing clause in the Constitution and the act of Congress of 1793, in 2 *Story Comm., sec.* 1811, 1812, *a*, the learned Commentator says:

"This clause was introduced into the Constitution solely for the benefit of the slaveholding states, to enable them to reclaim their fugitive slaves, who should have escaped into other states where slavery was not tolerated. The want of such a provision under the confederation, was felt as a grievous inconvenience by the slaveholding states; since in many states, no aid whatsoever would be allowed to the owners, and sometimes, indeed, they met with open resistance. In fact, it cannot escape the attention of every intelligent reader, that many sacrifices of opinion and feeling are to be found, made by the eastern and middle states to the peculiar interests of the south. This forms no just subject of complaint; but it should forever repress the delusive and mischievous notion, that the south has not at all times had its full share of benefits from the Union.

"It is obvious, that these provisions for the arrest and removal of fugitives of both classes contemplate summary ministerial proceedings, and not the ordinary course of judicial investigations, to ascertain whether the complaint be well founded, or the claim of ownership be established beyond all legal controversy. In cases of suspected crimes the guilt or innocence of the party is to be made out at his trial, and not upon the preliminary inquiry, whether he shall be delivered up. All that would seem, in such cases, to be necessary is, that there should be *prima facie* evidence before the executive authority to satisfy its judgment, that there is propable cause to believe the party guilty, such as upon an ordinary warrant would justify his commitment for trial. And in the cases of fugitive slaves, there would seem to be the same necessity of requiring only *prima facie* proofs of ownership, without putting the party to a formal assertion of his rights, by a suit at common law.

"Congress appears to have acted upon this opinion; and, accordingly, in the statute upon this subject have authorized summary proceedings before a magistrate, upon which he may grant a warrant for removal.

"In the case of *Prigg* v. *The Commonwealth of Pennsylvania*, 16 *Peters*, 608, this clause in the Constitution received a very careful consideration by the Supreme Court of the United States, and the constitutionality of the act of Congress of the 12*th February*, 1793, *ch.* 51, passed in furtherance of it, was fully discussed and affirmed. It was also the opinion of the court, that the power of legislation upon this subject is exclusive in the national government, and is not concurrent in the states; and that although the states possess full jurisdiction to pass regulations of police in respect to fugitive slaves, yet that such ragulations cannot be permitted to interfere with or obstruct the rights of the owner to reclaim the slave, derived from the Constitution, nor the remedies prescribed by Congress to aid and enforce such rights.

"The majority of the court held, however, that the states were not bound to provide means to carry the provisions of the Constitution as to fugitive slaves into effect, either by its courts or magistrates; but that the national government was bound, through its own proper departments, legislative, judicial, and executive, to enforce all the rights and duties growing out of this clause in the Constitution."

Sergeant in his *Comm. on Constitutional Law*, 398; says:

"From the whole scope and tenor of the Constitution and act of Congress, it appears, that the fugitive is to be delivered up on a summary proceeding, without the delay of a formal trial in a court of common law. If a certificate be given by a state judge, agreeably to the act of Congress, after a hearing, such certificate is a legal warrant to remove the same, and no writ of *homine replegiando* afterwards lies, on the part of the slave, in a court of the state where such certificate is given to try his right to freedom. Such writ is a violation of the Constitution. If the slave in such a case, has a right to freedom, he may try it in the state to which he is removed. Where, therefore, a judge of a state court, after a hearing on habeas corpus, gave a certificate agreeably to the act of Congress, and the slave sued out of the Supreme Court a *homine replegiando* against the keeper of the prison where he remained, the court quashed the writ." *Wright alias Hall* v. *Deacon*, 5 *Serg. & Rawle*, 62. See also *In the Matter of Martin*, 2 *Paine C. C. R.*, 348.

The validity of the act of Congress, 1793, has been affirmed in the several state courts, where it has been brought in question, and state laws conflicting therewith declared unconstitutional. *Wright* v. *Deacon*, 5 *Serg. & Rawl.* 62; *Glen.* v. *Hodges*, 9 *Johns. R.*, 67: *Jack* v. *Martin*, 12 *Wend. R.*, 311; *S. C.*, 12 *Wend. R.*, 507; *and Com.* v. *Griffin*, 2 *Pick. R.*, 11. In the first case, decided in 1819, *Ch. Justice Tilghman* in the course of his opinion, said:

"This is a matter of considerable importance, and the court has therefore held it some days under advisement. Whatever may be our private opinions on the subject of slavery, it is well known that our southern brethren would not have consented to become parties to a constitution under which the United States have enjoyed so much prosperity, unless their property in slaves had been secured. This Constitution has been adopted by the free consent of the citizens of Pennsylvania; and it is the duty of every man, whatever may be his office or station, to give it a fair and candid construction."

The case of *Prigg* v. *The Commonwealth of Pennsylvania*, 16 *Peters*, 608, came before the Supreme Court of the United States, on a writ of error to the Supreme Court of Pennsylvania, brought under the twenty-fifth section of the Judiciary Act of 1789, ch. 20, for the purpose of revising the judgment of that court, in a case involving the construction of the Constitution and laws of the United States.

The plaintiff in error was indicted in the court of Oyer and Terminer for York county, for having with force and violence taken and carried away from that county to the State of Maryland, a certain negro woman, named Margaret Morgan, with a design and intention of selling and disposing of, and keeping her as a slave or servant for life, contrary to a statute of Pennsylvania, passed on the 26th of March, 1826.

That statute, in the first section, in substance provides that if any person or persons shall, from and after the passing of this act, by force and violence take and carry away, or cause to be taken and carried away, and shall, by fraud or false pretence, seduce, or cause to be seduced, or shall attempt to take, carry away or seduce any negro or mulatto from any part of that commonwealth, with a design and intention of selling and disposing of, or causing to be sold, or of keeping and detaining, or of causing to be kept and detained, such negro or mulatto, as a slave or servant for life, or for any term whatever; every such person or persons, his or their aids or abettors shall, on conviction thereof, be deemed guilty of a felony, &c.

The plaintiff in error pleaded not guilty to the indictment, and the jury, on the trial, found a special verdict, which in substance states that the negro woman, Margaret Morgan, was a slave for life, and held to labor and service under and according to the laws of Maryland, to a certain Margaret Ashmore, a citizen of Maryland; that the slave escaped and fled from Maryland to Pennsylvania, in 1832; that the plaintiff in error, being legally constituted the agent and attorney of the said Margaret Ashmore, in 1837, caused the said negro woman to be taken and apprehended, as a fugitive from labor, by a state constable, under a warrant from a Pennsylvania magistrate; that the said negro woman was thereupon brought before the said magistrate, who refused to take further cognizance of the case; and thereupon the plaintiff in error did remove, take and carry away the said negro woman and her children, out of Pennsylvania into Maryland, and did deliver the said negro woman and children into the custody and possession of the said Margaret Ashmore. The special verdict further finds that one of the children was born in Pennsylvania, more than a year after the said negro woman had fled and escaped from Maryland.

Upon this special verdict the court of Oyer and Terminer of York county adjudged that the plaintiff in error was guilty of the offence charged in the indictment. A writ of error was brought from that judgment to the Supreme Court of Pennsylvania, where the judgment was *pro forma* affirmed. From this latter judgment the writ of error was brought to the United States Supreme Court. The court held the act of Pennsylvania under which the indictment was framed to be unconstitutional and void, inasmuch as it undertook to punish as a public offence against the state, the very act of seizing and removing a slave by his master, which the Constitution of the United States was designed to justify and uphold.

In the course of their remarks, the court say:

"It is historically well known that the clause in the Constitution of the United States relating to persons owing service and labor in one state escaping into other states, was to secure to the citizens of the slaveholding states the complete right and title of ownership in their slaves, as property, in every state in the Union into which they might escape from the state where they were held in servitude. The full recognition of this right and title was indispensable to the security of this species of property in all the slaveholding states; and indeed was so vital to the preservation of their domestic interests and institutions, that it cannot be doubted that it constituted a fundamental article, without the adoption of which the Union could not have been formed. Its true design was to guard against the doctrines and principles prevailing in the non-slaveholding states, by preventing them from intermeddling with, or obstructing or abolishing the rights of the owners of slaves.

"The owner of a fugitive slave has the same right to seize and to take him in a state to which he has escaped or fled, that he had in the state from which he escaped; and it is well known that this right to seize or re-capture is universally acknowledged in all the slaveholding states.

"The court have not the slightest hesitation in holding that under and in virtue of the Constitution the owner of the slave is clothed with authority in every state of the Union, to seize and recapture his slave, wherever he can do it without any breach of the peace or illegal violence. In this sense, and to this extent this clause in the Constitution may properly be said to execute itself.

"A 'claim' to a fugitive slave is a controversy in a case 'arising under the Constitution of the United States,' under the express delegation of judicial power given by that instrument. Congress, then, may call that power into activity for the very purpose of giving effect to the right; and, if so, it may prescribe the mode and extent to which it may be applied; and how and under what circumstances the proceedings shall afford a complete protection and guaranty of the right.

"The provisions of the sections of the act of Congress of February, 1793, on the subject of fugitive slaves, as well as relative to fugitives from justice, cover both the subjects; not because they exhaust the remedies, which may be applied by Congress to enforce the right, if the provisions shall be found, in practice, not to attain the objects of the Constitution, but because they point out all the modes of attaining those objects which Congress have as yet deemed expedient and proper. If this be so it would seem, upon just principles of construction, that the legislation of Congress, if constitutional, must supersede all state legislation upon the same subject, and by necessary implication prohibit it. The provisions of the act of February 12, 1793, relative to fugitive slaves is clearly constitutional in all its provisions; and, indeed, with the exception of that part which confers authority on state magistrates, is free from reasonable doubt or difficulty. As to the authority so conferred on state magistrates, while a difference of opinion exists, and may exist on this point, in different states whether state magistrates are *bound* to act under it, none is entertained by the court that state magistrates may, if they choose, exercise the authority unless prohibited by state legislation."

The master may arrest his absconding slave on Sunday; in the night time; in the house of another, if no breach of the peace is committed. *Baldwin C. C. Rep.*, 577.

And this right is the same as that by which special bail may arrest the principal in another state. *Id.* No person has a right to oppose the master in reclaiming his slave, or to demand proof of property. A judge or magistrate cannot order his arrest or detention without oath, warrant or probable cause. *Ib.*

By the act of Sept. 18, 1850, entitled "An act to amend and supplementary to 'An act respecting fugitives from justice, and persons escaping from the service of their masters,' approved Febuary twelfth, one thousand seven hundred and ninety-three," it is provided:

"Sec. 1. That the commissioners appointed, in virtue of any act of congress by the Circuit Court of the United States, and who in consequence of such appointment are authorized to exercise the powers that any justice of the peace or other magistrate of any of the United States, may exercise in respect to offenders for any crime or offence against the United States," &c., "shall be, and are hereby, authorized and required to exercise and discharge all the powers and duties conferred by this act."

Sec. 2. That the Superior Court of each organized territory shall have the same power as the Circuit Court of the United States, to appoint commissioners who shall "possess and exercise all the duties conferred by law upon the commissioners appointed by the Circuit Courts of the United States for similar purposes, and shall moreover exercise and discharge all the powers and duties conferred by this act."

Sec. 3. That said courts "shall from time to time enlarge the number of commissioners, with a view to afford reasonable facilities to reclaim fugitives from labor and to the prompt discharge of the duties imposed by this act."

Sec. 4. That such commissioners shall have "concurrent jurisdiction with the judges of the Circuit and District Courts of the United States, in their respective circuits and districts within the several states and the judges of the Superior Courts of the territories, severally and collectively in term time and vacation; and shall grant certificates to such claimants, upon satisfactory proof being made, with authority to take and remove such fugitives from service or labor, under the restrictions herein contained to the state or territory, from which such persons may have escaped or fled."

Sec. 5. That "it shall be the duty of all marshals and deputy marshals to obey and execute all warrants and precepts issued under provisions of this act, when to them directed; and should any marshal or deputy marshal refuse to receive such warrant or other process when tendered, or to use all proper means diligently to execute the same, he shall, on conviction thereof, be fined in the sum of one thousand dollars, to the use of such claimant on the motion of such claimant, by the Circuit and District Court for the district of such marshal; and after arrest of such fugitive by such marshal or his deputy, or whilst at any time in his custody under the provisions of this act, should such fugitive escape, whether with or without the assent of such marshal or his deputy, said marshal shall be liable, on his official bond, to be prosecuted for the benefit of such claimant for the full value of the service or labor of said fugitive in the State, Territory or District whence he escaped." Said commissioners may appoint suitable persons to execute "such warrants and other process as may be issued by them in the lawful performance of their respective duties; with authority to such commissioners, or the persons to be appointed by them, to execute process as aforesaid, to summon and call to their aid the bystanders, or *posse comitatus* of the proper county when necessary to insure a faithful observance of the clause of the constitution referred to, in conformity with the provisions of this act; and all good citizens are hereby commanded to aid and assist in the prompt and efficient execution of this law, whenever their services may be required as aforesaid, for that purpose, and said warrants shall run, and be executed by said officers anywhere in the state within which they are issued."

Sec. 6. "That where a person held to service or labor in any state or territory of the United States, has heretofore or shall hereafter escape into another state or territory of the United States, the person or persons to whom such service or labor may be due, or his, her or their agent or attorney, duly authorized by power of attorney, in writing, acknowledged and certified under the seal of some legal officer or court of the state or territory in which the same may be executed, may pursue and reclaim such fugitive person, either by procuring a warrant from some one of the courts, judges, or commissioners aforesaid, of the proper circuit, district or county, for the apprehension of such fugitive from service or labor, or by seizing and arresting such fugitive, where the same can be done without process, and by taking, or causing such person to be taken, forthwith before such court, judge, or commissioner, whose duty it shall be to hear and determine the case of such claimant in a summary manner; and upon satisfactory proof being made by deposition or affidavit, in writing, to be taken and certified by such court, judge, or commissioner, or by other satisfactory testimony, duly taken and certified by some court, magistrate, justice of the peace, or other legal officer authorized to administer an oath and take depositions under the laws of the state or territory from which such person owing service or labor may have escaped, with a certificate of such magistracy or other authority, as aforesaid, with the seal of the proper court or officer thereto attached, which seal shall be sufficient to establish the competency of the proof, and with proof also by affidavit of the identity of the person whose service or labor is claimed to be due as aforesaid, that the person so arrested does in fact owe service or labor to the person or persons claiming him or her, in the state or territory from which such fugitive may have escaped as aforesaid, and that said person escaped; to make out and deliver to such claimant, his or her agent or attorney, a certificate setting forth the substantial facts as to the service or labor due from such fugitive to the claimant, and of his or her escape from the state or territory in which such service or labor was due, to the state or territory in which he or she was arrested, with authority to such claimant, or his or her agent or attorney, to use such reasonable force and restraint as may be necessary under the circumstances of the case, to take and remove such fugitive person back to state or territory whence he or she may have escaped, as aforesaid. In no trial or hearing under this act, shall the testimony of such alleged fugitive be admitted in evidence; and the certificates in this and the first [fourth] section mentioned, shall be conclusive of the right of the person or persons in whose favor granted, to remove such fugitive to the state or territory from which he escaped, and shall prevent all molestation of such person or persons by any process issued by any court, judge, magistrate, or other person, whomsoever."

Sec. 7. Provides that "any person knowingly hindering the arrest of a fugitive, or attempting to rescue one from custody, or aiding to escape or harboring, shall be fined not exceeding one thousand dollars, and imprisoned not exceeding six months, and forfeit by way of civil damages to the party injured one thousand dollars for each fugitive lost.

Sec. 8. Provides for the fees of marshals and commissioners. The latter "shall be entitled to a fee of ten dollars in full for his services in each case, upon the delivery of the certificate to the claimant, his or her agent or attorney; or a fee of five dollars in cases where the proof shall not in the opinion of such commissioners warrant such certificate and delivery, inclusive of all services incident to such arrest and examination, to be paid in either case by the claimant, his or her agent or attorney."

Sec. 9. "That upon affidavit made by the claimant of such fugitive, his agent or attorney, after such certificate has been issued, that he has reason to apprehend that such fugitive will be rescued by force from his or their possession before he can be taken beyond the limits of the state in which the arrest is made, it shall be the duty of the officer making the arrest to retain such fugitive in his custody, and remove him to the state whence he fled, and there to deliver him to said claimant, his agent or attorney. And to this end the officer aforesaid is hereby authorized and required to employ so many persons as he may deem necessary to overcome such force, and to retain them in his service so long as circumstances may require. The said officer and his assistants, while so employed, to receive the same compensation and to be allowed the same expenses as are now allowed by law for transportation of criminals, to be certified by the judge of the district court within which the arrest is made, and paid out of the treasury of the United States.

Sec. 10. "That when any person held to service or labor in any State or Territory, or in the District of Columbia, shall escape therefrom, the party to whom such services or labor shall be due, his, her or their agent or attorney may apply to any court of record therein, or judge thereof in vacation, and make satisfactory proof to such court or judge in vacation, of the escape aforesaid, and that the person escaping owed service or labor to such party. Whereupon the court shall cause a record to be made of the matters so proved, and also a general description of the person so escaping, with such convenient certainty as may be; and a transcript of such record, authenticated by the attestation of the clerk and of the seal of the said court, being produced in any other State, Territory or District in which the person so escaping may be found, and being exhibited to any judge, commissioner or other officer authorized by the law of the United States to cause persons escaping from service or labor to be delivered up, shall be held and taken to be full and conclusive evidence of the fact of escape, and that the service or labor of the person escaping is due to the party in such record mentioned. And upon the production by the said party of other and further evidence if necessary, either oral or by affidavit, in addition to what is contained in the said record of the identity of the person escaping, he or she shall be delivered up to the claimant. And the said court, commissioner, judge or other person authorized by this act to grant certificates to claimants of fugitives, shall, upon the production of the record and other evidences aforesaid, grant to such claimant a certificate of his right to take any such person identified and proved to be owing service or labor as aforesaid; which certificate shall authorize such claimant to seize or arrest and transport such person to the State or Territory from which he escaped: Provided, That nothing herein contained shall be construed as requiring the production of a transcript of such record as evidence aforesaid; but in its absence the claim shall be heard and determined upon other satisfactory proofs competent in law." 9 *U. S. Stat. at Large*, 462.

SECTION II.

ARREST UNDER THE ACT OF 1850.

The detention under the act of September 18th, 1850, may be:

1st. Under the warrant of the judge or commissioner pending a hearing before him.

This being made to appear on return to the habeas corpus, the prisoner should be remanded; and this upon the ground that the jurisdiction of the United States officer having first attached it cannot be interfered with by a court having no *appellate* jurisdiction over him. *Ex parte Robinson*, 6 *McLean*, 355; *In the matter of Martin*, 2 *Paine C. C. Rep.*, 348.

2d. Under the *certificate* of the judge or commissioner.

This, by 6th section of the act, is declared to be "conclusive of the right of the person or persons in whose favor granted to remove such fugitive to the state or territory from which he escaped, and shall prevent all molestation of such person or persons by any process issed by any court, judge, magistrate or other person whomsoever."

The obligation of this provision depends upon the constitutionality of the act; and this has been questioned mainly on two grounds:

1st. That it deprives the alleged fugitive of the right of trial by jury.

2d. That it vests judicial power in officers who are not appointed as judges, as required to be appointed by the Constitution.

It is not proposed to discuss these points here, as they are known to be now pending before the Supreme Court of the United States. The weight of authority, so far as the cases reported show it to have been passed upon, is in favor of the constitutionality of the act. *Sims' case*, 7 *Cush.*, 285; *Ex parte Robinson*, 6 *McLean*, 355; *Henry* v. *Lowell*, 16 *Barb.*, 268.

The unconstitutionality of the act has, however, been maintained in an opinion of decided ability by a majority of the judges of the Supreme Court of Wisconsin, whose judgment is understood to be under review in the Supreme Court of the United States.

SECTION III.

ARREST UNDER THE AUTHORITY OF THE MASTER.

It would seem to follow as a corollary from the case of *Prigg*, 16 *Peters*, 708, that the master may not only arrest his slave without warrant, but may remove him out of the state without obtaining a certificate therefor; and that if it should appear at the hearing, upon habeas corpus, that the master was executing this right of private removal in a reasonable manner, and that the fugitive did owe him the service and was a fugitive, he should not be discharged although the hearing was before an officer who could not or would not grant a certificate to the master.

It has, however, been held under the act of 1793, that in the case of an arrest upon private authority it was the indispensable duty of the person making the arrest to take the person arrested immediately before the proper court or officer for hearing, &c.

In *New York*, *In the matter of Belt*, 1 *Parker Cr. Rep.*, 169, where a master arrested his slave, and instead of taking him before the proper officer for examination, removed him to a distance and concealed him for two days, and on his return to a habeas corpus claimed, not that he held him under the act of Congress for the purpose contemplated in the statute, but that he held him as his slave because he owed him servitude, it was held that the negro should be discharged. The court said: "There was only one case in which a fugitive slave could be held by his master in his personal custody in this state; that was under the law of Congress to take him without delay before the proper authorities in order to obtain the certificate necessary to justify the removal out of the state."

The act of Sep. 18, 1850, contemplates, if it does not require, an examination to be had as well in cases of arrest by the master or his agent as where the arrest is by the marshal under a warrant from the court, judge or commissioner. It provides in the 6th section, that the master or his agent duly authorized, "may pursue and reclaim such fugitive person, either by procuring a warrant from one of the courts, judges or commissioners aforesaid, of the proper circuit, district or county, for the apprehension of such fugitive from service or labor, or by seizing and arresting such fugitive where the same can be done without process, *and* by taking or causing such person to be taken forthwith before such court, judge or commissioner whose duty it shall be to hear and determine," &c.

It would appear, therefore, to be the duty of the master, under that act, to produce the alleged slave after the arrest and without delay, before the proper officer for examination.

SECTION IV.

LAW OF FREE STATES WHERE THE MASTER TAKES OR SENDS HIS SLAVE THERE.

It is not unusual for slaves sent on errands into the free states, to refuse to return. But instances of application for a habeas corpus are more common in cases where the master is present with the slave, claiming authority over him. In such cases it is to be expected that the laws of the state, where restraint is exercised and complained of, must be looked to for the determination of the status of the negro at the time of service of the writ.

It has sometimes been claimed that a master has a right to take his slave into a non-slaveholding state, upon a temporary visit for business or pleasure, or upon a journey from one slaveholding state to another; but it is believed to be a principle pervading the common law of all the non-slaveholding states, that whenever a slave, with the consent of his owner, comes within the limits of a non-slaveholding state for any purpose, he is free. This point was very elaborately argued, and very fully considered by the Supreme Court of Massachusetts, in the case of the *Commonwealth* v. *Aves*, 18 *Pick.*, 193, where it was held that if the owner voluntarily brings his slave into Massachusetts, he has no authority to detain him against his will, or to carry him out of the state against his consent.

There is no doubt in such a case that the slave would be held by the courts of any of the non-slaveholding states to be free, and would be discharged from the restraint of the master.

If the slave be an infant, not capable of exercising a reasonable discretion, the court will award it to the custody of some proper person willing to receive it other than the master.

It is not unusual in such cases for appointment of guardians to be made by the probate courts. And the court in the case of *Commonwealth* v. *Aves*, 18 *Pick.*, 193, ordered the child into temporary custody in order to give time for an application to the probate judge for letters of guardianship.

If the child be arrived at years of discretion and elects to continue in the custody of the master it is usual to permit it to do so.

There are oftentimes questions of embarrassment in determining whether the slave is really brought within the limits of a non-slaveholding state under such circumstances of actual or implied assent of the owner as to entitle him to assert his freedom in that state.

Some of these were suggested, but not decided, in the case of *Commonwealth* v. *Aves*, 18 *Pick.*, 193, as "where an owner of a slave is *bona fide* removing to another state where slavery is allowed, and in doing so *necessarily* passes through a free state; or where by *accident* or *necessity* he is *compelled* to touch or land therein, remaining no longer than necessary." The same court, eight years after, instead of answering the above suggestions, in effect repeated the last one *In the matter of Lucas*, 7 *Law Rep.*, 379, by saying "whether if a vessel, conveying slaves from one slave state to another, should be cast away on the coast of a free state, the slaves could be retained, is a question not now before us."

Cases have frequently occurred where steamboats upon which masters with their slaves have embarked in a slave state for a point in another slave state, have touched at landings in non-slaveholding states, for the purpose of landing or receiving passengers or freight, or of procuring the necessary stores for the voyage. In such cases they have frequently been discharged upon habeas corpus, the court holding that the landing of a vessel at a point usual for vessels to stop at for the purposes of travel and trade, might reasonably be supposed to have been foreseen by the master and so with his implied assent. That it was not coming upon free soil by an "irresistible necessity."

It was held, however, by Judge Read of the Supreme Court of Ohio in 1845, *In the matter of Watson*, 8 *Law Rep.* 83, that a person held to service or labor under [illegible] laws of one of the states, escaping from a boat on [illegible] Ohio river, within low water mark on the Ohio [illegible], a [illegible] fastened to the shore, and on which boat his master was conveying him from one place to another, is a fugitive from labor, within the meaning of art. 4, sec. 2, of the Constitution of the United States, and of the act of Congress 1793.

APPENDIX.

HABEAS CORPUS ACT, 31 CAR. 2.

ACT FOR THE BETTER SECURING THE LIBERTY OF THE SUBJECT, AND FOR PREVENTION OF IMPRISONMENT BEYOND THE SEAS.

WHEREAS great delays have been used by sheriffs, gaolers and other officers, to whose custody any of the king's subjects have been committed for criminal or supposed criminal matters, in making returns of writs of habeas corpus, to them directed, by standing out on alias or pluries habeas corpus, and sometimes more, and by other shifts to avoid their yielding obedience to such writs, contrary to their duty and the known laws of the land, whereby many of the king's subjects have been, and hereafter may be long detained in prison, in such cases where by law they are bailable, to their great charge and vexation:

II. For the prevention whereof, and the more speedy relief of all persons imprisoned for any such criminal or supposed criminal matters; (2) *Be it enacted, by the king's most excellent majesty, by and with the advice and consent of the lords spiritual and temporal, and commons in this present parliament assembled, and by the authority thereof,* That whensoever any person or persons shall bring any *habeas corpus* directed unto any sheriff or sheriffs, gaoler, minister, or other person whatsoever, for any person in his or their custody, and the said writ shall be served upon the said officer, or left at the gaol or prison with any of the under-officers, under-keepers, or deputy of the said officers or keepers, that the said officer or officers, his or their under-officers, under-keepers or deputies, shall within three days after the service thereof, as aforesaid (unless the commitment aforesaid were for treason or felony, plainly and especially expressed in the warrant of commitment), upon payment or tender of the charges of bringing the said prisoner, to be ascertained by the judge or court that awarded the same, and endorsed upon the said writ, not exceeding 12 pence per mile, and upon security given by his own bond to pay the charges of carrying back the prisoner, if he shall be remanded by the court or judge to which he shall be brought, according to the true intent of this present act, and that he will not make any escape by the way, make return of such writ; (3) and bring, or cause to be brought, the body of the party so committed or restrained, unto or before the lord chancellor, or lord keeper of the great seal of England, for the time being, or the judges or barons of the said court, from whence the said writ shall issue, or unto and before such other person or persons before whom the said writ is made returnable, according to the command thereof; (4) and shall then likewise certify the true cause of his detainer or imprisonment, unless the commitment of the said party be in any place beyond the distance of twenty miles from the place or places where such court or person is, or shall be residing; and if beyond the distance of 20 miles, and not above 100 miles, then within the space of 10 days, and if beyond the distance of 100 miles, then within the space of 20 days after such delivery aforesaid, and not longer.

III. And to the intent that no sheriff, gaoler or other officer may pretend ignorance of the import of any such writ; (2) Be it enacted by the authority aforesaid, that all such writs shall be marked in this manner; "Per statutum, tricesimo primo Caroli secundi Regis,"[1] and shall be signed by the person that awards the same; (3) and if any person or persons shall be or stand committed or detained as aforesaid, for any crime, unless for felony or treason, plainly expressed in the warrant of commitment, in the vacation time and out of term it shall and may be lawful to and for the person or persons so committed or detained (other than persons convict or in execution by legal process), or any one in his or their hehalf, to appeal or complain to the lord chancellor or lord keeper, or any one of his majesty's justices, either of the one bench or of the other, or the barons of the exchequer of the degree of the coif; (4) and the said lord chancellor, lord keeper, justices or barons, or any of them, upon view of the copy or copies of the warrant or warrants of commitment and detainer, or otherwise upon oath made that such copy or copies were denied to be given by such person or persons in whose custody the prisoner or prisoners is or are detained, are hereby authorized and required, upon request made in writing by such person or persons, or any on his, her or their behalf, attested and subscribed by two witnesses who were present at the delivery of the same, to award and grant an habeas corpus, under the seal of such court whereof he shall then be one of the

[1] By the 1 and 2 Ph. and M., c. 13, s. 7, it was enacted that "No writ of habeas corpus or certiorari shall be granted to remove any prisoner out of any jail, or to remove any recognizance, except the same writ be signed with the proper hands of the chief justice, or in his absence, of one of the justices of the court, out of which the same writ shall be awarded or made, upon pain that he that writeth any such writs, not being signed as aforesaid, to forfeit to our said sovereign lord the king and queen, for every such writ and writs, five pounds." And if not signed, the sheriff need not obey them. *Rex* v. *Roddam*, *Cowp.*, 672.

judges, (5) to be directed to the officer or officers in whose custody the party so committed or detained shall be, returnable immediate before the said lord chancellor or lord keeper, or such justice, baron, or any other justice or baron of the degree of the coif, of any of the said courts; (6) and upon service thereof as aforesaid, the officer or officers, his or their under-officer or under-officers, under-keeper or under-keepers, or their deputy, in whose custody the party is so committed or detained, shall within the times respectively before limited, bring such prisoner or prisoners before the said lord chancellor, or lord keeper, or such justices, barons, or one of them, before whom the said writ is made returnable, and in case of his absence, before any other of them, with the return of such writ and the true causes of the commitment or detainer; (7) and thereupon, within two days after the party shall be brought before them, the said lord chancellor or lord keeper, or such justice or baron before whom the prisoner shall be brought as aforesaid, shall discharge the said prisoner from his imprisonment, taking his or their recognizance, with one or more surety or sureties, in any sum according to their discretions, having regard to the quality of the prisoner and the nature of the offence, for his or their appearance in the Court of King's Bench the term following, or at the next assizes, sessions or general gaol delivery, of or for such county, city or place where the commitment was, or where the offence was committed, or in such other court where the said offence is properly cognizable, as the case shall require, and then shall certify the said writ with the return thereof, and the said recognizance or recognizances into the said court where such appearance is to be made; (8) unless it shall appear to the said lord chancellor, or lord keeper, or justice or justices, or baron or barons, that the party so committed is detained upon a legal process, order or warrant, out of some court that hath jurisdiction of criminal matters, or by some warrant signed and sealed with the hand and seal of any of the said justices or barons, or some justice or justices of the peace, for such matters or offences for the which by the law the prisoner is not bailable.

IV. Provided always, and be it enacted, That if any person shall have wilfully neglected, by the space of two whole terms after his imprisonment, to pray a habeas corpus for his enlargement, such person so wilfully neglecting shall not have any habeas corpus to be granted in vacation time, in pursuance of this act.

V. And be it further enacted, by the authority aforesaid, That if any officer or officers, his or their under-officer or under-officers, under-keeper or under-keepers, or deputy, shall neglect or refuse to make the returns aforesaid, or to bring the body or bodies of the prisoner or prisoners according to the command of the said writ, within the respective times aforesaid, or upon demand made by the prisoner or person in his behalf, shall refuse to deliver, or within the space of six hours after demand shall not deliver to the person so demanding a true copy of the warrant or warrants of commitment and detainer of such prisoner, which he and they are hereby required to deliver accordingly; all and every the head gaolers and keepers of such person, and such other person in whose custody the prisoner shall be detained, shall for the first offence forfeit to the prisoner or party grieved the sum of £100; (2) and for the second offence the sum of £200, and shall and is hereby made incapable to hold or execute his said office; (3) the said penalties to be recovered by the prisoner or party grieved, his executors and administrators, against such offender, his executors or administrators, by any action of debt, suit, bill, plaint or information, in any of the king's courts at Westminster, wherein no essoin, protection, privilege, injunction, wager of law, or stay of prosecution by "Non vult ulterius prosequi," or otherwise, shall be admitted or allowed, or any more than one imparlance; (4) and any recovery or judgment at the suit of any party grieved, shall be a sufficient conviction for the first offence; and any after recovery or judgment at the suit of a party grieved, for any offence after the first judgment, shall be a sufficient conviction to bring the officers or person within the said penalty for the second offence.

VI. And for the prevention of unjust vexation by reiterated commitments for the same offence; (2) Be it enacted, by the authority aforesaid, That no person or persons, which shall be delivered or set at large upon any habeas corpus, shall at any time hereafter be again imprisoned or committed for the same offence, by any person or persons whatsoever, other than by the legal order and process of such court wherein he or they shall be bound by recognizance to appear, or other court having jurisdiction of the cause; (3) and if any other person or persons shall knowingly, contrary to this act recommit or imprison, or knowingly procure or cause to be recommitted or imprisoned, for the same offence or pretended offence, any person or persons delivered or set at large as aforesaid, or be knowingly aiding or assisting therein, then he or they shall forfeit to the prisoner or party grieved, the sum of £500; any colorable pretence or variation in the warrant or warrants of commitment notwithstanding, to be recovered as aforesaid.

VII. Provided always, and be it further enacted, That if any person or persons shall be committed for high treason or felony, plainly and specially expressed in the warrant of commitment, upon his prayer or petition in open court, the first week of the term, or first day of the sessions of oyer and terminer or general gaol delivery, to be brought to his trial, shall not be indicted some time in the next term, sessions of oyer and terminer or general gaol delivery, after such commitment; it shall and may be lawful to and for the judges of the Court of King's Bench, and justices of oyer and terminer or general gaol delivery, and they are hereby required, upon motion to them made in open court the last day of the term, sessions or gaol delivery, either by the prisoner or any one in his behalf, to set at liberty the prisoner upon bail, unless it appear to the judges and justices upon oath made, that the witnesses for the king could not be produced the same term, sessions or general gaol delivery; (2) and if any person or persons committed as aforesaid, upon his prayer or petition in open court the first week of the term or the first day of the sessions of oyer and terminer and general gaol delivery, to be brought to his trial, shall not be indicted and tried the second term, sessions of oyer and terminer or general gaol delivery, after his commitment, or upon his trial shall be acquitted, he shall be discharged from his imprisonment.

VIII. Provided always, That nothing in this act shall extend to discharge out of prison any person charged in debt, or other action, or with process in any civil cause, but that after he shall be discharged of his imprisonment for such his criminal offence, he shall be kept in custody according to the law for such other suit.

IX. Provided always, and be it further enacted by the authority aforesaid, That if any person or persons, subjects of this realm, shall be committed to any prison, or in custody of any officer or officers whatsoever, for any criminal or supposed criminal matter, that the said person shall not be removed from the said prison and custody, into the custody of any other officer or officers; (2) unless it be by habeas corpus or some other legal writ; or where the prisoner is delivered to the constable or other inferior officer, to carry such prisoner to some common gaol; (3) or where any person is sent by order of any judge of assize, or justice of the peace, to any common workhouse or house of correction; (4) or where the prisoner is removed from one place or prison to another within the same county, in order to his or her trial or discharge in due course of law; (5) or in case of sudden fire or infection, or other necessity; (6) and if any person or persons shall, after such commitment aforesaid, make out and sign or countersign any warrant or warrants for such removal aforesaid, contrary to this act; as well he that makes or signs or countersigns such warrant or warrants, as the officer or officers that obey or execute the same, shall suffer and incur the pains and forfeitures in this act before mentioned, both for the first and second offence respectively, to be recovered in manner aforesaid by the party grieved.

X. Provided also, and be it further enacted by the authority aforesaid, That it shall and may be lawful to and for any prisoner and prisoners as aforesaid, to move and obtain his or their habeas corpus, as well out of the high court of chancery or court of exchequer as out of the Courts of King's Bench or common pleas, or either of them; (2) and if the said lord chancellor or lord keeper, or any judge or judges, baron or barons, for the time being, of the degree of the coif, of any of the courts aforesaid, in the vacation time, upon view of the copy or copies of the warrant or warrants of commitment or detainer, upon oath made that such copy or copies were denied as aforesaid, shall deny any writ of habeas corpus, by this act required to be granted, being moved for as aforesaid, they shall severally forfeit to the prisoner or party grieved, the sum of £500, to be recovered in manner aforesaid.

XI. And be it declared and enacted by the authority aforesaid, That an habeas corpus, according to the true intent and meaning of this act, may be directed and run into any county Palatine, the Cinque Ports, or other privileged places within the kingdom of England, dominion of Wales, or town of Berwick upon Tweed, and the islands of Jersey or Guernsey; any law or usage to the contrary notwithstanding.

XII. And for preventing illegal imprisonments in prisons beyond the seas; (2) Be it further enacted by the authority aforesaid, That no subject of this realm, that now is or hereafter shall be an inhabitant or resiant of this kingdom of England, dominion of Wales, or town of Berwick upon Tweed, shall or may be sent prisoner into Scotland, Ireland, Jersey, Guernsey, Tangier, or into parts, garrisons, islands, or places beyond the seas, which are or at any time hereafter shall be within or without the dominions of his majesty, his heirs or successors; (3) and that every such imprisonment is hereby enacted and adjudged to be illegal; (4) and that if any of the said subjects now is or hereafter shall be so imprisoned, every such person and persons so imprisoned, shall and may for every such imprisonment maintain, by virtue of this act, an action or actions of false imprisonment, in any of his majesty's courts of record, against the person or persons by whom he or she shall be so committed, detained, imprisoned, sent prisoner or transported, contrary to the true meaning of this act, and against all or any person or persons that shall frame, contrive, write, seal or countersign any warrant or writing for such commitment, detainer, imprisonment, or transportation, or shall be advising, aiding, or assisting in the same, or any of them; (5) and the plaintiff in every such action shall have judgment to recover his treble costs, besides damages, which damages so to be given shall not be less than £500; (6) in which action no delay, stay or stop of proceeding by rule, order or command, nor no injunction, protection or privilege whatsoever, nor any other than one imparlance, shall be allowed, excepting such rule of the court wherein such action shall depend, made in open court as shall be thought in justice necessary for special cause to be expressed in the said rule; (7) and the person or persons who shall knowingly frame, contrive, write, seal or countersign any warrant for such commitment, detainer, or transportation, or shall so commit, detain, imprison, or transport any person or persons, contrary to this act, or be any ways advising, aiding or assisting therein, being lawfully convicted thereof, shall be disabled from thenceforth to bear any office of trust or profit within the said realm of England, dominion of Wales, or town of Berwick upon Tweed, or any of the islands, territories or dominions thereunto belonging; (8) and shall incur and sustain the pains, penalties and forfeitures limited, ordained and provided in and by the statute of provision and præmunire, made in the sixteenth year of king Richard the Second; (9) and be incapable of any pardon from the king, his heirs or successors, of the said forfeitures, losses or disabilities, or any of them.

XIII. Provided always, That nothing in this act shall extend to give benefit to any person who shall by contract in writing agree with any merchant or owner of any plantation, or other person whatsoever, to be transported to any parts beyond the seas, and receive earnest upon such agreement, although that afterwards such person shall renounce such contract.

XIV. Provided always, and be it enacted, That if any person or persons lawfully convicted of any felony, shall in open court pray to be transported beyond the seas, and the court shall think fit to leave him or them in prison for that purpose, such person or persons may be transported into any parts beyond the seas; this act, or anything herein contained, to the contrary notwithstanding.

XV. Provided also, and be it enacted, That nothing herein contained shall be deemed, construed or taken to extend to the imprisonment of any person before the first day of June, one thousand six hundred and seventy-nine, or to anything advised, procured or otherwise done relating to such imprisonment; anything herein contained to the contrary notwithstanding.

XVI. Provided also, That if any person or persons at any time resiant in this realm, shall have committed any capital offence in Scotland or in Ireland, or in any of the islands or foreign plantations of the king, his heirs or successors, where he or she ought to be tried for such offence, such person or persons may be sent to such place, there to receive such trial in such manner as the same might have been used before the making of this act; anything herein contained to the contrary notwithstanding.

XVII. Provided also, and be it enacted, That no person or persons shall be sued, impleaded, molested or troubled for any offence against this act, unless the party offending be sued or impleaded for the same within two years at the most, after such time wherein the offence shall be committed, in case the party grieved shall not be then in prison; and if he shall be in prison, then within the space of two years after the decease of the person imprisoned, or his or her delivery out of prison, which shall first happen.

XVIII. And to the intent no person may avoid his trial at the assizes or general gaol delivery, by procuring his removal before the assizes, at such time as he cannot be brought back to receive his trial there; (2) Be it enacted, that after the assizes proclaimed for that county where the prisoner is detained, no person shall be removed from the common gaol upon any habeas corpus granted in pursuance of this act, but upon any such habeas corpus shall be brought before the judge of assize in open court, who is thereupon to do what to justice shall appertain.

XIX. Provided nevertheless, That after the assizes are ended, any person or persons detained may have his or her habeas corpus according to the direction and intention of this act.

XX. And be it also enacted by the authority aforesaid, That if any information, suit or action shall be brought or exhibited against any person or persons for any offence committed or to be committed against the form of this law, it shall be lawful for such defendants to plead the general issue, that they are not guilty or that they owe nothing, and to give such special matter in evidence to the jury that shall try the same, which matter being pleaded had been good and sufficient matter in law to have discharged the said defendant or defendants against the said information, suit or action, and the same matter shall be then as available to him or them, to all intents and purposes, as if he or they had sufficiently pleaded, set forth or alleged the same matter in bar, or discharge of such information, suit or action.

XXI. And because many times persons charged with petty treason or felony, or accessories thereunto, are committed upon suspicion only, whereupon they are bailable or not, according as the circumstances making out that suspicion are more or less weighty, which are best known to the justices of the peace that committed the persons, and have the examination before them, or to other justices of the peace in the county; (2) Be it therefore enacted that where any person shall appear to be committed by any judge or justice of the peace and charged as accessory before the fact to any petty treason or felony, or upon suspicion thereof, or with suspicion of petty treason or felony, which petty treason or felony shall be plainly and specially expressed in the warrant of commitment, that such person shall not be removed or bailed by virtue of this act, or in any other manner than they might have been before the making of this act.

INDEX.

CPSIA information can be obtained
at www.ICGtesting.com
Printed in the USA
JSHW012307281119
2682JS00001B/15